PAROCHIAL LECTURES

ON

THE PSALMS.

BY THE LATE

REV. DAVID CALDWELL, A. M.

PSALMS 1—50.

PHILADELPHIA:
WILLIAM S. & ALFRED MARTIEN,
No. 606 CHESTNUT STREET.
1859.

CONTENTS.

PAGE

LECTURE ON PSALM I. .... 13—24
PSALM II. .... 25—35
PSALM III. .... 35—45
PSALM IV. .... 46—58
PSALM V. .... 59—72
PSALM VI. .... 72—82
PSALM VII. .... 82—92
PSALM VIII. .... 93—103
PSALM IX. ....104—116
PSALM X. ....116—127
PSALM XI. ....128—138
PSALM XII. ....139—147
PSALM XIII. ....147—155
PSALM XIV. ....155—164
PSALM XV. ....164—175
PSALM XVI. ....175—188
PSALM XVII. ....188—201
PSALM XVIII. 1–27. ....201—213
PSALM XVIII. 28–50. ....213—225
PSALM XIX. ....226—240
PSALM XX. ....240—251
PSALM XXI. ....251—263
PSALM XXII. 1–13. ....263—277
PSALM XXII. 14–31. ....277—291
PSALM XXIII. ....291—305
PSALM XXIV. ....305—315
PSALM XXV. ....316—326

PAGE

LECTURE ON PSALM XXVI. ....326—337
PSALM XXVII. ....337—347
PSALM XXVIII. ....347—357
PSALM XXIX. ....357—368
PSALM XXX. ....368—378
PSALM XXXI. ....379—389
PSALM XXXII. ....389—403
PSALM XXXIII. ....403—413
PSALM XXXIV. ....414—427
PSALM XXXV. ....427—439
PSALM XXXVI. ....440—448
PSALM XXXVII. ....449—460
PSALM XXXVIII. ....461—471
PSALM XXXIX. ....472—480
PSALM XL. ....481—492
PSALM XLI. ....492—501
PSALMS XLII. AND XLIII. ....502—513
PSALM XLIV. ....514—525
PSALM XLV. ....526—538
PSALM XLVI. ....538—548
PSALM XLVII. ....548—557
PSALM XLVIII. ....557—568
PSALM XLIX. ....568—578
PSALM L. ....579—586

PUBLISHER'S ADVERTISEMENT.

THE author of the following work, the Rev. DAVID CALDWELL, was a well-known clergyman of the Protestant Episcopal Church in the diocese of Virginia. Ordained in 1841, by the venerable Bishop Moore, during the session of the Diocesan Convention at Alexandria, he took charge first of several country congregations in Amherst county, in that State; removed subsequently to St. Paul's church in the city of Norfolk: thence, after some years' useful service, returned again, with health exceedingly enfeebled, to the neighbourhood of his former charge. The healthful air and comparatively light duties of an upland and interior parish, sufficiently invigorated his exhausted strength to enable him, after two or three years of labour in the country, to venture once more on a city rectorship in Christ Church, Georgetown, District of Columbia. But here again his health, at all times feeble, failed; and he retired, after little more than two years, to Hanover county, Virginia, exchanging parishes with the Rev. Dr. Norwood. Discouraged in Hanover by a fire which consumed his dwelling, with an excellent library which he had been gathering for many years, he was induced, after no great length of time, to accept the wealthier rectorship of St. James's Church, Sherburne parish, Leesburg, Virginia, where, in the autumn of 1858, he died.

Clear in his views of doctrine; comprehensive in his

grasp of truth; with a penetrating intellect, a wonderful fertility of illustration, and a more than ordinary measure of logical and oratoric power; he was extensively popular both as a pastor and a preacher; drew always large audiences around him; and, but for his extreme fragility of constitution, might easily have taken rank with the most eminent of our American divines.

The idea of a practical Commentary on the Psalms of David, unincumbered with critical discussions, and adapted to the furtherance of the Divine life within the soul, was conceived by him while in charge of his last church in Leesburg, and carried out, in the form of Lectures to his people, as far as the present work extends. At the close of the Commentary on the Fiftieth Psalm, the hand that held the pen began to falter; and, after a few weeks of hopeful but vain struggle with disease, a calm and Christian death well closed a useful life.

Only one-third of his projected work upon the Psalms was finished at the time of his decease. But as this was entirely complete within itself; contained fresh and valuable thoughts on the sacred compositions it embraced; and had in it much that was "profitable for doctrine, for reproof, for correction, for instruction in righteousness;" his family have thought that the interests of religion, as well as the desire of friends, claimed of them the publication of it as far as it had gone. It is, accordingly, given to the world with the prayer that God may make it, through his Spirit, a means of enlarging men's acquaintance with his truth, and of promoting its benign and purifying influence on human character.

PHILADELPHIA, October, 1859.

INTRODUCTION.

PERHAPS there is no other portion of the word of God, except the Gospels, more generally read by Christians than the Psalms of David. We wonder not at this: for it matters not what our frame of mind may be, whether joyful, or sorrowful; hopeful, or full of fears, we here find words that express our feelings as no other words can. Nor is it the mind of the believer alone which these sacred lyrics describe, but also the mind of the man who says in his heart, "There is no God." They reveal the thoughts that fill and the feelings that agitate the heart of each. They also reveal the thoughts and feelings of one other heart, the thoughts and feelings of the heart of Him of whom it is written, "He is love." Moreover, there is not an aspect of nature, endless as it is in its scenes of beauty and sublimity, which is not here depicted with a vividness, fidelity of outline, filling up, and colouring, to which the highest achievements of the unaided human intellect in the same direction are but distant approaches. In their descriptions of nature, of God, and of man, the Psalms stand alone. But notwithstanding the lively and peculiar interest, as well as profit, with which even the general reader peruses the Psalms, there is no part of the word of God less understood in the *full import* of their meaning. This is owing in some instances to the extreme antiquity of the Psalms, and to their describing manners, customs, and institutions, which now exist, in many cases, only in the writings of the antiquarian. The imagery, too, that through which the thought and feeling of the inspired singer are generally expressed in their greatest force and beauty, is often obscure, and needs to be explained. Moreover, many of the Psalms are historical in their origin, and inexplicable till the historical key is discovered; personal, and not to be understood, until the person to whom they refer has been pointed out. This the author of the following Parochial Lectures on the Psalms has aimed to do. The Psalms are not only a *field* of jewels, where he who gathers only that which lies on their surface, enriches himself, but also a *mine* of spiritual wealth, where he who has sunk his shaft deepest, has always returned, reporting treasures in undiminished abundance and increasing richness still below the lowest depth to which he had carried on his work.

It has been the wish of the author of the following exposition of the Psalms, to put the reader in possession of the wealth *beneath*, as well as that *upon* their surface. This he has aimed to accomplish by so explaining the language, imagery, and allusions, historical or personal, of the verse or psalm, as to bring out the thought of the inspired singer, together with the feeling with which we may suppose him to have uttered it. His great aim has been to present all those who love our Lord Jesus Christ and his gospel, a book of thoughts on the Psalms, derived directly from a truthful exposition of the Psalms themselves. He has laboured to get at the mind of the Spirit in the psalm, and in every part of the psalm, and having, as he hoped, ascertained that, he has been satisfied with giving it utterance without blending words of his own with it. In treating the Psalms in this way only, did the author think that he could make them what they in fact are, utterances of the universal human heart, and also of the heart of Him in whose hand are the hearts of us all, to turn and fashion us as he will. Allowing the Psalms to utter themselves only in their own inspired voice, it is impossible to make them speak in the tones of any sect or party.

The publication of the following Lectures has been urged upon the author as, in some measure, meeting what has been felt by many to be really a want in the literature of our Church, viz. a plain, exegetical, evangelical, and practical exposition of the Psalms for the laity. The author hopes that his exposition may prove acceptable and useful to his brethren of the clergy: still he must say, that he has not written for the pulpit, but for the pew. We have never failed to feel the want of such an exposition on going through the Psalter of our Prayer Book. How many hundreds of times have we felt, as we were repeating its sacred words, that there was a deeper meaning, and in some cases, *another* meaning in the words, than that which appears in the *literal* sense, and which meaning, some brief explanation would bring out in all its force and beauty. It has been the aim of the author of the following Lectures to furnish the explanation required, and so to write, that an intelligent child could understand him. That he has in every instance succeeded in giving the right, or even more probable, explanation, would be a piece of extreme vanity in him to assume. He can only say that others, in whose judgment he confides more than he does in his own, have assured him that he has shed an amount of exegetical light over the Psalms in his Lectures, which not only justifies, but calls for their publication. Of the correctness of their judgment the reader of the Lectures must judge for himself. No one can be more conscious of their defects than the author is; and he regrets that delicate health obliges him to send them to the press in nearly the same imperfect form in which he delivered them to his people from the desk. He has forborne revising and re-writing, except to a very limited extent, lest he should consume strength which he will need in going on with the work to its completion.

Such, however, as it is, the author humbly consecrates his work to Him for the promotion of whose truth and glory he hopes it was undertaken—the blessed Messiah—seen more conspicuously in the Psalms, in greater power and majesty, than in any other portion of the Old Testament Scriptures.

The author would simply add in conclusion, that his work has been its own exceeding great reward. The hours spent in studying out* and composing these Lectures on the Psalms, have been among the happiest of his life. Day and night his meditation thereon has been sweet indeed. His walk through them has been as that through a garden, where, the farther you advance, the richer the flowers become in fragrance and colouring. If the reader shall experience a tithe of the pleasure in reading the follow-

* The author has read every writer on the Psalms he could lay his hands on—has gotten good from all—but acknowledges special indebtedness to Hammond, Horne, Poole, Calvin, and Hengstenberg.

ing exposition of the Psalms which the author has experienced in writing it, he will feel that his labour has not been lost, nor the reader's time thrown away.

Finally, as he has written his exposition for the laity, the author here dedicates it to the laity, and especially to those noble laymen of Virginia, and of one other dear place of the author's pastoral duty,* whose kindness to him has been so unparalleled! Such sympathy, such earnest co-operation in every good work; such ready acceptance of such services as could be rendered; such tender and persistent blindness to his many infirmities; and above all, such liberality as the author has experienced from so many noble men and noble women, he can never forget, and here records with gratitude. Often has the thought been present to his mind, while engaged in the onerous duties of his study, that if he should be led to write anything that would bring any increase of Divine light to their minds, or of Divine consolation to their hearts, it would be a reward abundantly sufficient to compensate him for all the labour of his work. God grant that this reward of his labour may not be denied, but abundantly granted to the author.

D. C.

LEESBURG, Virginia, *October* 1858.

* Christ Church, Georgetown, District of Columbia.

Parochial Lectures on the Psalms.

LECTURE ON PSALM I.

The Psalms have been justly regarded as an epitome of the whole Bible. They contain so much of the substance of both Testaments, of God and his law, of Christ and his gospel, that they may be considered as an abstract of both. Their inspiration is settled by our Lord, saying, "All things must be fulfilled which were written in the law of Moses, and in the Prophets, and *in the Psalms*, concerning me." Luke xxiv. 44. They are, in the highest conceivable sense, poetical, religious, and devotional compositions, set to music in the original Hebrew, and designed to be sung in both the public and private devotions of the people. They number one hundred and fifty in all; and are, in the Hebrew and Greek versions of the Scriptures, divided into five books; the first book ending with psalm the forty-first; the second, with the seventy-second; the third, with the eighty-ninth; the fourth, with the one hundred and sixth; the fifth, with the one hundred and fiftieth; and each final psalm with a doxology, except the last, which may be considered as being in itself the high-sounding doxology of the whole. The Septuagint, and the translations following it, in particular the translation used by the Roman Catholic Church, called the Vulgate, make but one psalm of the ninth and tenth, and also but one of the one hundred and fourteenth and one hundred and fifteenth; but separate the one hundred and sixteenth and one hundred and forty-seventh into two each, so that their numbering is in the end the same as ours and that of the Hebrew, one hundred and fifty. It is important to remember this diversity in division and numbering, especially as Roman Catholic writers for the most part cite according to the Greek and Latin versions of the Old Testament, the Septuagint and the Vulgate. Most of the psalms are ascribed to David, who is styled "the sweet Psalmist of Israel." 2 Sam. xxiii. 1. Many of them bear his name, and many more not bearing his name, are as confidently ascribed to his pen. His acknowledged effusions, however, so far out-number those of all the sacred poets beside, as those of Moses, Solomon, Asaph, Ezra, and others, that the whole collection is styled, THE PSALMS OF DAVID. The present arrangement of the Psalms, as to number, and also as to connection—where there is any connection between them, either of similarity or of contrast—is generally believed to be the work of Ezra, who is supposed to have lived until about the year four hundred and fifty-six before the advent of our Lord.

The first psalm is supposed to have been written by Ezra, and designed by him to serve as a preface to the whole collection. It is therefore general in its terms. It sketches with a graphic pen the opposite characters of the righteous and the wicked, and the invariable connection between virtue and happiness, vice and misery. It may, therefore, be regarded as the key-note of the teaching of every other psalm, indeed as the key-note of the teaching of the whole of inspiration, which is, *God loveth the righteous, but is angry with the wicked every day.* The righteous man, to whom alone blessedness belongs, it first describes negatively—then positively; tells us first what he is not—then what he is. He is one who has not only ceased to do evil, but learned to do well.

VERSE 1. Blessed is the man who walketh not in the counsel of the ungodly, nor standeth in the way of sinners, nor sitteth in the seat of the scornful.

We have in these words the first part of the answer to the question, "O where shall rest be found, rest for the weary soul?" The first step toward the attainment of the bliss for which we sigh, is *ceasing to do evil.* The words, *ungodly*, *sinners*, *scornful*, are thought by some to describe three separate grades or classes of transgressors; and the words, *walketh*, *standeth*, *sitteth*, three separate grades or degrees of sinning. The ungodly of this verse are therefore thought to be, not the openly wicked, but only those who are *without God in the world.* We meet with such in every community where the gospel is preached. They are moral, amiable, intelligent, cultivated, refined—but live only for this world. God is in none of their thoughts as an object of love and adoration, and his glory enters into none of their plans for life. They pursue earthly ends and earthly pleasures, as if God had given them being and endowed them with minds for no other purpose. Of course, too, living only for this world, their standard of right and wrong savours only of this world. They reckon that they are quite upright if they are, morally, not worse than their equals in social standing; that there can be no harm in conforming to the principles and practices of those with whom they are associated in life. Like to none of this class of persons is the man whom our psalm pronounces blessed. "He walketh not in the counsel of the ungodly.' He repudiates all rules of moral action so shifting and uncertain as human opinion. Though *in* the world, he is not *of* the world, and will not shape his conduct to its principles. And as he walketh not in the counsel of the ungodly, so he "standeth not in the way of sinners." Sinners in this clause may mean those who are morally worse than the ungodly just described; men who have fallen below the high-toned man of the world, and sin not only against what is good in human laws and customs, but also against the remonstrances of revelation, and of their own consciences. Though visited occasionally by remorse, their progress in evil is steadily onward. Their habits of sin are *fixed*—this is implied in the word *standeth*, a stronger term than *walketh*.

The blessed man of our psalm, however, standeth not in the way of sinners, of open and reckless transgressors. He eschews, so far as he can, both the maxims and the society of those who take pleasure in unrighteousness. He dreads, as worse than death, the sinful habits that hold them in bondage, and will choose none of their ways. Moreover, he "sitteth not in the seat of the scornful." Here is another stage and degree of wickedness that he will shun. Sitting in the seat of the scornful indicates more than a mere fixed habit of sinning. It indicates a scoffing at all religion, a deriding of every restraint put upon the human will. It describes the vile infidel, warring against the laws alike of God and man, maliciously violating both, and instigating others to do the same. He that standeth in the way of sinners would seem to be satisfied with being wicked alone—but he that sitteth in the seat of the scornful, labours to make other sas vile and wicked as he is himself. Such is the downward progress of the wicked. He begins with being simply *ungodly*, governing himself only by the maxims and practices of the world; he then passes on to be a *sinner*, an open, and, in many things, a reckless transgressor; and then to be a scoffer, deriding all religion, and labouring to make others as violently scoffing as he is himself. And where is the man who is simply ungodly, simply without God in the world, simply *unregenerate*, who can say that he will not take the second step in sin, and then—the third and last? No unregenerate man can say that he will not. The path of sin is an inclined plane pitched at a fearfully downward slope, and he who stands upon the plane at all, is sliding with a momentarily increasing velocity towards the bottom. The man, however, whom our psalm declares blessed, stands upon no part of this fearful slope—neither with the merely ungodly at its top, nor with the sinner at its centre, nor with the scornful at its base.

VERSE 2. But his delight is in the law of the Lord; and in his law doth he meditate day and night.

Here is the second part of the answer to the question, "O where shall rest be found, rest for the weary soul?" As the answer to the first part was, according to the teaching of the first verse, *ceasing to do evil*, so the answer to its second part is, according to the teaching of the second verse, *learning to do well;* is delighting in the law of the Lord, and meditating therein day and night. Combining these two—ceasing to do evil, and learning to do well—as the two are taught us in the word of God, will make us blessed, securing us the happiness for which the human heart everywhere and always hungers. And this is the reason that the good man is never found in *any* part of the way that leadeth unto destruction. It is because of his sincere love for the law of the Lord; a standard of right and wrong, that so clearly defines the two that he can never be at a loss to know what line of conduct truth and duty require of him. He knows by the testimony of every feeling of his heart, the truth of the words, "The law of the Lord is perfect, converting the soul: the testimony of the Lord is sure, making wise the simple: the statutes of the Lord are right, rejoicing the heart: the commandment of the Lord is pure, enlightening the eyes: the fear of the Lord is clean, enduring for ever: the judgments of the Lord are true, and righteous altogether. More to be desired are they than gold, yea, than much fine gold; sweeter also than honey and the honey-comb. Moreover, by them is thy servant warned; and in keeping of them there is great reward." Ps. xix. 7–11. The reading of the Divine word, combined with meditation and prayer, works a moral transformation in the soul; quickens its perceptions of the truth; forms it averse to sin, and fills it with a love for all that is holy, just, and good. There is a moral atmosphere investing the word of God, in which the humble mind finds itself at home, and all its powers of thought and feeling purified and strengthened. Bring such a mind into contact with the teachings of the Bible, and it *feels* that it has found *the truth*, and can rejoice in it as its element of life. It lays hold of the good man's conscience in a way that he cannot explain, and yet in a way to retain him a willing captive. His delight is in the law of the Lord, after the inner man. He feels that his soul was made to be conformed to its influences; and the effort of his life, day and night, is to render it complete. He labours without ceasing to fill his memory with its words, his understanding with its light, and his heart with its spirit. And what will be the effect upon the good man, of his thus delighting in the law of the Lord? The answer is:

VERSE 3. And he shall be like a tree planted by the rivers of water, that bringeth forth his fruit in his season: his leaf also shall not wither; and whatsoever he doeth shall prosper.

A beautiful illustration of the perpetual verdure and fruitfulness of the piety deriving its origin and sustenance from the word of God. It is compared to a tree whose roots are refreshed by never-failing streams of living water, and whose every part is instinct with the life flowing from its roots. It is the same with the piety nourished by the word of

God. As the sap of the tree imparts life, not only to its roots, and trunk, and larger branches, but also to the remotest twig and leaf, and to the very down upon the leaf; so the truly godly man's piety pervades his whole life, imparting its spirit, and character, and beauty to everything he does. He is not a religious man in one or two departments of life, but he is a religious man everywhere. His religion is a *mental habit*—a habit of thought, of feeling, of purpose, and of action, of which he never for a moment divests himself. He aims that not so much as a leaf on his tree of righteous living shall show signs of decay. The same spirit that actuates him in the largest, actuates him also in the least transaction of his life. He has respect unto all the commandments of the Lord; and whatever he does, aims to do all to the glory of God. His religion is not a thing that is *put on*—it is the man himself—*the* man *in* the man. Consequently, the storm that bows *mock* trees of righteousness to the earth, leaves *him* still standing; the drought that dries up *their* streams of life, leaves *his* still full, and fresh, and flowing. Vigour, verdure, and fruitfulness are his evermore. His source of strength can never fail. It is the river of life flowing from the throne of God and of the Lamb, reaching his soul through the law of the Lord, wherein is his delight and unceasing meditation. "And whatsoever he doeth shall prosper;" his worldly affairs generally, his spiritual affairs always. Whatsoever he doeth to perfect himself in holiness and pureness of living—wherever else he may experience failure, he will experience none here. God will strengthen him with might by his Spirit in the inner man, that he may stand in the evil day; and having done all, stand. His words to every one whose delight is in his law, are, "Fear thou not, for I am with thee; be not dismayed, for I am thy God: I will strengthen thee; yea, I will help thee; yea, I will uphold thee with the right hand of my righteousness." Isa. xli. 10.

VERSE 4. The ungodly are not so: but are like the chaff which the wind driveth away.

It is even so: the ungodly are not as the good man, whose delight is in the law of the Lord; they are not as he is, perpetually refreshed with streams from the "pure river of the water of life." There are no Divine influences flowing into their souls, to keep them evermore spiritually alive. They are not as a green tree with its roots deeply fixed in the earth, and fed by never-failing springs; nor even as a shrivelled tree, slightly rooted, and scantily watered; not yet indeed as any living thing—but they are chaff, worthless chaff, that the husbandman labours wholly to separate from the wheat. This is done in the East by throwing the grain with its chaff up against the wind, which the wind driveth away—our Prayer-book says, "away from the face of the earth." This translation expresses no more than the full force of the Hebrew verb rendered *driveth away.* As the word *chaff* expresses the worthlessness and helplessness of the ungodly, so the word *driveth-away* expresses the irresistible force that is brought to bear upon them. They are driven away from the face of the earth by wars, brawls, and secret murders; they are driven away from the face of it by themselves, by indulgences that hurry them into early and unhonoured graves. They are also driven away by the judgments of God, by the pestilence that walketh in darkness, and the destruction that wasteth at noon-day. Blown upon by the breath of mutual hatred, by the breath of their own passions, lusts, and appetites, and by the breath of incensed justice, the three combined do indeed drive them away as chaff from the face of the earth. Mutually destroying, self-destroying, and Divinely destroyed—such is the sad condition of the ungodly.

VERSE 5. Therefore the ungodly shall not stand in the judgment, nor sinners in the congregation of the righteous.

No, the ungodly shall not stand; if His winnowing judgments do not here separate them from the people of God, the winnowings of the judgment of the great day will certainly do it. The good and the bad, the chaff and the wheat are largely mingled here. They will, however, be wholly and for ever severed at the judgment of the great day. The Divine Husbandman will then, with his fan in his hand, for the last time, thoroughly purify his floor, winnowing out from among the pure and good, not only the ungodly, the sinner, and the scoffer, but also many who now have no fears for themselves—as the moralist, the formalist, the hypocrite, and the self-deceived. None will be able to stand in the judgment, be numbered in the congregation of the righteous, whose delight was not in the law of the Lord, and who did not exercise themselves therein day and night.

VERSE 6. For the Lord knoweth the way of the righteous; but the way of the ungodly shall perish.

This is the good man's consolation. The world may condemn and ridicule his way, and persecute him for persevering in it; yet the Lord knoweth, that is, *approveth* his way. His eye is evermore upon it for good. He marks well the good man's efforts to perfect himself in the virtues of a child of God, and strengthens him to go on from conquering to conquer. He protects him by his power, guides him by his wisdom, and sustains him by his grace. It was thus that he guided, protected, and sustained Noah in the deluge; Abraham in his wanderings; Joseph in his bondage; Moses in Egypt and in the wilderness; Daniel in the lions' den, and the Hebrew youth in the seven-times heated furnace. The Lord knoweth them that are his, and will never leave them, nor forsake them. The way of the righteous is his delight. But the way of the ungodly shall perish! The Lord abhors it. His eye is upon it for evil. He can never approve wicked men's thoughts or ways. His very nature, being infinitely perfect, binds him to defeat their plans, and punish them. He would not be God, if he could look upon evil and evil-doers with indifference. All the orderings of his providence, and all the arrangements of nature, are therefore in the long run against them to root them out.

Who then would not be the man whom our Psalm pronounces *blessed?* Who would not cease to do evil, and learn to do well, even as he did? He abounded in every good work and word, as the tree abounds with fruit, whose roots are fed by never-failing streams of living water. He so abounded in them because his delight was in the law of the Lord, and he exercised himself therein without ceasing. This was the whole secret of his blessedness, and will be the whole secret of ours, if the Lord shall ever delight in us, as he delighted in him. Our only safety, and our only happiness will be in amending our lives according to God's holy word. It is only as the waters of life reach our souls through the law of the Lord, that its palsied moral powers are quickened into life, and launch out upon an endless career of righteousness, purity, and bliss. And that all of us might have our moral powers thus quickened and directed, God gives his Holy Spirit to all of us who ask Him to put his laws into our minds, and to write them in our hearts. Heb. x. 16. It was to purchase for us this blessed Renovator and Restorer of all good in the soul, that his Son died on Calvary. Let us all then look to the gospel for strength to keep the law. We should use the law only as a schoolmaster to bring us to Christ, that we may be justified by faith. Gal. iii. 24. It is still our rule of holy living, but no longer the ground of our justification; and if any of us expect to reach a better world through the merit of our own obedience to the Divine law, and not through the alone merit of Christ's obedience, we shall be most deplorably disappointed. "For Christ is the end of the law for righteousness to every one that believeth." Rom. x. 4.

LECTURE ON PSALM II.

ONE greater than David is here, even the Son of David, whose kingdom ruleth over all. The main reference of this psalm is to Christ. Acts iv. 25–27, xiii. 33: Heb. i. 5, v. 5. It differs from the first, as the gospel differs from the law—that psalm is *moral*, showing us our *duty;* this is *evangelical*, showing us our Saviour. It is always thus that God exhibits the law and the gospel in his word. He never enjoins a duty without pointing us to Him through whom we may be enabled to perform it. If he require us to keep the whole law perfectly, it is in connection with the promise to write the whole law in living impulses upon our hearts. Heb. x. 16. If he tell us of our sins, he also tells us of Him whose blood cleanseth from all sin. If he tell us of our corruptions, he at the same time tells us also of a Divine Spirit, that can renew our souls in righteousness and true holiness. If, then, the sole object of the introduction of Messiah's kingdom be to restore man to purity and bliss—to bring him to delight in the law that is holy, just, and good—to transform him from a child of sin and Satan into a child of God, and elevate him to heaven, why should man oppose it? Why should he meditate its overthrow? Can he carry it against God? or, if he could, would not his victory be more disastrous to him than defeat? Some train of thought of this sort seems to be implied in the demand:

VERSE 1. Why do the heathen rage, and the people imagine a vain thing?

A vain thing as regards God—to attempt the overthrow of a kingdom upheld by Omnipotence, by Him who doeth whatsoever he pleaseth in the armies of heaven, and among the inhabitants of the earth, and whose hand none can stay. A vain thing, too, as regards themselves—for, supposing they should succeed, what would they have accomplished for themselves morally? The same that they would accomplish for themselves physically, if they were to strike the sun from its place in the heavens, henceforth to grope their way through a darkness that could be felt, and over an earth whence every form of beauty and life had fled. But vain as the undertaking must ever be, to attempt the overthrow of the kingdom of Christ upon earth, the ignorant, degraded, and easily excited multitude have not been the only persons to make it, but,

VERSE 2. The kings of the earth set themselves, and the rulers take counsel together, against the Lord, and against his Anointed.

Anointed here means the same as *Messiah*, and both words the same as *Christ* in the New Testament. How literally were the words of this verse fulfilled, when Herod, and Pontius Pilate, and the rulers of the Jews combined together to put Jesus to death! How cordially they hated each other; and yet how cordially they united in persecuting Jesus! This has been the history of our religion from the beginning. Men who would take counsel together in nothing else, have taken counsel together against the Lord, and against his Anointed. Christianity has been opposed by every other form of religion beneath the sun. The civil ruler has opposed it with the sword; the bigot with the screw, the wheel, and the stake; the philosopher with sophistry and derision; and the multitude with lawless violence. All have been alike eager to nail it to the cross, thrust a spear into its side, and place upon its head a crown of thorns. And when asked to spare it, the language of all has been, "Not this man, but Barabbas!" This feature of heterogeneous opposition to our religion, is conspicuous in all modern liberal and infidel conventions, where men of all beliefs, and of no belief, ignoring for the time being all their differences, unite heart and soul in a crusade against the word of God. They care little what stars occupy a place in the religious heavens of the world, provided the Star of Bethlehem be not of the number. They will tolerate any other form of religion sooner than the religion of the Lord, and of his Anointed. Of *their* religion, that is, of the religion revealed to us by the Father and the Son, by the Lord and his Christ, they say,

VERSE 3. Let us break their bands asunder, and cast away their cords from us.

These words, "bands and cords," suggest the secret of the world's great opposition to the gospel of Christ. It cannot abide the strictness of its laws. It is restiff under them, and would break them asunder and cast them off. It was not the strangeness of its *doctrines*, but the purity of its *precepts*, that so excited kings, and rulers, and people against the religion of the Son of Mary. If it had required them only to believe, or to profess to believe, and not also to *amend their lives according to God's holy word*, it would have experienced but little opposition. It is not requiring men to believe *mysteries*, but to *crucify every corrupt affection, and inordinate desire*, that sets them against the gospel. They love darkness rather than light, because they love their sins more than they love holiness. This was the case with the Jew and heathen of old. It is also the case with us. Our hearts are by nature as much opposed as theirs were, to being crossed in their desires by the law of God. None of our minds are subject to his law, till they are spiritually renewed. Till so renewed, they are enmity against God. We may not join hands with the revilers and persecutors of the religion of the Lord and of his Anointed, still if we fail to render its laws a loving obedience, the language of our hearts, in the ear of God, is, "Let us break their bands asunder, and cast away their cords from us."

VERSE 4. He that sitteth in the heavens shall laugh; the Lord shall have them in derision.

We can conceive of no feeling in the Divine mind toward any of his creatures that would lead him to literally laugh at and deride them. His feelings towards even those whom he dooms, are still feelings of pity. It was with tears that " God manifested in the flesh" exclaimed, "Behold, your house is left unto you desolate!" We may, therefore, understand by his laughing at and deriding the kings and rulers taking counsel together against him and his Anointed, only his *infinite consciousness of being able at any moment to defeat all their machinations.* As a man who was conscious of being able to deal in this way with his enemies would be likely to laugh at and deride them, till the time came for punishing them, so God, in order to our more vivid conception of the greatness of his own power and the utter impotence of his enemies, is said to do the same, though without any of the feelings that would, under similar circumstances, find their way into a human breast. Omniscient to plan, and omnipotent to execute, he can afford, till the right time comes for punishing them, to treat his enemies as if with supreme indifference. He can look, unmoved, upon their utmost opposition, as the opposition of worms. He is, therefore, never, by the fury of his enemies, hurried out of himself to take vengeance at once, but often leaves them to work out his own designs by their very wickedness, thus making their very wrath praise him. It was thus that he made the wrath of those crucifying his Son praise him. They thought they were destroying Messiah's kingdom. How mistaken! *They were laying its foundation!* It had its life and beginning in the blood which *they* thought would utterly extinguish it. Hence Luther's saying, "Who thought, when Christ suffered, and the Jews triumphed, that God was laughing all the time!" It was even so; for he saw them accomplishing—what they thought they were defeating—his own purposes of mercy toward a guilty world. He, therefore, still sat at ease upon his throne in the heavens, content to let the tide of human wrath roll on unchecked, till the time came for him to say, "Thus far—and no farther—here shall thy proud waves be stayed." This time is sure to come at the last: for He that sitteth in the heavens will not always act as if he ignored and derided the wickedness of the wicked. This has its bounds, beyond which God will not suffer it to pass; and when it reaches those bounds, then he visits for it.

VERSE 5. Then shall he speak unto them in his wrath, and vex them in his sore displeasure.

When God can no longer overrule the wrath of man to work out his own great purposes of truth and goodness, he restrains and punishes it. He dealt in this way with the Jews. As if contemptuously indifferent to what they were doing, he allowed them to go on until they had, as his death was necessary to the salvation of the world, crucified his Son: but when they pushed their hostility beyond, and aimed to drive the religion of Christ also out of the world, then, having laid aside his former apparent indifference, God spake unto them in his wrath, and vexed them in his sore displeasure. He sent the Roman legions against them, who besieged them till they endured horrors that shock the mind to relate, laid their city in ruins, levelled their beautiful temple to the ground, leaving not one stone upon another that was not thrown down; indeed ploughing up its very foundations, and then leading its former lovers and defenders away into hopeless captivity. And as he dealt with the Jews, so God at last dealt with the Romans also. He suffered them to take part in crucifying his Son, and punishing the Jews: but when they would have gone farther, he sent upon them a destruction even more sweeping than that sent upon the Jews. He subverted not only their political and military power, but gradually obliterated their very name. The history of other nations to whom God has spoken in his anger, is the same. So easily, when the time comes for him to do it, does He who who sitteth in the heavens discomfit his enemies. He frowns—and they are not! The places that knew them once, know them no more. Do what they may to overthrow the kingdom of his Son, God's never-failing answer to the fiercest and most formidable of its assailants is evermore the same.

VERSE 6. Yet have I set my King upon my holy hill of Zion.

Zion was the seat of Jewish royalty, but this King, against whom human malice would spend itself in vain, was a greater than David. He is the King of Zion; he is Head over all things to the Church; and hath all power given unto him in heaven and upon earth. Hence God calls him *his* King; that is, a King who shares the government of the universe with himself. Hence he says, "I have set *my* King upon my holy hill of Zion"—*my* King, not a king elected and consecrated to the office by man, but elected and consecrated by me. Who then is this divinely elected and divinely consecrated King, enthroned upon God's holy hill of Zion? The next verse answers,

VERSE 7. I will declare the decree: the Lord hath said unto me, Thou art my Son: this day have I begotten thee.

These are the King's own words, that the Lord himself had said unto him, "Thou art my Son."

His Son, too, in a sense which, as all approved commentators tell us, makes him equal with the Father Almighty. "Thou art my Son." Do we meet with words similar to these elsewhere? We do—once on the banks of the Jordan, at the baptism of Jesus of Nazareth. There came a voice from heaven, "This is my beloved Son, in whom I am well pleased." Matt. ii. 17. And so again, on the mount of transfiguration, issuing from the bright overshadowing cloud, there came a voice, "This is my beloved Son, in whom I am well pleased: hear ye him." Matt. xvii. 5. This divine Son-King then, enthroned upon God's holy hill of Zion, is he who was conceived by the Holy Ghost, and born of the Virgin Mary. "This day have I begotten thee." These words refer not alone to our Lord's miraculous conception, but to all the great acts of the Father Almighty—such as his raising Jesus from the dead, and exalting him to the right hand of power on high, whereby it was demonstrated that he was indeed the Son and equal of the Most High.

VERSE 8. Ask of me, and I will give thee the heathen for thine inheritance, and the uttermost parts of the earth for thy possession.

This is the price that Messiah was to receive for pouring out his soul unto death for us men and our salvation. The whole earth was in consequence to become his spiritual inheritance and possession—an inheritance and possession upon which he began to enter when the preaching of the gospel spread from the Jews to the Gentiles. Then began to be fulfilled that which will have been realized when the seventh angel sounds his trumpet, and there are great voices in heaven, saying, "The kingdoms of this world are become the kingdoms of our Lord, and of his Christ; and he shall reign for ever and ever." Rev. xi. 15.

VERSE 9. Thou shalt break them with a rod of iron; thou shalt dash them in pieces like a potter's vessel.

This cannot mean that Messiah's sway is a kingdom of *force*, but only that his enemies can no more withstand his power than an earthen vessel can withstand the blows of an iron rod. His only weapons of assault are truth and love; and if human power and institutions crumble at their touch and pass away, it is because there is something radically evil and defective in them. The northern oceans are often filled with mountains of ice, reaching not only far down into the deep, but towering also to the very clouds, and threatening to crush to atoms everything with which they come into collision. Nevertheless, how soon do a few days of the light and heat of the sun rob them of their strength, leaving the frailest barque to speed on its way over unobstructed waters! It is in this way that the Sun of Righteousness operates. By light and heat, truth and love, he clears the way over the frozen oceans of human life, for the onward progress of the ark of his salvation to the haven where it would be. The only way in which Messiah can be said to break his enemies with a rod of iron, and dash them in pieces like a potter's vessel, is his leaving them to the natural and fearful destruction that flows from resisting truth and love, the two great laws of his kingdom, and, indeed, the two great laws of all well-being. How appropriately then does our psalm close with the exhortation,

VERSES 10–12. Be wise now therefore, O ye kings; be instructed, ye judges of the earth. Serve the Lord with fear, and rejoice with trembling. Kiss the Son, lest he be angry, and ye perish from the way, when his wrath is kindled but a little. Blessed are all they that put their trust in him.

This exhortation to the great and mighty of the earth to serve the Lord and his Christ, with fear and trembling, is based upon the assumption that it is perdition to oppose them. And let none of us suppose that we are not opposing the rule of Messiah, the rule of the Son, because we were not among those who cried, "Away with him—crucify him!" An unregenerate heart places us in an attitude of hostility to him and his government. And if that heart be not removed from our breasts, and a heart of purity and love be put in its place, it will of itself alone work out for us a destruction far more fearful than that of being broken with a rod of iron, and dashed in pieces like a potter's vessel. Seek ye then this indispensable moral renovation; be melted by the light and heat, truth and love, of the gospel of Christ; for *blessed are all they that put their trust in him.* Blessed in this world—the waters of life begin at once to flow into the soul, filling it at times with a peace that passeth all understanding—a peace that nothing earthly can destroy, and that enables them to pass the valley of the shadow of death, fearing no evil. Blessed also in the world to come; the Son meets them on their entrance into that world with the cheering words, "Come, ye blessed of my Father, inherit the kingdom prepared for you from the foundation of the world." Blessed indeed are all they that put their trust in him—blessed here and hereafter, now and for ever. He maketh all things work together for their good; their very afflictions in this world to work out for them a far more exceeding and eternal weight of glory in the world to come.

LECTURE ON PSALM III.

This Psalm was composed by David when he was fleeing before his rebellious son Absalom. The history of that event, therefore, furnishes the key to its interpretation. David was a king, ruling in the fear of God, and success attended his every undertaking, until, in an unguarded hour, he was betrayed into illicit love, and then, to conceal it, into murder. It was not, however, wholly concealed, for God brought it home to David's conscience through the prophet Nathan; and though he remitted the law's express penalty, death, yet that he might punish David for his heinous offences, he said to him, "Behold, I will raise up evil against thee out of thine own house." 2 Sam. xii. 11. This evil, to rise up against David out of his own house, soon came, and in the same way too in which he himself had sinned—that is, in lewdness and blood; in lewdness first, his son Amnon dishonouring his own sister, (2 Sam. xiii. 14,) and then in blood, his son Absalom, to revenge his sister's disgrace, slaying Amnon. 2 Sam. xiii. 28, 29. This was evil indeed against David, out of his own house; and yet it was punishing him only by leaving his sons to repeat his own sins. His cup of shame and sorrow would even now seem to have been full; it was not, however. His ill-judged pardon of Absalom for the murder of his brother, and permitting him to return again to Jerusalem, increased his shame and sorrow, both as a father and as a king. Good himself, he was slow to suspect evil, and therefore suspected nothing evil in Absalom towards himself, till he had stolen the hearts of the people; till, by good words and fair speeches, he had persuaded them that it would be altogether to their advantage for them to place *him* upon the throne of Israel in his father's stead. Of this conspiracy to deprive him of his life and throne, David heard nothing and suspected nothing till it was ready to be executed. Then he learned that Absalom had been proclaimed king at Hebron, and that, with apparently few exceptions, the people had joined him. Unable to make head, at once, against so formidable and unexpected a conspiracy, and being, besides, unwilling to make Jerusalem, the holy city, the battle-ground of such an impious and unnatural war, David said to all his servants that were with him at Jerusalem, "Arise, and let us flee; for we may not else escape from Absalom: make speed to depart, lest he overtake us suddenly, and bring evil upon us, and smite the city with the edge of the sword." 2 Sam. xv. 14. And David, passing out of the city over the brook Kidron, with his few tried and still adhering friends, went up by the ascent of Mount Olivet, weeping as he went, with his head covered, and barefoot, in token of his going as a mourner, submitting himself to the mighty hand of God. It was while he was fleeing in this way before his ungrateful and unnatural son, that David conceived, if he did not actually write out at the time, the following psalm. How appropriate then, under such circumstances, are its opening words, addressed to Him who was then David's only hope!

VERSE 1. Lord, how are they increased that trouble me! Many are they that rise up against me.

If he could not commune freely with others, there is at least One to whom David can still go, and make his troubles known. Man may fail him, but the Lord will not. Man may refuse him aid and sympathy, but the Lord will refuse him neither. "Lord," says he, "how are they increased that trouble me!" All his old, and, as he once thought, fast friends, had revolted from him, and were seeking his life and throne; and, worst of all, his own son was heading the rebellion. And yet, what evil had he done them, that many were thus risen up against him? There was not one of those in rebellion against him who had received anything but good at his hands. What a commentary is this upon human gratitude—men seeking the life of one to whom they owed their blessings! It was in this way they treated David. It was in this way they treated the Son of David. He too experienced nothing but evil, where he should have experienced nothing but good. Many were they that rose up against Him. His whole nation clamored for his blood; nor did they rest till it flowed on Calvary. It has always been so. Christ has always been betrayed and crucified by those of his own household, the Church. It is of enemies within that he has oftenest been obliged to say with David, "Many are they that rise up against me." It is too, by enemies within that the Christian is oftenest betrayed to his ruin—sinful affections and ungoverned passions banishing Christ from his ruling place in the heart. David, however, was not so much distressed by the number of his enemies, as he was by what many of them said of him, namely,

VERSE 2. Many there be which say of my soul, There is no help for him in God.

This cut deeper into David's heart than anything else they could say or do. It was equivalent to saying, that he was such a wretch that mercy itself had cast him off. David was willing to admit that the Lord was afflicting him for his sins, but not that he had forsaken him. This is a mistake that the world are very apt to make—that is, to suppose a person who is greatly afflicted to be deserted of God. It was the mistake that Job's friends made in regard to him, and David's enemies in regard to him; hence Shimei, when he saw him fleeing before Absalom, cursed him as one forsaken of God. 2 Sam. xvi. 8. It was this mistake too that the enemies of the Son of David made in regard to him. Seeing him in the power of his enemies and nailed to the cross, they derided the idea that there was any help for him in God. Hence those taunting words upon Calvary, "If he be the King of Israel, let him now come down from the cross, and we will believe on him. He trusted in God: let him deliver him now if he will have him." Matt. xxvii. 42, 43. Nevertheless, both David and the Son of David found help in God.

Affliction is no certain evidence of Divine desertion. On the contrary, if it draw us, as it drew David, to a closer walk with God, it may be evidence that God is with us. Hence it is written, "Many are the afflictions of the righteous." Psal. xxxiv. 19. If, then, his afflictions lead him to a throne of grace, and to a holier life, let no one give place for a moment to the thought—whoever or whatever may say it, the world, the adversary, or his own heart—that "there is no help for him in God." Despair is one of the worst sins that man can commit. It disparages the Divine mercy—God's brightest and most cherished attribute—and distracts the soul as no other sin can. It is of Satan's fiery darts the most burning and consuming. And how are its fires to be quenched? David answers us in the words,

VERSE 3. But thou, O Lord, art a shield for me; my glory, and the lifter up of my head.

This is David's answer to the malicious taunt of his enemies, that "there was no help for him in God." "Thou, O Lord, art a shield unto me; my glory, and the lifter up of my head." Oppressive as his sense of sin was, his faith in God did not forsake him; it still sustained him in his sorest trials. He still believed that the Lord was a shield unto him on every side; "his glory" too; the source and author of his honours, and also "the lifter up of his head;" one who had delivered him in times past, and who would still deliver him. David did not cease to trust the Lord, because clouds and darkness were round about him, and he was fleeing before the storm. He recollected that other storms had spent their fury on him, and left him unharmed; and he believed that this would do the same. How important it is for the believer to remember, in the midst of *present* trials, *former* mercies and deliverances. How often does the retrospect serve to convince him that the Lord has *never* forsaken him, and therefore that he never will forsake him. Such was the effect upon David's mind of his review of the Lord's former dealings with him. The review strengthened and confirmed his faith. Nor did he combat his fears by faith only, but also by prayer, saying,

VERSE 4. I cried unto the Lord with my voice, and he heard me out of his holy hill.

David had been driven out from the visible presence of the Lord in his tabernacle on Mount Zion, nevertheless he still directed his prayer towards the holy hill, and received from thence an answer. This is one of the glorious privileges of the believer—his lot can be cast in no place whence his cry of distress cannot reach the mercy-seat upon God's holy hill on high. It cannot be said of the Lord, Lo, he is here; or, Lo, he is there. He is in every place where there is a heart sighing for his presence and aid. David found a mercy-seat in the wilderness, Jonah in the depth of the sea, Daniel in the lions' den, and the Hebrew youths in the seven-times heated furnace. It is always so. The Lord never fails any who seek him with the whole heart. In what way he answered David's cry for help we are unable to say; whether by some visible token of his favour, or secret communications of his grace. This only we know, that David's faith and prayers triumphed over all his fears, and so triumphed as to enable him to say,

VERSE 5. I laid me down and slept; I awaked, for the Lord sustained me.

"I laid me down, and slept." Could language more forcibly describe the tranquilizing effect of faith and prayer! David's situation was in every way calculated to drive sleep from his eyes, and slumber from his eye-lids: nevertheless, conscious of having the Lord as his shield, and having committed himself and cause to him in prayer, he composed himself to rest, and slept. His trust was not in vain. He awaked, for the Lord sustained him. How sweet it is to be able, in the midst of danger, to sink to rest without fear, secure of the protection of Him who never sleeps, who never even slumbers! This is the privilege of the believer alone—and the fulfilment to him of the promise, "Thou wilt keep him in perfect peace, whose mind is stayed on thee." Isa. xxvi. 3. It is the privilege of the believer alone, to say, as he composes himself to rest at the close of each day, and most of all, as he composes himself to rest at the close of life, "Father, into thy hands I commend my spirit;" and to do it without the least anxiety, confident that the same God that has watched over him in his bed, will also watch over him in his grave, and awake him, as he awaked his Son Jesus, even from *its* leaden slumbers. Nor was David enabled to sleep only, but also, his faith having been invigorated by prayer, to defy his enemies, saying,

VERSE 6. I will not be afraid of ten thousands of people, that have set themselves against me round about.

This was literally David's situation. Ten thousands of people were posted round about him, panting for his life. But he who has the Lord on his side, need not fear what man can do unto him. Numbers should have no terrors for him, knowing that He whose he is, and whom he serves, can as easily discomfit ten thousand as he can discomfit one. Engaged in the cause of truth and right, he has of course the God of truth and right on his side, and can therefore reckon upon certain victory. He need have no misgivings as to the result of the contest. The final result is certain, and can be but one. It is this thought of certain victory that girds the soul with supernatural strength and courage in all its conflicts with the powers of evil. "Were there as many devils in Worms as there are tiles on the housetops, still I will enter it," said Luther, on his way to the city of Worms, *alone*, to defend the word of God against the world in arms. The same fearlessness of man filled Luther's heart that filled David's; and, in one case, as in the other, must have come from the same source—the inspiration of the Almighty. The thought of each heart was, "I will not fear what man can do unto me." How many a martyr's, confessor's, and reformer's heart, has God filled with this sublime contempt of human power and malice! There is in the defiance, however, nothing of self-reliance—it is entirely the result of trust in God. This we learn from the words of David following his defiance, saying,

VERSE 7. Arise, O Lord; save me, O my God: for thou hast smitten all mine enemies upon the cheek-bone; thou hast broken the teeth of the ungodly.

This shows that David's expectation of victory was not in himself, in his personal prowess as a warrior, but in the faithfulness of the Lord his God. Hence his impassioned cry, "Arise, O Lord! save me, O my God!" It is true that David marshalled his forces as a skilful and experienced general should, and as carefully as if everything in the battle to ensue was to be accomplished by the sword alone;—and yet, he still looked to God alone for success. And to inspire himself with confidence that the Lord would give success, he refers to the victories he had given him in times past, saying, "Thou hast smitten all mine enemies upon the cheek-bone; thou hast broken the teeth of the ungodly." This imagery of breaking the cheek-bone and teeth of enemies, is likening them to those wild beasts whose great power is in the jaws and teeth, so that, when their jaws and teeth are broken, their power to injure is gone. The imagery, then, indicates that the Lord had always destroyed the power of David's enemies to injure him. And as the Lord had subdued his enemies before him hitherto, David could not but believe that he would subdue them still. This his belief was not in vain, as the speedy winding-up of Absalom's rebellion showed: for Absalom's forces, though outnumbering his father's, probably more than ten to one, were utterly routed and dispersed, and himself slain, in the first and only battle fought. The battle was the Lord's, the victory his, and to him David ascribes it in these words:

VERSE 8. Salvation belongeth unto the Lord: Thy blessing is upon thy people.

David's whole history proves the truth of this. And let none of us suppose that the history of David is peculiar. The salvation of every one of us is as much of the Lord, as David's was. If we have been preserved, it has been because his hand was over us. If we have not fallen into grievous sins, it has been because his grace restrained us. If we have not been overcome, either by external or internal foes, it has been because he was a shield about us, and a sustaining power within us. If we have been permitted to indulge the hope of pardon and future happiness, it has been because he so loved the world, that he gave his only begotten Son, that whosoever believeth on him might not perish, but have everlasting life. We seek in vain to mention any good which is not in some way the gift of God. The mind that thinks, the heart that feels, and the hand that executes, are his, and are blessings to us, only as he makes them such. How truly then may we say that "salvation belongeth unto the Lord!" "If he will save, none can destroy; and if he will destroy, none can save." This being so, how glorious is the assurance wherewith David closes this third psalm, saying,

"Thy blessing is upon thy people." The Lord is indeed good to all, and his tender mercies are over all his works; but then his *special* blessing is upon his people. He watches over them with an eye that never slumbers, and with a care that never fails. He is their good Shepherd, leading them forth into green pastures, and by the side of still waters, gently guiding the weak, and bearing the lambs in his arms, and carrying them in his bosom. Hear how David speaks, in another place, of this blessing of the Lord upon his people, (Psalm cxxi.) "He will not suffer thy foot to be moved: he that keepeth thee will not slumber. Behold, he that keepeth Israel shall neither slumber nor sleep. The Lord is thy keeper; the Lord is thy shade upon thy right hand. The sun shall not smite thee by day, nor the moon by night. The Lord shall preserve thee from all evil; he shall preserve thy soul." In promising, however, to deliver us from all evil, God has not promised never to *afflict* us. Many are the afflictions of the righteous. But to his people, affliction is not an evil, since he sustains them under it, according to his promise, (Isa. xliii. 2,) and makes it, with all things else, work together for their good. Who then, however weak he may be in himself, need despair? Salvation belongeth unto the Lord, and his blessing is upon his people: and the prayer of faith moves both his heart and his hand to give us the victory. However sorely then you may be afflicted, or tried, or tempted, believe not for a moment that there is no help for you in God. If you have forsaken your sins, and are looking to Christ for their pardon, and grace to sin no more, there is help, present and *everlasting* help for thee in him; and he is saying to thee, even now, "Fear thou not; for I am with thee: be not dismayed; for I am thy God. I will strengthen thee; yea, I will help thee; yea, I will uphold thee with the right hand of my righteousness. I will never leave thee, nor forsake thee."

LECTURE ON PSALM IV.

THIS Psalm is believed to have been written by David on the same occasion as the last—the rebellion of Absalom. It is written, however, in more general terms than the last, having no local or personal allusion in it, and is, on that account, better suited to express the sentiments of any suffering believer in the Church at large, and in all ages. It opens with the impassioned cry:

VERSE 1. Hear me when I call, O God of my righteousness: thou hast enlarged me when I was in distress; have mercy upon me, and hear my prayer.

This appeal of David to God as the God of his righteousness, or his righteous God, implies that he thought his cause one that a righteous God could espouse. This is a fact that we all should remember; that is, to ask of God only such things as he can grant consistently with his attributes. We should never ask anything, the granting of which would cause him to sacrifice one attribute to another. Even in asking things lawful, it is still to be done in submission to his will. It cannot, however, but increase our expectation of a favourable answer, that what we ask is for the glory of God. This was the conviction of David. He was suffering for the cause of his God, and therefore appeals to him as a righteous God to deliver him. It was not his own righteousness, but the righteousness of the cause for which he was suffering and contending, that emboldened him. It is well for us, that the moving cause for God's hearing our prayers, is out of our wretched selves; and that faith in Christ enables us to appeal to God, even as a God of justice, to pardon our sins, and save our souls—to pardon and save, as an act of justice to Christ, though still an act altogether of mercy to us. It is indeed true, that it is only as we ourselves are righteous, through faith in Christ, and lead, as the fruit of such faith, righteous lives, that we are authorized to assume that the Lord will hear us when we call upon him. It is not, however, this threefold, *evangelical* righteousness, that David pleads here; but the righteousness of his *cause*—the cause of God, of truth, and of right—of the Lord and of his Anointed.

"Thou hast enlarged me when I was in distress; have mercy upon me, and hear my prayer." David makes the Lord's former mercies to him an argument for their continuance and repetition. The import of his words is, As thou hast enlarged me when I was in distress, enlarge me again: as thou hast been merciful to me, be merciful to me again: as thou hast heard my prayers, hear them again: as thou hast been my deliverer, be my deliverer still. How strange an argument would this be, wherewith to urge man to help us—*because he had already helped us.* Nevertheless, this is the argument wherewith David urges the Lord: "Thou hast enlarged me when I was in distress;" therefore have mercy upon me now, and hear my prayer. Man is apt to reckon former benefits as a bar both to asking and granting other and newer ones. It is otherwise with the Lord. The more we pray, the more he loves to hear us pray; the more he gives, the more ready he is to add to his gifts. How like a God! And does not this fact alone prove the religion of the Bible to be of celestial origin? One benefit draws another after it, and still another, in endless succession. But wonderful as this aspect of the Divine goodness is, is it not in reality the feeling, when duly considered, of every pious mind used to prayer? That is, that the more frequently the Lord has heard our prayers in times past, the more certainly do we feel that he will answer them in time to come? that if he has delivered us out of one trouble, he will deliver us out of another, and still another; and that, if in answer to our intercessions he has saved one soul from death, he will save more? What a God is ours, to be moved by his past mercies to us, to repeat them; and to put it into the heart of his children to plead his past mercies as an argument for their repetition! He has nowhere reproved us for asking much, but often for not asking more.

VERSE 2. O ye sons of men, how long will ye turn my glory into shame? how long will ye love vanity, and seek after leasing? Selah.

What David here calls "his glory," may mean, first, his regal dignity and authority, to which he had been elevated from a shepherd boy. This dignity and authority he claimed as the direct and special gift of God. This claim, men of the world ridiculed, as they did also the claim of the Son of David, being the son of a carpenter, to be the King of Israel. Men can ill endure to see those whom, in their empty pride, they will not regard as their equals, elevated above them, even by God himself. Hence they persecuted both David, and the Son of

David, as upstarts and pretenders. It was not the rabble only who treated them in this way, but also the "sons of men," the great and the mighty ones of the earth. But they opposed them in vain—the throne of each was upheld by an Almighty God. David then could well demand, How long will ye attempt to subvert what Omnipotence has determined to establish? Your opposition can only end in your own ruin. This is one meaning of the words. But David's regal dignity was not his only glory; nor indeed his chief glory. His chief glory was his holy life, his faith in God, producing holiness and pureness of living. This also "the sons of men" ridiculed—turned into shame. They could as ill endure his holy life as they could endure his righteous rule. His good, therefore, was evil spoken of—he became the song of drunkards. They treated the Son of David in the same way. They not only derided his claim to be the King of Israel, but they were most of all offended at the reproving purity of his life and teaching. The light of truth, purity and love shining in everything he said and did, was too intense not to show them their own moral deficiencies; but instead of yielding themselves to the influences of that light, they laboured to turn it into contempt. And, unhappily, has not this too often been the treatment experienced by those of his followers, who would be, as he was, holy, harmless, undefiled, and separate from sinners? The world will smile upon you so long as your piety is not of a character to reprove them, by any marked and striking contrast between your course of life and theirs. Attempt, however, to be a *Christian indeed*—to govern yourself in all things by the law of God, insomuch that the world are obliged to see that if your course is right, theirs is wrong; that if yours alone can lead to heaven, they are lost—do this, and both their aspect and their language towards you change. The consistency of your life with the principles of your religion is stigmatized as weak, superstitious, austere; and to fix the stigma more indelibly, how many members of the Church join the cry, and add, "illiberal, narrow-minded, puritanical." It is thus that man's highest glory, his faith in God producing holiness and pureness of living, has always been disparaged by the world, and the allies of the world in the bosom of the Church. And David demands of the men of the world of his day, how long they would pour contempt upon this highest ornament of a rational nature—this only thing that brings the soul into communion with infinite purity, under the protection of infinite power, and spreads before it an inheritance of glory, honour, and immortality. To seek my happiness in this way, says David, I reckon "my glory;" you despise and disparage it, and turn it into shame. You are surprised and scandalized at my mode of seeking happiness; I am still more surprised and scandalized at yours. I demand, therefore, "How long will ye love vanity, and seek after leasing?" I seek honour and happiness in loving and serving God; you, in loving and serving the world. I seek honour and happiness in the true and eternal; you, in the false and perishable. What you love is vanity, emptiness, and nought; what I love is a substantial and everlasting good. What you seek after, is leasing, that is to say, a lie, a something that excites your hopes only to disappoint them; what I seek after, is truth, a something that can never deceive. In this way did David demonstrate that it was not his course, but theirs, that should be turned into shame. They could oppose him and his government, but their opposition could injure none but themselves. They could ridicule his trust in God as the only hope and portion of his soul, but their ridicule could be turned with infinitely greater force against what they had chosen as the hope and portion of their souls. The object of their love and pursuit was, as the words *vanity* and *leasing* mean, a *lying vanity*—a something full of deceit and full of emptiness. And has not this been the sad confession of thousands who have sought the things of this world as the satisfying portion of their souls? In the full enjoyment of every earthly good, they have still, even with bleeding hearts, been obliged to say, "Vanity of vanities! all is vanity, and vexation of spirit." And as this is invariably the final result of seeking happiness in the things of earth, there is even a startling emphasis in the words, "*How long* will ye love vanity, and seek after leasing?" But still farther to illustrate the certainty of his own happiness—not seeking it in the creature, but in God, the Creator, David adds:

VERSE 3. Know ye that the Lord hath set apart him that is godly for himself: the Lord will hear when I call unto him.

This is both the privilege and the glory of the man who loves, and is in turn loved by his Maker. The Lord hath set *him* apart for himself, to be the special recipient of his favours. It is of such that we read, "They shall be mine, saith the Lord of hosts, in that day when I make up my jewels; and I will spare them as a man spareth his own son that serveth him." Mal. iii. 17. It is useless, therefore, says David to those opposing his rule over them, and deriding his trust in God—it is useless for you to set yourselves against the godly man; he is under the special protection of the Lord Almighty.

It was in this way that God set apart his own Son for himself, for the accomplishment of his purposes of truth and mercy toward man. It is in this way, too, that he sets apart for himself every one bearing the image of his Son; and every one bearing that image can say, with the same assurance as David said it, "The Lord will hear me when I call unto him. The eyes of the Lord are upon the righteous; and his ears are open unto their cry." Psalm xxxiv. 15. It is for them, and for them alone, that the world exists; that seed-time and harvest, summer and winter, day and night, cease not; and that the rainbow spans the brow of the retreating storm. It may be a humiliating thought to the great and mighty of the earth, that God keeps the world in being, not for *them*—not to perfect any of *their* schemes—but for the godly man—to perfect his soul in holiness. If an hour should ever come in the history of our world, when there should be no longer a soul on earth qualifying for heaven, it is hardly to be doubted, that *that hour would be the last of time.* There would be, in that case, no longer anything here worth keeping the earth in existence for another moment.

VERSES 4, 5. Stand in awe, and sin not: commune with your own heart upon your bed, and be still. Offer the sacrifices of righteousness, and put your trust in the Lord.

The ungodly and the worldly-minded are here exhorted to repentance, and the three great steps leading to conversion are described. The first step is *solitary self-reflection.* "Stand in awe, and sin not: commune with your own heart upon your bed, and be still." It is for want of reflection that men do not fear God, and realize their dependence on his favour. Want of reflection is the great source of all irreligion. Convinced of this, the conductors of a certain seminary of learning made it one of the standing regulations of the institution, that every pupil should daily retire *alone* to her chamber for a half-hour's solitary reflection upon herself and her Maker. This solitary half-hour's daily communing with God and their own consciences was not without its legitimate effect. Many a pupil, who at first thought the half-hour would be an agreeable escape from the confinement of the school-room, began, when brought, as it were, face to face with God and their consciences, to entertain new and startling views both of Him and of themselves, and to ask the question, "What shall I do to be saved?" It was all, however, only the legitimate effect of solitary self-reflection. This, rightly pursued, must cause us to flee from ourselves and the creature, to the Lord. It was thus that reflection wrought on David. "I thought," says he, "upon my ways, and turned my feet unto thy testimonies. I made haste, and delayed not to keep thy commandments." Ps. cxix. 59, 60.

The second step is, "offer the sacrifices of righteousness"—that is, "cease to do evil; learn to do well." The offerings of righteousness here enjoined are not the material offerings of the Levitical law, but the offerings of love and obedience. It is thought by some that the words, "offer the sacrifices of *righteousness*," allude to Absalom's *hypocritical* sacrifices, and especially to his pretended vow to be paid at Hebron, when he went there only to raise the standard of rebellion. 2 Sam. xv. 7, 8. There is then an emphasis in the words, urging us to love God for himself alone, and to obey him, without pretence and without hypocrisy.

The third and last step is *faith;* for David adds, after enjoining solitary self-reflection and holy obedience, "and put your trust in the Lord." Here is the act that secures to us the pardon of our sins, the renovation of our hearts, the enlightening and sanctifying influences of the Divine Spirit. It is an act that renders sin hateful to the soul, and holiness its desire and delight.

VERSE 6. There be many that say, Who will show us any good? Lord, lift thou up the light of thy countenance upon us.

"Who will show us any good?"—or rather, as the word *any* is not in the original, Who will show us *good?*—that is, *the* good, the possession of which will leave man to desire nothing more. Believing that there must be such an all-satisfying good for him somewhere, and conscious of not possessing it, man has been evermore inquiring where it is to be found, and wherein it consists. Hence the endless disputations of the old philosophers in regard to the *chief good*, some placing it in one thing, some in another, and all missing the mark. This question, as to the *one only* thing that can render man perfectly and everlastingly happy—a question that must agitate every mind conscious of its weakness, and wants, and immortality—was propounded to the Psalmist; and how does he answer it?

Lord, lift thou up the light of thy countenance upon us. This is David's answer as to what constitutes man's chief good. It is the light of God's countenance shining upon the soul. It is that one *only* thing which will so fill and possess the soul, as to leave it nothing more to desire. The answer is, for substance, the same as the Levitical high priest's divinely worded benediction of old, saying, "The Lord bless thee, and keep thee: the Lord make his face to shine upon thee, and be gracious unto thee: the Lord lift up his countenance upon thee, and give thee peace." Num. vi. 24–26. The answer is also substantially the same as the benediction at the end of our communion service, which reads, "the peace of God, which passeth all understanding, keep your hearts and minds in the knowledge and love of God, and of his Son, Jesus Christ our Lord: and the blessing of God Almighty, the Father, the Son, and the Holy Ghost, be amongst you, and remain with you always." It is the blessing then of the triune God that enriches the soul for ever—gives it infinite power upon which to repose, infinite goodness to love—in short, infinite perfections of every kind upon which to exercise its endlessly expanding powers, both of feeling and of intellect. What more can the soul need, what more can it ask, than the secure and everlasting possession of such a good as this? Hear how David speaks of the effect which the Lord's lifting up the light of his countenance upon him had upon him:

VERSE 7. Thou hast put gladness into my heart more than in the time that their corn and their wine increased.

The worldly man knows no greater joy than that afforded him by the due returns of his labour. An abundant harvest, a prosperous commerce, a thriving trade, or a lucrative profession, puts its highest gladness into his heart. *He knows no joy independent of external circumstances!* It was otherwise with David. His joy was not only greater than any afforded by external circumstances, but wholly independent of them. If this psalm was conceived while he was fleeing before Absalom, he was dependent upon the charity of a faithful servant to keep himself and followers from literal starvation. 2 Sam. xvi. 1, 2. But in the midst of this utter destitution of every external comfort, he declares the joy of his heart to be greater than that of his enemies in the midst of their abundance. Such is the joy that the light of God's countenance, falling upon it, excites in the heart of the believer, even in the darkest hour of the darkest night of adversity. His joy lives an inextinguishable life even in such an hour; and well it may, for it is God himself who pours the living tide through his heart. And how sweetly does David describe its soothing and sustaining power when, in spite of all his dangers and privations, he says:

VERSE 8. I will both lay me down in peace and sleep: for thou, Lord, only makest me to dwell in safety.

The Hebrew word here translated *both*, would give the thought better if it were translated into the phrase *at once;* and so translated, how perfect a picture does it give us of a mind at ease! David was hemmed in by foes on every side, but instead of still watching, when the hour for rest had come, dismissing every fear, he says, "I will *at once* lay me down in peace, and sleep." A more helpless condition than that of profound sleep cannot be imagined; but David commits himself to it, as void of fear as a child in its father's arms. He explains, however, the origin of his supernatural composure in the words,

"For thou, Lord, only makest me to dwell in safety." Man was labouring to do him all the evil he could, but he knew that the Lord *alone*—though every friend besides should forsake him and combine against him—still that the Lord alone could make him dwell in safety. And with this thought still upon his mind, he falls asleep as sweetly and securely as if he had not an enemy in the world! How sublime a thing is faith! how it elevates a man above himself; and how certainly must it be the inspiration of Him in whose power and goodness it trusts!

This is a most instructive psalm. The first verse teaches us that, as a God of righteousness, God loveth and defendeth the right; and, as such, can grant even to our prayers, only that which is right in itself, or through the merits of his Son; and yet, that approaching him in this way, we may even plead his former mercies to us as an argument for their repetition. The second verse teaches us that man's highest glory is *faith*, is trust in the Lord, and that they who seek true, substantial glory in any other way, are chasing a shadow. The third verse teaches us that God's choicest treasure of earth is the godly man; that he has set apart every such man for himself, for the reception of his own glorious moral attributes and character. The third and fourth verses describe the process of conversion—that it begins with solitary self-reflection, communing with one's own heart; passes thence to a determined amendment of life; and ends in an unfaltering trust in the mercy of God alone for salvation. The sixth verse asks what that good is, the possession of which will make man so entirely happy as to leave him nothing more to desire, and answers the question, by declaring the favour of God, the light of his countenance upon the soul, to be that good; and then it is affirmed in the verse following, that his smile puts a joy and gladness into the heart above any that the world can bestow. The eighth and last verse describes the man who is filled with the consciousness of possessing this good, falling asleep sweetly and securely in the midst of the greatest dangers. Who, then, would not desire to possess this all-sufficing good? It can be obtained by faith in Him through whose death it was purchased. Possess yourselves of that faith, and then will the weakest and most timid of you be enabled to say, not only at the close of each succeeding day, "I will at once lay me down in peace and sleep," but to say it also when the hour comes wherein you must compose yourself for that sleep that shall know no waking, until the trumpet of the angel of the resurrection breaks up for ever the slumbers of the dead.

LECTURE ON PSALM V.

David seems to have been thoroughly persuaded that men ought always to pray, and not to faint; never to grow weary if an answer did not come as soon as was expected, or in the way desired. Prayer seems to have been as necessary to him as the play of his lungs and the pulsations of his heart. How many of his psalms open with a cry to obtain mercy and find grace to help in time of need! And so earnestly does his soul pant upwards to God, that he repeats the same thing over and over in nearly the same words; and yet always so that each succeeding repetition is still a variation, expressing another shade of the vehement intensity of his desires. Of this striking peculiarity of David's prayers we have an illustration in the first three verses of the psalm before us. Its fervid repetitions indicate a soul feeling that it cannot be denied. They remind one of the repetitions of Daniel pleading for the deliverance of captive Israel, saying, "O my God, incline thine ear, and hear; open thine eyes, and behold our desolations. O Lord, hear; O Lord, forgive; O Lord, hearken and do; defer not for thine own sake, O my God." They also remind one of the repetitions in the prayer of the Saviour in Gethsemane, a third time saying the same words. Matt. xxvi. 44. There is, however, although repetitions, no tautology in these petitions of David, for the petitions,

Verse 1. Give ear unto my words, O Lord; consider my meditation,

indicate two distinct forms and phases of prayer.

"Give ear unto my *words*, O Lord," indicates the offering up of such desires as can be adequately expressed in words, whereas, "consider my *meditation*," indicates the offering up to God of such desires as cannot be adequately expressed in words. The soul is capable of spiritual aspirations too intense for utterance. It is of such aspirations that the apostle speaks, when he says, "the Spirit itself maketh intercession for us with groanings which cannot be uttered." Rom. viii. 26.

This accords with the experience of every humble, earnest child of God. How often is he conscious of hungerings and thirstings after righteousness, that can be expressed only in sighs! Bishop Horne translates the word *meditation*, "dove-like moanings." The moaning of the dove is one of the most plaintive sounds in nature. Its tones remind one more of a broken heart, bemoaning the absence of its chief delight, than anything else that can be conceived. It is thus that the broken heart and contrite spirit bemoans the absence of its chief delight, the light of God's countenance. It can only sigh after the grace it needs. Hence, in the words, "give ear to my words," and, "consider my meditation," David prays the Lord to grant him, not only the desires he has been able to clothe in language, but also the desires which he has been able to express only in sighs and plaintive moans. For God's ear, however, these sighs and moans have a louder tongue than words. The Lord looks upon the heart, sees all its unutterable desires, and answers them all as prayer.

VERSE 2. Hearken unto the voice of my cry, my King and my God; for unto thee will I pray.

This verse describes an earnestness in prayer, which neither deliberately chosen words, nor sighs, nor moans, can adequately express. The vehemency of the desires finds utterance only in a *cry* for help. Of this form of prayer we have an illustration in the history of our Lord, who, in the days of his flesh, offered up prayers and supplications with strong *crying* and tears. Heb. v. 7. There are times when the powers of darkness so assail the soul, that an agonized *cry* for deliverance is its only language of prayer. They so assailed the soul of the Saviour, when he uttered that loud cry, "My God, my God, why hast thou forsaken me!" Matt. xxvii. 46. Such an hour of darkness seems to have come upon the soul of David, and is liable to come upon the soul of every believer. This fact David indicates in the words, "Hearken unto the voice of my cry, my King and my God." He appeals unto the Lord, first, as his King, as one who cannot but protect and deliver his servant and subject; and then to him as his God, all-sufficient to satisfy his every want and realize his every desire. To thee, therefore, he says, will I pray. Here then in the first two verses of our psalm are three distinct varieties of prayer. "Give ear unto my words," is prayer that can be clothed in deliberately chosen language. "Consider my meditation," is the prayer of unutterable desires. "Give ear unto my cry," is the prayer of agonized distress, of an overwhelming sense of sin and need of mercy. It is the cry of Peter sinking in the waves, "Lord, save! I perish!" These seem to have been David's prayers during the night; and he resolves that they shall be his prayer also in the morning; for he adds,

VERSE 3. My voice shalt thou hear in the morning, O Lord; in the morning will I direct my prayer unto thee; and will look up.

Having passed the night in communion with God, David resolved to begin the day with him; wisely, too, for there is much more need of the blessing of God upon us during the trials and temptations of the day, than there is during the repose of the night. The right way, however, is both to begin and end the day with God, to open it with prayer, and close it with the same key. It was the Saviour's practice. And if He, holy, harmless, undefiled, needed such incessant prayer, how much more must we need it! "In the morning will I direct my prayer unto thee, O Lord:" not at night only, but also in the morning, I will spread out my desires and petitions in order before thee, and look up; keep my eye henceforth fixed upon thee to watch what answer thou wilt return to them. This seems to be the import of the words. It is too much the habit of Christians to pray without watching for an answer to their prayers. It was not so with David. As his prayers ascended, he *looked up*, followed them with his whole soul, to learn what report they would bring back. No man prays in earnest, who does not earnestly expect an answer to his prayers.

VERSE 4. For thou art not a God that hath pleasure in wickedness: neither shall evil dwell with thee.

In praying that wickedness may come to an end, and righteousness be established in its stead, we know that we are asking things that are agreeable to the nature and purposes of God; and may therefore plead his nature and purposes as a motive with him to hear us, saying to him, as David does here, "For thou art not a God that hath pleasure in wickedness: neither shall evil dwell with thee." It is well for us, it is well for the universe, that God cannot endure moral evil, that sin is a thing that his soul hateth. If his infinite nature were not opposed to it, and bent on its destruction, every moral intelligence in the universe would become a fiend, and spend its immortality in finding in the lowest depths of degradation, "a lower depth, still opening wide." As much then as men may dislike the infinite holiness of God, it is our only guaranty that the entire universe will not become a hell, and every rational creature therein a fiend. God's infinite holiness, however, is not set upon the destruction of *evil* only, but also of evil-*doers*. Hence the words,

VERSE 5. The foolish shall not stand in thy sight: thou hatest all workers of iniquity.

God bears long with evil-doers, urges them long and affectionately to turn from their evil ways: but when they still persevere, he at last, though most unwillingly, overwhelms them. The foolish—not those who are deficient in natural capacity, but those who make no good use of their reason, who act like fools in opposing God's truth—shall not stand in his sight: he would not be God if he could endlessly tolerate such persons in their folly; for though his forbearance, up to a certain point, is the great glory of his character, if it were extended beyond that point, it would become a weakness and a crime.

VERSE 6. Thou shalt destroy them that speak leasing: the Lord will abhor the bloody and deceitful man.

To speak leasing is to utter untruths. As God abhors the gates of hell, so He abhors the man, or woman, that utters a falsehood. He has declared that all such shall have their part in the lake that burneth with fire and brimstone. Rev. xxi. 8. A want of truthfulness is a want of everything upon which we can reasonably build a hope of anything good for the soul. In the verse before us a want of it is associated with blood. He who abhors not the uttering of a lie, is likely to be a bloody, as well as a deceitful man. God, therefore, regards a want of truthfulness with the same abhorrence as that with which he regards murder: for, says another, "Let it be remembered that, in the Scriptures, lying and murder are invariable companions of deceit, treachery, and circumvention." God's whole soul is set against moral evil, to root it out of his universe. This was David's hope that he would deliver him from all moral evil, whether internal or external, the moral evil of his own heart, or that of the world around him. And this is the hope of every believer, praying to be delivered from the same. How bright in hope, then, even to us sinful creatures, is God's holiness, regarded as the source of human holiness, and as moving him freely to communicate it to all who ask it!

VERSE 7. But as for me, I will come into thy house in the multitude of thy mercy: and in thy fear will I worship toward thy holy temple.

It shall not fare with David as it shall with his enemies, the men who utter falsehood and make haste to shed blood. They shall perish, but he shall survive; nor survive only, but stand again in the presence of the Lord in his holy temple, and feel again the power of his presence over the mercy-seat in the holy of holies. Such is the privilege of the believer, still to believe, in the darkest hour of trial, that there is mercy in store for him; still to believe that he will yet stand in the Divine presence to render thanks for divine deliverances, and to receive new accessions of strength, to go on his way rejoicing and conquering.

VERSE 8. Lead me, O Lord, in thy righteousness, because of mine enemies; make thy way straight before my face.

How desirable that we should be enabled so to walk in the ways of truth and holiness, that our very enemies shall not be able to say any evil of us, unless they say it falsely. It is for guidance of this sort that David prays here. He knew that keen and hostile eyes were on him, watching him with ill intent. They so watched the Son of David. Satan endeavoured to seduce him, wicked men to entangle him, and both to destroy him. It is not otherwise with any of his followers. They, too, are watched by keen observers, and enemies of all righteousness. If the religion we profess be true, it convicts its adversaries of the greatest conceivable folly. They therefore fasten with eagerness upon anything that even *seems* to weaken its claims to a Divine origin, and especially upon the faults of its professors. A holy life is an argument in favour of the heavenly origin of our religion, whose force its adversaries feel more than they do that of any other. It silences their cavils, and extorts their homage. Hence, the

6*

moral importance of leading such a life, and, in order thereto, of the prayer, "Lead me, O Lord, in thy righteousness, because of mine enemies; make thy way straight before me." This leading God accomplishes for his people, sometimes by moving directly upon their own hearts, sometimes by moving upon the hearts of others in their behalf, and sometimes by the direct interpositions, as well as by the general orderings, of his providence.

VERSE 9. For there is no faithfulness in their mouth; their inward part is very wickedness; their throat is an open sepulchre; they flatter with their tongue.

This is a dark picture of the moral character of the men in the midst of whom David prays to be divinely guided. "There is no faithfulness in their mouth"—there is nothing certain in their words; they say, and do not; say one thing, and mean another; they conceal, evade, colour, and exaggerate the truth; or, what is the worst sort of falsehood, tell but half the truth; and though they see and know that they have made a false and injurious impression, they take no pains to remove it. "Their inward part is very wickedness;" the bent of their minds is to evil, and only evil continually; the heart is corrupt, the will perverse, and the understanding darkened. The whole inner spirit is depraved. "Their throat is an open sepulchre." The oriental sepulchre is generally constructed above the ground, and often excavated out of the solid rock, having a door that can be thrown widely open, and when so open, it sends forth putrid and pestilent exhalations, the pent-up malaria of decaying death. In a similar way, from an inward part of very wickedness, from a mass of corruption festering within them, the wicked send forth, through their throat, exhalations of moral and spiritual death. What else than such an open sepulchre is the throat of the profane, the obscene, the reviler, and the caviller? The wicked do not, however, always deal in gross attacks upon our religion. Failing sometimes to accomplish their aims and wishes in that way, they vary their tactics. They flatter with their tongue—some read the original, "they *smooth* their tongue." "By good words and fair speeches they deceive the hearts of the simple." Rom. xvi. 18. Discarding the profane and obscene ribaldry of the school of Paine and Voltaire, they adopt the polished style and phraseology of the school of Hume and Gibbon; urging at one time, historical, at another scientific, and at still another, some other learned objection to the doctrines or facts of our holy religion; doing all, however, with the air of men who sincerely *wished* their difficulties removed, to the end that they themselves might believe. There is often, therefore, no little praise and panegyric mixed up with their objections; but the praise is added only to give their objections greater force. They assume the air and language of friends, only to do the work of an enemy with more telling effect. Professing the greatest desire that the truth of Scripture should remain intact and unclouded, they nevertheless seize with the utmost eagerness upon any newly discovered fact, either of ancient history or of modern science, that seems to conflict with any of the statements of the sacred record, and never give it up, so long as it can be made to wear an infidel aspect.

"There is no faithfulness in their mouth; their inward part is very wickedness; their throat is an open sepulchre; they flatter with their tongue." How dark and revolting is the moral character here drawn of David's enemies! And yet it is the moral character of every one of us as we are by nature. It is *your* moral character, my reader, and *mine* too, if our hearts have not been changed by a power from on high. You may be as amiable and moral as the young man in the gospel, who fancied that he had kept all the commandments from his youth up; but if you have not been born again, you possess, in an unregenerate heart, the germs of every sin that can be named, and of every sin too in its darkest forms. Hence St. Paul quotes this very verse, among others, to prove that the character here delineated is not the moral character of a few very bad men, but of *all* men by nature. In reading, then, the darkest delineations of human character given us in the Bible, let even the purest and most amiable of us see, in those delineations, only what we ourselves are capable of becoming, and liable to become, unless a Divine power change or restrain us.

VERSE 10. Destroy thou them, O God; let them fall by their own counsels: cast them out in the multitude of their transgressions, for they have rebelled against thee.

This is the first of those psalms wherein David seems to pray for the destruction of his enemies, and thus, as some think, to manifest a spirit of revenge. To this objection—not of the infidel only, but also of many serious Christians—two answers can be given, either of which clears David of the charge of vindictiveness.

The first answer is, that the verbs here translated in the imperative mood, and in the form of a prayer, may be translated in the future tense, and consequently in the form of a prediction. The words, thus translated, would not be a prayer, but a prophecy; not a vindictive imprecation, but an inspired prophecy, and would read—Thou wilt destroy them, O God; they shall perish by their own counsels; thou wilt cast them out in the multitude of their transgressions, for they have rebelled against thee.

Supposing David's words, however, really to contain—what many eminent critics believe them to contain—an imprecation upon his enemies, we can still justify them upon the same grounds on which we justify prayer for the destruction of enemies with whom we are at war. And what patriot was ever yet blamed for praying God to destroy the enemies of his country? It was not for the destruction of his own *personal* enemies that David here prays—no man ever lived who was more forgiving of such—but for the destruction of the enemies of his country and of his God, the enemies of the government that God himself had instituted, and placed him at its head. Hence the reason David assigns why God should destroy his enemies, "For they have rebelled against *thee*." It was not as rebels against him as an individual, but as rebels against him as the head of a divinely established government, that David prays God to destroy his enemies. And what else is the voice of universal history than this very thing, that God does, sooner or later, destroy all those who oppose his kingdom, his Church on earth, with its divine laws, divine institutions, divine influences, and divine Head—that he destroys them, sometimes by leaving them to their own infatuated counsels, and the natural operations of multiplied transgressions; and again, by the unmistakable orderings of his providence? Regard David's words, then, either as an imprecation, or as a prediction, they by no means convict him of a spirit of revenge. Here, however, we come to the great contrast between God's dealings with the righteous and the wicked:

VERSE 11. But let all those that put their trust in thee rejoice: let them ever shout for joy, because thou defendest them: let them also that love thy name be joyful in thee.

To put one's trust in the Lord, and to love the name of the Lord, are words of the same import, and indicate the same temper and bearing of the soul towards its Maker. They indicate the complete affiance of the soul to God, and of God to the soul; their mutual rejoicing in each other, the soul in God, and God in the soul. Henceforth the Lord will suffer no fatal evil to befall the believer—only with his eyes shall he behold and see the reward of the ungodly. His defence can never fail him. His trust in the Lord, too, shall be within him a well-spring of joy and peace. He knows whom he has trusted, and is persuaded that He is able to keep that which he has committed unto him against that day. The past has been forgiven him; the present is in consequence joyful, and the future radiant with glory, honour, and immortality. Such present happiness and future hope have all they that trust in the Lord, and love his name.

VERSE 12. For thou, Lord, wilt bless the righteous; with favour shalt thou compass him as with a shield.

God's blessing not only makes us happy, but renders us secure, and is as a shield to us on every side. The shield here intended, was not armour of defence only, but also of repulsion. Its bulging centre was thick set with sharpened spikes and pointed spears, so that the enemy against whom it was thrust, or who threw himself against it, was not repelled merely, but repelled, pierced through and through. Such a shield is the favour of the Lord to the righteous. It not only so *protects* the righteous behind its ample circuit, that no weapon of his enemies can reach him to do him harm, but it *repels* them, pierced, bleeding, and dying. It so repelled man's last great enemy, death, enabling him to exclaim, as he looked down upon his fallen and expiring foe, "O death, where is thy sting? O grave, where is thy victory? Thanks be to God which giveth us the victory, through our Lord Jesus Christ!" Such is the God with whom we have to do. He so hates sin that he cannot but render us every assistance in his power, to rid our hearts and lives of every vestige of it. He so loves holiness that he beholds the feeblest beginnings of it in the soul with infinite delight—beginnings as feeble as the bruised reed, and as easily extinguished as the last remaining spark of an expiring wick. Let none of us, then, despair of escaping from the power and pollution of our sins, and perfecting our souls in the holy affections that qualify for heaven. And let us, to this end, having closed each previous day with a prayer equally fervent and full of faith, begin each succeeding day of our lives with the petition and promise, "Give ear to my words, O Lord; consider my meditation. Hearken unto the voice of my cry, my King and my God: for unto thee will I pray. My voice shalt thou hear in the morning, O Lord; in the morning will I direct my prayer unto thee, and will look up," until thou, for Christ's sake, pardon my sins, and surround me with the shield of thine everlasting love.

LECTURE ON PSALM VI.

It has been objected to some of the Psalms of David, and especially to the sixth, that they discover a spirit of complaint unbecoming true manliness of character; that sighs, moans, tears, impassioned cries, are ill suited to such a man as David is claimed to have been. They who make this objection, mistake the *cause* of David's lamentations. That cause was not so much his sufferings in themselves, as the sins that had made them necessary. It was not the lacerating rod, but the consciousness that he needed such a rod to bring him to repentance and a better mind. This weeping from a sense of sin, is by no means inconsistent with even heroic fortitude. It is what the martyr has done, standing by his stake, and refusing to be bound to it, while its flames were flashing their fiercest heat around him. It was what Cranmer did, his eyes streaming with tears from a sense of his sins, while at the same time he thrust his guilty, recanting right hand, into the flames of his stake, and held it there, without shrinking, till it was burned to ashes. It is not for want of enduring firmness under affliction that the believer so often weeps, but from a vivid recollection of the sins that have rendered affliction necessary to reclaim him. It is under altogether another aspect that affliction presents itself to the man who regards all suffering as the result of accident, or as a link in an adamantine chain of fate. There being, to his mind, no wise reclaiming love, no God, in such a dispensation, he has to meet it only with stoical indifference. If his own strength suffice to sustain him, well—if not, he is miserable indeed; for he acknowledges no other and higher power of support and resistance than that to be found within the soul itself. It is otherwise with the believer. Let the rod of God touch *him*, and his heart melts, his eyes run down with tears, and there ascends the impassioned cry for the pardon of that which has brought the rod upon him—his sins. It was evidently under feelings and convictions of this sort, that David conceived and penned the sixth psalm. It accordingly opens with the cry,

VERSE 1. O Lord, rebuke me not in thine anger, neither chasten me in thy hot displeasure.

On what occasion the Psalmist was brought so to realize the exceeding sinfulness of sin, we do not know. He had, however, evidently been made to feel that sin is such, in its nature, as to demand the vengeance of God upon the sinner for it. This feeling is sometimes wrought in the soul by a divine providence; sometimes by an operation of the Holy Spirit; and sometimes by both combined. But in whatever way David's vivid sense of his ill-desert, because of sin, was roused, it thrilled through his soul a moral electricity, quickening his every thought and feeling into intense activity. He saw how odious sin must be in the sight of the infinite purity of God, and how certainly he must punish for it. And yet he also saw that, if God did punish for it, he must utterly perish. Hence his cry of distress and deprecation, "O Lord, rebuke me not in thine anger, neither chasten me in thy hot displeasure!"—I deserve thy wrath, but spare, O spare me! He saw God standing before him with, as it were, a drawn sword in his hand, ready to destroy him; and yet, notwithstanding the fearful sight, he flees directly to him. The thought of his heart was, "though he slay me, yet will I trust in him; I will never leave him nor forsake him. If he wounds, he can heal; if he bruises, he can bind up. He alone has the words of eternal life, and to him will I cleave." The worldly man's convictions of sin drive him away from God, to seek relief in something that will lead to self-oblivion. His only refuge is, *not to think* of the God who has made him feel that he is a sinner. It is otherwise with the believer. If God afflicts him, he receives it as a call to a closer walk with him, and a holier life. If he convicts him of his sins, and ill-desert because of them, he receives it as an invitation to seek the pardon of his sins with renewed and augmented earnestness. However much the believer may be troubled or distressed in mind, body, or estate, he never for a moment thinks of turning away from his God, but only the more earnestly deprecates his wrath, and implores his mercy. He knows that there is help for him nowhere else, and he seeks it nowhere else. So David thought and did, and adds:

VERSE 2. Have mercy upon me, O Lord, for I am weak: O Lord, heal me, for my bones are vexed.

David had done and suffered as much for his God as any other man that had ever lived; and yet mercy, unmerited favour, is his only plea here. He has no merit nor goodness of his own, to offer as a reason why the Lord should not rebuke him in his wrath, and chasten him in his hot displeasure. "Have *mercy* upon me, O Lord, for I am weak: O Lord, heal me, for my bones are vexed." The physical effects of God's chastening hand upon David for his sins are here graphically described. He is weak, and his bones are vexed. Joy infuses life, strength, and activity; sorrow takes them away. Such was the effect of David's religious sorrow upon him. It had induced faintness in his heart, and a tremor in his limbs. He was like Belshazzar when he beheld the fingers of a viewless hand writing upon the plaster of his wall. The sight, filling his soul with a sense of guilt, changed his countenance, troubled his thoughts, and smote his knees one against another. It was a sense of guilt, too—of the world's guilt laid upon him—that prostrated the Saviour upon the ground, and made him sweat big drops of blood. It is not unusual for intense conviction of sin to exert a depressing effect upon the physical energies; so depressing as sometimes to produce sickness. We see it especially in the case of the religious hypochondriac—his melancholy producing sickness, and his sickness deepening his melancholy, and each mutually aggravating the virulence of the other, till it is hard to tell to which the means of cure should be first applied—whether to the mind's or to the body's disease. Sometimes the patient is in need of one treatment, and sometimes of the other, and sometimes of both, the physical and spiritual, combined, to effect a cure. Often, however, a distressed and doubting believer needs a physician more than he needs his pastor. Yet in all ordinary cases of physical prostration from intense conviction of sin, David indicates the only adequate means of recovery when he cries to the Lord to heal him. When the hiding of God's face has depressed us, nothing but the light of it lifted upon us again, can elevate us. Therefore whenever, in view of merited punishment, your heart faints within you, and your knees tremble under you, let your cry be, "O Lord, heal me: O Lord, lift thou up the light of thy countenance upon me." The joy poured into your heart by that light shining on you, will give new colour to the cheek, animation to the eye, elasticity to every movement, and vigour to every limb. So have I seen the critically balanced scales of death begin to turn lifeward, from the moment the mind of the patient took hold of Christ, by faith, as the Saviour of the soul. Physicians themselves have acknowledged that the turning point was then.

VERSE 3. My soul is also sore vexed: but thou, O Lord, how long?

Here was the climax of David's suffering. His soul also was sore vexed: and a wounded spirit who can bear? Physical sufferings are as nothing when compared with the kindlings of Divine wrath in the conscience. When conscience is touched by the hand of God, and gives way, man is helpless indeed! This was David's case. An awakened and accusing conscience was exciting in him a certain fearful looking for of judgment and fiery indignation. Little does man know of suffering, till he has been made to feel in his soul the unmitigated evil of sin. There is no other torment equal to the torment of an awakened and exasperated conscience. It makes the soul feel the evil and bitterness of sin indeed. You recollect how the Saviour felt this in his hour of darkness in the garden, from the mere pressure of the sins of others. "My soul," said he, "is exceeding sorrowful, even unto death:" and his sweat was as it were great drops of blood falling down to the ground. Behold also in the events of his crucifixion how much harder mental than bodily sufferings are to bear. He had been smitten, buffeted, scourged, had his brows compressed with puncturing thorns, and been nailed also to the cross, and yet, under all this physical suffering, he opened not his mouth: not even a sigh is recorded to have escaped his lips. What then means that agonized cry, "My God, my God, why hast thou forsaken me?" Ah! the frown of God, for our sins, has fallen upon his soul! That was "the sharpness of death;" and not his physical sufferings. He bore all in silence till his "soul also was sore vexed:" and then, what a cry! what a rending shriek! what consternation of spirit! And this consternation of spirit in view of the ill-desert of sin was also upon David's soul, and under its overwhelming pressure, his only cry is, "But thou, O Lord, how long?" Hope deferred has made his heart sick, and allows him to think only of the delayed relief, and to ask again and again when it will come. When some great sorrow oppresses the heart and fills it with anxieties to the utmost bounds of endurance, how expressive, and how natural, too, are these words of David, "How long, O Lord, how long?"

VERSE 4. Return, O Lord, deliver my soul: O save me for thy mercies' sake!

However heavily David's sins pressed upon his soul, he certainly takes himself to the right source for help. The Lord has made him feel his sins, and to the Lord he flies for salvation. He asks deliverance, however, not as a thing of debt, or of right, but altogether of grace. "O save me for thy mercies' sake!" His sins were great: yet there was one other thing still greater—the mercy of his God. David, therefore, pleads it: and pleads it, too, as redounding more to the glory of his God to show mercy, than to execute justice. And that is what the guiltiest of us may plead: for our God delighteth in mercy, and never feels himself so much honoured as he does when his needy creatures hope in his mercy, and make it the ground of confidence in their prayers. Hence David's prayer, "O save me for thy mercies' sake!"

VERSE 5. For in death there is no remembrance of thee: in the grave who shall give thee thanks?

There is some obscurity in these words *literally* understood. They at least *seem* to teach that all thought and consciousness ceased with man at his death. If that be their meaning, they certainly show that David's views of a future life were quite defective. If that be their meaning, we may well say, he that is least in the kingdom of heaven is greater than he—that the very child, with the New Testament in his hands, has clearer views of immortality than David had. We can hardly believe, however, that David meant to teach that thought and consciousness ceased with man at death. The death here intended is probably the second death, and the grave intended, the prison of the lost: *that* is the death, and *that* the grave, from which David prays to be saved—the death and grave of "both soul and body in hell." And surely, there is no grateful remembrance of, and giving thanks to God, there. On the contrary, all who have experienced that death, and descended into that grave, gnaw their tongues for pain, and blaspheme the God of heaven. In view of such an issue, well might David pray, "Return, O Lord, deliver my soul: O save me for thy mercies' sake!" For surely, a more terrific thought cannot be presented to the human soul, than the thought that it must remain a sinning and suffering creature for ever, a moral blot in every part of the universe to which it may flee: hateful in its own eyes, and hateful in the eyes of God.

VERSES 6, 7. I am weary with my groaning; all the night make I my bed to swim: I water my couch with my tears. Mine eye is consumed because of grief; it waxeth old because of all mine enemies.

David still continues to describe, by its physical effects, his conflict with the fear of eternal death. It has excited his groans, till he is wearied with them; his tears, till his bed is wet with them; and extinguished the sight of his eyes, as if premature old age had come upon him. It may be thought by some a weakness, so to grieve over one's sins. Those who think so, little understand what sin is—what ravages it commits in the soul, what it robs us of here and hereafter, and what it at last consigns us to. He is not the weak man who weeps over sin, but he who makes light of it. It is the only thing we should fear. He who fears it not is mad. He fears not the infinite God who has forbidden it, and will punish for it. He fears not his own conscience, which, awakened at last, will fasten upon his soul with a vulture's clutch, for ever. He fears not the worm that ever gnaws, and never dies; the fire that ever burns, and is never quenched! Brave, indeed! but it is the bravery of the moral maniac. No, no! instead of such bravery, give me the heart that melts, and eyes that weep, at the recollection of sins. Sooner than make light of sin, I would say, with the prophet, "O that my head were waters, and mine eyes a fountain of tears, that I might weep day and night." Who the enemies were that had caused David so much grief, whether visible or invisible, tangible or intangible, internal or external, we have no means of ascertaining. One thing, however, we do know with certainty, that he triumphed over them. Hence the words:

VERSES 8, 9. Depart from me, all ye workers of iniquity; for the Lord hath heard the voice of my weeping. The Lord hath heard my supplication; the Lord will receive my prayer.

Here is a change indeed! Joy and gladness, thanksgiving, and the voice of melody! Sighs have given place to smiles, tears to laughter, groans to songs, and cries of despair to shouts of triumph! He defies his enemies, whoever and whatever they may be, and bids them leave him. Once more the Lord is on his side, and he will not fear what man, or fiend, can do unto him. The Lord hath heard the voice of his weeping, his supplication, and will receive his prayer. It is strange how quickly God can send light into the darkest mind, and peace to the most agitated breast. He speaks, and it is done; he commands, and it stands fast. It is hard to realize that the David of the two verses now before us, is the same person to whose plaintive voice we have been listening through the whole of the previous part of the psalm. And how completely is David's experience herein the experience of many a believer—many to whom the brightest light has succeeded the greatest darkness! They battled long with the powers of darkness and their own hearts, but victory came at last; and such a victory! They then learned that not a sigh had been heaved, nor a tear shed, nor a groan given, nor a prayer offered, in vain; but that all had been answered, and returned in blessings on their heads; and that their dross had been consumed, and their gold refined. The enemy had gained nothing by the sore trials to which he had subjected them; but they came out of the conflict better qualified than they had ever been before, to fight the good fight with augmented vigour and success. This also was David's experience, and he accordingly closes with the words:

VERSE 10. Let all mine enemies be ashamed and sore vexed: let them return and be ashamed suddenly.

The struggle referred to in this psalm has been left on record for our instruction and guidance. It teaches us that whatever calamity may befall us, whether in mind, body, or estate, we are to receive it as the chastening of a loving Father, striving thereby to bring us to repentance, and to a closer walk with him. It also teaches us that it is by no means an evidence of Divine desertion, for God to excite within us a conviction of sin, and apprehension of evil in the world to come, so intense as to make our knees to tremble under us, and our hearts die within us. "Whom the Lord loveth, he chasteneth, and scourgeth every son whom he receiveth." Then let every one, so chastened and scourged, say continually, "O Lord, rebuke me not in thine anger, neither chasten me in thy hot displeasure," but "save me for thy mercies' sake," in Jesus Christ. Then, in due time, God will turn your darkness to light, and your sorrow into joy.

LECTURE ON PSALM VII.

To a mind conscious to itself of rectitude, there is no accusation so hard to be borne as that of having the heart set upon evil. That is the painful position of David in the psalm now before us. He has evidently been charged with plotting against the life and throne of Saul. It is indeed true that he himself had been consecrated to the throne of Israel, (1 Sam. xvi. 13,) but not under circumstances that would justify him in violently removing its present incumbent. Nor had David done anything to induce in any fair mind the belief that he was aiming to do so. On the contrary, he had time and again fought the battles of Saul, won his victories, and spared him when he had him in his power. Yet Saul seems to have been embittered against him by "the words of Cush, the Benjamite." The word *cush*, means *black*, and is thought by some to have been chosen by David to indicate the malevolent character and designs of some accuser of him to Saul. Others think, as Saul was a Benjamite, and a man of dark purposes, that the name was chosen to designate Saul himself. But in whatever way Saul's mind was exasperated against him, whether by the jealous thoughts of his own heart, or by the calumnies of others, David could not but keenly feel the injustice done him. He had been outlawed, and a price put upon his life. No man dared to own him as a friend. Hunted down in all the ways, and by all the means that a king could command, sustained only by the consciousness of his innocence, and despairing of human relief, David therefore sends up the cry,

VERSES 1, 2. O Lord my God, in thee do I put my trust: save me from all them that persecute me, and deliver me: lest he tear my soul like a lion, rending it in pieces, while there is none to deliver.

Though it was nowhere to be found on earth, yet David knew there was help for him in heaven; that there was One reigning there whose very nature moved him to vindicate suffering innocence, even the Lord his God, Jehovah-Elohim; the God in whom all the eternal perfections of absolute Godhead infinitely reside. In him he trusts; to him he appeals to save. His persecutors were many indeed, and mighty. But his defence against them all is, *faith in God;* he seeks no other, he desires no other. Nor is the God in whom he trusts a strange God, but his *own* God. Hence his words, "O Lord *my* God." Such is the power and privilege of faith. It makes God the soul's *own.* It appropriates his infinite power to protect it; his infinite wisdom to guide it; and his infinite goodness to satisfy its every want. David has indeed but One ally, but that ally is God—the Lord *his* God. He knows in whom he has believed, and is persuaded that he is as willing as he is able to fulfil the desires of his heart. He first desires to be delivered from *all* his persecutors, and then singles out one from whom he especially desires to be delivered, lest he tear his soul like a lion, rending it in pieces, while there is none to deliver. This specially deprecated enemy is believed to have been the infuriated Saul. He was a king—one whose mandate every one was bound to obey; and if he came upon him, how certainly would resistance be vain, and destruction seem inevitable! He would be as helpless in Saul's hands as the feeble fawn in the fangs of the enraged king of the forest. And yet, this lion in human form was upon his trail, and would be satisfied with nothing less than David's blood; and from his rending clutch and devouring jaws, God alone could save him. This prayer is full of instruction. Every one of us may have some powerful enemy that may tear the soul like a lion, rending it in pieces, while there is none to deliver. This enemy may be Satan, the prince of devils, assaulting the soul with some horrible temptation; or it may be some easily besetting sin, as pride, avarice, love of pleasure, impetuosity, vindictiveness, the lust of the debauchee, or some giant appetite—like that for intoxicating drinks—an appetite that binds the strongest in chains, and precipitates them headlong into hopeless and dishonoured graves. A lion indeed!—frenzied, infuriated, and ravening! Whatever the specially dangerous enemy our souls have cause to fear, while praying for deliverance from all spiritual adversaries, we should, as David did, single out that one for special prayer.

VERSES 3–5. O Lord my God, if I have done this; if there be iniquity in my hands: if I have rewarded evil unto him that was at peace with me; yea, I have delivered him that without cause is mine enemy: let the enemy persecute my soul, and take it; yea, let him tread down my life upon the earth, and lay mine honour in the dust. Selah.

What David claims for himself here, is not a spotless and universal righteousness, but only that he is not guilty of what had been laid to his charge—that is, of plotting against the life and throne of Saul. If he had done that, he freely consents that Saul may persecute him, and put him to the most ignominious death, and cover his memory with all manner of disgrace; tread down his life upon the earth, and lay his honour in the dust. But he denies that he has requited kindness with ingratitude, confidence with treachery, or good with evil. On the contrary, he declares, "Yea, I have delivered him that without cause is mine enemy." He probably refers to his having twice spared Saul when he had him in his power; in one instance cutting off the skirt of his robe, (1 Sam. xxiv. 11,) and in the other, taking away his spear and a cruse of water at his head, while he was asleep, (1 Sam. xxvi. 12;) in both instances leaving him unharmed, and restraining his men also from slaying him. David's whole bearing towards Saul was that of a good and loyal subject. He could safely declare that he was innocent, and invoke evil upon himself, if he were not so. And his doing it, indicates the most thorough consciousness of his integrity, and persuasion of God's purpose to defend the right. There is nothing either of levity or of profanity in the asseveration and invocation, but such as a God-fearing and innocent man may blamelessly make when unjustly accused. Very different, however, are such words in the mouth of the wicked. How often do we hear them asseverating their innocence, and invoking destruction upon themselves if they are guilty, when, if God were to deal with them according to the truth in the matter, they would drop down dead at the instant, and go at once to their own place!

VERSES 6–9. Arise, O Lord, in thine anger; lift up thyself, because of the rage of mine enemies; and awake for me to the judgment that thou hast commanded. So shall the congregation of the people compass thee about: for their sakes, therefore, return thou on high. The Lord shall judge the people: judge me, O Lord, according to my righteousness, and according to mine integrity that is in me. O let the wickedness of the wicked come to an end; but establish the just: for the righteous God trieth the hearts and reins.

Although David knew that Saul had been rejected from being king over Israel, and that he himself had been divinely designated to rule in his stead, he would do no act of wrong or violence to accelerate his own accession to the throne. He left it to his God to pave the way for him to the throne in his own time and mode. But as Saul's overthrow seemed the only cure for the evils that his misrule had produced, he prays God to bring it about in such a way as that all should see that it was the "Lord's doing;" and then adds, as the effect of its being seen that He had done it, "so shall the congregation of the people compass thee about;" so shall there be a returning from their backslidings, and a revival of pure and undefiled religion; "for their sakes, therefore, return thou on high;" let it appear by some special judicial interposition of thy power, whom thou hast chosen to lead thy people in the ways of truth and peace, Saul, or me. "Judge me, O Lord, according to my righteousness, and according to mine integrity that is in me." As was before said, it is not universal righteousness that David here challenges for himself, only integrity in regard to Saul; he had not sinned against him; on the contrary, had rendered him good, and good only, and often good for evil. And this is what many a man can say in regard to his fellow-man, that, in regard to him, he is righteous, and his integrity intact; and that, if impeached by him, he may appeal even to infinite justice for an acquittal with commendation. It is far otherwise, however, with every one of us, when we speak of righteousness and integrity in regard to God. When he shall impeach us, and bring us to trial for our treatment of him, we shall have no merit of our own to plead in bar of judgment. The only righteousness that will avail us aught in that day will be the righteousness of Jesus Christ, made ours by faith. It is no human, but only a Divine righteousness that will avail us then. It is therefore only in regard to Saul that David asks God to judge him according to his righteousness, and according to his integrity; and then adds, "O let the wickedness of the wicked come to an end; but establish the just; for the righteous God trieth the hearts and reins." He does not say here who is wicked, or who is just, himself or Saul; he leaves it to the Searcher of hearts to decide the question, and, deciding it, to deal with each according to his deserts. Doubtless, however, David's own heart told him who was guilty, and who innocent, and that he had nothing to fear; hence the fervour of his appeal. A blessed thing it is for the heart to speak peace to the soul in the hour of trial; for if our heart condemn us not, then may we have confidence towards God. It was, however, not his blamelessness alone that inspired David with such confidence towards God, but also God's own love of righteousness and hatred of sin in his creature; a love and hatred that David now proceeds to describe in words of no ordinary strength and fulness of meaning, saying,

VERSES 10, 11. My defence is of God, which saveth the upright in heart. God judgeth the righteous, and God is angry with the wicked every day.

David's faith here becomes assurance: his defence is of God, who saveth the upright in heart. His very nature moves him to save them: he must cease to be God, before he can cease to be their helper. God judges the righteous; espouses their cause, vindicates it, recognizes it as his own, and can never allow it finally to fail. "And God is angry with the wicked every day:" disapproves their plans, abhors their spirit, and so orders all things in nature and in providence as ultimately to overthrow them. In God's very nature, therefore, in his innate, eternal, and ever-active love of rectitude and hatred of moral evil, David is assured, doubly assured, that he shall stand and Saul fall. And this double assurance of finally triumphing over the evil within us and around us, we all have, who have put our trust in the Lord. He loves the righteousness that we are seeking, and will help us to attain it: hates the evil with which we are contending, and will help us to overcome it. It is otherwise that he bears himself towards the ungodly and the sinner.

VERSES 12, 13. If he turn not, he will whet his sword; he hath bent his bow, and made it ready. He hath also prepared for him the instruments of death; he ordaineth his arrows against the persecutors.

The Lord here stands before the guilty as a mighty warrior, with sword and bow in hand, and the arrow in place upon the string: and as the sinner goes on in his trespasses, the sword grows sharper, and the arrow is drawing nearer to its head, until the Divine forbearance being at last exhausted, the sword descends and the arrow speeds to the heart. The Lord's hand has taken hold on judgment, and the sinner lies prostrate before him. It is well, however, to consider what it is that whets God's sword of vengeance, bends his bow, draws the arrow to its head, and at last speeds it on its mission of death. It is the sinner's sins: but for them, his glittering sword would remain in the scabbard, his arrows in their quiver, his bow unbent and unstrung. It is only indirectly that it can be said of the Lord in his dealings with the sinner, "He hath also prepared for him the instruments of death; he ordaineth his arrows against the persecutors. He has ordained the sudden and violent death of the opposers of his truth, only as there exists, in the very nature of things, an immutable and eternal connection between a career of violence and a corresponding termination of it. This has been signally verified in the death of the persecutors of his Church. It would seem as if God had indeed prepared the weapons of death for them, and wielded them with his own hand: so suddenly and miserably have most of them perished! And it is remarkable that Saul himself perished by the very weapons here named: first pierced with an arrow, and then falling upon his own sword. 1 Sam. xxxi. 3, 4. The sword and the arrow, however, were no otherwise the Lord's, than as he makes use of wicked men to inflict his wrath upon each other. Nor are wicked men destroyed only by the orderings of Divine Providence, but often also by the very means employed by themselves for the destruction of others. Hence it is said of the sinner,

VERSES 14–16. Behold, he travaileth with iniquity, and hath conceived mischief, and brought forth falsehood. He hath made a pit, and digged it, and is fallen into the ditch which he made. His mischief shall return upon his own head, and his violent dealing shall come down upon his own pate.

The man that travaileth with iniquity, who is big with thoughts and purposes of evil, shall experience, as the issue of his birth-throes, nothing but mischief and falsehood, misery and disappointment. Sin is a thing that recoils upon its perpetrator, and inflicts its heaviest blows upon the soul conceiving it, intending it, and giving it life and form. He that digs a pit for another shall fall into it himself. "His mischief will return upon his own head, and his violent dealing come down upon his own pate." It was in accordance with this self-avenging power of sin, that Saul was slain by the Philistines, (1 Sam. xxxi. 2–4,) whom he had designed to be the slayers of David, (1 Sam. xviii. 21, 25;) that Haman was hanged upon the gallows he had erected for another, (Esther vii. 10;) and that the Jews themselves were destroyed by the Romans, whose aid they had invoked and received to crucify their Messiah. This recoiling, self-revenging power of sin, is conclusive proof that a holy, just, and living God is moving everywhere in nature, and in the affairs of men, to paralyse the arm of the evil-doer, and to make man feel in every blow that he inflicts upon truth and right, upon innocence and virtue, a counter blow of overwhelming force. It was the conviction of this great truth, as a principle permeating the government of God, that makes David speak of the discomfiture of his enemies as a thing already accomplished. He sees every blow aimed at him, recoiling upon themselves; every machination concocted for his overthrow, rendering their own still more inevitable. A fearful thought this, to the wicked, that *his own evil shall slay him:* and yet, to others, a thought full of hope, that God has so ordered things in his universe that *evil must destroy itself.* Hence it is that David closes his psalm with the words,

VERSE 17. I will praise the Lord according to his righteousness: and will sing praise to the name of the Lord most high.

And who of us have not the same reasons for praising God "according to his righteousness," a righteousness moving him always and everywhere to succour virtue and abase vice, defend innocence and overwhelm guilt. Glorious truths are these two: "God judgeth the righteous: God is angry with the wicked every day." It was his conviction of these truths that stayed David's soul in the hour of his persecution for righteousness' sake. And upon these two great truths we, too, may plant our feet, as upon the Rock of Ages. Our God must cease to be God, before he can cease to make these truths the basis principles of his government of the world. It is verily true that we have no righteousness of our own to recommend us to the righteous protection of our God. There is a righteousness, however, that makes us virtually righteous in the sight of even Infinite Righteousness, *the righteousness of Jesus Christ*, made *ours* by faith. Clothed in that righteousness, we participate at once in all the protections, privileges, and blessings promised to the righteous in the word of God; come at once within the omnipotent sweep of that righteousness of God that maketh all things work together for good to them that love him. Let us all then, ceasing to do evil, and learning to do well, seek to be clothed in the righteousness of Christ, for he is the end of the law for righteousness unto every one that believeth. Rom. x. 4. He tasted death for every man, and his blood cleanseth us from all sin—

> "Is of sin the double cure,
> Saves from wrath, and makes us pure."

LECTURE ON PSALM VIII.

It is difficult to conceive of anything more eminently calculated to inspire the mind with awe and loving admiration, than the contemplation of the works of God's visible creation; the alternations of night and day, the regular return and reproduction of the seasons, and the undisturbed position of the stars in their places, from generation to generation. It is evidently under feelings excited by the contemplation of these things, that David wrote the eighth psalm. It therefore opens with the words:

Verse 1. O Lord our Lord, how excellent is thy name in all the earth! who hast set thy glory above the heavens.

Everywhere upon the earth around him, David beheld the impress of God's name—the handwriting of his glorious attributes of power, wisdom, and goodness. It is not improbable that he had in mind the whole process of the original creation, as it stands recorded in the first chapter of Genesis—the heaven and the earth called into being out of nothing; the earth being without form and void, and the abode of darkness, until at last, under the successive touches of the hand that created it, it abounded in every form of life and beauty, mineral, vegetable, and animal, rational and irrational; and man was placed over the whole as its designated lord and head. He saw everything that God had made, and that it was indeed what God had pronounced it—very good. He did not wonder that "the morning stars sang together, and all the sons of God shouted for joy," (Job xxxviii. 7;) when the earth at last stood forth complete in all its arrangements for the abode of man, addressing itself in its minutest creations to his understanding and his heart. He discovered wisdom everywhere, love everywhere, perfection everywhere. "How excellent is thy name in all the earth!" There is vegetable and animal life under the tropics; there is vegetable and animal life in the regions of perpetual snow; and God has so adapted each to its place, and its place to each, that each finds its own location a home, and its own climate the element of a joyous existence. It matters not how far, nor in what direction, we push our investigations into the works of terrestrial nature; each new step serves to reveal more and more the fashioning hand of God upon them. "Who hast set thy glory above the heavens." Here David's eye glances from the contemplation of the terrestrial, to that of the celestial creation—the works of God in the spacious firmament on high:

> In reason's ear they all rejoice,
> And utter forth a glorious voice,
> For ever singing, as they shine,
> "The Hand that made us is divine."

Day, with its illuminating sun and revealing light, had its lessons for David in the things immediately around him; and yet night, with its darkness, had its lessons of sublimer range and more solemn import. Then it was that the heavens appeared with their shining hosts, as the *crown* of God's creative glory—a crown, having for its diamonds, suns and stars, stretching away in every direction into depths illimitable. No audible voice did they utter, yet to David's ear their silent majesty spoke more potently of the power of God than anything that he had ever heard upon earth. But with our fuller knowledge in respect to them, that they are worlds, and systems of worlds, some of them perhaps millions of times larger than our own, and that the name of God is excellent amidst them all; that all are filled with the riches of his power, wisdom, and goodness, O what a voice issues from the silent depths of midnight heavens, to tell us of the greatness of the Lord our God! How it steals into the soul, with a power to hush its every unbelieving thought to silence! God speaking in nature, in the silent teachings of the heavens above, and of the earth beneath, finds a ready and willing listener in every one in whose heart there is no guile. Hence David adds:

VERSE 2. Out of the mouth of babes and sucklings hast thou ordained strength, because of thine enemies; that thou mightest still the enemy and the avenger.

We are here taught that the loving admiration with which a child beholds the glory of God in creation, in the beauty and fragrance of the flower, and the bright shining of the stars, is enough to rebuke those denying the hand of God in them. There is something extremely beautiful in this making the child's susceptibility to the beautiful in nature, an argument to silence the gainsayer. Nor is it alone in their quicker perceptions of natural beauties, that children often discover the Divine in things sooner than others. They discover moral beauties sooner—the divine in character and conduct. They discovered the Divine in the Saviour's character and works, crying, "Hosanna to the Son of David!" while others were denouncing him as an impostor. Indeed, the Saviour cites these very words against those who desired him to silence their hosannahs, saying, "Have ye never read, Out of the mouth of babes and sucklings thou hast perfected praise?" Matt. xxi. 16. Children urged their way into his presence, for his smile and blessing, while the Pharisees viewed him askance, and with "jealous leer malign." It is even so, and always so. The pure in heart see God in every manifestation of himself. The Divine, whether uttering itself in nature, or in revelation, goes direct to the heart of childhood, and to the hearts of those who, in temper and disposition, are as little children. It is out of the mouths of such that God's praise has been perfected in his Church, from generation to generation. Their simple-hearted, unquestioning piety, *the piety of admiring love*, has done more than the mightiest arguments of the advocate and controversialist, to silence the infidel, disarm the prejudiced, win over the hostile, and confirm the wavering. The world was forced to believe the religion Divine, that found its readiest and most congenial home in the minds of the guileless; that such comparatively pure minds were the soil in which a Divine thing would soonest take root, and bear fruit. And to this temper of mind we all must come, before we can meet God in peace: "For verily I say unto you, Except ye be converted, and become as little children, ye shall not enter into the kingdom of heaven." Matt. xviii. 3. David, however, here passes to another aspect of his subject, saying,

VERSES 3, 4. When I consider thy heavens, the work of thy fingers; the moon, and the stars, which thou hast ordained; what is man, that thou art mindful of him? and the son of man, that thou visitest him?

This is a question that has troubled others besides David—whether a Being so great as his visible creation proclaims the Lord our God to be, can be mindful of man. A view of the immensity of the Divine rule and empire, overwhelms many a man with a sense of his nothingness; makes him feel that he is a mote, an atom, a molecule, floating in the bosom of illimitable space—true, indeed, a thinking mote, a thinking atom, yet all the more wretched for being so, since thought reveals his situation to him; a creature whose very name, in Hebrew, means *weakness:* will he not be overlooked and lost in the midst of such infinite surroundings? Doth the great, the mighty God, the Lord of hosts, care for such an one, feel an interest in him and his welfare? Hear His own answer to the question: "Thus saith the high and lofty One that inhabiteth eternity, whose name is Holy: I dwell in the high and holy place, with him also that is of a contrite and humble spirit, to revive the spirit of the humble, and to revive the heart of the contrite ones." Isa. lvii. 15. "Thus saith the Lord, The heaven is my throne, and the earth is my footstool, ... but to this man will I look, even to him that is poor and of a contrite spirit, and trembleth at my word." Isa. lxvi. 1, 2. Here is God's own answer to the question, whether or not he is mindful of man. Nor is he simply mindful of him, but has given him a position of eminent superiority in his creation.

VERSE 5. For thou hast made him a little lower than the angels, and hast crowned him with glory and honour.

In describing man as having been made a little lower than the angels, as wanting but little of a celestial elevation, David refers to the peculiar dignity conferred upon man at his creation. He was created in the image of God. "God said, Let us make man in our image, after our likeness. . . . . So God created man in his own image, in the image of God created he him." This image of God in the soul of man is what constitutes his great and peculiar dignity in the scale of being. The image itself consists in an immortal, intelligent, and, originally, a holy spirit—a spirit capable of seeing truth as God sees it, right and wrong as he sees them, and of advancing in its similitude to him in these things more and more for ever. It can therefore commune with God, and God with it, as natures in living and intelligent sympathy with each other. It is this—God's having created man, as it were, a minor repetition of himself—that excited David's adoring wonder, and is that of which he speaks in the words, "Thou hast crowned him with glory and honour." Physically contemplated, man is the master-piece of creation, its crowning glory and honour; and yet the crowning glory and honour of man, is his rational soul—a soul bearing the moral and intellectual impress of Him whose inspiration it is. It is this that elevates him infinitely above every other creature of earth, and constitutes him the appropriate lord and sovereign of the world. It is this that qualifies him for, and entitles him to exercise the dominion of which David speaks in the words,

VERSES 6–8. Thou madest him to have dominion over the works of thy hands: thou hast put all things under his feet: all sheep and oxen, yea, and the beasts of the field; the fowl of the air, and the fish of the sea, and whatsoever passeth through the paths of the sea.

Man was made for this dominion over all terrestrial nature; it was the end had in view when God said, "Let us make man in our image, after our likeness;" for he immediately adds thereto, as if it were the purpose for which he was about to create man in his image, "and let him have dominion over the fish of the sea, and over the fowl of the air, and over the cattle, and over all the earth, and over everything that creepeth upon the earth." Gen. i. 26. It is the image of God in his soul that gives man dominion over everything earthly besides; that enables him to subject the strongest and most irresistible of nature's agencies to his control; to make earth and air, fire and water, his servants to do his bidding; to arrest and direct even the lightning in its course, and send it the bearer of his wishes thousands of miles in an instant. It is also the image of God in his soul that enables him to subject to his control the strongest, fiercest, and most intractable of nature's irrational tribes. "For every kind of beasts, and of birds, and of serpents, and of things in the sea, is tamed, and hath been tamed by man." Jas. iii. 7. The fear of him, and the dread of him, is upon them all, Gen. ix. 2; not one of them, not even the lion, can endure the steady gaze of his eye, but under it shrinks and slinks away as from the presence of a superior nature. Some mystic influence surrounds man, and goes out from him. No doubt he lost much of his supremacy over the brute creation by falling into sin; but sufficient vestiges of it remain to indicate what it must have been; that there was a time when the little child could lead the lion as easily as it could lead the lamb; and play with the asp and the cockatrice unharmed. Isa. xi. 6, 8. And even now, though it is only the wreck of what it was, what ascendency does the image of God in his soul give man over the earth, and all that therein is! What can man not accomplish that he sets his heart upon accomplishing? Time and space he has annihilated; lifts the mountain from its bed, or makes a passage for himself through its everlasting rocks; spans fathomless abysses with bridges of iron, and lays the wires for the transmission of his lightning voice and will through the paths of the seas. Yea, more—the image of God in his soul enables him, having only earth as his stand-point, his observatory, to commune with the stars—to tell their distances, their orbits, the period of their revolutions, measure their magnitudes, weigh their densities, and to tell also when the erratic comet, viewless for hundreds of years from its remoteness in space, will return, and come sweeping over his own meridian again. No wonder that, in view of the workings of such a mind and will in man, David should say to his God, "Thou hast crowned him with glory and honour, and made him a little lower than the angels."

VERSE 8. O Lord our Lord, how excellent is thy name in all the earth!

The psalm ends as it began, still celebrating the greatness of God as manifested in his goodness to man; manifested in an earth vocal everywhere with the love of its Creator, in heavens telling the same story in still louder tones, and in an immortal soul endued with powers of thought and feeling that proclaim it to be, in its moral and intellectual dignity, kindred to God himself. Such was man, and in such wise did the heavens and the earth speak to his consciousness, when he first stood forth the representative of God in his terrestrial creation. But, alas! how soon the crown fell from his brow, and the sceptre from his hand!—so soon, that for the last six thousand years all that we have seen of his greatness has been but glimpses of the image in which he was created, and of the dominion for which that image qualified him.

Does some one ask here, Is there no way of restoring man his lost crown and sceptre? of renewing in his soul, in original brightness and integrity, the image in which he was created? Yes, a way has beed devised and perfected for accomplishing all this, and even more. When Christ united his Divine with human nature, he raised man as much above what he was in the beginning, as the possession of a rational soul in the beginning raised him above the merely animal creation by which he was surrounded. Man was no longer a little lower than the angels—the union elevated him to a dignity above them. Hence we read, "Do ye not know that the saints shall judge the world? Know ye not that we shall judge angels?" 1 Cor. xv. 2, 3. As our human nature appears upon the judgment-seat in the person of Jesus Christ, who is man as well as God, we are said to participate with him in his judgment of men and angels; that is, because of the part that our human nature takes in the judgment. We participate in all the honour which that nature receives in being united with the Divine in Christ. And that our humanity might be clothed with this glory and honour, Christ himself was, for a short time, made a little lower than the angels, became man, that he, by the grace of God, might taste death for *every* man, for the whole human race, (Heb. ii. 9,) and so render us all capable of becoming partakers of the Divine nature. 2 Pet. i. 4. Angelic nature has never been so honoured. It is human nature alone that has been honoured with the union, a union that holds out to the hopes and aspirations of every man a holiness, purity and bliss, like those of Christ himself. If this were the thought in David's mind, he might well demand, "What is man, that thou art thus mindful of him? and the son of man, that thou so visitest him?" This was crowning man with honour and glory indeed! the union of his human with the Divine nature elevating him above not only what he was before he fell, but also above the angels! This being so, David could well omit what he had said of "the heavens" in the first verse of the psalm, and repeat at its close only the words, "O Lord, our Lord, how excellent is thy name in all the earth!" However brightly God's love shone in the heavens, among the angelic hosts, it was altogether eclipsed and cast out of mind by the manifestations of his love to man. When the angels fell, they fell to rise no more; no hand from on high was stretched forth to rescue them, and re-instate them in pristine glory. It was otherwise with man: when he fell, he was not only re-instated in the glory he had lost, but raised above it. Nor did this elevation extend only to his mind, but also to his body: "It is sown in corruption, it is raised in incorruption: it is sown in dishonour, it is raised in glory: it is sown in weakness, it is raised in power: it is sown a natural body, it is raised a spiritual body." And as God has advanced the material and natural in man to the spiritual, he has advanced that which is spiritual in him to the celestial—made it a partaker of a Divine nature. Man, therefore, can have a just and adequate conception of himself, of the dignity to which he is capable of being raised, only as he contemplates his entire nature, physical and intellectual, as it is seen in Christ, glorified and in living union with the Divine. Let us all, then, strive to attain unto the glory and honour that God has prepared for us by uniting our human nature with his Divine nature in the person of his Son Jesus Christ. Under his feet as man, God hath put all things, even death itself. All power is given unto the Son in heaven and in earth, that he may help and protect with almighty power, all those in whom the moral and intellectual image of God has been renewed. He regards all such, not simply as his creatures, as the angels are, but as his *children*. Let us, then, by continual prayer for the Holy Spirit, seek to be renewed in the spirit of our minds, after the image of Him who created us: and then, being so renewed, however much we may adore the goodness of God in the heavens, to angel and archangel, when we consider how much more he has done for us men and our salvation, the beginning and the end, the opening and the close of our every hymn of thanksgiving, our every anthem of praise, will be, "O Lord, *our* Lord, how excellent is thy name in all the earth!" how unspeakable is thy love to man! And if any man perishes after God has done all this for him, how fearful will his perdition be! As much more fearful than that of the angels, as he has been, in the Divine design and intention, elevated above them.

LECTURE ON PSALM IX.

To a generous nature, no other exercise can be more delightful than that of rendering to God praise and thanksgiving for his mercies. It is the exercise to which every harp in heaven is tuned, and especially the harps of the redeemed. They cease not, day nor night, celebrating the deliverances wrought out for them by their God. The loudest and most ceaseless voice heard in heaven is the anthem, "Alleluia: Salvation, and glory, and honour, and power, unto the Lord our God." And a voice issues also from the throne, saying, "Praise our God, all ye his servants, and ye that fear him, both small and great." Rev. xix. 1, 5. Such is the song of the Church in heaven. The same is the song, though in a modified key, of the Church on earth. Hence David, representing not only himself, but the whole Church militant, opens the ninth psalm with the words:

VERSES 1, 2. I will praise thee, O Lord, with my whole heart; I will show forth all thy marvellous works. I will be glad and rejoice in thee: I will sing praise to thy name, O thou Most High.

It is God's marvellous works that determined David to praise him with his whole heart; not the works of his visible creation, but the works of his providence, wrought for the maintenance of true religion, and virtue, and the punishment of wickedness and vice. It is the contemplation of his works as the moral Governor of the universe, that leads David to be glad and rejoice in him, and to sing praises to his name, as to the Most High. He sees him everywhere smiling upon the righteous, frowning upon the wicked, and so ordering all things as to secure the final triumph of the one, and the final overthrow of the other. The thought is, The Lord shows himself everywhere a righteous Governor, therefore he must be a righteous God: he exists only to do right, and to the accomplishment of that every energy and attribute of his infinite nature is directed. All this David had seen in his government of the world for thousands of years, and especially in his marvellous works—his miracles of power and grace, wrought in behalf of the people whom he had chosen to be peculiarly his own—those to whom he would reveal himself in all the infinite perfections of his nature and character. It is the revelation that God had thus made of himself, that inspired David to speak of him as he does in the opening of the psalm, as a Being altogether worthy of the soul's unbounded love, and trust, and adoration. He then proceeds to enumerate some of the marvellous works of the Lord, as the moral Governor of the world, making them, as he passes on, alternately the basis of prophecy, praise, and prayer.

VERSES 3, 4. When mine enemies are turned back, they shall fall and perish at thy presence. For thou hast maintained my right and my cause; thou sattest in the throne judging right.

How vivid an idea does David give us here of the power of God! His enemies fall and perish at his presence! If they but realize that they are before him, faintness seizes upon their hearts, and they sink. "Whom seek ye?" said our Lord Jesus Christ, God manifested in the flesh, to those who had come out to arrest him, and they answered, "Jesus of Nazareth." No sooner had he said unto them, "I am he," than they went backward, and fell to the ground. John xviii. 4–6. God, by his very presence, fills the heart of guilt with fears that overcome it. The Holy Spirit also makes the guilty soul hear the words, "I am He: I am thy God, now before thee," and takes away its strength. He makes the soul feel itself to be in the presence of One whom it cannot withstand, and with whom it is madness to contend. This interpretation of David's words, lets us into the meaning of the promise God made to Moses, when about to leave Egypt to make the conquest of Canaan, saying, "My presence shall go with thee, and I will give thee rest;" and also the meaning of Moses' reply, "If thy presence go not with me, carry us not up hence." Exod. xxxiii. 14, 15. The symbol of God's presence with his people was the *shekinah*—the luminous cloud of the bush, seen by Moses, and the guide of the Hebrew people in all their subsequent wanderings in the wilderness. This cloud, however, was one thing to the people of God, and quite another to his enemies: to one, it was a guiding pillar of light; to the other, a mass of bewildering darknesss. Exod. xiv. 19, 20, 24. So it has been, so it is now, and so it will ever be—the presence of God, life to his friends, death to his enemies. Nor is this order of things the result, on his part, of arbitrary will, but the result of the maturest deliberation. "For," says David, "thou hast maintained my right and my cause: thou sattest in the throne judging right." God's every procedure is that of an impartial judge. He examines well every cause before he acts. He sits on the throne judging right; and the right of a cause determines him infallibly to favour it, as the absence of right determines him just as infallibly to oppose it. It was therefore David's conviction of his being in the right that enabled him so confidently to predict that his enemies would fall and perish at the presence of the Lord. At this point, however, he passes from prophecy to history, saying,

VERSES 5, 6. Thou hast rebuked the heathen, thou hast destroyed the wicked, thou hast put out their name for ever and ever. O thou enemy! destructions are come to a perpetual end; [or, the destructions of the enemy are come to a perpetual end,] and thou hast destroyed cities; their memorial is perished with them.

Such is the doom of all those who array themselves against a righteous cause and a righteous God. The Lord so rebukes them as to destroy them; to put out their name for ever and ever; to bring their destruction of others to a perpetual end, raze their own cities to the ground, and bury their memorial with them in the dust. So it was in David's days, so it had been before, and so it has been since. Where now are the many and powerful nations of Canaan who opposed themselves to the people of God? Gone! Their power to destroy ceased; they themselves perished; and their cities, not even a memorial of them remains to tell us where they stood. The land in which they once lived, and reigned, and waged war against the God of heaven, is as barren of any vestige of them, as if they had never existed! Their very ruins have perished! And what more can we say of Tyre and Sidon, Babylon and Nineveh? Little indeed. Though they were at one time the most powerful cities upon which the sun ever shone, they have long since been "empty, void, and waste." And where too, is Rome—imperial Rome—the eagle of whose power touched with one wing the rising, and with the other the setting sun, and cast its shadow over a world? She too is gone; her name living only in history. She has a national existence nowhere on the earth which she once called her own. Whatever of her former greatness is still visible in the world, is visible only in ruins! Verily "thou hast rebuked the heathen, thou hast destroyed the wicked, thou hast put out their name for ever and ever."

VERSES 7, 8. But the Lord shall endure for ever: he hath prepared his throne for judgment: and he shall judge the world in righteousness: he shall minister judgment to the people in uprightness.

David here draws a contrast between changing man and the unchanging God; between evermore vanishing human thrones, and the throne of God high and lifted up—his throne of judgment—a throne erected to try and determine the cause, not of David only, nor of his people only, but of all men—to judge the world in righteousness. He teaches that right and wrong everywhere are objects of the Divine regard, and will be through all time, and will be when time shall be no more; that the Divine judgment, like the Divine omnipresence, embraces every creature in the vastness of its range. In this way David ascends in his reasoning from the particular to the general, and from the general to the universal, making the Lord's dealings with him and his people Israel the basis of the conclusion, that *so* he will deal with all men. He thus encourages all men everywhere to pursue the right, assuring them that, in pursuing it, the God of all righteousness is with them, and will, in due time, decide it in their favour. None of us then should ever either fear or hesitate to do right, leaving the issue in the hands of Him whose peculiar province it is to defend it, and avenge it. Nor does he only defend and avenge the right, but,

VERSES 9, 10. The Lord also will be a refuge for the oppressed, a refuge in times of trouble. And they that know thy name will put their trust in thee; for thou, Lord, hast not forsaken them that seek thee.

The Lord is not only the righteous Judge and Vindicator of the cause of the oppressed, but he is also a Refuge for them—a refuge in times of trouble; a high place unto which they may flee, and be safe; a citadel of rock, whence they can look down upon their enemies, secure and defiant. The most that a human judge can do, is to acquit the innocent, and leave them to themselves. It is otherwise with the Lord; where he acquits, he afterwards protects; he never forsakes them that seek him. He henceforth surrounds them with the shield of his presence, power, and love. It is this aspect of the Lord's dealings with those seeking him that leads David to say, "they that know thy name, will put their trust in thee." It is only necessary to know the name of God, to learn his moral character as it is exhibited from generation to generation, in his opposite dealings with the righteous and the wicked, to inspire the soul with unlimited confidence in him as its Judge and Refuge. The revelation that history, as a whole, makes of him is, that he is holy, just, and good. And what the whole Church can testify to, as the result of all of God's dealings with it, every individual believer can at last testify to, as the result of all His dealings with him—that is, the thorough persuasion that the Lord ever judges aright, is a refuge from the oppressions of every enemy, and never fails any who seek him. How readily, then, may every believer join in the words,

VERSES 11, 12. Sing praises to the Lord, which dwelleth in Zion: declare among the people his doings. When he maketh inquisition for blood, he remembereth them: he forgetteth not the cry of the humble: the cry of the afflicted.

It is the Lord dwelling in Zion, to whom David exhorts us to sing praises. We see God in his works of nature and of providence, but we see him there through a darkened glass, as compared with the view he gives us of himself in Zion—in the ordinances of his house, the revelations of his will, and the exhibitions of his love. He there reveals himself glorious in holiness, fearful in praises, doing wonders. It was there that he spake to the believer's eye, in the ever-burning sacrifice and ascending incense; to his ear, in the voice issuing from the holy of holies; and to his heart in all things. He stood there with his nature and attributes, as it were unveiled to the eye of the beholder. The cloud that shrouded him was not a cloud of darkness, but a cloud of light, above the brightness of the sun. Speaking to them in nature and in providence, his creatures might sometimes mistake his meaning and the import of his words. It was otherwise when he spake to them from his dwelling place in Zion. Who can mistake any part of the character that he gives himself in the words, "The Lord, the Lord God, merciful and gracious, long-suffering, and abundant in goodness and truth, keeping mercy for thousands, forgiving iniquity, and transgression, and sin, and that will by no means clear the guilty." Exod. xxxiv. 6, 7. How plainly do these words tell us that the Lord, who dwelleth in Zion, is infinitely merciful, infinitely holy, and infinitely just. And all his doings are in strict accordance with these his infinite attributes. Hence the exhortation to declare among the people his doings. His doings will bear the scrutiny of every one. He never deviates from his nature in anything he does. He feels every wrong inflicted upon the innocent as a wrong inflicted upon himself, and when he maketh inquisition for blood, he remembereth them: the voice of their blood crieth unto him from the ground, and he will avenge it: they may sometimes think otherwise, but he forgetteth not the cry of those afflicted for his sake: their cry enters into his ear, and sinks down into his heart. Such is the Lord which dwelleth in Zion, and dwelleth there for the express purpose of teaching man what He is, and what He will do. I am holy, I am just, I am good, the friend of the righteous, and the enemy of the wicked, are words written out in letters of living light upon every page of the statute book of his sanctuary. Sing praises, then, sing praises unto the Lord which dwelleth in Zion; unto Him who hath there revealed himself to us, as our hiding place from the tempest, and our refuge from the storm.

VERSES 13, 14. Have mercy upon me, O Lord; consider my trouble which I suffer of them that hate me, thou that liftest me up from the gates of death: that I may show forth all thy praise in the gates of the daughter of Zion. I will rejoice in thy salvation.

Strange, that in the midst of such jubilant songs

of praise and thanksgiving, David should so suddenly betake himself to prayer! Strange! did we say? No: it is not strange: for none of our joys here are without something of sorrow still:

> "E'en the rapture of pardon is mingled with fears,
> And the cup of thanksgiving with penitent tears."

We no sooner experience one deliverance than, taught by our weakness, we know that we shall quickly need another. If one pulsation of our hearts be that of praise and thanksgiving for the past, the next will be a pulsation of fear for the future. However many enemies God may have subdued under us, there will be some still remaining to hate and harm us: there will at least still be,

> "Temptation without, and corruption within."

Our prayer unto the Lord, therefore, should evermore be to lift us up from the gates of death, the deep-sunk and strong-barred prison of the lost—*sheol*—whence his Son delivered us by dying for us upon the cross, and back into which prison we shall certainly glide and fall, unless he *at every moment* sustain us by the grace that lifted us thence. Nor should we seek this grace simply for the comfort that it may bring ourselves, but for the glory it will bring to God, that we may show forth all his praise in the gates of the daughter of Zion, tell his Church on earth, and at last his Church in heaven, how good and gracious he has been to us. If we ask deliverance, or any other blessing, for any other purpose than this, we ask it amiss. The heart of fire and the tongue of flame are to be desired, only that we may adequately praise God for his mercies to us. This is the thought of David when he says, "I will rejoice in thy salvation." He desires life only that he may serve the Lord of life. And when we so forget ourselves in serving and glorifying him, he will forget himself infinitely more in serving and glorifying us, and inspire us with an all-absorbing assurance of final victory over all our enemies. Of such a victory David was assured, and he immediately speaks of it as a victory already obtained, saying,

VERSES 15, 16. The heathen are sunk down in the pit that they made: in the net which they hid is their own foot taken. The Lord is known by the judgment which he executeth: the wicked is snared in the work of his own hands.

Higgaion—meditate upon that. *Selah*—pause, to consider it. Here is a repetition of what we have had before, (Ps. vii. 15, 16,) "the wicked sunk down into their pit, and caught in their own net." It is so always. Wickedness sooner or later overreaches itself, and defeats its own aims. This, we are assured, is a result of the Divine ordering. The Lord is known by the *judgment* which he executeth. His judgments are always of a character to manifest, on the one hand, his own immutable justice; and on the other, that vice is self-destructive, that the wicked is snared in the work of his own hands. Nothing that a wicked man does to the injury of others, can end to his advantage. By Divine appointment the evil of the evil-doer hems him in as by a circle of fire, contracting more and more till it consumes him. It is his thorough conviction of the existence of this order of things that enables David to speak of the overthrow of his enemies as a thing already accomplished. Nor does he stop at this, but adds,

VERSES 17, 18. The wicked shall be turned into hell—*sheol*—and all the nations that forget God: for the needy shall not always be forgotten: the expectation of the poor shall not perish for ever.

Here the Psalmist's eye glances from God's judgments in this world, to his judgment in the world to come. This is the last thought wherewith he encourages the persecuted for righteousness' sake, to continue steadfast and immovable. Clouds and darkness may be round about them, in their way through life, and at their exit out of it, but the Lord hath not forgotten them: their hope shall yet be realized: their expectation of a final triumph shall not perish for ever. There is a day coming when their character shall be vindicated before an assembled world, and their enemies go away into everlasting punishment. "One day is with the Lord as a thousand years, and a thousand years as one day." He who is from everlasting to everlasting can take his own time to redress the wrongs of those hoping in his mercy: though we feel assured that he will take the earliest moment dictated by wisdom. Let us all then, without one impatient or repining thought, leave all judgment, and the time of executing it, in his hands, even as David does, saying,

VERSES 19, 20. Arise, O Lord; let not man prevail; let the heathen be judged in thy sight. Put them in fear, O Lord; that the nations may know themselves to be but men. Selah.

David here prays the Lord to arise above those who, in their pride and arrogance, had risen above him—forgotten him, and forgotten themselves; forgotten that they were but men. To what heights of arrogance has the pride of man not carried him! what titles has it not led him to assume! what power not to claim! and how signally has God sometimes punished him for it! For claiming that Babylon had been built, and his kingdom become great by the might of his own power, Nebuchadnezzar was the same hour bereft of reason, and driven forth to eat grass as the ox, till he should acknowledge that the Most High ruleth in the kingdom of men, and giveth it to whomsoever he will. Dan. iv. 30—32. And Herod, too, was similarly dealt with when he exulted in his kingly authority as a thing of his own achieving, and listened with pleasure to the people shouting under the spell of his eloquence, "It is the voice of a god, and not of a man." Immediately the angel of the Lord smote him, because he gave not God the glory; and he was eaten of worms, and gave up the ghost. Acts xii. 22, 23. The Lord is known by the judgment which he executeth. There is not another thing that he so hates and detests, loathes and abhors, as he does human pride. "Put them in fear, O Lord, that the nations may know that they are but men." And what can be more eminently calculated to inspire men with fear, than what David has taught us in this psalm, namely, that, by Divine appointment, the wicked are snared in the work of their own hands; moreover, that the Lord pursues them with his judgments in this world, or, if he allows them to escape his hand in this world, he overtakes them with judgment in the world to come? Beloved readers, this God is our God; all that this psalm says he will do for the righteous he will do; and all that it says he will do to the wicked, he will do. Let us then seek the mercy of Him whose justice we cannot endure. "Believe on the Lord

Jesus Christ, and thou shalt be saved." He will vanquish your every enemy, even death itself, and enable you to hear the voice that breaks up the slumbers of the dead, not only undismayed, but with joy and thanksgiving, and to ascend to the last judgment confident of an acquittal with commendation. Blessed are all they that put their trust in him!

LECTURE ON PSALM X.

However thoroughly we may be persuaded that God worketh all things after the counsel of his own will, in the heavens above, and on the earth beneath, and worketh all things in wisdom and in righteousness, still there are times when we cannot but wonder that he should allow innocence to suffer, and guilt to prosper, so long as he sometimes does. This wonder often fills the heart of the patriot, convinced of the entire righteousness of his cause, but experiencing defeat after defeat, till his heart dies within him. It sometimes possesses the soul of the believer too. It disturbed many a Reformer before the Reformation; many an humble Christian during the dark ages of the Church. They saw innocence broken upon the wheel, burning at the stake, toiling in the galleys, and pining away in dungeons; while guilt was arrayed in purple and fine linen, and fared sumptuously every day. But though they saw these things, they never ceased to believe that the Lord was righteous; their only anxious thought in regard to him was, whither he had betaken himself. This was evidently the thought in David's mind when he composed the tenth psalm; a psalm in several respects so like to the one going before it, that the translalors of the Septuagint and Vulgate editions of the Old Testament have made but one of the two. David could not but believe the Lord to be the righteous Governor he had represented him in the preceding psalm; but seeing the righteous depressed, and the wicked rampant, and unwilling to abate his faith in God's perfect justice, he demands the reason for what he beheld, saying,

VERSES 1, 2. Why standest thou afar off, O Lord? why hidest thou thyself in times of trouble? The wicked in his pride doth persecute the poor: let them be taken in the devices which they have imagined. [Or, they, the poor, are taken in the devices which they, the wicked, have imagined.]

Here is a posture of things well calculated to excite an appeal to a righteous God—the righteous trodden under foot by the wicked, and taken in their plots. David had said in the preceding psalm, "the Lord also will be a refuge for the oppressed; a refuge in times of trouble." And is not such his faith now? Undoubtedly; and it is this faith that leads him to demand, "Why standest thou afar off, O Lord? why hidest thou thyself in times of trouble?" He believes that a righteous God cannot look with indifference upon what is passing before him; that he cannot connive, as it were, at the pride and persecutions of the wicked, and the sufferings of the innocent. David speaks to God as a loving and confiding child speaks to his father, reasoning with him out of his own attributes and character, assuming that it is in his very nature to minister justice, and judgment, and equity; and that therefore he must, in the present instance, interpose to put an end to the wickedness of the wicked, and establish the just. All this is implied in the reiterated "why," with which the psalm opens. It indicates, on David's part, no abatement of faith in the righteousness of his God, now that clouds and darkness surround him, but rather an appealing to it with increased confidence and energy. The pressure of external evil served only to develop David's faith in God, that he will not leave the persecuted poor in the toils of the enemy, but in his own good time rescue and deliver them.

VERSE 3. For the wicked boasteth of his heart's desire, and blesseth the covetous, whom the Lord abhorreth. [Or, the covetous blesseth himself; he abhorreth the Lord.]

Here is a sad picture of depravity—the wicked boasteth of his heart's desire; unblushingly proclaims the evil upon which his heart is set, and, having accomplished it, glories in it. Evil has become his good, and he pursues it with his whole soul. This is not an unusual character; we often hear men boasting, not only of the evil they will do, but of the evil they have done. Nor does the wicked man always rejoice only in his own evil, but also in the evil of others. Hence we read, "he blesseth the covetous, whom the Lord abhorreth." He taketh pleasure in the griping, the grasping, the extortionate; in men who are God's abhorrence. Or, if we give the other rendering, "the covetous blesseth himself, he abhorreth the Lord," we have the character of the wicked man still more darkly delineated.

Right and wrong are alike to him, provided they bring him gain. His ungodly gains induce contempt of his Maker. He has made gold his hope, and fine gold his confidence. He fancies that he has become rich without God, and that he will remain rich in spite of him. And let none of us suppose that such is not the general effect of riches upon the human heart; and especially of riches unscrupulously obtained. That which any of us imagine we have obtained without God, we are very apt to think we can retain without him; that the same tact and talent which gained us our wealth, will, irrespective of any other means, secure it to us in perpetuity.

VERSE 4. The wicked, through the pride of his countenance, will not seek after God: God is not in all his thoughts. [Or, all his thoughts are, "There is no God."]

Here is an advance in the wickedness of the wicked. Success has so elated his pride, that he will not seek after God. He makes no inquiry whether God regards human actions; nor whether there exists, in the nature of things, or by Divine appointment, any such things as right and wrong. Practically, he acknowledges no god but his own will, and the desires of his heart. Or, as some render the first part of the verse, The wicked, in his pride, thinks that God will not seek after him, will take no notice of, and make no inquiry into his conduct. He thinks that he is in none of God's thoughts, as God is in none of his. All his thoughts are, "There is no God." *Thoughts* here mean plans, purposes, enterprises. Not one of his plans for life bespeaks his belief in the existence of an overruling power. If he acknowledge the existence of such a power, it is only in words; it is a bed-ridden thought in his soul, and gives neither shape, nor colour, nor direction to anything he does. And, alas! is there not much of this at least practical atheism in the heart of every one of us? How few of our plans for life bespeak our belief in the existence of a God who made us what we are, and gave us what we have—to whom we are accountable, and who will bring us into judgment for our lives on earth! Every man is practically an atheist, who does not live, and act, and plan for eternity.

VERSE 5. His ways are always grievous; thy judgments are far above out of his sight: as for all his enemies, he puffeth at them.

These words describe the external condition of the man whose pride leads him to practical atheism. His ways are always prosperous. So the best critics understand the word "grievous": everything goes according to his wishes; not one of his plans appears to fail. As for the judgments of God, they are far above out of his sight; he sees them not, he feels them not, and therefore does not believe in their existence for himself. As for all his enemies, he puffeth at them; treats them with supercilious contempt, hisses them out of his sight, scatters them by the veriest breath of his displeasure, as leaves are scattered by the wind. His character is that of the unjust judge, so tersely and darkly described in the parable, who feared not God, nor regarded man, (Luke xviii. 4;) a being of supreme selfishness, himself his sole centre of hope, happiness, and care. And let none of us suppose that uninterrupted prosperity may not have the same effect upon our hearts; rendering us as fearless of God, and regardless of man.

VERSE 6. He hath said in his heart, I shall not be moved; for I shall never be in adversity.

Impunity in the past, makes the wicked confident of the future. He says "in his heart, I shall not be moved." God, if there be a God, does not choose to interfere in my affairs; and no man, if he would, dare to interfere. I shall therefore never be in adversity; I have my fortunes in my own keeping, and no power can mar them. How naturally this feeling glides into every heart, whose desires have been long indulged and gratified. The rich man spoke about many years of self-indulgence, as if the years were in his own hands; and while the words were yet in his mouth, "God said unto him, Thou fool, this night shall thy soul be required of thee." Luke xii. 20.

VERSE 7. His mouth is full of cursing, and deceit, and fraud; under his tongue is mischief and vanity.

Here the thoughts of the wicked pass into words, into cursing, deceit, and fraud. He imprecates curses upon himself, to conceal his deceit; and he labours for such concealment, that he may more successfully practice fraud. He frames his speech, not to benefit others, but to accomplish his selfish ends. Who can tell how much poison there is in our words! So much, that St. James says, he that offendeth not in word, is a perfect man, and able to bridle the whole body. James iii. 2. "Under his tongue is mischief and vanity," or oppression. The poison-sacks of serpents are under the tongue; and as the serpent

11

ejects the poison from them only to kill, so the wicked man uses language only for mischief and oppression.

VERSE 8. He sitteth in the lurking-places of the villages: in the secret places doth he murder the innocent: his eyes are privily set against the poor.

A vivid description of the active principle of evil, as it manifests itself in countries where systems of espionage and secret police prevail. The secret, governmental spy sitteth in the lurking-places of the villages, watches his victims from his concealment of place or character, as the lion watches his prey from his hiding-place. "In the secret places doth he murder the innocent;" drags them away to some secret tribunal—such as the Inquisition was and is—where their cry of anguish, and the voice of their wrongs, are smothered together. "His eyes are privily set against the poor:" no man knows, in such countries, who is acting the spy upon him. If he worship God after the dictates of conscience, or speak of human liberty as a human right, out springs some spy from his concealment of place or character, and tells him of a sentence against him to be executed speedily.

VERSE 9. He lieth in wait secretly, as a lion in his den; he lieth in wait to catch the poor; he doth catch the poor, when he draweth him into his net.

Here the wicked man is compared first to the lion, watching his prey from his lurking-place; and then, to a hunter casting his net. So it is; how often does wickedness combine the ferocity of the brute with the intelligence of man, to accomplish its selfish ends! Nor does it stop at this; if it fail to realize its aims by force, it then changes its tactics. Hence we read of the wicked:

VERSE 10. He croucheth, and humbleth himself, that the poor may fall by his strong ones.

The lion comes crouching and fawning to your feet, but only that, having thus thrown you off your guard, his spring may be the more deadly; that he may break you with his jaws, and rend you with his claws, more fearfully. If the Church of Rome had sat for this picture of the wicked man, the likeness could not have been more accurate. Her policy, and the policy of all the governments whose policy she has been able to control, has always been, first force, then fraud. Nevertheless, whether employing force or fraud, threatening or persuasion, bulls of excommunication, or enticing words, having but a single end in view, the subjugation of the universal human will and conscience to her control. Her strong ones, into whose power the weak have finally fallen, have at last always been fire and faggot, wheel and screw, inquisition and sequestration. If, however, any of us suppose that the character she has developed is anything else than the unrestrained natural wickedness of the human heart, we are mistaken. "As in water, face answereth to face, so doth the heart of man to man." Prov. xxvii. 19.

VERSE 11. He hath said in his heart, God hath forgotten: he hideth his face, he will never see it.

David here recurs to the prolific source of all the wickedness of the wicked—his practical disbelief in the existence of an overruling Providence. He does not believe that God sees, remembers, and will bring every work into judgment. It is surprising what strides men will take in iniquity when once the idea of an avenging God is banished from their minds! Into what a pandemonium did it convert the whole of France! Sin ran riot, till men were glutted with it; and one of the chief anarchists said, "If there were no God, I would decree the existence of one, for there is no governing the world without at least the idea." The whole nation learned, almost too late to save themselves from ruin, that God was not a listless spectator of their doings; that they whose motto and battle-cry in regard to Jesus was, "Crush the wretch!" were themselves felled to the earth by the blows they aimed at him in the persons of his followers.

VERSES 12, 13. Arise, O Lord; O God, lift up thy hand: forget not the humble. Wherefore doth the wicked contemn God? He hath said in his heart, Thou wilt not require it.

Having set forth in the previous portions of the psalm how the long-suffering forbearance of God had served only to increase the wickedness of the wicked in word, thought, and deed, and emboldened him to affirm that there is no God, or that, if there be, he does not concern himself with the affairs of men, David here calls upon God to vindicate himself from the blasphemous aspersion—to arise, and cast off his seeming indifference; and now, as if he had been standing with his hand in his bosom, to lift up his arm for some signal stroke of avenging justice, he appeals to the Lord his God to do this for his own sake, for the vindication of his character for righteousness, saying, "Wherefore should the wicked contemn God, by saying in his heart, Thou wilt not require it?" Thou wilt not recognize any such distinctions as right and wrong, righteous and unrighteous. Arise, O Lord, and rebuke this impious incredulity in regard to thy real character, and so rebuke it that all men shall see that there is no oblivion with thee, no want of inquiry, and no want of retributive justice.

VERSE 14. Thou hast seen it; for thou beholdest mischief and spite, to requite it with thy hand: the poor committeth himself unto thee; thou art the helper of the fatherless.

The wicked had declared that God regarded neither the oppressor nor the oppressed; David here replies that he regards both, and will deal with both according to their characters. The Lord may delay long before he deals with the wronged and the wrongdoer according to their deserts; but that is no evidence that he in the meantime regards both alike—that is, both with indifference. Faith still contemplates him as only awaiting the fittest time to avenge the one, and punish the other.

VERSE 15. Break thou the arm of the wicked and of the evil man: seek out his wickedness till thou find none.

Destroy all his power to do evil, ferret out his wickedness till none remains to be found; convince him that not only atrocious acts, but the thoughts of the heart come within the scope of thy judgments. Such is the clearance of moral evil that God will at last make in his universe—so complete that even his own all-searching eye shall not be able to discover a vestige of it remaining.

VERSE 16. The Lord is King for ever and ever: the heathen are perished out of his land.

Here is the faith that sustains the heart of the believer in the darkest hour of the darkest night of providence: "the Lord is King for ever and ever;" of his government there is no end; its lines run on parallel with the ages of eternity; guilt, therefore, can never escape its vengeance, nor innocence fail of its vindication. "The heathen are perished out of his land." David here speaks of a thing to come, as if it were already passed, so certainly would it be brought about under the eternal rule of God. Such is the privilege of faith, fixing its eye upon a righteous God, seated upon an everlasting throne of empire, it is enabled to speak of things that are, as if they were not; and of things that are not, as if they were.

VERSES 17, 18. Lord, thou hast heard the desire of the humble: thou wilt prepare their heart, thou wilt cause thine ear to hear: to judge the fatherless and the oppressed, that the man of the earth may no more oppress.

Here is the conclusion to which faith is sure to arrive at last. However rampant sin may become in the earth, however long innocence may suffer, the assurance at last glides into the heart of the believer, that these things will not continue always so. God himself, by the operations of his Spirit, inspires the assurance. He prepares the heart, in the midst of the worst things, to hope for the best; in the midst or a world groaning and travailing in pain for sin, to hope for new heavens and a new earth, wherein dwelleth righteousness; where the wicked shall cease from troubling, and the weary be at rest. In this way the Lord heareth the desire of the humble. He heareth them, either by granting them their heart's desire at the present time, or by giving them such an inward assurance of granting it in the future, that peace, the peace of God, enters into and possesses the soul. Nor does he give us this assurance of peace only in regard to external, but also in regard to all internal enemies. He gives us assurance of a time when the heart shall rest for ever in its God—when all its conflicts with its own weakness and corruptions will have ceased, and it be filled with a joy unspeakable and full of glory.

One thought more, before we close. Let none of us mistake who the wicked man of this psalm is. Beloved reader, his character may be yours or mine. It is that of every one whose natural wickedness has been left to develop itself unmodified by the restraining or transforming grace of God. Everything that this wicked man is herein described as thinking, saying, and doing, you and I would think, and say, and do, if left to ourselves. He is designed to represent in every age, the man who has no hope, and is without God in the world. You and I, beloved reader, see in this wicked man, only what we are capable of becoming, and what, in all the dark essentials of his character, we surely will become, if God do not change us by his grace, renew us in the spirit of our minds, and then evermore strengthen us with might by his Holy Spirit in the inner man, that we may be enabled to withstand in the evil day, and having done all, to stand. Let us then seek at once the grace that will save us from the character and the doom of the wicked man of our psalm, and seek it till God inspire in our hearts the assurance that he has heard our prayers.

LECTURE ON PSALM XI.

It is by no means always an easy question for the good man to decide, when he shall flee, and when resist, the storm of immorality and irreligion that may be prevailing in the community to which he belongs. He may err as widely in precipitating the time for doing a thing, as he can in allowing the time to pass by unimproved. It is as much the part of a good general to know when to halt, as when to advance; when to retreat, as when to attack; when to save life, as when to cast it away. The only question for him to settle, is, which course for the time being, will, in the end, best promote the cause he has in hand. Our Lord both spoke and acted on this principle, counselling his disciples at one time to save themselves by flight; at another, to remain at their posts, even at the cost of their lives. He counselled them to determine their line of conduct, not by its consequences to themselves, but by its consequences to the cause by which they were identified. If flight would best promote its interests, they were to flee; if remaining at their posts, they were to remain, and, if needs be, die there. This was our Lord's counsel to his disciples, and his own conduct was in keeping with it. He saved his life by flight, till the interests of his cause demanded the surrender of it, and then he laid it down without resistance and without regret. Many a bishop, too, in the primitive Church did the same: fleeing, so long as flight could best serve their Master's cause; but, when it demanded the surrender of their lives, giving themselves up freely to martyrdom. David, too, is an example of a good man pursuing, at different times, two directly opposite lines of conduct: but pursuing each with the same definite end always in view, namely, the advancement of God's kingdom of truth and righteousness in the earth. For years after he had been divinely designated to the throne of Israel, we see him fleeing before his persecutors, like a terrified bird. In the psalm before us, however, his affairs are no longer as they have been. The time has come when the cause with which he has identified himself can no longer be promoted by his flight. It demands champions and defenders, and it may be, martyrs. Hence, to those counselling flight now, he answers,

VERSE 1. In the Lord put I my trust: how say ye to my soul, Flee as a bird to your mountain?

This reply of David to the advice of timid friends, or designing enemies, reminds one of Luther's reply to the message, that he would proceed to the Diet of Worms at the peril of his life. His only reply to the intimidating message was, "If there were as many devils in Worms as there are tiles upon the roofs of its houses, I would go on." Hitherto Luther had evaded all open encounter with the fierce lion of Rome; but now the time had arrived when he felt that it was his duty to beard him, break his jaws, and pluck his mangled prey, the Church of the living God, out of his mouth. The whole Roman world were in arms against him, and thirsting for his blood; but ,in the name of God, he defied them all. He asked no other mountain of refuge, and would betake himself to no other. David occupied a similar position, and manifests a similarly determined spirit in the words, "In the Lord put I my trust: how say ye to my soul, Flee as a bird to your mountain?" On what especial occasion David felt himself called on to assume this bold and defiant attitude, we are not informed. It is enough for us to know, that he assumed it, and no doubt under circumstances that demanded the assumption. He feared not what man could do unto him, and would resort to no devices of human contrivance for relief. His trust was in the living God; and the exhortation to flee the post of duty, pierced him to the soul: "In the Lord put I my trust." I know that I am fighting his battles, and that he will not leave me to fight them alone. Think ye that he who has God for his champion, needs any other defence?

VERSE 2. For, lo, the wicked bend their bow, they make ready their arrow upon the string, that they may privily shoot at the upright in heart.

With what graphic vividness do David's timid friends, or designing enemies, here describe his danger to him! They liken him to a bird flying in the open plain, while on every side, in the groves and thickets surrounding that plain, archers lie concealed, with bows bent, and arrows ready upon the string, to shoot at him!—a description of one's danger well calculated to fill the heart with fears and misgivings. Most men have courage to contend with a visible and tangible foe; few, indeed, with an invisible and intangible one. The presence of such a foe on every side had, however, no terrors for David. Upright in heart himself, he felt assured that the upright God would be his shield. He has therefore no occasion to flee the open plain for some mountain fastness. He dreads neither the open force nor the undermining cunning of the enemies of his God. Their sharpest arrows, even bitter words uttered in secret, may fly all around him, and darken the air over him, but not one of them shall touch him. He is safe; and he reveals the secret of his safety in the words, "in the Lord put I my trust,"

VERSE 3. If the foundations be destroyed, what can the righteous do?

It is here sought to operate still farther upon David's fears; all is represented as lost beyond recovery; that the foundations of society are destroyed; that truth and justice have ceased to govern the actions of men. How often has this anarchy of affairs been realized in the history of the world; law and order trodden under foot, and violence reigning supreme in their stead! And how often is this state of affairs urged upon the good man as a sufficient reason for his deserting his post! The cry is, "All is anarchy—what can the righteous man do? Unsupported and alone, what can he do to stem and turn back the tide of wickedness rising and raging everywhere around him?" *What* can he do? Let the effect of Luther's speech before the Diet at Worms answer the question. Acknowledging all his writings, and confronting the greatest and mightiest of the whole earth, he concluded his speech to them in the following words: "Let me then be refuted and convinced by the testimony of the Scriptures, or by the clearest arguments, otherwise I cannot and will not retract; for it is neither safe nor expedient to act against conscience. Here I take my stand; I can do no otherwise, so help me God! Amen." Luther's was but a single voice against the world; but how its tones rung through the earth, startling the nations from Rome to the Orkneys. It was a single voice, saying, authoritatively, to the usurpations of the great Antichrist, "Here shall thy proud waves be stayed!" The inundations of wickedness, surging and dashing over the earth, began immediately to recede. How often, too, in many a church, and in many a community, and in many a country, is a similar effect produced by a single voice! All is anarchy, all lawless violence, and good men in despair, till some one fearless spirit confronts, rebukes, and defies wickedness in power—mounts the whirlwind and directs the storm, and brings it down in due time upon those who raised it. It matters not how entirely the foundations of society may be destroyed, truth and justice trodden under foot, he who undertakes its reformation by taking counsel, not of his fears, but of truth and right, will in the end succeed? If he can say, "in the Lord put I my trust," he can smile at, as he certainly should spurn, all suggestions of flight when the hour for decisive and definitive action has come. For such a man to flee his post at such a time, would be virtually denying the existence of a righteous God.

VERSE 4. The Lord is in his holy temple, the Lord's throne is in heaven: his eyes behold, his eye-lids try, the children of men.

David here recurs to the sentiment expressed in the first words of the psalm, "in the Lord put I my trust;" only here he expands the sentiment, and shows why he should trust in the Lord. "The Lord is in his holy temple;" he is evermore in his Church to protect and perpetuate the religion he has revealed to it; dwelling therein by his word and Spirit, and so taking up his abode in the hearts of some, that he shall never want a seed to serve him. He may sometimes leave his Church to be tossed, and agitated, and sifted, but he will never altogether forsake it, but still carry it on, after every reverse, to new victories. It was his conviction of this truth that led David so vehemently to repudiate the advice given him to flee. As God is evermore in his holy temple, his Church, he felt assured that He would defend all those whom he had called to defend it. "The Lord's throne is in heaven:" here David gives us another reason why he should not flee, why he should not cease to reprove error, and bear testimony to the truth—his Defender's throne is in heaven, far above the reach and malice of men. The wicked may assail and overturn human thrones, but there is one throne whose stability they can never affect—God's throne in heaven. All things else may reel, and totter, and fall, but that remains unmoved. And upon that immovable throne David here fastens the eye of his faith, knowing that whenever there shall issue thence the voice, "Peace, be still!" the moral and social anarchy raging around him will subside, and a great calm ensue. He knows too, that even while the storm is raging in its fury, it cannot overwhelm him till the occupant of that throne give the word. And he is quite sure that that word will not be given till he has fulfilled his earthly mission, whatever that mission may be. This, too, seems to have been the thought in the mind of the Saviour, when, in reply to the message of the Pharisees, "Get thee out, and depart hence; for Herod will kill thee," he answered, "Go ye and tell that fox, I cast out devils, and I do cures to-day and to-morrow, and the third day I shall be perfected: nevertheless, I must walk to-day, and to-morrow, and the day following." Luke xiii. 31–33. He knew that he was safe so long as any part of his mission remained to be fulfilled, whoever might hate him, and whoever might seek his life. Such is the confidence inspired by faith in Him whose throne is in heaven, whose kingdom ruleth over all, and who suffereth not even a sparrow to perish without his permission. His eyes behold, his eyelids try the children of men. He is not an indifferent spectator of human conduct; on the contrary, his eye is fixed upon it with a scrutiny so intense, and a vision so piercing, that nothing can escape him. He sees our thoughts, beholds them afar off, even while they are as yet but just emerging above the horizon of our own consciousness. To the terror of the one, and the comfort of the other, he beholds everywhere the evil and the good.

VERSE 5. The Lord trieth the righteous: but the wicked, and him that loveth violence, his soul hateth.

"The Lord trieth the righteous;" he tries them for their own good, that they may know themselves. He tries them for the good of others, that the world may learn how powerful a thing faith in God is, when it has once laid fast hold of his promises. It was for this purpose that he tested Abraham, when he commanded him to offer up his son Isaac, with his own hand, a burnt-offering unto the Lord. The trial taught Abraham what he could never have known of himself without it—the character of true evangelical obedience; that it falters at no sacrifice known to be required by the will of God. It is these testing trials of the righteous that bring out their graces, develop and perfect their virtues. The hand of God is in them all, seeking higher praise for himself, and working out a far more exceeding and eternal weight of glory for the believer. "The Lord trieth the righteous;" only, however, to consume their dross and refine their gold. The wicked have no just cause for triumphing over him, when they see the righteous man in affliction. The hand of God is thus upon him only for his good. His trials are no evidence that the fact is otherwise. And, on the other hand, let not the wicked man suppose that his prosperity is evidence that God approves him, or his ways. "The wicked, and him that loveth violence, his soul hateth." His whole nature revolts alike at their characters and their conduct. He abhors them none the less, because he does not overwhelm them at once. In this way David encourages himself and all other believers in the Lord, teaching that the trials of the righteous are only for their good, the prosperity of the wicked by no means indicative of the Divine approbation, and that, consequently, the former will in due time be delivered, and the latter overthrown. He describes the overthrow of the latter in the verse following, saying,

VERSE 6. Upon the wicked he shall rain snares, fire and brimstone, and an horrible tempest: this shall be the portion of their cup.

The allusion here is undoubtedly to the destruction of Sodom and Gomorrah, fire descending from above, and rising up from beneath, to consume them. Gen. xix. 24, 25. The wicked lay snares for the righteous; upon the wicked themselves God rains snares, showers them down upon them as if the heavens were full of them. God rains snares upon the wicked when he overwhelms them by the orderings of his providence. They may for a long time have had things their own way; a single reverse, however, comes at last—why, or how, they cannot tell—but followed so quickly and rapidly by others, that they soon feel themselves safe nowhere; that flight is impossible, resistance vain, and destruction inevitable. It is always so with the wicked when God at length pours out his judgments upon them. Amos ix. 1. They cannot move but they find themselves in still another snare of the infinite net of snares cast abroad for them by the hand of God. "Upon the wicked he shall rain fire and brimstone." The Hebrew words here translated *fire* and *brimstone*, do not indicate a fire that merely flashes its heat upon us, like the lightning's blaze, and then passes away, but a molten, liquid, and adhesive fire; such a fire as that afforded by burning pitch, being at the same time both fuel and flame—a flame that sticks and clings to one like his very flesh, and as if it were a part of it. And what else than such a sticking, clinging, and adhesive fire, at last, is the lust of the debauchee and wanton, the appetite of the inebriate, the cravings of the glutton, and the temper of the impetuous and vindictive man? The fire that consumes all such, sticks and adheres to them like burning pitch. The lust, the appetite, and the irritable temper, are each, in itself, both fuel and flame. And when at length Divine wrath, fire from above, shall mingle, as it did with the bitumen of the cities of the plain, with the self-fed and self-sustained flame in the sinner's own body and soul, how intense and insufferable must the heat become! Upon the wicked he shall rain an horrible tempest; a tempest of horrors, a wrath-wind! The allusion is to the pestiferous simoom of Arabia—beautiful in its approach, tinting the air along its course with the hues of the rainbow, but leaving behind it not a living creature in whose face it has breathed! A wrath-wind and tempest of horrors indeed! And yet, fearful as it is, it only shadows forth the tempest of remorseful terrors that sometimes sweeps through the guilty soul in the dying hour. It is needless to tell the man so dying, the man whose conscience God has armed with something of the retributive power that it possesses in the world to come, what is meant by an horrible tempest. He feels it in his soul as no language can describe it. "Upon the wicked he shall rain snares, fire and brimstone, and an horrible tempest; this shall be the portion of their cup."

VERSE 7. For the righteous Lord loveth righteousness; his countenance doth behold the upright.

Here is the secret, the source and spring of all of God's dealings with man—*his love of righteousness.* It is the source of all his judgments upon the wicked, and of all his blessings upon the righteous. He cannot treat the two otherwise than he does, without contradicting his very nature. Righteousness is the essence of his being; the attribute that governs every other attribute of his infinite nature. It controls his power, his love, and his will. Our only safety then, is to identify ourselves with him in righteousness: to adopt his cause as our own, and to reckon no sacrifice too great to be made, that will promote it. It was to promote the cause of righteousness in the earth, that his own Son descended to earth, laboured, suffered, and died. We are to make him our Exemplar. He never, in anything he did, calculated its consequences to himself, but only to the cause he had espoused. We are to do the same. We are not to consult what will be most agreeable to our feelings, nor what will be most for our temporal interests, but how we can best serve the cause of truth and right in the church or community in which God has cast our lot. Nor is there any member of any church or community to which this responsibility does not attach. It attaches to every one: to the servant, as well as to the master; to the man under authority, as well as to the man in authority. All are equally bound to identify themselves and all that they have with the cause of righteousness, to the maintenance of true religion and virtue, and the punishment of wickedness and vice; and to that end, all are equally bound to seek a personal interest in the atoning blood of Him through whom alone we can be righteous in the sight of God. All who fail to become righteous through faith in him, and to live for the cause for which he lived, and laboured, and suffered, and died, will at last be among those upon whom the Lord will rain snares, fire and brimstone, and an horrible tempest. May God, of his infinite mercy in Jesus Christ, give us all grace to love righteousness as he loves it, and to seek its universal prevalence as earnestly!

LECTURE ON PSALM XII.

On what occasion David wrote this psalm cannot be determined. It describes a state of public morals well calculated to fill the heart of the patriot and believer with grief and sad forebodings: good men and true everywhere disappearing, and those who would carry everything by bold and reckless, or specious and flattering speech, occupying their places. Truth and fidelity seemed for the time to be displaced by falsehood and treachery. With this conviction oppressing his heart, David opens the twelfth psalm with the impassioned cry,

Verse 1. Help, Lord; for the godly man ceaseth; for the faithful fail from among the children of men.

To one reflecting that God's kingdom of truth and righteousness in the earth is to be maintained through human agencies, it is a saddening sight to see one after another of its champions and defenders disappearing from the conflict. The sight often smites the heart of the survivor, as it would have smitten the heart of the Israelite to have seen David fall in his combat with Goliath. Few indeed are the communities, whether civil or ecclesiastical, whose histories do not exhibit epochs and crises in which their whole future well-being seemed to depend upon the life of a single man, or, at most, upon the lives of a very small band. And when such men fall in the conflict, or depart hence in the course of nature, good men feel that society has suffered a loss that cannot be easily repaired. But how much more severely is the blow felt when the champions of a cause are lost to it, not by death, but by turning traitors: when a Judas betrays the Church, and an Arnold the State. Now it is in this latter sense that we are to understand David's words, "the godly man ceaseth; the faithful fail from among the children of men." It was not by the sword of an enemy, nor by natural death, that they had been lost to the cause of law and order, truth and right, but by betraying it and fighting against it. David's own son, and subjects, and generals, and ministers, had conspired to overthrow the cause they had sworn to defend: and thus situated, he appeals to the only power that can now avail him, saying, "Help, Lord;" man has failed me: thou alone canst now deliver: for,

VERSE 2. They speak vanity every one with his neighbour: with flattering lips and with a double heart do they speak.

Confidence in each other's word, the belief that men speak their real sentiments, and will realize them in their actions, is the great bond of human society. Society cannot exist without such confidence and belief as the general sentiment. Wherever these are wanting as the general sentiment, society is not a cemented union, but only an aggregation and juxtaposition of individuals. And this is the state of society described in the words, "they speak vanity, falsehood, lies, every one with his neighbour: with flattering lips and a double heart do they speak." There is an utter want of sincerity in their words, having its origin in universal suspicion and distrust. Believing that they will not have the truth spoken to them, they do not speak it to others: they flatter the powerful, that they may secure their favour; the weak, that they may use them. All is done, however, with a double-heart, to deceive: all their fine speeches to each other are secretly intended to promote only the interests of the speaker, and this every one of them knows and feels. So it is: such is a part of the curse of wickedness, it has no confidence in itself, and thinks it can succeed only by falsehood and deceit. Hence, to promote their own ends, the wicked often flatter, where they despise; and profess confidence, where they feel nothing but distrust. This has been signally verified in the conduct of eminent infidels, fulsomely flattering one another by letter, and face to face, but in their words and letters to others, expressing unmitigated distrust and contempt. And what we find so largely exhibited in the conduct of infidels, every one of us will find more or less of, in our own hearts and lives. There is a great deal more duplicity and double dealing in our intercourse with each other than we imagine, till we compare our every word with the standard of truth and the real feelings of our hearts at the time. There is more need to us all, than many of us imagine, of the Divine exhortation, "Putting away lying, speak every man truth with his neighbour." Eph. iv. 25.

VERSES 3, 4. The Lord shall cut off all flattering lips, and the tongue that speaketh proud things: who have said, With our tongue will we prevail; our lips are our own: who is lord over us?

The language of agitators, of men who think to carry everything by free speech, a free press, and a free pulpit! God forbid that we should ever see the day when either of these three great agencies for enlightening, exciting, and directing human thought, shall not be free. They are the earthly trinity that preside over all that can be dear to us as American citizens and American Christians. However much they may be abused, they are still the chief glory of our country. It is not to be denied, however, that they are abused. Instead of being used only for the defence of truth and right, they are often prostituted to stirring up the most fearful passions that can agitate the human breast; to arraying brother against brother, citizen against citizen, section against section, and church against church. You may remonstrate with the men so engaged, but the only answer you can obtain from them is likely to be, "With our tongue will we prevail; our lips are our own: who is lord over us?" They act as if freedom of speech implied the right to say whatever fancy may dictate, when it may dictate, where it may dictate, and as it may dictate. Hence the recklessness with which not only opinions, but character and motives are assailed. The right of free discussion is often indulged by its advocates, till they seem to have forgotten that men have any other rights. Nor is this lawlessness of tongue confined to partizan leaders and to those in authority; it pervades and embitters private life. We meet, in every walk of society, persons who pride themselves on their fearlessness of speech, and who, in sheer wantonness, inflict wounds upon the characters and feelings of others, that time can never heal. They forget that there are words worse than blows, and insinuations to which death would be a kindness. Still, they pride themselves upon their outspokenness as a virtue. A virtue! Heaven save us from all such virtue, and the virtuous impulses of all such characters. Virtuous as they may fancy themselves, because of their candour, they come under the condemnation of this psalm. "The Lord shall cut off all flattering lips, and the tongue that speaketh proud things:" they who use their tongues to the injury of others shall in due time receive their reward. There is a God of truth and justice, who hears their words. He abominates alike their flattery, and their abuse of others; sees what was spoken with a desire to do good, and what with a purpose to do evil; what proceeded from the wisdom which is from above, and what from a heart actuated only by its own likes and dislikes, preferences and aversions. God is not an indifferent listener to what men say.

VERSE 5. For the oppression of the poor, for the sighing of the needy, now will I arise, saith the Lord: I will set him in safety from him that puffeth at him. [Or, I will set him in safety who sigheth after it.]

We are apt to think lightly of wrongs inflicted by the tongue. It is otherwise with Him who sees their evil effect. He sees how they oppress the poor, and extort sighs from the needy; not specially the world's poor and needy, but the Lord's poor and needy; those of an humble and contrite spirit, whom, because neither their feelings nor their principles allow them to avenge themselves, the world assail, because they can assail them with impunity; prefer charges, impute motives, and insinuate suspicions, because they can do so without being called to account for it. How often do the wicked speak of believers as they would not dare to speak of each other. The believer, however, is not so helpless as the world think him to be. There is at least one Being who never ceases to regard his wrongs—the Almighty Because of the oppression of the poor, because of the sighing of the needy, now will I arise, saith the Lord: I will establish him in *safety* who sigheth after it. Safety is what David sighed after in the very first word of the psalm; and safety is here promised him in the same Hebrew word repeated. The Lord establishes the believer in safety, sometimes by silencing for ever the tongues that would ruin him; sometimes by making their flattery or abuse so gross and palpable as to deprive them of all power to injure; and sometimes by so strengthening the integrity of the believer, that no smooth words can undermine it, and so bringing it out to the light that no harsh words can obscure it. God is not an indifferent spectator of the assaults made upon the integrity, character, or feelings of those hoping in his mercy. For all those sighing after safety from the tongue of flattery or abuse, he will, sooner or later, silence in some way every tongue that would either drive or decoy them from the path of duty; for,

VERSE 6. The words of the Lord are pure words; as silver tried in a furnace of earth, purified seven times.

Here is a contrast instituted between the words of God and the words of man. Man's words may deceive and disappoint, but the Lord's will not. "Hath he spoken, and shall he not do it? or hath he said, and shall he not make it good?" No word of his has ever been tried, and not found true; and no promise of his believed, and not made good. However severely tested, every saying of his comes out at last bright and clear. The infidel has tried the Divine sayings in his crucible, and they have stood the fires of even his furnace. The Christian too has tried them in the furnace of affliction, and the fiercer the fires burned, the brighter the sayings shone. He has come forth from every trial of the Divine faithfulness, proclaiming with increased fervour, "His promise is for ever sure." It was thus that Joshua spoke of the Divine faithfulness to the Israelites, saying to them, "Ye know in all your hearts, and in all your souls, that not one thing hath failed of all the good things that the Lord your God spake concerning you: all are come to pass unto you, and not one thing hath failed thereof." Josh. xxiii. 14. In view of such faithfulness on the part of his God, in the fulfilment of his every promise to his people, David is fully justified in adding:

VERSE 7. Thou shalt keep them, O Lord, thou shalt preserve them from this generation for ever.

However false, deceitful, selfish, and overreaching the generation was that David has been describing, he assures those trusting in his mercy, and striving to walk blamelessly, that the Lord will keep and preserve them unharmed in the midst of it all. It was thus that he preserved Noah in his generation, Lot in Sodom, and Daniel in the court at Babylon. In the midst of the most wicked community, God will preserve uncorrupted those who seek his face and favour, and endure as seeing him who is invisible. He will so operate upon their hearts, or upon the hearts of others, or so order the events of his providence, that they shall pass unscathed by the wickedness which consumes all around them. We are, then, not to seek safety in flight from the position in which God has placed us by his providence, but, by faith and prayer, submitting ourselves to his protection and guidance.

VERSE 8. The wicked walk on every side, when the vilest men are exalted.

In this last verse David gives us both the effect and the cause of the wickedness of the times, namely, the elevation of unworthy men to places of power and authority. Having obtained their places by falsehood and corruption, they surround themselves with men of the same character, and generally as the reward for their mendacity in serving them. It is humiliating and alarming to witness the extent to which this order of things is carried. The purest are assailed with the same unrelenting recklessness of assertion and fabrication. The question with the partisan, in both Church and State, is not, What only can I say of my opponent and his cause that is just and true? but, What can I say of them, that will injure them most?" The consequence of this disregard of truth is, that good men will not offer for places which good men alone should fill, and, as a thing in course, power and authority fall too often into the hands of those who will use them to promote only their own selfish aims. It must be acknowledged, however, that the people themselves are in a great measure responsible for this deplorable state of morals. We are not sufficiently regardful of the moral character of those whom we elect to make, interpret, and execute our laws. We act upon the absurdity of supposing that a man may be false to his God, and still true to us; habitually violate the Divine, and still be obedient to human law. It is true that perfect men cannot be found anywhere on earth, in Church or State; still, it cannot be doubted that we should elevate to positions of trust and power only men who have the fewest imperfections. Nor can it be denied that we should look still more scrutinizing to our own characters than to the characters of our rulers. It is our duty to cultivate an uncompromising adherence to truth both in our words and actions. We may have the power to say what we please, but we have no right to say anything to another's injury. However much we may boast of our freedom of speech, saying "our lips are our own," and demanding "who is lord over us?" there is, nevertheless, a Lord over us, even the Lord God of truth, who requires his creatures to be truthful, even as he is truthful. And this fact should lead us all to seek to be renewed in the temper of our minds by the Divine Spirit of truth, purchased for us by our Lord Jesus Christ, and, through his intercession, vouchsafed to all who seek its influences.

LECTURE ON PSALM XIII.

THERE are times in the believer's experience when God seems to him to have forgotten him; when, though a child of the light, he walks in darkness—and that, too, while endeavouring to approve his every act and thought to Him who searches the heart. It is one of the mysteries of his grace that God should so deal with those hoping in his mercy, and walking according to his laws. David complains elsewhere, "Lord, why castest thou off my soul? why hidest thou thy face from me?" Ps. lxxxviii. 14. Job says, "O that I were as in months past, as in the days when God preserved me; when his candle shone upon my head, and when by his light I walked through darkness." Job xxix. 2, 3. Isaiah intimates the same idea of desertion, saying, "Who is among you that feareth the Lord, that obeyeth the voice of his servant, that walketh in darkness, and hath no light? let him trust in the name of the Lord, and stay upon his God." Isa. l. 10. So also Jeremiah complains: "I am the man that hath seen affliction by the rod of his wrath. He hath led me, and brought me into darkness, but not into light." Lam. iii. 1, 2. The believer who, when in spiritual darkness, thinks that his trials are peculiar, and says, "Behold, and see if there be any sorrow like unto my sorrow, which is done unto me, wherewith the Lord hath afflicted me," (Lam. i. 12,) may learn, in the Scriptures here recited, that holy prophets were tried in the same way thousands of years ago. What particular spiritual grief pressed so heavily upon David's heart at the time he wrote this psalm, he does not tell us. His words, therefore, are applicable to any spiritual desertion that the believer may experience. And where is the earnest believer who has not experienced some spiritual sorrow so intense, and so long-continued, as to force him to cry out,

VERSES 1, 2. How long wilt thou forget me, O Lord? for ever? how long wilt thou hide thy face from me? how long shall I take counsel in my soul, having sorrow in my heart daily? how long shall mine enemy be exalted over me?

This four times repeated "how long?" and once with the addition "for ever?" indicates an intensity of feeling that can be expressed in no other words.

The believer finds no other suffering so hard to bear, as he does the suffering caused by the loss of sensible communion with God; the loss of the feeling that God is with him by his sustaining and cheering presence in his soul. O what a thought! that God has forgotten him, and turned his face away from him in anger! It is this that brings the believer to his wit's end—to taking counsel in his soul what he shall do to escape, what he shall do to regain what he has lost; and to having sorrow in his heart daily, because every means used for obtaining relief fails of it, leaving him still under a cloud and in the dark. Nothing that he can do gives him a moment's abatement of his distress. David, too, seems to have had some particular enemy whom he specially dreaded. "How long shall mine enemy be exalted over me?" This enemy may have been Saul, of whom David had often thought in his heart, "I shall surely perish one day by the hand of Saul." 1 Sam. xxvii. 1. And who of us have not, besides our spiritual sorrows, besides our days and nights of distracted thoughts and aching hearts—also our specially dangerous enemy?—our Saul, our easily besetting sin?—and, most dangerous of all, the great spiritual Saul that overthrew the bliss of Eden, tempted the second Adam in the wilderness, and leaves no means untried to destroy all who would be such as he was. But in what way did David seek deliverance from the despair filling his soul, and from the enemy exalted over him? By prayer to God, saying,

VERSES 3, 4. Consider and hear me, O Lord my God; lighten mine eyes, lest I sleep the sleep of death; lest mine enemy say, I have prevailed against him; and those that trouble me rejoice when I am moved.

Dark, dense, and chilling as the cloud is that overshadows David, he still sees God through it, or rather, trusts him behind it. "Consider and hear me, O Lord *my* God"—still *his* God, though he seemed to have forgotten him, and hid his face from him. He hopes against hope; hopes and despairs, despairs and hopes. Such is always the working of the heart that has been touched by the regenerating grace of God; like the magnetic needle, however much agitated by external force and disturbing influences, continually struggling to regain its pole. It is impossible for such a soul altogether to despair; it will retain, in the lowest depths, still enough of hope to send up winged words to the throne of grace. Its language evermore is, "out of the depths have I called unto thee, O Lord: Lord, hear my voice." However broad the arc of its oscillations of despondency may be, they are evermore at least crossing the line that points to the Star of Bethlehem. "Lighten mine eyes, lest I sleep the sleep of death." It is well known to those who are familiar with its approaches, that the immediate precursor of death is failing vision—the sure indication to the dying man that he is passing away, that life's strength will soon be wholly gone. Something of this failing vision David experienced. The sorrows of his heart, like those of the Saviour in the garden, had been so severe, that soul and body appeared sinking beneath the load. Neither seemed able longer to bear up under the hidings of God's face. Hence the prayer, "lighten mine eyes," restore my expiring strength, revive my fainting soul by the enlivening beams of thy love and mercy, or I die, body and soul. "Lighten mine eyes, lest mine enemy say, I have prevailed against him; and those that trouble me rejoice when I am moved." David here advances another reason why God should restore unto him the joy of his salvation, and uphold him by his grace. His fall would give the enemies of religion occasion to revile it, as vain, and worthless, and powerless to save. David asks God to deliver him, because it would be for the honour of religion for him to do so. And his example in this respect is one that we cannot imitate too closely. We should seek deliverance from the evils that may beset us, not merely for the comfort which the deliverance will bring ourselves, but for the honour it will bring to the religion we profess, and the God whom we serve. In every petition we offer unto God we should seek his glory and the advancement of the religion of his Son. We should ask light and grace of him, only that light and grace may be conspicuously manifested in our lives, to the silencing of enemies and gainsayers, and the encouraging of those that hope in his mercy.

VERSES 5, 6. But I have trusted in thy mercy; my heart shall rejoice in thy salvation. I will sing unto the Lord, because he hath dealt bountifully with me.

Here is indeed a pleasing change! despair exchanged for faith, complaints for thanksgiving, and prayer for praise. We hear no longer the voice of sorrow, but in its stead, the voice of gladness and melody. God has at last given his servant "beauty for ashes, the oil of joy for mourning, the garment of praise for the spirit of heaviness." First, we hear the voice of faith, "I have trusted in thy mercy;" then the voice of joy, "I will rejoice in thy salvation;" and then the voice of thanksgiving, "I will sing unto the Lord, because he hath dealt bountifully with me." Light is sown for the righteous, and gladness for the upright in heart. The sincere believer may travel on through many a weary day under a cloud, but not always. The Sun of Righteousness shall at length appear to him with healing in his beams. It is not to be denied, however, as already remarked, that the hiding of God's face from his children is oftentimes a mystery. Much spiritual darkness is no doubt caused by the mind's sympathizing with a morbid condition of the body: a condition not always known to the sufferer, and often not even suspected. Nevertheless, the morbid condition exists, and prevents the mind from rightly estimating the evidences of its conversion. No sooner, however, is the believer's health restored, than he finds himself in a new world of religious hope and feeling, and yet without a single new evidence of his being a child of God. His repentance is not more sincere, his faith more entire, nor his purpose to serve God more determined: his restoration to health alone has invested his evidences of conversion to God with pleasurable emotions: he has of course more enjoyment in his religion, but not an iota more of genuineness and safety in it than there was before.

We have in mind an illustration of this. Several years ago, at one of our large watering-places, I made the acquaintance of an invalid, who, though suffering severely from physical disease, was suffering still more from religious despondency. A more sincere, simple-hearted, intelligent Christian, I thought I had never met. I did everything I could to remove his doubts, and show him that he had nothing to fear; but without success. I at length said to him, "Major S., if you were standing at the bed-side of a dying fellow-creature, who gave you the same evidence, in his thoughts, feelings, and purposes, of being a child of God, that you have just given me of your being such, would you not be perfectly satisfied in regard to his safety in the world to come?" "O, yes!" he promptly replied, "but Mr. C., I cannot bring these things home to my own heart." I replied, "No, sir, because your mind sympathizes so painfully with the morbid condition of your body—the moment you are relieved of your physical sufferings, you will be relieved also of your mental." He replied, with a deep drawn sigh, "I hope it may be as you say, but I fear that it will not." We soon after separated to go to other springs, to meet again two or three weeks afterwards. In the meantime he had been relieved of his physical malady. I saw the change the moment we met, and taking him by the hand, said to him, "You are a well man." "O yes," he replied with animation, "I am no longer the sufferer I have been." I here interposed, "But how are your religious hopes?" He replied, with a joyfulness of expression in his look that I can never forget, "Not a cloud, not a cloud!" I then, looking him full in the face, significantly inquired, "Well, Major, have you been favoured with any *new* evidence of being a child of God?" To which he replied, with a smile in which a full recollection of all our past conversations seemed to be blended, "Not one, not one! it has turned out as you said it would."

Again: much spiritual darkness is caused by

ignorance and misconception of what constitutes the true evidence of conversion. Some make that evidence to consist in being able to tell the time and place when the great change occurred; others, in certain frames and feelings; and still others, in holding to certain views of Divine and human agency: whereas the only sure and necessary evidence of conversion is, that we have *so repented of our sins as to have forsaken them, looking to Christ for their forgiveness; and are humbly endeavouring, God helping us, to live according to his laws.* If this be the prevailing temper of our minds, we need not trouble ourselves about other evidences of a spiritual change. We need no other. Again: there is much spiritual darkness caused by God's leaving us to feel the evil of our sins long after he has forgiven their death-penalty. He does this, that we may not so readily fall into the same, or similar sins again. He dealt thus with David after his two great sins, forgiving their death-penalty, yet making David feel the evil of them to the end of his days. This is taught us in his subsequent history, and especially in the fifty-first psalm. The most prolific source, however, of spiritual darkness and sorrow is some knowingly, or unconsciously indulged sin, on account of which God withdraws the cheering influences of his grace, till the known sin is confessed and forsaken, the unknown detected and dealt with in the same way. Such are the four great causes of our walking in spiritual doubts, darkness, and sorrow. There may be other causes for God's hiding his face from us, for withdrawing the sustaining, guiding, and enlivening influences of his Spirit—but we can only imagine them, we cannot positively affirm them upon the testimony of his word. But whatever the cause may be for God's leaving us in the dark, and filling our souls with sorrow, we cannot err, if we do as David did: betake ourselves to him in prayer, asking him to strengthen us with might by his Spirit in the inner man, to overcome every sin, and particularly the sin by whose power our safety is specially endangered. We would, therefore, close with the words of Isaiah, already once recited, "Who is among you that feareth the Lord, that obeyeth the voice of his servant, that walketh in darkness, and hath no light? let him trust in the name of the Lord, and stay upon his God." Isa. l. 10.

LECTURE ON PSALM XIV.

VERSE 1. The fool hath said in his heart, There is no God. They are corrupt, they have done abominable works, there is none that doeth good.

THE man here called a *fool*, is not a man deficient in understanding and natural endowments, but a man who makes no good use of them. He has eyes, but sees not; ears, but hears not; a mind, too, but he never thinks. It would be better for him if he were indeed a fool, than to be what he is. God is visible and speaking in his works everywhere: this fool sees and hears him nowhere. He proclaims his existence and attributes in the soul and conscience more loudly than anywhere else; and yet "the fool hath said in his heart, There is no God." He has said it to his conscience, that he may sin without fear and without remorse. He wishes there were no God to call him to account; and so he at last persuades himself into saying it. He cannot sin without apprehension of after retribution, till all thoughts of a living, omniscient, and righteous God are banished from his mind. But whence cometh this strange infatuation among men, of saying, "There is no God"? It cometh from a depraved moral nature. They are corrupt—that is the secret of their wishing there were no God. "They have done abominable works"—and this, while it strengthens the atheism originating in corruption, renders a firm belief of it on their parts still more necessary to their peace of mind; the more men sin, the more stoutly must they strive to believe that "there is no God." "There is none that doeth good:" no, doing good lies not at all in the atheist's line of life; since the world began we never heard of one of their number who went about doing good. Infidelity and uniform well-doing are so antagonistic, that the two are never found in the same person. It is impossible for a truly good man to be an atheist. It is a wicked life that beguiles men into believing that there is no God. Where the heart is right, and the life right, the mind seizes upon the doctrine of an overruling Divine Providence as one of the sweetest and most consoling of thoughts.

VERSE 2. The Lord looked down from heaven upon the children of men, to see if there were any that did understand, and seek God.

God examines carefully before he decides. He does nothing in haste, but makes his decision not until after the most scrutinizing examination. This is especially the case when he passes judgment on man's moral character. It was not until after such an examination that he rendered the verdict in regard to man before the flood: "The wickedness of man is great in the earth; and every imagination of the thoughts of his heart is only evil continually." Gen. vi. 5. In the first verse the fool had said in his heart, "there is no God;" but here the Being whose existence he had denied, is looking down upon him from heaven—nor upon him alone, but upon all the children of men, to see if there were any that did understand; any that made a better use of their faculties than the fool just described; any that did seek God as their protector, guide, and portion. But, alas! he finds the fool who had said in his heart, "there is no God," repeated in every one of the children of men upon whom his eye falls—hence his words:

VERSE 3. They are all gone aside, they are all together become filthy; there is none that doeth good, no, not one.

Such is the moral character of the whole world by nature. The whole are gone aside; have missed the truth and the life to which it leads. "They are all together become filthy." Moreover, of this entire mass of humanity, "there is none that doeth good, no, not one." All are as far removed from righteous lives as they are from the truth and pure hearts. In losing the truth, they therewith lost the holiness whereby alone the human soul can be kept from moral putrefaction. Holiness is the soul's only element of spiritual life. Remove the salt from the ocean, and its mass of waters would become a stag-

14

nant sea of death. A similar effect has been produced in our human nature, by the loss of the holiness in which it was originally created; the loss has converted the ocean of our human life into a stagnant sea of moral death. "All together have become filthy;" not a single drop of its many waters—not a single soul of the whole mass has escaped the contagion, save one only—the Son of Mary. Many think that these dark pictures of human nature apply only to the heathen world. That is a mistake. They apply essentially to every one of us who still retain, unchanged, the moral nature wherewith we are born into the world.*

VERSE 4. Have all the workers of iniquity no knowledge? who eat up my people as they eat bread, and call not upon the Lord.

Not to call on the Lord, and to be a worker of iniquity, are phrases descriptive of the same character. They teach the fact that he that calleth not on the Lord, is sure to be a worker of iniquity; that prayerlessness and wickedness are apt to be united. Prayer and the practice of sin cannot exist together. Praying withdraws men from sin, and sets their feet in the ways of righteousness. Hence, when the Lord would satisfy the timid Ananias that Saul of Tarsus

* Between the third and fourth verses of this fourteenth psalm, as the verses are numbered in our English Bible, there have been inserted in the Psalter of our Prayer Book, several verses taken from other portions of the inspired record, (see Rom. iii. 13—18, and also Psalms v. 9; x. 6; xxxvi. 1; cxl. 3; and also Isa. lix. 7, 8.) These intervening verses, though confessedly a portion of the inspired word of God, are rejected by judicious critics as an interpolation here. They harmonize so entirely with the teachings of the psalm in regard to human depravity, that some early Christian transcriber was probably tempted to insert them from the New Testament as they are there cited by St. Paul. We omit them, therefore, in our exposition of the psalm, and pass on to the next verse, according to the numbering of our English translation.

was no longer making havoc of his Church, he said to him, "Behold, he prayeth." Acts ix. 11. "Who eat up my people as they eat bread:" these words specify one of the forms, and the most fearful form, in which the wickedness of the human heart, as described in the preceding verses, has manifested itself—that is, in the persecution of the righteous. The darkest and bloodiest page in human history is just here. Men have been persecuted for righteousness' sake more than for anything else. The persecution began with the shedding of the blood of righteous Abel; and at what time since has the tide of righteous blood ceased, when it was in the power of an infidel and ungodly world to keep it still flowing? We mean by the term "world," in this connection, not merely those who have made no profession of godliness, but also those who, though having made such a profession, have manifested a spirit as intolerant, and at times even more intolerant, of true righteousness than the world itself. It was not a heathen man and professed infidel who shed the first righteous blood, but a brother, worshipping at the same altar with the brother whom he slew. Gen. iv. 1–8. They were not heathen who cried out, "Away with him! crucify him!" He was not an avowed atheist who breathed threatening and slaughter against the disciples of the Lord, (Acts ix. 1,) but the pride of his nation and its church—the church claiming to be the Church of God! With how keen a zest did these consume the true Israel of God, and with as little compunction as they ate their bread. No pagan power, before or since, ever engaged in the work with greater delight. It is to be doubted whether more righteous blood has not been shed by bigotted ecclesiasticism than by paganism. The former has shown an intolerance of real godliness certainly equal to that of the latter. Hence the demand in regard to both, "Have all the workers of iniquity no knowledge?"—do they not know that in acting thus, they are but acting out a nature that is utterly perverted?—that in thus arraying themselves against the righteous, they are arraying themselves against God himself? This would seem to be the import of the demand in regard to the knowledge which workers of iniquity, and especially persecutors, may have of the origin and import of their acts. That they do not always know what they are doing, is proved by what our Lord said of his crucifiers, "Father, forgive them; for they know not what they do." Luke xxiii. 34. And that they do not always understand the character of the impulses under which they are acting, is also proved by what our Lord said to his disciples: "Yea, the time cometh, that whosoever killeth you, will think he doeth God service," (John xvi. 2;) and by the fact that Saul of Tarsus verily thought with himself that he ought to do many things contrary to the name of Jesus of Nazareth. Acts xxvi. 9. All this, however, only goes to prove how fearful the blinding power of that heart of wickedness is, wherewith we are born into the world, and to confirm the words of inspiration in another place, "The heart is deceitful above all things, and desperately wicked; who can know it?" Jer. xvii. 9. But however persecuted, whether by those who know what they are doing, and persecute them maliciously, or by those who do not know what they are doing, and thus may persecute them conscientiously, God will not long leave the righteous in the hands of either.

VERSE 5. There were they in great fear: for God is in the generation of the righteous.

Hitherto "the workers of iniquity," they that "call not upon the Lord," are represented as having had things all their own way, with none to molest or make them afraid. Here, however, the God whose character they had misconceived, or whose existence they had in their hearts denied, has made his appearance in the midst of them, filling them with fear. "There were they in great fear." There, in the midst of their fancied security and belief that there was no power to call them to account for their doings, some Divine providence had made them feel that there is a God, and that he is a God greatly to be feared. It is remarkable how quickly God sometimes turns the triumphs of the wicked into consternation and dismay. The providence, too, is generally of such a character that it cannot be mistaken as a Divine interposition on behalf of righteousness against wickedness, on behalf of the people of God against their enemies. "Let us flee from the face of Israel," said the Egyptians, as the waters of the Red Sea were pouring their waves back upon them, "for the Lord fighteth for them against the Egyptians." Exod. xiv. 25. The same conviction of the Lord's fighting for Israel against their enemies, made the inhabitants of Canaan as helpless as lambs before their invaders. Such have been, in the main, the orderings of Divine Providence in regard to the enemies of the righteous and righteousness. When the measure of their iniquity is full, how suddenly he overwhelms them, and generally at the moment of their greatest exultation. It was thus that he overwhelmed Sennacherib before Jerusalem, destroying a hundred and four-score and five thousand of his soldiers in a single night, and sending him back to his own country alone. It was thus that he overwhelmed Nebuchadnezzar, depriving him of reason, while he was yet exulting over the vastness of his empire as a thing of his own achievement. It was thus that he overwhelmed Belshazzar, while he and his nobles were profaning the sacred vessels of the temple in their feast, and thus pouring contempt upon the people of God and their religion; the same hour there came forth the fingers of a man's hand, and wrote his doom on the plaster of the wall; and that night, Belshazzar, king of the Chaldeans, was slain. It was thus too that God overwhelmed Spain, bearing down with her Invincible Armada upon the shores of England, to extinguish the only pure, unadulterated light of Christianity then on earth. God met it with a storm—blew, and the vast armament disappeared; and Spain has been living but a dying life ever since. "God is in the generation of the righteous;" is ever in the midst of his faithful people, and can never fail, at the right juncture of their affairs, to deliver them and punish their enemies. His providence so hems the wicked in, that he cannot escape. "Knowest thou not this of old, since man was placed upon the earth, that the triumphing of the wicked is short? . . . The heaven shall reveal his iniquity, and the earth shall rise up against him. . . . He shall flee from the iron weapon, and the bow of steel shall strike him through." Job xx. 4, 5, 27, 24.

VERSE 6. Ye have shamed the counsel of the poor, because the Lord is his refuge.

Ye wicked, ye workers of iniquity, ye that call not upon the Lord, manifest the extreme wickedness of your heart in another way, ye ridicule the counsel of the poor, the righteous man's making the Lord his refuge. How powerful a weapon of persecution is this of ridicule! and with what effect has it not been used against the Church of God and individuals, drawing from its quiver at one time the simple banter; at another, the sneer of the blackguard; and at another, the keen sarcasm and polished irony of the would-be philosopher. You recollect with what malicious zest our Lord's enemies used this weapon of ridicule against him on the cross, saying, "He trusted in God; let him deliver him now if he will have him." But while the words were yet in their mouths, the darkened heavens, a shuddering earth, and a lightning-riven temple, turned their triumph into consternation. Luke xxiii. 48. They thought, however, that they had surely falsified the crucified One's trust in God when they consigned his body to a sealed and guarded grave. But here also they were disappointed: the third day dawned, and he was not where they had laid him. *He had risen from the dead!* Another and final proof that God never forsakes those who make him their refuge. He follows them down into the grave and brings them up even thence; thus turning the good man's sighs into songs, and the bad man's derision into dismay.

VERSE 7. O that the salvation of Israel were come out of Zion! When the Lord bringeth back the captivity of his people, Jacob shall rejoice, and Israel shall be glad.

Yes, the only cure for the evils described in this

psalm must come from Zion, from the religion revealed in its sacred oracles, and typified in the sacrifices and ritual of its temple. If the Lord bring us not back from the moral captivity in which we all are by nature, through the operations of that religion, there is no help, no redemption for us. But let none of us fear. He who died for us upon Calvary, tasted death for every man, and his blood cleanseth us from all sin. Salvation is come out of Zion, and is offered to all without money and without price, who will receive it in the name of Christ. Let us all then gladly accept this so great salvation; then shall we, renewed in the moral image of Him who redeemed us, not wish there were no God, but the glad saying of every thought and feeling of our hearts will be, "Whom have I in heaven but thee? and there is none upon earth that I desire besides thee." Ps. lxxiii. 25.

LECTURE ON PSALM XV.

VERSE 1. Lord, who shall abide in thy tabernacle? who shall dwell in thy holy hill?

DAVID is not asking here what will purchase him heaven, but what line of conduct will lead him up to the heaven already purchased for him by another. It was as a justified believer that David asks, "Lord, *who* shall abide in thy tabernacle? *who* shall dwell in thy holy hill?" It is asking what course of life a professor of godliness is bound to lead. If Christ has purchased a heaven of righteousness, purity, and love, for us, no other than a life of righteousness, purity, and love, can conduct us to it. It is not the life that purchases us the inheritance, it only fits us for it. Who then is the man whose steps take hold on eternal life, and conduct him as a welcome and everlasting guest into the temple of God on high?

VERSE 2. He that walketh uprightly, and worketh righteousness, and speaketh the truth in his heart.

He walketh uprightly, endeavours so to live that he can say to all who know him, "Which of you convicteth me of sin?" He worketh righteousness, aims to be strictly just; never inquires what custom may allow, nor what human law may allow, nor what expediency may seem to demand, but what only is in itself just and right. No earthly advantage is, in his estimation, great enough to be obtained at the sacrifice of justice. He reckons it by no means necessary for him to become rich, or great, or powerful, or even to live; he does, however, reckon it absolutely necessary for him to do right. Threatened with evil for refusing to assist in the perpetration of a wrong, Socrates replied, "I will never willingly assist an unjust act. I expect to suffer a thousand ills, but none so great as to do unjustly." Such is the temper of every just man's mind. He worketh righteousness: it is the labour and habit of his life to render unto every man his due. He cannot conceive of anything as right, which will not bear the scrutiny of a just and omniscient Judge. He never forgets that the Being in whose holy hill he would dwell for ever, is a being of infinite rectitude. He labours, therefore, to have every act of his life such as that righteous being can approve. Moreover, "he speaketh the truth in his heart;" labours to preserve an entire harmony between his outer and inner life, to be in act what he is in thought. He will no more act, than he will utter, a falsehood. His outer life is an image and transcript of the inner; his righteousness is not a something put on, but the simple and truthful development of what he is in his heart. As he never forgets that the Being whose everlasting favour he covets, is a Being of infinite rectitude, so he never forgets that he is also a Being of infinite truth. The language alike of his heart and of his lips is, "Search me, O God, and know my heart: try me, and know my thoughts: and see if there be any wicked way in me, and lead me in the way everlasting." He walketh uprightly, he worketh righteousness, he speaketh the truth in his heart.

VERSE 3. He that backbiteth not with his tongue, nor doeth evil to his neighbour, nor taketh up a reproach against his neighbour.

"He backbiteth not with his tongue:" he will no more inflict a wound upon another's reputation, than he will upon his person or property. The backbiter, so called, because, like the dog, he steals behind those in whom he wishes to flesh his teeth, deals in innuendos, insinuations, evil surmisings, significant shrugs and looks, double-entendres, words meaning one thing in their literal sense, and altogether another thing from the tone in which they are uttered, and so destroys a good name, that no open assault could have affected. In this way the weak often overwhelm the strong; the vilest, the most pure. The blow from behind and in the dark, accomplishes its work of ruin before danger is even suspected. The truly good man, however, will assail no man's good name. If he cannot speak good of another, he will say nothing. He thinks, and justly too, that he has no more right to injure another's character, than he has to injure his health; to destroy another's good name, than he has to destroy his life: he "backbiteth not with his tongue, nor doeth evil to his neighbour." If he discover his neighbour's faults, he does not noise them abroad, but tries to conceal them; and so, if he discover his neighbour's necessities, he does what he can to relieve them. Moreover, he taketh not "up a reproach against his neighbour." Some understand these words to mean, he will not *originate* a reproach against his neighbour; others understand them to mean, he will not *listen* to a reproach against his neighbour. The willing listener is as bad as a talebearer. If there were none to listen to the tale of scandal, there would be none to start it, and none to repeat it. The slanderous ear, then, is as detestable as the slanderous tongue. And yet, when the scandal is once started, how few hesitate to circulate it, thinking themselves guiltless, because they did not originate it! We have, however, yet to learn that, in order to convict a man of murder, it is necessary for him to have made, with his own hands, the knife with which he dealt the deadly blow; that he used the knife, is quite enough to convict him of the crime. So it matters not who originates a scandal; all who repeat it are involved in the guilt of the evil it does. He who administers a poison, is as guilty as he who compounds it. And he who repeats a calumny, what else is he doing but administering the poison compounded by another? The talebearer's usual preface, "they say," or "people say," or "have you heard?" in nowise exculpates him from the guilt of an originator. The truly good man, however, will not originate a tale of scandal; he will not circulate it, he will not listen to it. He treats the talebearer as the pest of society, frowns him into silence, and out of his sight.

VERSE 4. In whose eyes a vile person is contemned; but he honoureth them that fear the Lord: he that sweareth to his own hurt, and changeth not.

The sincere worshipper of God holds vileness in contempt: he would still despise it, though it should wear a crown, sit upon a throne, and wield a sceptre. It is impossible for a pure mind to render any sort of homage to vice. Such a mind will, for the sake of society, honour the office that a bad man may hold, but he will not honour the man himself. St. Paul honoured Ananias, as high priest, while he still stigmatized him as a whited wall, for commanding him to be smitten contrary to the law. Acts xxiii. 3. To receive the homage of the world, it is only necessary for vileness to be gilded with gold, arrayed in purple and fine linen, or invested with power. It is otherwise with the man whose moral sentiments qualify him for the society of heaven. Though his heart's desire and continual prayer to God is, that all men may become pure and godlike, still a vile person can never occupy a place where he will not be, in his eyes, contemned. He is obliged to regard every such man as a leprous spot upon the moral system of the world; "but he honoureth them that fear the Lord." He honours virtue wherever found, in whatever garb it may appear. As vice can never put on a garb, nor occupy a place where it will not excite his contempt, so virtue can never wear a garb, nor occupy a place where it will not excite his sincere respect. He honours everywhere the man who honours God. He looks upon such a man as co-operating with God himself in endeavouring to render the world in which we live like the heaven to which we should aspire, the abode of purity, righteousness, and bliss. The good man renders this homage to virtue, not of compulsion, but spontaneously. It is the homage of a kindred spirit, of a spirit filled with the same love of truth and rectitude. This never-failing homage to virtue is, however, predicated of the godly man of our psalm: "He honoureth them that fear the Lord;" all in whom he discovers the faintest resemblance to Him who closed his earthly career upon Calvary. Moreover, if he has sworn to his own hurt, he changes not. However much it may cost him, he keeps his word. If he sweareth unto his neighbour, he disappointeth him not, though it should be to his own hinderance. Though willing to submit to all such forms, he does not require to be obliged by bond and security to fulfil his engagements. He is not of those who seem to regard nothing binding upon them, but what can be enforced by process of law. His simple word is to him a law. His love of truth and right is more to him than any human law can be, and would, if there were no law, lead him still to keep his promise inviolate. He will never excite an expectation in any mind, which he will not do his best to realize. Others may reckon themselves released from their promises, when they prove to be injurious to them;

15

but he still adheres to his, to the letter, and to the last, unless he is voluntarily released by the person to whom it was made. It may sometimes be unjust in a neighbour to enforce the fulfilment of a promise hastily or incautiously made; still a truly godly man will not falsify his word by refusing to fulfil even such promises. The only promise which he will not endeavour to fulfil, is a promise involving in its fulfilment something morally wrong. All such promises are a nullity, however made, and to whomever made, and binding upon no man to fulfil. No man is bound by a promise to do a thing that is morally wrong.

VERSE 5. He that putteth not out his money to usury; nor taketh reward against the innocent. He that doeth these things shall never be moved.

He will not increase the poor man's distress by taking advantage of his necessities to exact an exorbitant interest upon what he may lend him. If he can help the poor man at all, he helps him without remuneration for the aid rendered. The law delivered to the Israelites reads, "If thou lend money to any of my people that is poor by thee, thou shalt not be to him as a usurer, neither shalt thou lay upon him usury." Exod. xxii. 25. "Thou shalt not give him thy money upon usury, nor lend him thy victuals for increase." Lev. xxv. 37. "Thou shalt not lend upon usury to thy brother; usury of money, usury of victuals, usury of anything that is lent upon usury." Deut. xxiii. 19. This law against usury does not forbid the lending of money and other things on interest to persons engaged in trade—to those whose business is buying and selling to get gain; it only forbids the taking of interest upon things lent to the straitened poor. It requires us, being able to do so, to help such without remuneration, and to be satisfied with the naked return of what we have lent them. It requires us to help to save the little property of the poor for them by a well-timed liberality. And yet how many, who pass for honourable men in the world, sacrifice the poor man to their cupidity—make his extremity their opportunity! The poor man wants money—they lend it to him at an exorbitant interest, secured by a lien upon his little all; the property has to be sold to pay the debt, and they are present to bid it in at the lowest possible price—for themselves! God has a word for such persons: "He that by usury and unjust gain increaseth his substance, he shall gather it for him that will pity the poor." Prov. xxviii. 8. The man who would dwell for ever with his God, putteth not out his money, nor anything else of his, to usury to the poor. He will not enrich himself by another's misfortunes, but do what he can to lighten them. He obeys, in its literal sense, the precept, "Give to him that asketh thee, and from him that would borrow of thee, turn not thou away." Matt. v. 42. He regards himself as God's almoner to the needy. "Nor taketh reward against the innocent." The man who has his face set heavenward, will never do anything to deprive an innocent person of his rights. If he is a witness, neither fear, nor favour, nor reward, will restrain him from telling the truth, the whole truth, and nothing but the truth. If he is a judge, he will receive no bribe of any sort to influence his decision. If an advocate, he will not lend himself to obtain for his client what does not belong to him of right; he will not, as Isaiah styles such pleading, "justify the wicked for reward." Isa. v. 23. The highest legal talent is not unfrequently prostituted to the defence of known and acknowledged guilt. Such lending of one's talents is taking reward against the innocent, against those whom the guilty one has wronged, and against society at large, thus doomed to become again the victim of his crimes. Such defence makes the advocate an accessory after the fact. Moreover, the advocate who lends himself to setting a bad man loose again upon society, unwhipped of justice, is as responsible for whatever evil the man may afterwards do, as he would be for the evil done by a wild beast that he had been feed to unchain. We rejoice to believe that not a few of the legal profession regard the defence of guilt against innocence in this light. Many of the brightest and purest lights of our American Church are to be found on the bench and at the bar—men who would sooner thrust their right hands into the fire than soil them with a fee to clear the guilty, or oppress the innocent. It is impossible to conceive of a higher attribute of moral character than this fixed determination, to know nothing but right in the advocacy and administration of justice. It is one of the attributes of moral character ascribed to the good man of our psalm, "he taketh not reward against the innocent." If the controversy in which he may be called to act as a witness, a judge, an advocate, or simply to give the influence of his name, were a controversy between a king and a peasant, a millionaire and a beggar, a master and his servant, he would wholly ignore the social position of the parties litigant, and be found siding only with him who was in the right.

"He that doeth these things shall never be moved." He that doeth what things?—"he that walketh uprightly, and worketh righteousness, and speaketh the truth in his heart; he that backbiteth not with his tongue, nor doeth evil to his neighbour, nor taketh up a reproach against his neighbour; in whose eyes a vile person is contemned; but he maketh much of them that fear the Lord: he that sweareth to his own hurt, and changeth not; he that putteth not out his money to usury, nor taketh reward against the innocent." These are the moral virtues of the man who would obtain a kingdom that cannot be moved—of the man who would dwell for ever in the tabernacle of God on high. Do you answer, that we are saved by faith? Granted—but not by an idle and barren faith; but by a faith that worketh—worketh by love, purifieth the heart, overcometh the world, and aboundeth in good works. The faith that saves the soul, produces all the moral virtues. "Add to your faith," says St. Peter. Add what to your faith? "Add to your faith, virtue; and to virtue, knowledge; and to knowledge, temperance; and to temperance, patience; and to patience, godliness; and to godliness, brotherly kindness; and to brotherly kindness, charity." 1 Pet. i. 5–7. Quite an addition to faith! Very like golden rounds in a ladder reaching from earth to heaven. Such are the *virtues* of faith; its *graces* are as follows: "The fruit of the spirit is love, joy, peace, long-suffering, gentleness, goodness, faith, meekness, temperance." Gal. v. 22, 23. These words are as bright an exhibition of what the true believer is internally, as the words repeated just before them are of what he is externally. The faith that saves the soul, purifies both heart and life. The word of God knows of no other way leading up to heaven than heavenly tempers and a heavenly life. The atonement made for our sins by Christ, in no wise releases us from the obligation to lead such a life, to cultivate such dispositions, and practise such works as would become an actual resident of the heavenly world. It is the glory of our religion that the salvation it offers to the lost, is altogether of grace. If it offers pardon to the guilty, purity to the polluted, and mansions of everlasting rest to the weary and the homeless, it offers the whole as a free gift. Eternal life is the gift of God through our Lord Jesus Christ. The song sung by every human spirit in heaven is one and the same, namely, "Unto Him that loved us and washed us from our sins in his own blood, and hath made us kings and priests unto God and his Father, to Him be glory and dominion for ever and ever. Amen." So it ought to be. God forbid that we should teach that heaven is purchased for us by any other merits and obedience than the merits and obedience of God's own Son, made ours by faith. The faith, however, that makes the purchase of Christ's blood ours, is a faith that infallibly leads to holy obedience. Christ himself makes holy obedience to his laws the great and only infallible evidence of a saving faith in him. "Not every one," says He, "that saith unto me Lord, Lord, shall enter into the kingdom of heaven, but he that doeth the will of my Father which is in heaven. Therefore, whosoever heareth these sayings of mine, and doeth them, I will liken him unto a wise man which built his house upon a rock; and the rain descended, and the floods came, and the winds blew, and beat upon that house; and it fell not, for it was founded upon a rock. And every one that heareth these sayings of mine, and doeth them not, shall be likened unto a foolish man, which built his house upon the sand; and the rain descended, and the floods came, and the winds blew, and beat upon that house, and it fell; and great was the fall of it." Whoever builds his hopes of heaven upon a faith not leading to holy obedience, is destined to have them all swept away. He who died to redeem us and exalt us to everlasting life tells us so. He ignores as a saving faith the faith that makes light of the very least of his commandments. "Whosoever," says he, "shall break one of the least of these commandments, and shall teach men so, shall be called least in the kingdom of heaven; but whosoever shall do and teach them, shall be called great in the kingdom of heaven." Matt. vii. 24–27.

LECTURE ON PSALM XVI.

VERSE 1. Preserve me, O God: for in thee do I put my trust.

THIS is the cry of one surrounded by dangers, in the midst of which he feels that Divine power alone can save him. However great the soul's self-reliance, there are times when it feels that it needs a strength greater than its own to sustain it. This was David's feeling, when he uttered the cry, "Save me, O God!" Whether the dangers he dreaded were actual and urgent, or only anticipated, he does not in so many words inform us. It is clear, however, that the danger that David most dreaded was death—the loosening of the vital cord, and the return of the spirit unto God who gave it: death, not in its physical aspects, but death as the beginning of endless happiness, or endless misery. Of such an existence for the soul, this psalm gives clearer intimations than any that have preceded it. Hitherto in the psalms human immortality has been seen only through a veil: in this psalm the veil is lifted. It tells us that the grave cannot retain the soul, and that there is for it in the presence of God fulness of joy and pleasures for evermore. It is this revelation of another and eternal life for the soul that gives to this psalm its title, Michtam, *golden:* or, as others understand the word, a *secret*, a *mystery*, a doctrine of profound import. Of profound import indeed, revealing human immortality, and joys in reserve for that immortality, such as eye hath not seen, nor ear heard, nor have entered into the heart of man to conceive. It is in this sense, that of a doctrine of profound import about to be revealed, that St. Paul says of the everlasting life of the body, "Behold, I show you a mystery; we shall not all sleep, but we shall all be changed, in a moment, in the twinkling of an eye, at the last trump: for the trumpet shall sound, and the dead shall be raised incorruptible, and we shall be changed. For this corruptible must put on incorruption, and this mortal must put on immortality." 1 Cor. xv. 51–53. It would seem that it was in view of the dangers besetting the immortal life in reserve for his soul, that David cries out, "Preserve me, O God: for in thee do I put my trust."

VERSE 2. O my soul, thou hast said unto the Lord, Thou art my Lord: my goodness extendeth not to thee.

"Whom have I in heaven but thee? and there is none upon earth that I desire besides thee," is the language of David's soul, the language of his inmost being, the one feeling that absorbs every other. He knows in whom he has trusted, and is persuaded that he is able to keep, for time and eternity, that which he hath committed unto him—his soul. He feels that his soul has in the Lord all that it needs. The language of his heart is, Thou wilt guide me with thy counsel, and afterwards receive me to glory. The prospered husbandman's choice for his soul, was this world's goods. He said to his soul, "Soul, thou hast much goods laid up for many years: take thine ease; eat, drink, and be merry." David's choice for his soul, was the *Lord:*—the great *Fountain* of good: not much goods laid up for many years, but an all-sufficing good for eternity. He chose an immortal good for an immortal nature: an inexhaustible good for a nature that will ever have wants to be supplied. David was conscious, too, that he had no good of his own, no element of eternal happiness in himself, no moral excellence not derived from above. "My goodness," says he to his Maker, "extendeth not to thee:" that is, I can do nothing to increase thy essential glory and happiness, and so merit good at thy hands. Others, however, understand the original words to mean, My good is not without thee, is from thee, is thy gift. This is the teaching of our twenty-first hymn:

"Thou all our works in us hast wrought,
Our good is all divine;
The praise of every holy thought
And righteous word is thine."

This is the teaching also of St. Paul, where he says, "By the grace of God I am what I am." These words being read in the presence of the holy John Newton, after he had become old and blind, he uttered the following affecting soliloquy:—"I am not what I *ought* to be! Ah! how imperfect and deficient! I am not what I *wish* to be! I abhor that which is evil, and would cleave to that which is good! I am not what I *hope* to be! Soon, soon I shall put off mortality, and with mortality all sin and imperfection. Yet though I am not what I ought to be, nor what I wish to be, nor what I hope to be, I can truly say I am not what I once was, a slave to sin and Satan; and I can heartily join with the apostle, and acknowledge, 'By the grace of God I am what I am!'" So, too, David thought, and says, in the words, "my goodness extendeth not unto thee:" thou, Lord, who art my soul's chosen and chief good, art the source of all that is good in me.

VERSE 3. But to the saints that are in the earth, and in the excellent, in whom is all my delight.

This choosing of the Lord as his soul's highest good, and only source of unmixed good, and committing the everlasting welfare of his soul to his keeping, David does not confine to himself, but extends to God's holy ones everywhere—to the saints that are in the earth, and to the excellent. They are called saints, because having looked to God for help, he has made them holy. They are called excellent, because God has adorned them with the moral attributes of his own nature; because he has renewed them in the Divine image in which he created them. The great conservative grace of the soul, and, at the same time, also its highest ornament—holiness—has been restored to them. The regenerating and sanctifying love of God has been shed abroad in their hearts by the Holy Spirit. It is of such that David says, "in whom is all my delight." Though a king at the time, he says elsewhere, "I am a companion of all them that fear the Lord." Ps. cxix. 63. The divine beauty of holiness attracted David wherever he saw it. He hailed it as an emanation from the great uncreated Source of light and goodness. He delighted in all whom God had thus honoured and adorned.

VERSE 4. Their sorrows shall be multiplied that hasten after another god: their drink-offerings of blood will I not offer, nor take up their names into my lips.

There is no other fact more incontrovertibly established than the fact that idolatry of every sort is a system of sorrows. Forsaking the one living and true God, to serve other gods, has written the scroll of human history, within and without, with mourning, lamentation, and woe. The command, "thou shalt have no other gods but me," is a command grounded in the nature of things, and the necessities of the human soul. The human soul cannot have any other god, without piercing itself through with many sorrows. The moment it adopts, as the object of its supreme love and adoration, any other being than the Lord God, it begins to degenerate. The result is the same—degeneracy—where the attempt is made even to blend with the worship of the true God, the worship of other beings. Saint-worship has proved as disastrous to human progress, as the worship of pagan gods and heroes. Italy has been as sadly degraded by Papal, as it ever was by pagan Rome. Jupiter, and Venus, and Bacchus, and Mars, have only been displaced by saints as little entitled to our respect. It is only as the soul chooses for its worship an object of supreme excellence, that it rises in the scale of moral and intellectual dignity. Such an object David's soul had chosen as the God of its worship: "Their drink-offerings of blood will I not offer, nor take up their names into my lips." Drink-offerings of wine were offered by the Israelites; but all such offerings of blood were forbidden them. Lev. xvii. 9–14. The heathen, however, in their worship, both drank and offered blood. It will be recollected by the reader of history, that Cataline pledged his accomplices in a goblet of blood, binding them by fearful oaths to the performance of fearful deeds, previous to explaining to them his plan for the massacre of the Roman Senate and people. Hannibal, too, is said to have made a blood-drinking vow. We have read also of a tyrant, who, piercing his enemies with hot irons, and gathering the blood in a cup, as it flowed, drank one-half of it, and offered up the other half to his god. These illustrations go to prove that worshipping other gods than the true God, degrades man more and more, until the words *brute* and *fiend*, are the only words that accurately describe him. Nothing but worshipping the true God, in spirit and in truth, can render any man either good or happy. This is taught us by God himself, saying to all those not so worshipping him, "Behold, my servants shall eat, but ye shall be hungry: behold, my servants shall drink, but ye shall be thirsty: behold, my servants shall rejoice, but ye shall be ashamed: behold, my servants shall sing for joy of heart, but ye shall cry for sorrow of heart, and shall howl for vexation of spirit." Isa. lxv. 13, 14. Verily, "their sorrows shall be multiplied who hasten after another god."

VERSE 5. The Lord is the portion of mine inheritance and of my cup: thou maintainest my lot.

Having divided the land of Canaan among the Israelites by lot, and set apart Aaron to the work of the priesthood, the Lord spake unto Aaron, "Thou shalt have no inheritance in their land, neither shalt thou have any part among them; I am thy part and thine inheritance." Exod. xviii. 20. David alludes to this fact in the words, "The Lord is the portion of mine inheritance and of my cup." There is a fulness of meaning in this declaration, that other words can hardly increase. The Lord himself is mine inheritance! The Lord himself, with all his infinite attributes! It is as if David had said, Am I weak? The Lord's omnipotence is mine, to do for me all that omnipotence can do. Am I ignorant? His infinite wisdom is mine, to teach me. Am I guilty? His infinite mercy is mine, to pardon all my sins. Am I polluted? His infinite holiness is mine, to cleanse me from all my impurities. Would any injure me? His infinite justice is mine, to avenge my wrongs. Am I poor and needy? His all-sufficiency is mine, to supply my every want. Do any hate me? His infinite love is mine, to give me perfect and everlasting rest. O what words can adequately describe the inheritance that the believer has in the Lord himself!—an inheritance that can never fail him, a cup of bliss that can never become empty. If the believer has many of this world's goods, he enjoys God in them all; if he has nothing, he still enjoys everything in God. His happiness can no more be reached and destroyed, than He can be reached and destroyed who constitutes it. God maintains his lot with all the attributes of his infinite nature. David may well add, as he does in the next verse,

VERSE 6. The lines are fallen unto me in pleasant places; yea, I have a goodly heritage.

A goodly heritage, indeed! Not a world, nor a universe of worlds, but the Lord and Maker of all worlds! Go where he may, he is still in pleasant places; for, go where he may, he can never get beyond the bounds of his heritage. If he ascend up into heaven, behold his heritage is there: if he make his bed in the grave, behold his heritage is there: if he take the wings of the morning, and dwell in the uttermost parts of the sea, even there shall his heritage lead him, and his right hand hold him. God is everywhere, and God is the believer's heritage. If prosperity come, it is a pleasant place; if adversity come, it is a pleasant place; if affliction come, it is a pleasant place; if death come, it is a pleasant place, for the believer knows that all things, under the direction of Him whom his soul has chosen for its portion, shall work together for his good. David's words remind one of Habakkuk, declaring that, though he should be stripped of every earthly comfort, he still would rejoice in the Lord, and joy in the God of his salvation. Hab. iii. 18. So that the Lord was still left him, his joy should know no abatement, knowing that, having him as his heritage, no loss could impoverish him.

VERSE 7. I will bless the Lord, who hath given me counsel; my reins also instruct me in the night seasons.

The counsel given him by the Lord is the revelation of his character and will, contained in the history and laws of Moses, the services of the tabernacle, and the teachings of the prophets. It was as the God of revelation that the Lord had given David counsel. He had spoken to him in his word, telling him who he is, and what service he requires of his creatures. He had spoken to him in the services of the sanctuary. While its services spoke of wrath, they spoke also of mercy; while they spoke of pollution, they spoke also of purity; while they spoke of sin, they also shadowed forth the atonement to be made for sin. All the services of the sanctuary prefigured the grace that was to come to us through the gospel. The victim that bled, prefigured the victim that would afterwards bleed upon Calvary. The fire that descended from heaven to consume the sacrifice, prefigured the wrath of God that would, for man's sake, descend upon his own Son, and burn into his soul, until justice itself would cry out, Hold, enough! The water used, prefigured the purifying efficacy of the Divine Spirit, creating within us clean hearts, and renewing within us right spirits. The incense mingled with so many sacrifices and offerings, prefigured the precious merits of Him whose merits, perfuming our worship, would render all our offerings pleasant and acceptable unto his Father. David no doubt saw all these things in the letter of the law and the types of its services—saw those types as a veil thrown around Christ, yet a veil so transparent to him, that he saw Christ through it. It is a mistake to suppose that the devout worshipper of the tabernacle and temple did not see the Divine substance in the shadow. Christ himself says, "Abraham rejoiced to see my day; and he saw it, and was glad." John viii. 56. And the light of revelation enjoyed by Abraham was dim indeed compared with that enjoyed by David.

Nor was it alone by the written word and significant type, that the Lord had given David counsel as to the way of life, but also by the illuminations of his Holy Spirit. Hence his words, "My reins also instruct me in the night season." These words indicate the mysterious movings of the Divine Spirit upon David's mind and heart, (so the word *reins* means,) thoughts and feelings, in seasons of solitary retirement. The Divine Spirit would come to him, having been engaged during the day in the study of the law and the ritual services of the tabernacle, to teach him the spiritual import of that in which he had been engaged; to enlighten his understanding to perceive the truth, and to open his heart to love and embrace it. It was while he communed with his own heart upon his bed, and was still, that the Divine Spirit brought to his remembrance all things whatsoever he had seen and heard, opening up the full spiritual meaning of the precept and the rite, the law and the ceremony, until the whole became to David's mind luminous with Divine light, and prophetic of a perfect and everlasting salvation to come.

VERSE 8. I have set the Lord always before me: because he is at my right hand, I shall not be moved.

The Lord, such as he has revealed himself to me in his word, and in the services of his house, is always before me: a just God, and yet a Saviour; just, yet justifying him that believeth; commanding an innocent animal to be slain and burned upon the altar, to remind me that I deserve the same fate; and yet, through the same sacrifice, also carrying my mind forward to another and a Divine victim to be slain for the sins of the world. "Because He is at my right hand, I shall not be moved." Surely, the God who will not spare his own Son, but in due time deliver him up to die for all, cannot refuse me any thing else necessary to secure his favour. It is evidently God in Christ, whom David sets always before him. It is difficult to give another and lower meaning to his words. It is only as he is seen in Christ that God can become to a guilty creature an object of love, hope, and trust. Out of Christ, God is a consuming fire. It is not to Sinai, flashing with flames and shaken by the voice of the Lawgiver, that the guilty dare to go for shelter and safety, but only to Calvary, flowing with the blood that cleanseth us from all sin. To Calvary, through the operations of a lively anticipative faith, David had betaken himself.

VERSE 9. Therefore my heart is glad, and my glory rejoiceth; my flesh also shall rest in hope.

David's assured confidence of the Divine favour and protection fills his heart with gladness, and his soul with joy. "My glory rejoiceth." He means by his *glory* the purely intellectual and rational part of his nature. This, along with the emotional part of it, his heart, was affected by his faith. The faith that makes God the portion of the soul, engrosses both the rational and emotional nature, both the understanding and the heart. It is not an act of the will alone, nor of the intellect alone, but an act of both together. Reason must approve what the will chooses, and in order to its choosing it. Such was David's faith; both his rational and emotional nature, both his reason and his heart, found rest and happiness in its object. Nor did his faith cause him to hope well for his soul only, but also for his body. Hence his words, "my flesh also shall rest in hope." These words certainly sound very like a prediction of the resurrection of the body. We do not see that any other meaning can be given to them, and especially when we read in the next verse,

VERSE 10. For thou wilt not leave my soul in hell; neither wilt thou suffer thine Holy One to see corruption.

It is true that this verse is applied by St. Peter, (Acts ii. 27, 31,) and by St. Paul, (Acts xiii. 36, 37,) to the resurrection of Christ, to show that the return of his soul to his body, before the latter saw corruption, had been foretold. As found in our English Bible, and also in the Greek, the words, "thine Holy One," are in the singular form: in the most approved copies of the Hebrew Scriptures, however, the words are in the plural, "thine holy ones." There is, however, no real conflict between the two renderings, inasmuch as the resurrection of God's "Holy One," the resurrection of his own Son, was the beginning, the earnest, and the guaranty of the resurrection of all those whose nature he had assumed. His resurrection was virtually the resurrection of *all* holy ones; a unity embracing within itself a countless plurality. This idea harmonizes the plural form of the prediction, with the singular form of its application. "Holy ones" shall indeed see corruption, but not to remain under its dominion for ever: they shall indeed see the grave, but not to remain its everlasting prisoners. Their flesh shall rest in hope to rise.

VERSE 11. Thou wilt show me the path of life; in thy presence is fulness of joy; at thy right hand there are pleasures for evermore.

It has often been said by those not over friendly to revelation, that human immortality and eternal life are not revealed in the Old Testament Scriptures. How any can read the sixteenth psalm, and especially the last verse of it, and still make such a declaration, we are unable to see. It is indeed true that human immortality and eternal life are not so clearly revealed in the Old Testament Scriptures as they are in the New. It is the gospel that brought life and immortality into light, unobscured by even a shadow. It is, however, taxing our credulity too heavily, to ask us to believe that David did not expect another and better life. If he did not, what mockery is there in such words as these to his Maker, "Thou wilt show me the path of life; in thy presence is fulness of joy; at thy right hand are pleasures for evermore." We urge all to walk in the way of life that God hath showed; to seek for the fulness of joy and the pleasures for evermore, which he hath prepared for those who serve him in the gospel of his Son. Choose

Christ as the portion of your souls, and you will possess yourselves of a good that will never fail you, and never cease to satisfy. He was God manifested in the flesh, and the soul that is inwardly united to the living God, nothing, not even death itself, can harm. Around that soul are the omnipotent and everlasting arms, and its fountain of bliss is the Infinite Love.

LECTURE ON PSALM XVII.

VERSE 1. Hear the right, O Lord, attend unto my cry; give ear unto my prayer, that goeth not out of feigned lips.

THAT God may hear us when we cry unto him, we must pray for a right thing in the right way. If we regard iniquity in our hearts, the Lord will not hear us. To have prayer answered, the heart must be in moral harmony with the petition urged. Accordingly, while David prays, "Hear the right, O Lord," he adds, "my prayer goeth not out of feigned lips." His heart, and his whole heart, was in the prayer offered. He asked for right with a heart in love with right. In affirming that his prayer proceeded not out of feigned lips, David does not claim for himself sinless righteousness, but only sincerity. And this is all that any man can claim, namely, that he truly loves the right he asks, and desires that God may be glorified in granting it. So loving right, David appeals to the righteous Lord to vindicate it between him and all who would injure him. We learn from this verse, that, to secure the Divine co-operation and protection, it is not enough that we advocate a righteous cause; we must advocate our righteous cause with the only righteous motive—that is, the simple desire to please and glorify God. They who seek only their own glory, the glory of their country, or the glory of a party, in advocating a righteous cause, cannot, with any reasonable hope of being favourably answered, ask God to help them. "God heareth not sinners; but if any man be a worshipper of God, and doeth his will, him he heareth." John ix. 31. *His* prayer goeth not out of feigned lips.

VERSE 2. Let my sentence come forth from thy presence; let thine eyes behold the things that are equal.

Not claiming for himself sinless obedience, nor a nature without its frailties, but only evangelical righteousness, uprightness of heart, sincere purpose to promote the cause of truth and right, David asks that his sentence may come forth from the Divine presence; that, through some unmistakable interposition of his providence, God would decide the contest between him and his adversaries. "Let thine eyes behold the things that are equal." David here invites Omniscience to investigate the justice of his cause, and scrutinize the motive with which he had espoused it. He asks nothing for himself, except in so far as he is identified in heart and soul with His cause, the cause of truth, right, and righteousness. Nor is there in this feeling of David anything of self-righteousness. It is only the feeling of which St. John speaks—"if our heart condemn us not, then have we confidence towards God." 1 John iii. 21. And again: "Herein is our love made perfect, that we may have boldness in the day of judgment."

1 John iv. 17. David's fearlessness of the Divine sentence was not the result of conscious innocence, but the result of a conscious participation in the merits and atonement of Christ. It was a feeling that had been wrought into his heart by the regenerating power of the Divine Spirit; and that Spirit can so work the same feeling into the heart of the guiltiest of us, that we too can look forward to the Divine sentence in our own case with the same confidence. Clothed in the full righteousness of Christ, and filled with his Spirit, the guiltiest of us can say, even to infinite Justice, "Let my sentence come forth from thy presence."

VERSE 3. Thou hast proved mine heart; thou hast visited me in the night; thou hast tried me, and shalt find nothing: I am purposed that my mouth shall not transgress.

God himself had proved David; had tried him in the night; had set him to examining his heart when none but the Divine eye could see him; when the external world no longer tempted him to appear to be what he was not; when conscience gives its most unbiassed decisions, and when the soul, cut off from the consideration of everything but its own history and character, stands alone, as it were, looking itself full in the face. It is solitude, and especially the solitude of night, that gives men the truest views of themselves. Its silence, its secresy, and its security against detection, leave the soul to follow, unrestrained, the real bent of its own character. Vice, like wild beasts of prey, shunning the light and the day, ravins at night. Yet, coming to him even at night, and searching into his heart with the gaze of Omniscience, God found nothing in David's heart to reprove; no trace, no vestige of the particular sins of which his enemies had accused him. And this is all that David claims for himself—not universal righteousness, but only entire freedom from certain specified sins laid to his charge. In this limited claim, his mouth had not transgressed, his words had not gone beyond the real feelings of his heart. And so it is with many a believer; he cannot lay claim to universal righteousness—he can, however, claim entire freedom from many things laid to his charge, and appeal to the omniscient Searcher of hearts to attest the truth of his claim. To visit one in the night, sometimes means to visit with affliction. So understood, David's words teach us that even affliction, which so often weakens and destroys other men's integrity, had only strengthened his, and rendered it more conspicuous. Fires had not consumed him, but only shown that, in regard to the things laid to his charge, he had not anything, not even dross, to be consumed.

VERSE 4. Concerning the works of men, by the word of thy lips I have kept me from the paths of the destroyer.

The works of men here referred to, are the works of unregenerate men, of men yet in their sins, loving sin, serving sin, in bondage to sin;—the works of men—the entire spirit, principles, and practices of the world—living for self, indulging self, avenging self, rendering evil for evil, and often evil for good; and, in so doing, so wasting self, and each other, that every man so living is called a destroyer. David had in him by nature the same bias to evil as other men have, the same root of every evil work, but he had restrained it, and given his better nature the ascendency. How? He answers, "by the word of thy lips I have kept me from the paths of the destroyer." He had cleansed his way of the sins that defiled other men's ways, by taking heed thereto according to God's word. He lived a pure life, because he walked by a pure rule, and prays the Lord that he may not be left to deviate from that pure rule—saying in the next verse,

VERSE 5. Hold up my goings in thy paths, that my footsteps slip not.

How merciful a God is ours! If he impose a law, he gives us grace to keep it; if he enjoin a duty, he gives us the strength necessary to perform it. David knew this, and hence, to enable him to walk by a Divine rule, he asks for Divine help. "Hold up my goings in thy paths; work within me both to will and to do the things required by thy law. That my footsteps slip not, make me pure within, and put thy Spirit within me, and so cause me to walk in thy statutes, and keep thy judgments, and do them." God is not a hard master, reaping where he has not sown, and gathering where he has not strewed. He strengtheneth with might by his Spirit in the inner man, all those sincerely endeavouriug to live according to his laws. There are eminent critics, however, who give another rendering of the Hebrew of the fifth verse, namely, "My steps have laid hold of thy paths, my feet have not swerved." This rendering would make out of the original, not a prayer for moral strengthening, but a still further affirmation by David of his integrity, of his entire sincerity—not saying more than he felt.

VERSES 6, 7. I have called upon thee, for thou wilt hear me, O God: incline thine ear unto me, and hear my speech. Show thy marvellous loving-kindness, O thou that savest by thy right hand them which put their trust in thee from them that rise up against them.

It is first as to a prayer-hearing God that David appeals unto God here; and then as the Saviour of all those who trust in him. "Show thy marvellous loving-kindness:" put forth some special manifestation of thy power to encourage me, and silence mine adversaries. God's right hand is ever in reserve for the defence of all those who hope in his mercy. For their sakes he is a prayer-hearing God, to answer their prayers by any exercise of his omnipotence that their necessities may require. Every cry of theirs for help enters into his ear, and sinks down into his heart, as a cry that must be answered. His whole nature is excited into the intensest activity by the cry of those striving to be righteous as he is righteous, holy as he is holy. Such a striving after holiness and righteousness identifies them with him, and him with them, and makes of both but one.

VERSES 8, 9. Keep me as the apple of the eye, hide me under the shadow of thy wings, from the wicked that oppress me, from my deadly enemies, who compass me about.

The world is no friend to righteousness; its spirit cannot endure the restraints that holiness imposes upon its workings. Hence the world's hostility to all those who live truly godly lives. So David complains, The wicked oppress me, my deadly enemies, enemies against the soul, compass me about. These words, however, had their more signal fulfilment in the experience of the Son of David. He was verily "oppressed" by the wicked, and "compassed about" by deadly enemies, experiencing nothing but evil, where he should have experienced nothing but good. It is from such men that David prays, "Keep me as the apple of the eye, hide me under the shadow of thy wings." There is thought by some to be in both these images an allusion to God's tender care of Israel in his forty years wanderings between Egypt and the land of promise. "He found him in a desert land, and in the waste howling wilderness; he led him about, he instructed him, he kept him as the apple of his eye. As an eagle stirreth up her nest, fluttereth over her young, spreadeth abroad her wings, taketh them, beareth them on her wings; so the Lord alone did lead Israel, and there was no strange god with him." Deut. xxxii. 10–12. To understand the full force of keeping one as the apple of the eye, it is necessary to consider, first, how the *whole* eye is protected, sheltered by bones and sinews, opening and closing doors, light-softening and dust-excluding curtains; and then that the *pupil* of the eye, located farther in, is protected by guardians equally wonderful and peculiarly its own. There is no other part of the human body so wonderfully protected, and no other part that, when endangered, we so instinctively try to shelter from harm. And so God guards his people, as tenderly as we guard the pupil of our eye: yea, as tenderly as he guards the pupil of his own eye. So saith Zechariah, "He that toucheth you, toucheth the apple of his eye." Zech. ii. 8. So too, to understand the full force of the words, "hide me under the shadow of thy wings," it is necessary to consider the habits of a parent bird, sheltering her young under her wings, alike from the heat and the cold, the storm and the enemy that would destroy them. It matters not what it may cost her, the parent bird never fails to hide her young under the shadow of her wings. How touchingly the Saviour applies this image to himself, saying, "O Jerusalem, Jerusalem, thou that killest the prophets, and stonest them that are sent unto thee, how often would I have gathered thy children together as a hen gathereth her chickens under her wings, and ye would not." So illustrated, what beauty and tenderness are there in David's words, "keep me as the apple of the eye, hide me under the shadow of thy wings."

VERSE 10. They are inclosed in their own fat: with their mouth they speak proudly.

To be enclosed in one's own fat, means to be wrapped up in pride and self-complacency, the effect upon weak and ignoble minds of worldly prosperity. It is said that the purely fatty part of the human body, having no nerves of sensation, can be cut and pierced without experiencing any feeling of pain. Hence, in Scripture phraseology, to say that one's heart is fat, is equivalent to saying that it is hard and insensible, void of moral and sympathetic feeling, and not to be affected by any appeal made to its pity, or sense of right. It indicates a haughtiness and insolence of bearing towards others hard to be borne. Alas! how a little worldly elevation sometimes changes the best character into the worst! How it renders the man proud, who before was humble; the heart hard, which before was tender! To be delivered from the tender mercies of mindless wealth, of heartless prosperity, is a prayer that others besides

David have breathed into the ear of Divine mercy. It was not the poor, but the proud, the prosperous, the high in station and authority, that chased the Son of God to the cross and reviled him there.

VERSES 11, 12. They have now compassed us in our steps, (1 Sam. xxiii. 26:) they have set their eyes bowing down to the earth; like as a lion that is greedy of his prey, and as it were a young lion lurking in secret places.

The eagerness with which David's foes sought his destruction, is here compared to the eagerness of a lion seeking his prey, of a lion on the trail of his game, having his eyes fixed upon the earth to detect every print of its foot, to track it along every path it may have taken. It was thus that Saul hunted David, tracking him from the city to the wilderness, from the wilderness to the rocks of the wild goats, and from the rocks of the wild goats to the wilderness again. 1 Sam. xxiv. 2; xxvi. 2. It was thus, too, that the Jews hunted down the Son of David, tracking him wherever he went, and also laying wait for him, like a lion lurking in secret places for his prey. No lion ever sought the blood of his prey more eagerly than the Jews sought the blood of their Messiah. And let none of us suppose that, if we had lived in the days of the Saviour, we would not have persecuted him as the Jews did. As face answereth to face in water, so answereth the heart of man to man. The Jew's heart was only a human heart: no worse by nature than it is found in the bosom of every descendant of Adam. Goodness has always been hunted down and preyed upon by wickedness, where wickedness has not been restrained by the grace or providence of God. It is due alone to his grace and providence that righteousness has not altogether disappeared from the earth. There is a roaring lion on the track of every one of us, panting to devour us, and he would devour us, if God did not restrain him. 1 Pet. v. 8.

VERSES 13, 14. Arise, O Lord; disappoint him, cast him down: deliver my soul from the wicked, which is thy sword: from men which are thy hand, O Lord, from men of the world, which have their portion in this life, and whose belly thou fillest with thy hid treasure; they are full of children, and leave the rest of their substance to their babes.

This is an appeal to the Divine rectitude. David knows that his prayer will be heard only as he loves and imitates that rectitude himself. And even in praying God to deliver him from the wicked, he acknowledges that the wicked are God's sword, and men of the world his hand, to correct for sin. Knowing, however, God's unchanging favour to those hungering and thirsting after righteousness, David asks, if he needs correction, that it may be administered, not by the wicked, but by God himself. He knew that God could be moved to pity and to spare when the wicked would not. If this is the thought that was in David's mind, it is the same that was in his mind when, to correct him for his pride in taking the census of his people, the Lord required him to choose either seven years' famine, or three months' flight before his enemies, or three days' pestilence, and David answered, "Let us fall now into the hands of the Lord, for his mercies are great; and let me not fall into the hand of man. So the Lord sent a pestilence." 2 Sam. xxiv. 14, 15. In the hand of a merciful God, the pestilence was less to be dreaded than the sword in the hand of merciless man. But more than ever are the wicked the sword of God, when, to punish them for their sins, he lets them loose upon each other, as he did the heathen nations of old, and the French in their great Revolution. From such, and also from men of the world, David prays to be delivered.

"Men of the world, who have their portion in this life!" What more appalling words can be found in the Bible! And who are men of the world?—all who have imbibed the spirit of the world, and live according to the principles of the world; all who seek no good for themselves but such as this world can bestow, and no honours but such as this world can confer. They may be clothed in purple and fine linen, and fare sumptuously every day—but they have their portion in this life; this life ended, there remains for them nothing but the rich man's bed of flame and burning tongue. They may have much goods laid up for many years, wherein to take their ease; to eat, drink, and be merry—but their portion is in this life. And when the soul is required of them, whose shall those things be which they have provided? Their children's? Yes—and, if you please, even their children's children's, for some so render the latter part of the verse—thus: "Their sons shall be full"—that is, satisfied—"and leave their residue to their babes." They have enough for themselves, and for their children, and for their children's children; and yet their portion is all in this life; there remains to them in the world to which they have gone but one wish in regard to their surviving families, and that wish is, that they could send some one from the dead to warn them, lest their families also should come to their place of torment. So the rich man wished, and so many a man of the world has wished that he could warn his family. O, if he could only see them once more, or send but a single message back to them, how different an estimate would he teach them to place upon this world! He would tell them in such tones of anguish as no earthly tones can imitate, what it is to have all our good things here! God, in mercy, save us all from being men of the world, who have their portion in this life! "For what shall it profit a man, if he should gain the whole world and lose his own soul?"

VERSE 15. As for me, I will behold thy face in righteousness: I shall be satisfied, when I awake, with thy likeness.

However much the wicked may be prospered, and the righteous depressed, David is persuaded that God will in due time vindicate the righteous and his own righteousness. Hence his words, "As for me, I shall behold thy face in righteousness." Whatever clouds may hang over the Divine providence in its present treatment of the good man and the man of the world, David is convinced that those clouds will ultimately be dissipated. The seeming severity of the Divine providence towards the good man never destroys his faith in a final adjustment of all present inequalities. He forgets not, in the darkest hour of his history, that a book of remembrance is written before the Lord for them that fear Him, and think upon his name; and that the Lord hath said, "they shall be mine in that day when I make up my jewels, and I will spare them as a man spareth his own son that serveth him." In that day the good man will discern between the righteous and the wicked, between him that serveth God and him that serveth him not. It is his thorough conviction of this—namely, that God will at last show that he hath done all things right, that determines David, whatever may be the complexion of his outward affairs, still to serve God in righteousness; not to allow the prosperity of the man of the world, nor the adversity of the good man, to betray him into believing that God is not a righteous God, and the rewarder of righteousness in his creatures. "I shall be satisfied, when I awake, with thy likeness." In these words David evidently refers to the portion of those whose portion is not in this life—to the portion of those whose portion is fulness of joy, and pleasures for evermore in the presence of God. It was not for an earthly, but for a heavenly portion that David's soul hungered and thirsted. He panted to be like to his God in knowledge and true holiness. The words, "I shall be satisfied, when I awake, with thy likeness," teach the doctrine so clearly taught in the New Testament, that, to be qualified for heaven, we must be renewed in the image of God. It is only as the image of God is drawn anew in the soul, that it becomes capable of eternal happiness. "Except a man be born of water and of the Spirit, he cannot enter into the kingdom of God." "Marvel not that I said unto thee, Ye must be born again." These are the words of Him who redeemed us with his blood, assuring us that, unless his Spirit also renew us, we can never see the bliss of heaven, and are incapable of it. And yet he who redeemed us, tells us that the divine Spirit is free to all who ask it in His name. Let us all then seek His regenerating and sanctifying influences—those influences that unite the soul to Christ as the branch is united to the vine, to be constantly receiving spiritual life and nourishment from his fulness. So united to Christ, the weakest of us may dread the Divine judgment as little as David dreaded it, and, sustained by our divine Redeemer, descend even into the sleep of death and the grave, repeating the words of David, "As for me, I will behold thy face in righteousness; I shall be satisfied, when I awake, with thy likeness."

LECTURE ON PSALM XVIII. 1—27.

Having fought the battle of life nearly to its close, and been, through the help of God, successful in every conflict, David commemorates his manifold dangers and deliverances in the psalm before us. Its superscription reads, "A Psalm of David, the servant of the Lord, who spake unto the Lord the words of this song in the day the Lord delivered him from the hand of all his enemies, and from the hand of Saul." The whole psalm is found also in the twenty-second chapter of the second book of Samuel, where it appears with several variations; but none, however, materially changing its general meaning. The psalm in both places is believed to have been composed by David. Its form in Samuel is thought to be best suited to making it a part of David's history; its form here to its being sung in the public worship of

God. Which of the two is the original, and which the copied form, we cannot decide; nor need we, to enable us to perceive at once that it is one of the sublimest poetical and devotional effusions of even David's inspired pen. The psalm opens with the words,

VERSE 1. I will love thee, O Lord, my strength.

The original word here translated *love*, denotes the strongest and tenderest form of that affection—the form of it that glows in the heart of an affectionate child towards a loving and beneficent parent. It is love animated by an unceasing sense of benefits received. It is love excited by love—the love of which St. John speaks, where he says, "We love Him, because he first loved us." 1 John iv. 19. True love to God is not a cold admiration of his character: there enters into it, as its most invigorating element, a grateful and affectionate remembrance of benefits received. It is in this sense that David uses the word *love*, when he says, "I will love thee, O Lord, my strength.

VERSE 2. The Lord is my rock, and my fortress, and my deliverer; my God, my strength, in whom I will trust; my buckler, and the horn of my salvation, and my high tower.

David here adds metaphor to metaphor, figure to figure, to describe the Being whom he loves so tenderly for his mercies to him. The Lord is his rock, an high and inaccessible place, to which, having fled, none can reach him:—the Lord is his fortress, a muniment of enclosing walls on every side round about him:—the Lord is his deliverer, an active, intelligent, and omnipotent friend, ever at hand, a very present help in trouble:—the Lord is his strength, his stone, or stronghold of undecaying strength, whence, having taken refuge in it, no created power can dislodge him:—the Lord is his buckler, interposing his hand between him and danger, on whatever side it is threatened:—the Lord is the horn of his salvation, to thrust away from him every assault made upon him; the allusion being to those animals whose power both of attack and defence is in the horn:—the Lord is also David's high tower, his impregnable citadel, whence he can securely overlook and destroy all those who would approach to destroy him. There is no qualification necessary to constitute a perfect defender, that David does not find in the Lord. In his infinite attributes is everything he needs. He therefore loves him, trusts in him, and asks no other guardian. Some eminent critics think David's words in this second verse are addressed to Christ, the "Rock of Ages."

VERSE 3. I will call upon the Lord, who is worthy to be praised: so shall I be saved from mine enemies.

David flees to the Lord as his only refuge; not as many flee to him, willing to flee to any other refuge, if there were any other competent to afford them protection. David preferred the Lord as his refuge and deliverer, to all others. He knew the Being in whom he trusted, that he was "worthy to be praised;" that he was possessed of every excellence necessary to constitute him an all-sufficient help. To pray as we ought, and so as to be heard, we must address our prayers to God as "worthy to be praised;" as a Being whose excellence we understand. "I will call upon the Lord, who is worthy to be praised: so shall I be saved from mine enemies." It is calling upon the Lord, with a full understanding and loving appreciation of his praiseworthy character, that secures us his favour. It is an intelligent, loving, and praising faith, a faith still loving and praising under every dispensation of the Divine providence, that enlists the Divine power upon our side.

VERSES 4, 5. The sorrows of death compassed me, and the floods of ungodly men made me afraid. The sorrows—[or, as the margin has it, the cords]—of hell compassed me about: the snares of death prevented me.

These several phrases, "sorrows of death," "snares of death," and "cords of hell," indicate the most imminent dangers, and the sorest mental sufferings. The authors of these dangers and sufferings were, David tells us, ungodly men, laying snares for him, as hunters lay snares for game. His enemies were as floods surrounding him; and every one of them had either spread a net for him, or stood, as it were, with noose in hand, to fling around him, the moment they could reach him. So death stands round every one of us, lasso in hand, to bring us down. The snares of death, however, never beset the paths of any besides, so thickly and incessantly as they beset the paths of David, and the Son of David. No sooner did they lay claim to a mission from God, than the ungodly prepared sorrows indeed for them, laid snares for them—Satan himself, in the case of the Son of David, being the first to attempt to ensnare him—insomuch that each of them continually felt that the cords for lowering them into the grave were being drawn around them.

VERSE 6. In my distress I called upon the Lord, and cried unto my God: he heard my voice out of his temple, and my cry came before him, even into his ears.

The man whose heart has been touched by the regenerating grace of God has but one refuge in distress—the mercy of his God. It matters not from what source his distress arises, whether from himself or others, or from the hand of God, his refuge is the Lord. If he is weak, he knows that God alone can strengthen him. If he is guilty, he knows that God alone can pardon him. If he is wounded, it matters not how or by whom, he knows that God alone can heal him. If he is in danger, he knows that God alone can rescue him. If he has sinned against Him, even grievously, he still flees to the Lord as his hope and help—making his very sins an argument for the exercise of the Divine mercy, saying, "Lord, be merciful unto me: heal my soul, for I have sinned against thee." Ps. xli. 4. It is one of the marvels of Divine grace that the soul which has been touched by its regenerating power, will allow nothing, not even its own sins, to prevent it in the hour of distress from calling upon the Lord, and crying unto its God, till its prayer comes before him and enters into his ears.

VERSE 7. Then the earth shook and trembled: the foundations also of the hills moved and were shaken, because he was wroth.

Here is the beginning of God's answer to David's prayer for deliverance from his enemies. His presence in wrath is indicated by the shaking and trembling of the earth, and the quaking of the hills to their foundations. It was thus that the earth was moved when the law was delivered on Sinai; and thus that it was moved when the law's great victim expired on Calvary. The convulsions described in this verse are those of an earthquake, produced by the special Divine agency, not, however, an ordinary, but a volcanic earthquake.

VERSE 8. There went up a smoke out of his nostrils, and fire out of his mouth devoured: coals were kindled by it.

Here the convulsed and reeling earth sends forth its pent up elements of destruction, smoke, fire, and burning lava. All, however, is represented as sent forth by God himself, as an expression of his wrath, as the smoking, burning, and kindling breath of his omnipotence.

VERSE 9. He bowed the heavens also, and came down: and darkness was under his feet.

The belching smoke and flames soon surcharge the heavens and seem to bow them down as a mass of solid darkness to the very earth. This deepening and descending darkness looks indeed like the descent of an angry God on a mission of vengeance. None but those who have witnessed this heralding stage of a volcanic storm, can fully understand the imagery. It seems to such, using language none too strong, to speak in every part of it as the movement of an angry God, beneath whose feet is the dark, though, as yet, silent thunder-cloud.

VERSE 10. And he rode upon a cherub, and did fly; yea, he did fly upon the wings of the wind.

He who holds the winds in his fist, has here let them loose. Nor do they move as inanimate things, but like his angels that excel in strength, even his cherubim, who do his commandments, and hearken unto the voice of his word. Neither do his winds go forth alone: He himself rides upon their wings, directs them in their courses, and indues them with their strength. This fearful rush of winds is followed by another scene in course:

VERSE 11. He made darkness his secret place; his pavilion round about him were dark waters and thick clouds of the skies.

Clouds dark with waters surround him on every side, like a sable tent, clouds charged with waters ready to empty themselves in torrents upon the earth. God is represented in another place, (1 Tim. vi. 16,) as dwelling in light that no human eye can endure: here he dwells in darkness that no human eye can penetrate. Darkness, clouds, and thick darkness, are his secret place and pavilion. Light, however, here permeates the scene, but a fearful light.

VERSES 12, 13. At the brightness that was before him, his thick clouds passed, hail-stones and coals of fire. The Lord also thundered in the heavens, and the Highest gave his voice; hail-stones and coals of fire.

There is said to be something peculiarly terrific in an oriental thunder-storm. Its vivid light and intense darkness, succeeding each other with startling rapidity, are appalling. This is indicated in the words, "at the brightness that was before him, his thick clouds passed;" that is, passed away. So intense is the light of the lightning's flash, that the whole mass of dark clouds seems to pass away, and their place to be occupied for an instant by a mass of solid light, shedding its beams over everything upon the earth like a mid-day sun. The light, however, is only for an instant—and then a darkness, that may be felt, shuts up the whole from every vision but His, to whom the darkness and the light are both alike. Meanwhile the roar of the thunder, the voice of the Most High in the clouds, is incessant; the lightnings flashing from cloud to cloud, from the clouds to the earth, and from the earth back again to the clouds. Moreover, it seems as if He who measureth the waters in the hollow of his hand had poured them out, for the rain descends in torrents, mingled at times with destructive hail, while coals of fire, *balls of meteoric flame*, run along the ground. Exod. ix. 23.

VERSE 14. Yea, he sent out his arrows, and scattered them; and he shot out lightnings, discomfited them.

It is not at random that God allows the hail to descend, and the lightnings to play. He gives to each its direction and its object. He shoots out his lightnings as the archer shoots his arrow from its string, with definite aim and unerring precision. He sees his mark, and never misses it. No shield can turn his arrows off, nor can an enemy know that he has been shot at, till the arrow pierces. It seems to have been by such a storm as here described, that the Lord discomfited his people's enemies at Hebron, Josh. x. 10, 11; and again at Mizpeh, 1 Sam. vii. 10–12.

VERSE 15. Then the channels of waters were seen, and the foundations of the world were discovered at thy rebuke, O Lord, at the blast of the breath of thy nostrils.

As David began, in the seventh verse, with describing the incipient convulsions of an earthquake, he ends here with giving us its final effects. The channels of waters were seen—a frequent effect of volcanic action being the cleaving of the earth into fissures that reach down to the subterranean reservoirs, and forcing them to the earth's surface in overflowing streams. The foundations of the world, its foundations of everlasting rock, were discovered, rent asunder, and thrown to the earth's surface, "at thy rebuke, O Lord, at the blast of the breath of thy nostrils." He maketh a channel for the waters through the rocks, and a passage for his lightnings through the clouds, with the same ease. A breath of his accomplishes both.

VERSE 16. He sent from above, he took me, he drew me out of many waters.

Many waters, indeed! Thick clouds of the skies pouring themselves down in deluging torrents, and the great channels of waters underneath the earth rising up to swell the flood! These many waters, however, only represent the floods of ungodly men, of whom David has spoken before. It was they who had caused his life to be, as it were, a continuous volcanic storm. But the earthquake which they hoped would have engulfed him, engulfed themselves; and the storm they raised to overwhelm him, spent its fury upon their own heads. The Lord caused their violence to recoil upon themselves.

VERSE 17. He delivered me from my strong enemy, and from them which hated me: for they were too strong for me.

David here passes from the highly poetical description of his enemies, dangers, and deliverances, to a more quiet and literal representation of them. His "strong enemy" was probably Saul; and they that hated him, the followers of Saul. They were too strong for him single-handed; but not too strong for him with the Lord on his side.

VERSE 18. They prevented me in the day of my calamity; but the Lord was my stay.

David's enemies seized upon every reverse in his fortunes to ruin him—even his professed friends, in the day of his calamity, would have betrayed him. 1 Sam. xxiii. 12, 20. Nevertheless, in the midst of open enemies and secret traitors, he still says, "but the Lord was my stay." No man ever yet made the Lord his stay, in the hour of temptation and trial, and failed of his assistance. David knew this from experience. Hence he says of his stay,

VERSE 19. He brought me forth also into a large place: he delivered me, because he delighted in me.

From dens, and caves, and mountain fastnesses, where he had long been obliged to conceal himself for safety, the Lord had brought David forth, as from a prison, into the open air and largest liberty, having in some way subdued every enemy that could molest him or make him afraid. All this the Lord had done for David, because he delighted in him. The Lord delighted in David for his integrity and uncompromising adherence to the truth; not that David was without sin, but that he was sincere in all his purposes and endeavours to serve God. Godly sincerity can never fail of the Divine assistance in time of need.

VERSE 20. The Lord rewarded me according to my righteousness; according to the cleanness of my hands hath he recompensed me.

It was because of the general rectitude of his conduct, that the Lord had delivered David from his enemies, and placed him at last upon the throne. This he mentions, not in a spirit of self-righteousness, but to encourage others to live a life of holy obedience to the will of God; this being the path of safety and salvation. It was the rendering to them according to their ways in this, that made all the difference between the Lord's dealings with David and with his enemies.

VERSES 21, 22. For I have kept the ways of the Lord, and have not wickedly departed from my God. For all his judgments were before me, and I did not put away his statutes from me.

Here is David's righteousness, according to which the Lord had rewarded him. It is the righteousness of sincerely endeavouring to live according to the laws of God. These laws David's enemies repudiated—he did his best to obey them. For this the Lord rewarded him, even when, in every instance of obedience, it was his own grace that enabled David to will and to do as he did.

VERSE 23. I was also upright before him, and I kept myself from mine iniquity.

In claiming to be upright before the Lord, David means, that he had never abjured his service. This praise God himself accords to him, saying, "My servant David kept my commandments, and followed me with all his heart, to do that only which was right in mine eyes, . . . save only in the matter of Uriah the Hittite." 1 Kings xiv. 8; xv. 5. "I have kept myself from mine iniquity;" the iniquity into which I am by nature most liable to fall. Happy is the man who, like David, conscious to himself of general rectitude, of labouring to have a conscience void of offence towards God, and towards man, has, among his other transgressions, only one great and deplorable sin, casting its chilling shadow over him! How earnestly should every man strive to keep himself from his iniquity, from the sin, whatever it may be, which doth most easily beset him!

VERSE 24. Therefore hath the Lord recompensed me according to my righteousness, according to the cleanness of my hands in his eye-sight.

This is the sentiment of the twentieth verse literally repeated; and both verses are only a simple declaration that God, in his dealings with men, makes a difference between the righteous and the wicked, in favour of the righteous. "The ground," it has been said, "on account of which David here so presses his righteousness, is not a bepraising of self, but the design of inspiring others also with zeal for the fulfilment of the law."

VERSES 25—27. With the merciful thou wilt show thyself merciful; with an upright man thou wilt show thyself upright; with the pure thou wilt show thyself pure; and with the froward thou wilt show thyself froward. For thou wilt save the afflicted people; but wilt bring down high looks.

Having, in the previous portions of the psalm, narrated the deliverances God had wrought for him, not when he was a king among kings, and at the head of armies, but while he was poor, and persecuted, and alone, rewarding him according to his righteousness, David here, in these verses, declares that God acts *universally* on the principle of being unto men what they are to him; of meeting them on their own grounds, and dealing with them just according to the character they choose to enact. If they choose to enact the character of righteous men, he deals with them as righteous men, saves them when they are afflicted for righteousness' sake, employing every element and agent of his power to rescue them from harm. If they choose to enact the character of wicked men, he deals with them as wicked men; he brings down their high looks, employing every element and agent of his power to overwhelm them. It remains therefore a matter for each of us to decide, what God shall be to us, and how he shall deal with us. If we walk in his ways, he will walk with us, nor forsake us, nor cease to bless us. If we do not walk in his ways, he will never cease to oppose us, nor to employ the agents of his power against us. Let us all, then, take refuge in the mercy of him whose justice we cannot endure. Let us recollect that he who was David's rock, is the Rock of Ages, since cleft on Calvary, to afford a hiding-place for us all—a hiding-place not only from all the storms of this life, but also a sure hiding-place from the storm of fire that shall sweep over the earth when it shall be shaken for the last time, and removed out of its place. Who of us will not need a hiding-place then, and who of us can need a better hiding-place then, than that offered to us all in Christ?

LECTURE ON PSALM XVIII. 28—50.

VERSE 28. For thou wilt light my candle; the Lord my God will enlighten my darkness.

To light one's candle is to give prosperity; and to enlighten one's darkness is another mode of expressing the same thought. Whoever else might oppose him, David's experience of His past dealings with him, persuaded him that the Lord would not; that, having defended and delivered him when he was friendless and persecuted, he would still continue to bless him now that he had reached the throne. Hitherto in the psalm David describes himself as the object of the Divine mercy, miraculously delivered from all his enemies, and especially from Saul; henceforward, however, to the end of the psalm he describes himself as the instrument of the Divine mercy, God co-operating with him, and he with God, in subduing his enemies under him. David's history in this respect is like to the history of Christianity; its beginnings, were in miracles, its subsequent victories by a power inherently its own. In the first twenty-seven verses he speaks of the deliverances he had experienced; in the last twenty-three, he speaks of the conquests he had achieved, and would achieve—for he speaks both historically and prophetically—and in speaking prophetically, carries the mind forward to the conquests of Him whose dominion shall be from sea to sea, and from the river unto the ends of the earth.

VERSE 29. For by thee I have run through a troop; and by my God have I leaped over a wall.

Strengthened by his God, David had routed his enemies drawn up in battle array against him. "By thee I have run through a troop." By the same help, he had stormed and taken their strongholds and fortified places; "by my God have I leaped over a wall." David's overcoming the most formidable foes and obstacles by the help of the Lord, reminds one of St. Paul's words, "thanks be unto God, which always causeth us to triumph in Christ." 2 Cor. ii. 14. "I can do all things through Christ, which strengtheneth me." Phil. iv. 13. They who contend in the strength of Christ can never fail of overcoming. To the weakest of his followers, under the sorest conflicts, his words are, "My grace is sufficient for thee; for my strength is made perfect in weakness."

VERSE 30. As for God, his way is perfect; the word of the Lord is tried: he is a buckler to all those that trust in him.

David's experience had taught him what every man's experience will teach him in this world, or in the world to come—that is, that God's way is perfect; that there is no taint of injustice in any of his dealings with his creatures. This Nebuchadnezzar acknowledged after God had punished him for his pride, (Dan. iv. 37;) and this they who sing the song of Moses and of the Lamb, proclaim in the heavens above, saying, "Just and true are thy ways, thou King of saints." Rev. xv. 3. "The word of the Lord is tried;" tried by the severest tests of human experience, it increases in lustre more and more as immutable truth. The sky of David's hopes had been overcast with many a cloud, and rent with many a storm, but no promise of his God had failed to be fulfilled. "He is a buckler to all those who put their trust in him;" a buckler of infinite wisdom, power, and goodness.

VERSE 31. For who is God save the Lord? or who is a rock, save our God?

"Who is God save the Lord?"—that is, just, true, and the helper of all who flee to him for succour? This could not be said of any that the heathen called gods. According to their own account of them, their gods were unjust, false, and failed them in their hour of need. The Lord alone had manifested a character that entitled him to be called God. "Or who is a rock save our God?" In calling God a rock, David indicates the immutability of his nature; that he is of one mind and changes not, but retains from age to age the same love of justice, the same love of truth, and the same settled purpose to serve and save all who serve Him. It was otherwise with the gods of the heathen; they were as fickle as men, and quite as variable in their principles of action.

VERSE 32. It is God that girdeth me with strength, and maketh my way perfect.

He who is infinite in strength girded David with strength, and made his way perfect; removed out of his way, by His grace or providence, every obstacle to his progress onward to a final and crowning victory. It was in this way that he made St. Paul's way perfect before him, leading him on from conquering to conquer, from victory to victory, until, when the time of his departure came, he leaves, shouting, "I have fought a good fight, I have finished my course, I have kept the faith: henceforth there is laid up for me a crown of righteousness, which the Lord, the righteous Judge, shall give me at that day; and not to me only, but unto all them also that love his appearing." 2 Tim. iv. 7, 8. Such is the strength wherewith God girdeth all those who serve him in the gospel of his Son.

VERSE 33. He maketh my feet like hinds' feet, and setteth me upon my high places.

In the twenty-ninth verse David represents himself, through the strengthening of his God, as breaking through and routing serried lines of troops drawn up in battle array against him, and also as storming their strongholds and driving them thence. Here, aided by the same power, he represents himself as pursuing his enemies with the fleetness of the hind to their mountain fastnesses. The hind, the female of the antelope, is the swiftest and most sure-footed of animals, its feet being peculiarly fitted to scaling mountains with ease, and running along the most precipitous heights with safety. It was along paths, comparable to such for danger, that the Lord had prepared David to run with feet that never missed their hold. And if we could see the Lord's dealings with us, as David saw his dealings with him, how many of us might see that he had strengthened us to run along ways equally difficult and dangerous? How many of us might see that he had given his angels charge over us to bear us up in their hands, lest we should dash our foot against a stone, that would have precipitated us to the earth, never to rise again? Happy the man whom the Lord so setteth upon the high places of victory over all his spiritual foes!

VERSE 34. He teacheth my hands to war, so that a bow of steel is broken by mine arms.

God raises up men specially qualified to meet the exigencies of human society—the soldier, the statesman, the lawgiver, the teacher of religion, the ready writer, the eloquent man, and the cunning artificer. He had need of a soldier to accomplish the purposes of his will, and he qualified David for the work; and so long as David prosecuted his wars, free of ambitious and malevolent feelings, and solely with the desire of accomplishing the will of God, he served God as acceptably in the field, as he could have served him in his temple. Provided his cause be just, and he prosecute it with right motives, the patriot soldier is engaged in as holy a work as the priest at the altar. God so taught David the art of war, that "a bow of steel was broken by his arms." It required the use both of hands and feet to bend the ancient bow of steel; how great then must David's strength have been, to break it with his arms. This verse has, of course, a spiritual application, showing how easily God can clothe with overcoming might all who are engaged in the good fight of faith, enabling them to overcome, with a moiety of their strength, the strongest weapons with which they may be assailed.

VERSE 35. Thou hast also given me the shield of thy salvation: and thy right hand hath holden me up, and thy gentleness hath made me great.

This is what every one can say who has been preserved and upheld by the power of God: "thy gentleness hath made me great." David's words here recall the Saviour's, "take my yoke upon you, and learn of me: for *I am meek and lowly in heart;* and ye shall find rest unto your souls." Matt. xi. 29. The lowliness of the Lord in stooping to our infirmities, bearing with our sins, speaking the word of tender reproof here, and of encouragement there, and so training us up for our heavenly inheritance, excites the wonder of the believer more and more. O the gentleness, the lowliness, and condescension, of the high and lofty One! is the thought which at last occupies the mind of the believer to the exclusion of almost every other.

VERSE 36. Thou hast enlarged my steps under me, that my feet did not slip.

Having had his way before him cleared by the Lord, and been also endued with strength by him, David pushes on in his victories with a strong, steady, and far-reaching step. He runs, and is not weary; he walks, and is not faint. It is so with all who wait on the Lord as David did. Isa. xl. 31.

VERSES 37, 38. I have pursued my enemies, and overtaken them: neither did I turn again till they were consumed. I have wounded them that they were not able to rise: they are fallen under my feet.

David's rapid and subjugating victories teach the Christian an important lesson, that is, that the warfare he wages against sin should be, not as a warfare of resistance only, but also of aggression: that he should anticipate the onsets of evil and guard against them;

inflict blow after blow upon sin in his life, blow after blow upon sin in his heart: neglect no means of weakening the power of sin over him. It was not by resistance alone that Christ achieved his victories. He did indeed repel the onsets made upon him by the adversary: but having done that, he carried the war into the adversary's own domains, took his strong holds, silenced his oracles, threw down his temples, and liberated his captives. The kingdom of Christ is essentially an aggressive kingdom, it aims at the conquest of the world, and will not cease its holy warfare till it has made the conquest of the world. Its King will go on from conquering to conquer, till not an enemy remains to be subdued. And every believer should strive to be able to say of his sins, what David says of his enemies, "I have pursued them, and overtaken them: neither did I turn again till they were consumed. I have wounded them that they are not able to rise: they are fallen under my feet."

VERSES 39, 40. For thou hast girded me with strength unto the battle: thou hast subdued under me those that rose up against me. Thou hast also given me the necks of mine enemies, that I might destroy them that hate me.

Whatever his triumphs and successes, David never for a moment forgets the Author of them; that he prevailed only because he was "strong in the Lord;" that it was through "the power of his might" that insurgent subjects at home were subdued, and enemies abroad bowed the neck in submission, or turned their backs in flight. No enemy can withstand us, when girded with the power of his might. The seventy returned again with joy, saying, "Lord, even the devils are subject unto us through thy name."

Luke x. 18. Strengthened with might by his Spirit in the inner man, the believer overcomes temptation without, and corruption within—Satan himself—death itself. His language to the believer, so strengthened, is, "Come, put your feet upon the necks of these kings;" the king of devils, and the king of terrors. Josh. x. 24.

VERSE 41. They cried, but there was none to save them: even unto the Lord, but he answered them not.

This is by no means an unusual occurrence: the enemies of God calling upon him in their extremity to save them. Voltaire died alternately supplicating and blaspheming the Son of God! "Will not this God," he exclaimed, while foaming with impotent despair, "whom I have denied, save me too? Cannot infinite mercy extend to me? O Christ! O Jesus Christ!" He said to his physician, "Doctor, I will give you half of what I am worth, if you will give me six months' life." The doctor answered, "Sir, you cannot live six weeks." Voltaire replied, "Then I shall go to hell, and you will go with me;" and soon after expired. He cried, but there was none to save him; even unto the Lord, but he answered him not. Paine's end was equally fearful. While free from intense suffering, he was still the bold and defiant infidel, but when distress and anguish came upon him, he would repeat, without intermission, "O Lord help me, God help me, Jesus Christ help me!" in a tone of voice that would alarm the whole house; and when asked, "Mr. Paine, what must we think of your present conduct? Why do you call upon Jesus Christ to help you? Do you believe that he can help you? Do you believe in the Divinity of Jesus Christ?" he replied, after a pause of several minutes, "I have no wish to believe on that subject." An infidel hypocrite! consistent to the last! How fearfully do the last hours of such men as Paine and Voltaire illustrate the words, "Because I have called, and ye have refused; I have stretched out my hand, and no man regarded; but ye have set at naught all my counsel, and would none of my reproof; I also will laugh at your calamity; I will mock when your fear cometh; when your fear cometh as desolation, and your destruction cometh as a whirlwind; when distress and anguish cometh upon you; then shall they call upon me, but I will not answer; they shall seek me early, but they shall not find me." Prov. i. 24–28. "They cried, but there was none to save them; even unto the Lord, but he answered them not." We referred to this verse in the third verse of our psalm, where we endeavoured to show that none can pray to God as they ought, without an intelligent, appreciating and approving estimate of his praiseworthy character. This estimate of the Divine character the wicked cannot have, and of course in the hour of need, flee unto God merely as a refuge from danger which they cannot hope to escape in any other way. They flee unto him, not because they love him, but because they cannot withstand, and therefore dread, his power. To the call of all such men God is deaf, even as they have been deaf to his call, when he would have had mercy upon them.

VERSE 42. Then did I beat them small as the dust before the wind; I did cast them out as the dirt in the streets.

How weak and worthless a thing man becomes when God refuses to hear his cry for mercy! The "small dust before the wind" represents his weakness; the "dirt that is cast out into the streets," represents his worthlessness. Such were the most powerful of his enemies before David, when God had forsaken them. May a merciful God save us all from Divine abandonment!

VERSE 43. Thou hast delivered me from the strivings of the people; and thou hast made me the head of the heathen: a people whom I have not known shall serve me.

Blessed with victories at home over the uprisings of his own people, and with victories abroad over the heathen, David is persuaded that nation after nation would be added to his conquests, and the conquests of his successors; even nations which, at the time of uttering this prophecy, he knew not. This can of course have its complete fulfilment only in Christ, David's Divine and final Successor on the throne of Israel. It is under his rule that the strivings of his own people, the Jews, shall at length cease, the fulness of the Gentiles be gathered into his church, and nations that now know him not, shall serve him in the gospel.

VERSES 44, 45. As soon as they hear of me, they shall obey me; the strangers shall submit themselves unto me. The strangers shall fade away, and be afraid out of their close places.

Such was the moral effect of David's victories upon the nations around him, that many who had only heard of them, voluntarily submitted themselves to his rule. 2 Sam. viii. 10. Even those who had secreted themselves in the holes of the rocks, and in the caves of the earth, were afraid of him out of their close places, and rendered him a feigned submission. That is the meaning of the word here translated "submit." "Thine enemies," says Moses, "shall *feign* to thee." Deut. xxxiii. 29. David, however, in the verses before us, speaks in the future tense, and in so doing, predicts what would take place under the rule of his Divine Son. And what David here predicted, has since taken place; many have submitted to Christ as soon as they heard of him; some rendering him sincere obedience; others, over-awed by the external manifestations of the Divine power resident in the laws and ordinances of his kingdom, only a feigned obedience. Times of great outward prosperity to the Church are the times when hypocrites are readiest to profess its faith. This fact was signally verified in the accessions to the Church consequent upon the conversion of Constantine. It grew by the accession not only of those who loved, but also of those who hated the truth. Its opponents faded away like the vanishing cloud. It is no slight compliment to Christianity, that it can compel the homage of minds that hate it, and would, if they could, destroy it. The fact bespeaks its Divine power as nothing else can. Despotism feels its power, and trembles before it; superstition dreads its presence; infidelity invokes its aid in the dying hour.

VERSE 46. The Lord liveth; and blessed be my Rock; and let the God of my salvation be exalted.

Here begins what is not improperly regarded as the doxology of the whole eighteenth psalm. "The Lord liveth." He alone is the living God. He alone hath life and immortality in himself, and imparteth it to others; other gods are dead idols; they have mouths, but they speak not; eyes have they, but they see not; they have ears, but they hear not; noses have they, but they smell not; they have hands, but they handle not; feet have they, but they walk not; neither speak they through their throat."

Ps. cxv. 5–7. "Blessed be my Rock;" the Lord alone is the only immutable Helper, a Rock, strong and unchanging. "And let the God of my salvation be," or he is "exalted;" whatsoever can give beauty, dignity and glory to character, is his. The gods of the heathen are nothing—the Lord is everything.

VERSES 47, 48. It is God that avengeth me, and subdueth the people under me. He delivereth me from mine enemies; yea, thou liftest me up above those that rise up against me; thou hast delivered me from the violent man.

David is continually recurring to the only Source of his strength, conquests, and deliverances. The thought was ever present and operative in his mind, that in God alone he lived, and moved, and had his being; and in him alone accomplished anything of good. This thought and feeling is the believer's only safety; the moment he thinks he can of himself accomplish anything good, he falls. If David had ceased to cherish this feeling, the Lord would never have delivered him from all his enemies, and from the violent man, Saul.

VERSE 49. Therefore will I give thanks unto thee, O Lord, among the heathen, and sing praises unto thy name.

St. Paul, in his Epistle to the Romans, quotes these words as the words of Christ himself, saying, "I will confess to thee among the Gentiles, and sing unto thy name." Rom. xv. 9. St. Paul's application of the verse before us, shows that David was here speaking of his Divine Son, as well as of himself, and spoke of his own conquests achieved for his own people Israel, only to shadow forth the still greater conquests that his Son would achieve for the whole world—for the Gentiles as well as for the Jews.

VERSE 50. Great deliverance giveth he to his king; and showeth mercy to his anointed, to David, and to his seed for evermore.

Here is a clear reference to a King, and an anointed One, greater and higher than David, even to the seed of David, conceived by the Holy Ghost, and born of the Virgin Mary. To Him the Lord hath indeed given great deliverance—the deliverance, not of a single nation only, but the deliverance of a world from the bondage of sin and corruption. He overcame our great spiritual Saul, and every other enemy; encountered the hosts of darkness, and put them to flight. Before Him, Satan himself fell, like lightning from heaven, from his high places of power. He descended into the grave, and came up a Conqueror even thence, leading captivity captive. He ascended in triumph to the skies, and is set down at the right hand of the Majesty on high, the crowned and anointed King of his Church; crowned and anointed, not as David was, for an age only, but for evermore. His is an eternal crown, an eternal throne, and an eternal dominion, upheld by all power in heaven and in earth. It is mercy indeed that the Lord showeth to his Anointed, to his Messiah—mercy for others, mercy for the guilty—pardoning and saving all those who ask pardon and salvation in His name. Let us all then submit ourselves to Messiah's loving rule; so shall we at last reign with him in his kingdom for evermore.

LECTURE ON PSALM XIX.

VERSE 1. *The heavens declare the glory of God, and the firmament showeth his handy-work.*

THE object of the nineteenth psalm is not to *contrast*, but to *identify* the God of nature with the God of revelation, as one and the same infinite Being; to show that the God who in the beginning created the heavens and the earth, is the same God who speaks to us in the law; and thus to do away the impression, so prevalent with many, that the Jehovah of Israel was a local God. It shows that the God who is the author of the most glorious thing in the physical world, the bright orb of day, is also the author of the most glorious thing in the moral world, the Divine law. The first verse of the psalm affirms that the heavens declare the glory of God, and the firmament showeth his handy-work; that eternal power and Godhead are manifested in their existence. Out of nothing, nothing could be made, except by the preexistence of such a power. Just so sure as anything now is, something has always been, and that always existing something is God. If at any time in the flow of eternal ages, there was nothing, there would be nothing still. Or, supposing matter to be eternal, if there ever was a time when all was chaos, all would be chaos still; for eternal power and Godhead are no more necessary to call matter into being out of nothing, than they are necessary to give previously existing matter its present properties and arrangements. It is also equally absurd to suppose the present forms of matter to be eternal; for our own earth, and we may suppose the same of all other planets, is continually changing—its very rocks and mountains wearing down, its valleys and even seas filling up, so that ultimately they will require a re-adjustment and new arrangement. The simplest and most rational account of the origin of things, is given us in the very first verse of the Bible, in the words, "In the beginning God created the heavens and the earth." The moment eternal power and Godhead are introduced into the scene, as the author of creation, all mystery disappears. We see at once that such a Being could make the heavens what they are; and that what he could do, he has done, stamping every creation of his in the heavens over us with the insignia of his Divinity.

VERSE 2. Day unto day uttereth speech, and night unto night showeth knowledge.

The story that the heavens tell of their Author is without intermission. They are telling it forth day and night. An Oriental understands this unceasing testimony of the heavens to a Divine original, much better than we do. Our skies by day, and starry canopy by night, are often glorious; but their glory can hardly be compared with that of an Asiatic sky. It was said of the latter, by Niebuhr, the father of the historian, long after his return from the East, and when he had become blind from age, that the glittering splendour of the nocturnal Asiatic sky, as also its lofty vault and azure by day, on which he had so often gazed in his wanderings, imaged itself to his mind in the hours of stillness, and afforded him his sweetest enjoyment. Day and night had each a voice full of Divinity to him; and each told the tale of its beginning, order, and beauty, to his musing spirit, and that its beginning, order, and beauty, were in God, and worthy of God. So Niebuhr felt, whether gazing upon the heavens by day or by night; and so David felt.

VERSE 3. There is no speech nor language where their voice is not heard.

Taking these words as they stand in our English Bible, they teach us that the testimony borne by the heavens to a Divine Author, is a testimony that addresses itself to men everywhere, to all endowed with the faculty of speech. That is undoubtedly true; it is not however, exactly the meaning of the Hebrew. Literally rendered, the Hebrew original reads, "There is no speech, and there are no words; their voice is not heard." The unceasing testimony borne by the heavens to the glory of God, is not an *audible* testimony, is not uttered in words and articulate language. Their testimony is a silent testimony; and yet in what power do they speak of the Divine greatness! Who can gaze long and alone upon the silent majesty of the heavens, without exclaiming, There is a God! We gaze upon their silent wonders as we gaze upon the things surrounding us in some vast gallery of art. The painted canvass is indeed silent, and the chiseled marble dumb, but though voiceless, how potently does each speak to our minds of the skilful hands that executed them, and made them what they are! In the same way, and more potently, do the heavens speak of the hand that made them what they are. They are silent, but what language could speak to the heart, as their deep and everlasting silence speaks to it of the grandeur of their Author?

VERSE 4. Their line is gone out through all the earth, and their words to the end of the world. In them hath he set a tabernacle for the sun,

The line mentioned here is a measuring-line, a line used to ascertain areas, and especially the extent of a given territory. The measuring line of the heavens embraces the whole earth within its compass; the testimony they bear to the glory of God extends to the ends of the world. They look down upon us with the same calm majesty at the equator, the tropics, and the poles. Their blue star-enameled depths tell the same story to all; to savage and to sage, to every creature endowed with reason and reflection. The gospel of Christ, God's great moral manifestation of himself, possesses the same inherent power of speaking to the human heart in every clime, in all the earth, and unto the ends of the world. Rom. x. 8. "In them," that is, in the heavens, "hath he set a tabernacle for the sun." The oriental royal tent, tabernacle, or pavilion, is composed of the richest material, dyed in splendid colours, and ornamented with beautiful embroidery. The heavens are such a pavilion for the sun, overcanopying and surrounding it like a curtain—a curtain of simple blue, by day; at night, however, of blue, studded with gems of light and beauty, that no man can number. How vivid a conception of the power of God, who "stretcheth out the heavens as a curtain, and spreadeth them out as a tent (for the sun) to dwell in." Isa. xl. 22.

VERSE 5. Which is as a bridegroom coming out of his chamber, and rejoiceth as a strong man to run a race.

In beauty and in power, in splendour and in might, the sun comes daily forth from its chambers in the east. No bridegroom could be more gorgeously arrayed, and no giant pursue his course with stronger step. It *rejoices* to run its course. It goes shining on, as if its journey were a pleasure to it. It neither faints, nor grows weary, but still goes onward from age to age with strength undiminished. It set out in its race this morning as fresh as it was on the day it first started in the orbit marked out for it by the hand of Omnipotence. A strong man, indeed! And yet how many such strong men are there in the universe! Immensity is filled with suns, running their courses, as glorious, as unceasing, and as untiring, and every one of those suns overcanopied by a pavilion as magnificent as that which overcanopies our own. How forcibly does all this proclaim the glory of Him whose goings forth have been from of old, even from everlasting! Micah v. 2.

VERSE 6. His going forth is from the end of the heaven, and his circuit unto the ends of it: and there is nothing hid from the heat thereof.

It is not a useless race that the sun runs in its ceaseless circuit through the heavens—a race intended merely for display. Its course is not more glorious and untiring than it is beneficial. There is nothing hid from the heat thereof. Its light brings warmth and life to everything it visits, and it visits everything. Ocean depths are not beyond the reach of its influences, and either pole feels the energy of its power. It paints the flower blooming upon the floor of the ocean, as well as that blooming upon the surface of the earth. There is another sun that visits the moral world in the same way and with equal power—the Sun of Righteousness. *His* light, too, brings warmth and life to every soul it visits.

VERSE 7. The law of the Lord is perfect, converting the soul; the testimony of the Lord is sure, making wise the simple.

Having described the glory of God, visible in the creation of the heavenly bodies, and especially of the sun, and shown that all is perfect, all glorious, David here affirms that the *law* given by the same Being is also perfect. He evidently takes it for granted that such a Being could give no other law, without denying himself, and contradicting the revelation of his attributes legible in nature. The law of the Lord is *perfect;* it is wanting in nothing to a perfect revelation of the Divine will and character—wanting in nothing to a perfect rule of human conduct—wanting in nothing to a full exhibition of the human soul once bearing the Divine image, and of what changes it must experience to be restored to that image. It is a mirror whence we see reflected in rays of living light the image of God as he was, is, and ever will be; the image of man as he was, is, and should be. There is nothing of excess, or of deficiency, in the instruction God has given man to guide him in the way everlasting. The law of the Lord is perfect, *converting the soul.* David of course speaks here of the Divine law as it is applied to the heart by the Divine Spirit. So applied it quickens the soul from the death of sin to the life of righteousness. The testimony of the Lord is *sure*, certain, and trustworthy, whether speaking of himself, or of man—making wise the simple, that is, the honest, the sincere, persons open to conviction and persuasion. To the hearts of such, the teachings of God's word come home as the teachings of Divine and eternal truth. To one bantering a plain uneducated Christian on the absurdity of believing the Bible to be a revelation from the Supreme Being, he replied, "I know nothing about what learned men call the *external* evidences of revelation, but I will tell you why *I* believe it to be from God. I have a most depraved and sinful nature, and, do what I will, I find I cannot make myself holy. My friends cannot do it for me, nor do I think all the angels in heaven could. One thing alone does it—the reading and believing what I read in that blessed book—*that does it.* Now, as I know that God must be holy, and a lover of holiness, and as I believe that book is the only thing in creation that produces and promotes holiness, I conclude that it is from God, and that God is the author of it." The man who has been born again by the Divine Spirit, through the instrumentality of the truth, knows and is sure that the Bible is the word of God, by its effects upon his own heart. This testimony of the Lord to the truth of his word, is as sure, as certain, and as trustworthy to the ignorant as it is to the intelligent; it maketh both of them "wise unto salvation."

VERSE 8. The statutes of the Lord are right, rejoicing the heart: the commandment of the Lord is pure, enlightening the eyes.

The statutes of the Lord rejoice the heart, because, in obeying them, there is a consciousness of right that can never fail of bringing pleasure to the mind. The commandment of the Lord enlightens the eyes, because its purity, like the rays of the sun, removes all mental and moral darkness, enables the soul to see its own and the Divine character in the clearest possible light. Some, however, understand the *statutes* of the Lord here, as meaning the ritual and sacrificial ordinances of his house, rejoicing the heart by setting forth salvation through atonement; and the *commandment* of the Lord, as meaning the code of civil laws given by him for the government of his people Israel, a code of laws so perfect and humane in their provisions, as to have excited the admiration of the most eminent statesmen and jurists; a code, too, that has been modifying and elevating the legislation and jurisprudence of the world, ever since it was delivered to Moses, and that, too, in many cases where its very existence was unknown, or ignored. But in whatever sense you understand the words *statutes* and *commandment* in this verse, in a moral, ceremonial, or civil sense, it can still be affirmed of them, that they bring joy to the heart, and light to the eyes. However understood, they still proclaim themselves emanations of the Divine mind.

VERSE 9. The fear of the Lord is clean, enduring for ever: the judgments of the Lord are true and righteous altogether.

The fear of the Lord, in this verse, is the sense of religion wrought in the soul by the Divine Spirit, using the word of God as its instrument. The sense of religion in the soul is elsewhe.e called the beginning of wisdom—the divinely opened and divinely fed fountain whence everything good in man flows. It is clean, undefiled, enduring for ever; a pure fountain of hallowed emotion, sending forth the never-failing streams of holy obedience. Its thought of the great Lawgiver is, that his judgments are true and righteous altogether. Touched by his regenerating grace, the soul sees nothing but truth and righteousness in every enactment of his will and revelation of his character. Its reverential fear of God is as unceasing in its operations as the Divine law exciting it is unceasing in its demands. It is the feeling that gives rise to the anthem unceasingly heard in heaven, "Holy, holy, holy, Lord God Almighty, which was, and is, and is to come:" "heaven and earth are full of thy glory."

VERSE 10. More to be desired are they than gold, yea, than much fine gold; sweeter also than honey and the honey-comb.

The divinely enlightened mind values the word of God more highly than it does any earthly blessing beside. To every such mind that word is more precious than rubies. No money could induce the primitive Christians to give up their copies of the Scriptures. They would sooner give their bodies to be burned, than surrender the holy word to the flames. "Will you sell me this book?" was the question asked of a pious servant reading her Bible. "No, sir," she replied; "if you would give me my freedom for it, you should not have it." Even that which of all earthly things is dearest to the human heart, freedom, this Christian slave would not compare, for preciousness, with her single copy of the word of God. "Sweeter also than honey and the honey-comb"—or, as the margin of our English Bible renders it, "than the droppings of the honey-comb"—honey exuding in drops from the comb being richer, purer, and sweeter than any other. There is, however, no honey so sweet to the natural taste as the word of God to the spiritual taste of his children. Its precepts and promises glide into the spirit with a sweetness that renders all other sweets insipid. Lady Jane Gray said to friends, who wondered how she could deny herself the amusements of the court, and sit at home alone reading her Bible, "All amusements of that description are but a shadow of the pleasure which I enjoy in reading this book." How little do most of us realize the sweet and unspeakable pleasures of which we rob ourselves in not studying the word of God, and exercising ourselves therein day and night. So studied, it distills sweetness as well as healing balm into the wounded spirit. This was David's experience, and his experience has been the experience of thousands.

VERSE 11. Moreover, by them is thy servant warned: and in keeping of them there is great reward.

The word *warned*, in this place, means instructed, admonished, enlightened—the ever-increasing light that the study of the Divine laws and ordinances shed through the mind in regard to every question of truth and duty—a light beaming more and more unto perfect day. Of this light in the soul it is elsewhere said, "When thou goest, it shall lead thee; when thou sleepest, it shall keep thee; and when thou walkest, it shall talk with thee: for the commandment is a lamp, and the law is light." Prov. vi. 22, 23. The whole law becomes light in the mind of the believer. He comes at last to doubt the verities of the Divine word, as little as he doubts his own existence. It is to him a revelation discovering ever-increasing heights and depths of moral light and beauty; and "in keeping of them there is great reward." "Godliness is profitable unto all things, having promise of the life that now is, and of that which is to come." 1 Tim. iv. 8. It is impossible to obey any law of God, whether a physical, an intellectual, or a moral law, without experiencing pleasure in and through the very act of obedience. This is specially true of obedience to moral laws. "In keeping of them there is great reward;" great reward in the pleasure afforded by the simple act of obedience. But besides this great reward in the act itself, God has added to obedience a reward of grace, rewarding the very obedience inspired by His own truth and grace, as if it were altogether the believer's own, and rendered in his own strength. It was thus that he treated those to whom he committed the talents, rewarding them for what they had acquired only through his bounty. The reward was conferred, not as wages and in the way of merit, but as a token of the Divine approbation.

VERSE 12. Who can understand his errors? cleanse thou me from secret faults.

Taught the spirituality of the Divine law, as reaching to the thoughts, the feelings, and the motives, and comparing therewith the operations of his own heart, David demands "who can understand his errors?"—who can tell how oft he offendeth?—who can tell in what thought, word, or deed of his, there has not been some taint of sin?—who can tell, judging himself by the purity of the Divine law, whether that which he thought no sin at all, is not altogether sinful? It is through the teachings of the Divine law, that the soul learns its extreme sinfulness. "I had not known sin," says St. Paul, "except by the law." And no man is so ready to cry out, "Cleanse thou me from secret faults," as the man who has studied that law longest, and kept it most perfectly. He sees himself filled with infirmities of which he once had never suspected himself; and he knows that He whose eye searches through all, must see faults of which he is still unconscious. Hence, even from secret, unconscious, unknown faults, David prays God to deliver him—faults of ignorance, of prejudice, of thoughtlessness. There is a fearful passage in Leviticus respecting sins committed through an ignorance which a diligent use of means might have removed. It reads, "If a soul sin, and commit any of these things which are forbidden to be done by the commandments of the Lord, though he wist it not, yet is he guilty, and shall bear his iniquity." Lev. v. 17. None but an invincible ignorance, an ignorance that could not have been overcome, extenuates the guilt of sin.

VERSE 13. Keep back thy servant also from presumptuous sins; let them not have dominion over me: then shall I be upright, and I shall be innocent from the great transgression.

Having in the preceding verse prayed that his sins of ignorance and infirmity may be pardoned, David here prays that he may be preserved from sins of presumption. The sentiment of the last verse is, "forgive us our trespasses;" the sentiment of this verse is, "lead us not into temptation, but deliver us from evil." That verse is a prayer for pardoning mercy; this for preventing and preserving grace. There were sacrifices appointed to make atonement for the sins of the man who had sinned ignorantly; but there were none appointed for him who had sinned knowingly and presumptuously. Numb. xv. 27–31. Hence St. Paul's saying, "If we sin wilfully, after that we have received the knowledge of the truth, there remaineth no more sacrifice for sin, but a certain fearful looking for of judgment and fiery indignation, which shall devour the adversaries." Heb. x. 26–28. It is a perilous thing to do what we know to be wrong; and of this the profane swearer is guilty every time he utters an oath, and the Sabbath-breaker every time he passes the Sabbath in a way not sanctioned by the law of God. The man gathering wood on the Sabbath is an instance of wilful and presumptuous sinning; he knew, when he did it, that he was violating a Divine law, and being consulted as to what should be done with him, God commanded him to be put to death. Num. xv. 32–36. David, then, had good reason for praying to be preserved from known, presumptuous, and daring sins. It was only as he should be preserved from such, that he could continue evangelically upright, and innocent of the great transgression—final apostasy; or, as some render the words, of much transgression, a career of reckless sinning, that would at last so harden the soul as to render the attainment of eternal life impossible. To falling into such sins every man is liable who is not continually restrained by the grace of God. "The Lord left me but for a moment, and see what I have done!" said an eminently gifted, devoted, and laborious clergyman to his family, as they rushed into his room and found him weltering in his blood—a suicide!

VERSE 14. Let the words of my mouth, and the meditation of my heart, be acceptable in thy sight, O Lord, my strength, and my redeemer.

David's strength is the Lord; his redeemer is the Lord. His only hope and trust is the Being whose *natural* attributes of infinite power, wisdom, and goodness, the heavens declare; and whose *moral* attributes of infinite holiness, truth, and mercy, his law proclaims. David does not speak of God's physical works, to contrast them with his moral manifestations of himself, but to show that he who framed such heavens as those which overcanopy our earth, and stretch away through space, could not do otherwise than give a perfect moral law for the government of his rational creatures; a law that would do for the soul, what the sun does for the earth—clothe it with light, and life, and beauty; a law, too, that claims the right to control the whole man; the outward act, and the inward thought; the words of the mouth, and the meditation of the heart. To be wholly governed by this law, is every man's duty. It is the only way in which any man can be happy in the presence of a holy God. It is a law which the angels in heaven could not cease to obey, without becoming wretched. Indeed, it is a law which God himself could not cease to obey, without sending the shock of infinite and eternal woe through his whole being. It is the basis even of the Divine happiness, as it is a transcript of the Divine character. It is every rational being's only element of eternal bliss. Do you wonder, then, beloved reader, that David speaks of the law of the Lord as he does? or that those desiring your everlasting welfare, urge upon you the study of this law as they do? Or do you wonder that even Christ, the Lord from heaven, died to purchase for you the Holy Spirit, to enable you to love and obey it; to put it into your minds, and write it in your hearts, in lines that shall never fade, and impulses that shall never cease? God himself must cease to be what he is, and the soul cease to be what it is, before it can be eternally happy, without loving and obeying the law of the Lord. It tells us, in words that none can fail to understand, of Him in knowledge of whom standeth our eternal life. "It has God for its author, salvation for its end, and truth, without any mixture of error, for its matter." The more we learn of this law, and the more we imbibe of its spirit, the more vehemently shall we pant after its purity, hunger and thirst after its righteousness, and make our incessant prayer what David's was, "Let the words of my mouth, and the meditation of my heart, be acceptable in thy sight, O Lord, my strength, and my Redeemer."

LECTURE ON PSALM XX.

VERSE 1. The Lord hear thee in the day of trouble: the name of the God of Jacob defend thee.

THE twentieth psalm is a sacred war song, sung by the Israelites, as their king was going out to battle; a song wherein they express, in a direct address to their king, their heart's desire and prayer to God, that he would lead him forth to victory. It was customary, in the earlier ages of the world, for the king to lead his people in their wars. The preservation of his life while so engaged, was of course a matter of extreme interest to his people. Nearly all the nations of antiquity, therefore, preceded their campaigns with solemn rites and religious ceremonies. As they were about to engage in a war with the Philistines, Samuel said to his countrymen—"Gather all Israel together at Mizpeh, and I will pray for you unto the Lord." 1 Sam. vii. 5. With the prophet's prayers there were also fasting, confession of sin, and sacrifice, (verses 6, 9.) A like proceeding is described in the psalm before us, wherein we have not only the sacrifices offered, but also the prayer used. Its beauty and propriety no one can fail to perceive, who considers the circumstances that called it forth. The nation is moved.

Their country is about to be invaded by powerful and relentless enemies; and the man through whom, under God, their liberties have been achieved, and through whom alone they can be perpetuated, must lead the onset, and direct the battle. How many a time since the world began have the hopes of a nation centered in a single man, and expired when he fell! When, therefore, David's loving and confiding subjects saw him compelled to lay aside for a time, the sceptre of the king for the sword of the general, how natural the fervid wish they express for him in the words, "the Lord hear thee in the day of trouble: the name of the God of Jacob defend thee!" It was wishing help for him from the only source whence effectual help can come. "*The Lord* hear thee in the day of trouble." The day of trouble in this place means the day of battle. It was then, when violence and death would be on every side, that David's subjects pray the Lord to cover his head, and hear his prayer—"The name of the God of Jacob defend thee:" it is not an "unknown God" to whom David's friends appeal. It is *the God of Jacob*, whose name is the synonym of infinite power, wisdom, and goodness: who had covenanted with Abraham, Isaac, and Jacob, to be a God to them, and to their seed after them, for ever: and who proclaims his name in the words, "the Lord, the Lord God, merciful and gracious, long-suffering and abundant in goodness and truth, keeping mercy for thousands, forgiving iniquity, and transgression, and sin, and that will by no means clear the guilty." Exod. xxxiv. 5–7. Indeed, this whole character of the Divine Being, as here given by himself, a character of infinite holiness, truth, mercy, and justice, God had developed in his dealings with his covenant people. Consequently in *desiring Jacob's God to defend their king*, the Israelites were only desiring him to be to David in the day of battle what he had been to Abraham, and Moses, and Joshua, and Gideon, and Jephtha—his sword, and shield, and banner.

VERSE 2. Send thee help from the sanctuary, and strengthen thee out of Zion.

It is surprising to see with what heroism the grace of God can inspire the weakest and most timid of human beings. It finds them when the day of trouble comes upon them, fearing no evil. They may have had many fears before, but there is no fear then. The Spirit in their hearts forbids the feeling. It enables them to smile at that which drives others mad; to feel secure in the midst of dangers; and to hail as manifestations of love, what others can regard only as tokens of wrath. All this the grace of God does for us. It is certain, however, that nothing but help from the sanctuary, and strength out of Zion, can accomplish it. No other religion can, save that prefigured in the rites and ceremonies of the tabernacle, and perfected by Christ. It is only the religion setting forth atonement for sin, and purification from its stains, that so strengthens the heart, makes the weak strong, and the timid bold. All other religions have been broken staves, and bruised reeds, piercing all those who have leaned upon them for support. "Who is he that overcometh the world, but he that believeth that Jesus is the Son of God?" 1 John v. 5; is a claim for the peculiar power of the Christian religion set up eighteen hundred years ago. The claim has never been disproved. Faith in a divine Saviour, in Jesus the Son of God, as seen in the services on Mount Zion, or on the cross upon Calvary, is the only thing that has endued the soul with strength to withstand in the day of evil, and having done all, to stand. How full of meaning, then, is the people's prayer for their king, "the Lord send thee help from the sanctuary, and strengthen thee out of Zion."

VERSE 3. Remember all thy offerings, and accept thy burnt-sacrifice. *Selah.*

Many suppose the *Selah* of this verse to indicate a pause in the song at this point, to allow time to make the sacrifice and offerings mentioned. The burnt-sacrifice was that wherein the animal being slain, and its blood sprinkled round the altar, every part of it was laid upon the altar and burned to ashes. Its being *wholly* consumed is the reason why it is sometimes called a holocaust. The *whole*-burnt offering, was a sacrifice of atonement, a sacrifice wherein the offerer acknowledged that he himself deserved to die as his victim died, and to be consumed as it was consumed. This being done in reliance on God's mercy, secured the offerer the pardon of his sins. This accomplished, he then makes a bloodless offering, an offering, with incense and oil, of some product of the earth. This latter offering was an offering of communion between him and his now reconciled God, and also a consecration of himself and of all that he had to the service of God. Following the sacrifice of atonement just made, and believed to have been mercifully accepted, it is the consecration of which St. Paul speaks, where, after having set forth the fulness of the atonement made for our sins by Christ, he says, "I beseech you therefore, brethren, by the mercies of God, that ye present *yourselves a living sacrifice*, holy, acceptable unto God, which is your reasonable service." Rom. xii. 1. Such is the import of the words, "Remember all thy offerings, and accept thy burnt-sacrifice." It was desiring for their king, not only the pardon of his sins, but also the acceptance of his person and of his services; that he might go forth to fight their battles for them, justified, accepted, and in communion with God. It is a desire that the people of God cannot cherish too fervently, nor offer up too frequently, for those whom God in his providence has appointed to lead them in their Christian warfare.

VERSE 4. Grant thee according to thine own heart, and fulfil all thy counsel.

Supposing the prayer of the preceding verse to have been vouchsafed, the people may safely pray God to grant their king the desires of his heart. If his heart had been touched by the regenerating grace of God, the Spirit itself would indite his petitions, and would, of course, indite only such things as were agreeable to the will of God. "This is the confidence," says St. John, "that we have in Him, that if we ask anything according to his will, he heareth us." 1 John v. 14. The prayer of a truly devout and righteous man is nothing less than the breathings of the Divine Spirit, making intercessions for him; and what God the Spirit inspires, God the Father can never fail to answer. David's heart's desire, to subdue his and their enemies, being so inspired, his people could without risk ask God to grant it. David's situation was an enviable one! having a people continually praying God to grant him his heart's desire! O how the consciousness of having such a people encourages the heart of the Christian leader!

It fills him with hope, and zeal, and energy, when he would otherwise faint by the way. His people's prayers for him are the right arm of a minister's strength.

VERSE 5. We will rejoice in thy salvation, and in the name of our God we will set up our banners: the Lord fulfil all thy petitions.

The people still continue their address to their king, declaring that they will rejoice in his preservation, and that, to encourage him to engage without fear in the conflict before him, they will set up *their* banners in the name of their God. Setting up their banners in the name of God, means that the whole nation would go forth to battle with their king, each tribe marching under its own banner—a banner on which, tradition says, was painted the symbol of the tribe, corresponding to Jacob's blessings. Gen. xlix. It was a custom with the nations of antiquity to inscribe their banners with the insignia of their religion. It may have been under banners of this sort, inscribed also with sacred mottos, that the Israelites promised to set themselves in martial array. Or, setting up their banners in the name of God, may mean that they would unfurl their banners upon every mountain top, till the whole nation should rally to the help of their king. It matters little which explanation we adopt as the more probable; either exhibits the same glorious spectacle—a whole nation ready and eager to follow their king wherever he may lead them, and fight with him unto death against every enemy that would come against them! A nation that so unites with its head deserves to conquer, and will conquer. No other nation, or church, has any right to expect the Divine blessing. Great as he was as a general, David would have made no head against the hostile powers surrounding him if he had been left to contend alone. He could only direct the battle, and if his people did not choose to fight with him, it must be lost. It is the same with the commissioned soldier of Christ now. If his people will not wage the great spiritual battle with him, it must be lost. Leaving its battles to be fought, and its victories won, mainly by its commissioned officers, has come to be the great calamity of the Christian Church. The consequence is that every year the Church of God is becoming more and more an army without leaders. We thank God that its officers are not found shrinking from the contest, but having often to wage it so nearly alone, how many of them fill a soldier's grave years too soon! "The Lord fulfil all thy petitions." This, with the Israelites, was no idle, unmeaning prayer; what they asked God to grant their king, they laboured to realize by their co-operation with him. They did not regard him as their champion to fight their battles for them, but only as their leader to conduct them to the field.

VERSE 6. Now know I that the Lord saveth his anointed; he will hear him from his holy heaven with the saving strength of his right hand.

What token God had given the Israelites that he would preserve their king in the midst of the dangers to which he was about to be exposed, we are not informed. It may have been fire descending from heaven to consume the sacrifice and offerings. This was the token of the Divine favour vouchsafed to Elijah in his contest with the prophets of Baal. "The fire of the Lord fell, and consumed the burnt-sacrifice, and the wood, and the stones, and the dust, and licked up the water that was in the trench." 1 Kings xviii. 38. This token of the Divine favour—miraculous fire consuming the sacrifice—was not uncommon. Lev. ix. 24; Judges vi. 21; 1 Chron. xxi. 26; 2 Chron. vii. 1. On this occasion, however, the token of the Divine acceptance may not have been miraculous fire; it may have been the conviction that God sometimes works in the hearts of those offering prayer to him, that their petitions will certainly be granted. It is sometimes the believer's privilege to rise from his knees with the burthen removed from his heart, filled with the assurance that his prayer, in God's own good time, will be answered. In this way the dying parent receives assurance that his children, who are yet in their sins, will in due time be gathered into the Ark of safety. "*Now* know I that the Lord will save them," is the language both of his heart and of his lips. An assurance of this sort filled the Saviour's heart when about to raise Lazarus from the dead. While he was yet on his way to the grave, he said, "Father, I thank thee that thou hast heard me." John xi. 41. Before he uttered the words, "Lazarus, come forth!" he knew that they would be obeyed. So each particular Israelite says, "Now know I that the Lord saveth his anointed." It was the assured conviction of every mind that the right hand of the Divine power would be over their king, to preserve him alive, and give him success. It is a bright omen when the faith of an entire church becomes one and the same. It is an indication that the Lord's Anointed, the Lord's Messiah, is about to lead his people forth to such spiritual conquests as are seldom made. This faith of a multitude expressed as the faith of one only, is the faith contemplated by our own Church. In our prayers and praises, we speak in the plural number, saying, "Almighty and most merciful Father, *we* have erred and strayed from thy ways;" "*we* praise thee, O God; *we* acknowledge thee to be the Lord." But when we come to the creed, though thousands may be repeating it with us, we drop the plural, and speak only in the singular number, saying, "I—*I* believe in God the Father Almighty; *I* believe in Jesus Christ, his only Son our Lord; *I* believe in the Holy Ghost." It is this personal, individualizing faith—and yet also consolidating, embracing in the unity of its spirit the blessed company of all believing people, because inspiring all with one heart and one mind—it is this faith that prevails with God. It was this individualizing, and yet also consolidating faith, that called down the Holy Ghost on the day of Pentecost, and ushered in the Christian dispensation in its fulness. It is indeed true, that all the disciples were seeking the same promised blessings, yet the secret of their prevalence was, that they "all continued with one accord in prayer and supplication." Acts i. 14; ii. 1.

VERSES 7, 8. Some trust in chariots, and some in horses: but we will remember the name of the Lord our God. They are brought down and fallen; but we are risen, and stand upright.

Both the chariot and the horse were forbidden the Israelites in war. The prohibition may have been because the generally mountainous character of Judea rendered them comparatively useless as an arm of military power. Yet horsemen and war-chariots were the right arm of the military power of the nations around them. And a fearful engine of destruction the war-chariot was! Armed with a spear-pronged pole, with long scythes projecting from both ends of its axle, and drawn by horses, breaking the ranks of an enemy, it mowed men down like grass! Those supplied with these chariots and iron-mailed horses and horsemen, were the most formidable enemies with whom the Israelites had to contend, their own weapons being for the most part only the sword, the spear, the sling, and the bow. Their enemies also often counted their horsemen and chariots by the thousands and tens of thousands. In these they trusted; but in their contests with Israel their trust failed them. Through the help of God the Israelites discomfited and laid them low. No power of human device can stand against the power of God. "Thou comest to me," said David to Goliath, "with a sword, and with a spear, and with a shield, but I come to thee in the name of the Lord God of Hosts, the God of the armies of Israel, whom thou hast defied." 1 Sam. xvii. 45. A pebble of the brook from a simple sling felled the boasting giant to the earth. And God can always cause means of defence, simple as a sling and stone, to repel the assaults of the mightiest. The believer should never fear what man can do unto him. He who has right on his side, may be sure that God will in due time vindicate his character. He who takes the avenging of his wrongs into his own hands, rather than leave their avengement to a just and omnipotent God, is an infidel. He acts as if there were no God, and no hereafter. Invisible guardians are round about those who make God their trust, and his laws their rule of conduct. "Fear not," said Elisha to the young man terrified at the sight of the Syrian hosts, with chariots and horsemen surrounding them, "for they that be with us are more than they that be with them." "And the

Lord opened the eyes of the young man; and he saw; and behold the mountain was full of horses and chariots, of fire round about Elisha." 2 Kings vi. 16, 17.

VERSE 9. Save, Lord: let the King hear us when we call.

The King the people here invoke, is one greater than David; even the King whose mission is to go on conquering and to conquer, till all the nations of the earth submit to him; the King of kings, and Lord of lords. Rev. xix. 16.

This psalm teaches the Church of God a lesson which they should never forget, which is, that they should pray God with one mind and one heart and without ceasing, to grant their spiritual head strength and wisdom to lead wherever duty points the way, and then grace to follow as one man. Every member of the Church of God is a soldier of Christ, and bound to fight manfully under his banner unto his life's end. It is mockery for a Church to wish their spiritual leader God-speed in his contest with evil, while they do not wage the contest with him: to say to him, "The Lord hear thee in the day of trouble; the name of the God of Jacob defend thee: send thee help from the sanctuary, and strengthen thee out of Zion," unless they add thereto, immovably resolved to make their words good, "We will rejoice in thy salvation, and in the name of our God we will set up *our* banners." In nine cases out of ten, a pastor will be to his people just what they choose to make him, a savour of life unto life to them, or of death unto death. Praying for him and co-operating with him, they make his ministry a ministry of life to them; refusing him their prayers and co-operation, they make his ministry a ministry of death to them. To insure the Divine blessing upon the word spoken, there must be faith and prayer, self-renunciation and self-devotion, in the pew as well as in the pulpit. Though it should be presented with all the argumentative power of a Paul, and all the eloquence of an Apollos, the word preached does not profit, where it is not mixed with faith in them that hear it. Heb. iv. 2. Faith in those receiving or asking his blessing is the one indispensable condition on which Christ confers it; we accordingly read, that where faith was wanting, He could *there* do no mighty work, save that he laid his hands upon a few sick folk and healed them. Mark vi. 6. Few indeed are the spiritually sick whom Christ heals in a church the faith of whose members is not alive, and operative, and continually praying God to put forth his power to save.

LECTURE ON PSALM XXI.

VERSE 1. The king shall joy in thy strength, O Lord; and in thy salvation how greatly shall he rejoice!

THIS is said by the people of their king, that he shall rejoice, rejoice greatly, even exult, in the strength and salvation of the Lord. The world have but one mode of estimating the power and security of a nation; they estimate both by the wisdom of its statesmen, the strength of its armies and navies, and the magnitude of its revenues. If these abound, the nation glory in them, and reckon upon the future as theirs, to dispose of as they list. We read, however, as a check upon this spirit of self-reliance, "Let not the wise man glory in his wisdom, neither let the mighty man glory in his might, let not the rich man glory in his riches; but let him that glorieth, glory in this, that he understandeth and knoweth me, that I am the Lord, which exercise loving-kindness, judgment, and righteousness in the earth: for in these things I delight, saith the Lord." Jer. ix. 23, 24. No legitimate human means of success are to be neglected, but to be used—to be used, however, with the feeling that God alone can give them efficiency. Using human means with this feeling, is joying in the strength of the Lord, in his strength as rendering the simplest means adequate to overcome the greatest obstacles and the most powerful enemies; the lifting up of a rod adequate to open a highway for the people of God through the depths of the sea; the blowing of a trumpet to shake down the strongest walls, and a pebble from a sling to prostrate a giant in the dust. Israel's king could well rejoice in such strength, and exult in his preservation by such a Being! It was strength that rendered his human strength virtually omnipotent, and insured his safety in the midst of dangers. "The king shall joy in thy strength, O Lord; and in thy salvation how greatly shall he rejoice!" Happy are the people who can say this of their leaders and rulers, that they are men who glory only in the help and protection of God, and who, helped and protected by him, are labouring to make the world they live in like the heaven to which they aspire. God grant that neither the church nor the state may ever want for men actuated by this faith.

VERSE 2. Thou hast given him his heart's desire, and hast not withholden the request of his lips.

The God with whom we have to do, is a discerner

of the thoughts and intents of the heart. I may be so ignorant as not to know how to pray; dying, and unable to pray; or filled with emotions that stifle utterance. It makes no difference; I am not thereby cut off from communion with the Father of my spirit. He looketh into the heart, seeth all its desires, and interprets them as prayer. Hence the promise, "It shall come to pass, that before they call, I will answer; and while they are yet speaking, I will hear." Isa. lxv. 24. God is so ready to hear prayer, that he will answer it not only while its words are yet upon the lips, but while it exists in the unuttered desires of the heart. It was thus that he dealt with David, granting him the desire of his heart as well as the request of his lips, conferring on him the success implored in the preceding psalm.

VERSE 3. For thou preventest him with the blessings of goodness; thou settest a crown of pure gold on his head.

The goodness of God continually anticipates our wants. The blessings of his goodness often come on us while we are not expecting them, and not even thinking of them. Satisfied with his humble condition as the keeper of his father's sheep, there were no thoughts of a kingdom in David's mind when the Lord sent Samuel to anoint him to the throne of Israel. David's whole history is full of blessings and honours coming upon him as unexpectedly. And we are the subjects of this preventing, anticipating goodness, as really as David was. The whole scheme of our salvation, conceived and virtually consummated before the world was, is an illustration of the fact. And the effectual carrying home of that salvation by the Divine Spirit is also equally anticipative, that Divine Agent having actually to overcome an innate

22

opposition in the soul to its reception even as a free gift. Not one of us seeks the mercy of God in Christ, till the Divine Spirit first predisposes us to the work. "Thou settest a crown of pure gold on his head." David once had a crown of gold, adorned with precious stones, set on his head; a crown of immense value that he took from one of the kings he had conquered. 2 Sam. xii. 30. It is believed, however, that there is no reference to that crown here. In this place, "a crown of pure gold" means the glorious kingdom with which David had been honoured—a kingdom of Divine laws, Divine institutions, and Divine superintendence—a kingdom which, through one of David's successors on the throne of Israel, would become universal and eternal—Messiah's kingdom of everlasting righteousness! In the glory of this kingdom, perfected in the Son of David, all may share who will submit themselves to the laws of its Head—Divine Mercy incarnate, exalted to supreme power, to confer glory, honour, and immortality, upon all those seeking them in His name.

VERSE 4. He asked life of thee, and thou gavest it him, even length of days for ever and ever.

David's utmost ambition seems to have been to live in his posterity, upon the throne of Israel, unto the end of the world; 2 Sam. vii. 13–16; and this God had promised him; not however in the sense in which David had asked it, but in a much sublimer sense. It was not life to the end of the world that God granted him, but length of days for ever and ever. This was a clear pre-intimation of the eternal life that God hath given us in his Son. God put into the words of David's prayer, a fulness of meaning of which he had not conceived, a fulness which nothing but the advent of his Divine Son has adequately revealed. In him alone we have "length of days for ever and ever." *He* is the King to whom God granted it: he asked life for himself, and the grave surrendered its victim: he asked life for those who should become subjects of his kingdom, and we hear them singing, "O death, where is thy sting? O grave, where is thy victory? Thanks be to God which giveth us the victory through our Lord Jesus Christ." 1 Cor. xv. 55, 56. "For we know that if the earthly house of this tabernacle were dissolved, we have a building of God, an house not made with hands, eternal in the heavens." 2 Cor. v. 1.

VERSES 5, 6. His glory is great in thy salvation: honour and majesty hast thou laid upon him. For thou hast made him most blessed for ever: thou hast made him exceeding glad with thy countenance.

While apparently speaking only of their living king the people are continually using language that can, in all the fulness of its meaning, be applied to One much greater than he. God can, indeed, lay glory, honour, and majesty upon a king of finite powers; and he had laid them upon David to a degree unparalleled in the history of the world. But when it is said, "Thou hast made him a blessing for ever," a blessing to *eternity*, the mind is carried forward to Him whom David only represented, to the Only-Begotten of the Father, full of grace and truth. He is the King whom God has constituted the source and fountain of *eternal* blessings. The word *blessed*, or *blessing*, is plural in the Hebrew, denoting the fulness of the blessings coming to us through Christ, so full that they will leave the soul nothing more to desire. "Thou hast made him exceeding glad with thy countenauce:" this is believed to refer to the gladness that Christ experienced in gaining the victory over sin for man in man's nature, and then being exalted in that nature to the right hand of the Majesty on high, to intercede there for all those asking mercy in his name, and evermore receiving it for them as the purchase of his blood. Our Lord is never so happy as when he sees us thankfully embracing the salvation he has wrought out for us. He then sees the travail of his soul, and is satisfied. Isa. liii. 11.

VERSE 7. For the king trusteth in the Lord, and through the mercy of the Most High he shall not be moved.

David's trust in the Lord was strong, and through the mercy of the Most High it seldom failed to sustain him. Even when, on one occasion, the people spake of stoning him, he still encouraged himself in the Lord his God. 1 Sam. xxx. 6. There were times, however, when David's faith wavered, and when, as he fell into grievous sin, it seems for the time being to have failed him. In speaking then of a king whose trust in the Lord would not allow him to be moved, the words could, in their highest sense, refer only to Him whose faith in God still sustained him under every trial; to him whose faith, using the simple words, "it is written," repelled every assault that Satan himself could make upon it, and enabled him, when dying under the frowns and execrations of a world, and even under the hidings of his own Father's face, to say, "Father, into thy hands, I commend my spirit." Luke xxiii. 46. His faith in God was tried more frequently and more severely than that of any other, and it was never found wanting. And when we see him still believing, still trusting, still confiding in the Divine mercy to sustain him under trials, the very recital of which appal us, we are apt to suppose that he was sustained by some power not accessible to us. We are mistaken in that supposition. In all his conflicts with evil he was sustained by only such communications of Divine grace as are free to all who will seek them as he sought them. It was *as man* that he contended, and *as man* that he prevailed, strengthened only by those communications of Divine grace that he died to purchase for us all. If he had contended and prevailed by any other power than that of simple faith in God, he could not be an example for our imitation. We read, however, that, even in the most trying passages of his life, he has left us an example, that we should follow his steps. 1 Peter ii. 21. Trusting in the mercy of the Most High, he was not moved: trusting the same mercy through him, we shall not be moved, but finally overcome even as he overcame. It was no vain boast in St. Paul, saying, "I can do all things through Christ, who strengtheneth me." Philip. iv. 13.

VERSE 8. Thy hand shall find out all thine enemies; thy right hand shall find out those that hate thee.

There is no mistaking the hand of which mention is here made. It is the hand of which we elsewhere read, "if I take the wings of the morning and dwell in the uttermost parts of the sea; even there shall thy hand lead me, and thy right hand hold me." Ps. cxxxix. 10. It is the hand of the anointed King of Zion, of him who, being in the form of God, thought it not robbery to be equal with God. Philip. ii. 6. How his hand has found out his enemies, and his right hand those that hate him, is shown in the his-

22*

tory of his Church. The orderings of Divine Providence have always in the end overwhelmed its enemies with confusion. Every effort to retard its progress has in the end accelerated it. The progress of "the truth as it is in Jesus" has been like to that of some mighty river, obstructed at points in its course by barriers thrown across it. The barriers, however, in nowise checking the swelling of the tide above, but being, by the increasing pressure of that tide, themselves swept away, serve in the end no other purpose than that of giving the river a larger volume of waters, a deeper channel, and a more irresistible current with which to urge its way. Fed by fountains that can never fail, he who, by throwing dams across it, attempts to interrupt the Mississippi in its flow, will be swept away for his pains. The higher he builds his dams, the greater will be the deluge with which he is doomed at last to be overwhelmed. So has it always been with every attempt to arrest the onward course of our religion. Every such attempt has in the end only added to its strength, inspiring its friends with new hopes, and covering its enemies with new disgraces. All who have opposed have at last been made to feel and own that He who claimed to be the Author of our religion was indeed a King whom it was vain for man to resist. The apostate emperor Julian acknowledged this. Having done everything he could do to extirpate the religion of Jesus, calling him, in derision, the Galilean God; overcome at last, he died, exclaiming, "O Galilean, thou hast prevailed!" The hand of the King had found him out, as it has found out all who have refused submission to his rule. All who have laid profane hands upon the ark of the Lord, have been smitten to the earth—all who have attempted to falsify the truth as it is in Jesus, have encountered balls of fire bursting forth from Mount Zion to consume them.

VERSE 9. Thou shalt make them as a fiery oven in the time of thine anger; the Lord shall swallow them up in his wrath, and the fire shall devour them.

In predicting that Messiah would make his enemies and haters like a fiery oven in the day of his wrath, the prophet only predicts what necessarily results from opposition to truth and righteousness. Opposition to Divine truth involves a state of things inherently self-destructive, a state of moral feeling essentially disastrous in its operations. Unholy passions are fuel that make an oven indeed of the soul. And how fiercely their fires burn, when left to act unrestrained, we have fearful illustration in the history both of individuals and of nations. France once said, We will not have this man to rule over us; and with what intensity of heat did the nation soon burn! every opposer being a burning brand in himself, and also a fire to consume others. The conflagration spread till the whole nation became, as it were, a burning oven, the wild and malevolent passions of the individual constituting the fuel that gave the oven its all-consuming heat. The fire devoured them; but it was the fire of their own kindling. When the time comes for God to rid the earth of an individual, or of a nation, he has no need to rain down fire upon them from heaven. He has only to leave them to themselves, when the fire of their own unholy passions will consume them. And God can be said to consume his enemies, only as he can be said to do what he does not *interfere to pre-*

vent. Hence he is said to *send* strong delusions upon those whom he does not withhold by his preventing grace from falling into such delusions. 2 Thess. ii. 11. This, in the general orderings of his providence, seems to be the only way in which the wrath of God is manifested in the destruction of his enemies.

VERSE 10. Their fruit shalt thou destroy from the earth, and their seed from among the children of men.

Fruit and seed are words of the same signification here; both words meaning children, offspring. It is impossible for any man to sin, without involving those connected with him in the evil consequences of his sin. The curse that falls upon the guilty parent extends more or less of its bane to his children. The lightning cannot smite the trunk, and leave the branch unscathed. The same deluge that swept away the antediluvians, swept away their children also; even as the same ark that saved Noah, saved his children too. This general identification of the child's destiny with that of the parent, cannot be destroyed without destroying the parental relation, and all the blessings growing out of it. This identification of his child's destiny with his own, should be the parent's strongest earthly stimulant to virtue. If, however, love for his offspring does not deter a man from sin, the course of Divine Providence is not thereby interrupted. Children are made partakers of their parents' sins, and, making them their own by adoption, follow their parents to a disgraceful end. Brief indeed is the history of those families in which irreligion has prevailed. Some secret curse seems to cleave to such families, silently wasting them, until not a member remains to tell who they were, or what were their names. We search society nearly in vain for the descendants of those who have at any time made themselves conspicuous as the enemies of the cross of Christ. Who now inherit the names of Voltaire, Rousseau, Hume, Paine, or Aaron Burr?

VERSES 11, 12. For they intended evil against thee: they imagined a mischievous device, which they are not able to perform: therefore shalt thou make them turn their back, when thou shalt make ready thine arrows upon thy strings against the face of them.

Even for *intending* an evil, and *imagining* a mischief which they are not able to perform, God brings men into judgment. He deals with men according to the *purposes* of their hearts, and not according to their actual performances. Hence the severity of his dealings with those who have opposed the kingdom of his Son. He has meted out punishment to them according to the thoughts and intents of their hearts. The sharp arrows of his providence have pierced them as deeply as if they had actually accomplished what they intended. Each particular providence has its own mission, and is as unerring and resistless in its course, as the arrow directed by Omniscience and sent home to its mark by Omnipotence.

"Therefore shalt thou make them turn their back, when thou shalt make ready thine arrows upon thy strings against the face of them." When Messiah meets his enemies through the orderings of his providence, he not only makes them turn their backs in flight, but his arrows often transfix them fleeing. They who will not be saved by his mercy, must perish under the blows of his justice. "He that believeth on the Son, hath everlasting life: and he that believeth not the Son, shall not see life; but the wrath of God abideth on him." John iii. 36.

VERSE 13. Be thou exalted, Lord, in thine own strength; so will we sing and praise thy power.

As the people began this psalm in a direct address to the Lord, they close it in the same way, saying, "Be thou exalted, Lord, in thine own strength." God is exalted in his own strength, when he uses his power to the punishment of wickedness and vice, and the maintenance of true religion and virtue. It is God in Christ whom we may especially desire to see exalted; the God who so loved the world that he gave his only begotten Son to die for its redemption; the God who can be just to his law, and yet justify the believer in Jesus—be infinitely just, and at the same time infinitely merciful. "So will we sing and praise thy power:" nowhere else is the Divine power to save so seen as it is seen in Christ. He is emphatically the power of God; and in him, moved to it by the Divine Spirit, the people rejoiced—rejoiced that the Lord had laid help upon One who is mighty to save unto the uttermost all that would come to God through him. They rejoiced in his victories, and longed for the time when not an enemy would remain to be subdued. We should long, and pray, and labour for the same. It is only as we identify ourselves with Christ in his spirit, aims, and labours, that we can be saved. If we refuse to be ruled by the sceptre of his love, we must be broken by the rod of his wrath. If he dwell not in our souls, changing them into his own image, they must become the everlasting abode of evil passions, that cannot but make them a fiery oven, an ever-glowing furnace of self-generating wo! How earnestly, then, should we all pray, "Thy kingdom come"—thy kingdom of righteousness, purity, and bliss, come into every heart! Even so come,

Lord Jesus: "For thine is the kingdom, and the power, and the glory, for ever and ever. Amen."

LECTURE ON PSALM XXII. 1—13.

VERSE 1. My God, my God, why hast thou forsaken me? why art thou so far from helping me, and from the words of my roaring?

THE first of these words found utterance in the most agonized shriek that ever burst from human lips. They are the "Eli, Eli, lama sabachthani," with which the Son of God bowed his head and gave up the ghost. It was at the close of the three hours of supernatural darkness that he uttered them. During those three hours the darkness upon his soul was denser than even that which overspread the earth. He was then, by the grace of God, tasting death for every man, and felt its bitterness as it had never been felt before. He was enduring the wrath of God as the Surety and substitute of guilty man. The Lord had laid upon him the iniquities of us all. The cup of a world's transgressions was being pressed to his lips, and he was drinking it off to its dregs. The bitterest ingredient however in his cup of trembling, was the loss of his Father's sensible presence. Because of this, amazement seems to have seized upon his spirit. His Father *seems* to have forsaken him—seems to have given him up to contend alone with the powers of evil; and yet he can with difficulty bring himself to believe that his Father has done so in reality. That he hopes against hope, and still believes even in his despair, is indicated in the emphatic *why* with which he addresses his Father—"why hast thou forsaken me?—why art thou so far from helping me?—why art thou so far from the words of my roaring?" We see a still confiding faith shining through this reiterated *why*, and shining still more clearly through the reiterated "my God, my God." If not to his feelings, yet to his faith, the Father Almighty is still his God. He will not judge the Lord by feeble sense, but still trust him for his grace. What a lesson may the believer learn from Christ in this verse—still trusting in God under the darkest hidings of his countenance, and the loss of every sensible evidence of his favour. His example teaches us that we must indeed "walk by faith, and not by sight." 2 Cor. v. 7. There may be mystery in many of the Divine dealings with us; but to the believer it is all a mystery of love, for he knows that God is thereby working out for him a far more exceeding and eternal weight of glory. It was so with Christ; it will be so with all who trust in God as he trusted.

VERSE 2. O my God, I cry in the day-time, but thou hearest not; and in the night-season, and am not silent.

It is not improbable that our Lord here refers to the many prayers which he had offered up long before, to be sustained in the hour of his final conflict with the powers of darkness. He offered up "prayers and supplications, with strong crying and tears." He prayed till his sweat became, as it were, great drops of blood. He also continued all night in prayer to God. There was no one duty of the believer that he practised more incessantly than he practised prayer. It was his vital breath. He knew, too, that God is more ready to hear than we are to pray. And yet he here complains that his prayers seem to have been offered in vain. The fact amazes him. The evil day has come upon him, and the strength for which he had so long and earnestly prayed to sustain him in that day, is for some reason withheld. How painfully this sometimes accords with the experience of believers in Jesus. For years, it may be, they have been praying for grace to sustain them under the trials of some day in the future. The day of trial comes, but not the sustaining strength—at least, to the degree expected. Immediately the thought arises in the mind, that God cannot be so ready to hear prayer as he is represented to be, and the distressed believer is tempted to give over praying. The example of the Saviour should rebuke such despondency. He did not cease to cry unto God because his prayers were not answered at the time he had hoped they would have been. He still prayed without ceasing, leaving it to his Father to determine the times and the seasons when his petitions should be granted.

VERSE 3. But thou art holy, O thou that inhabitest the praises of Israel.

However intense his sufferings may be, the Saviour knows that there can be no taint of wrong in them, because He who leaves him to endure them, is holy, and incapable of the least injustice. Though clouds and darkness are round about him, "righteousness and judgment are the habitation of his throne." Psalm xcvii. 2. However little he may be able to explain the Divine dealings with him, the believer can never conceive of them, except as being dictated by infinite love and infinite wisdom. Hence the sentiment of his heart, even when crushed as the Saviour's was, is evermore the same, "But thou art holy, O thou that inhabitest the praises of Israel." "It is the Lord, let him do what seemeth him *good." 1 Sam. iii. 18. "Not my will, O Father, but* thine be done." Faith, however much it may suffer, would not, for a universe of worlds, have anything otherwise than just as God hath ordered it. The believing soul shudders at the thought of taking its destiny into its own hands.

VERSES 4, 5. Our fathers trusted in thee; they trusted, and thou didst deliver them. They cried unto thee, and were delivered: they trusted in thee, and were not confounded.

Messiah here contrasts his condition with that of those who had called upon God in other days. To them he had always proved himself a refuge and strength, a very present help in trouble. They had never trusted without being delivered. No small part of the history of the Divine dealings with the patriarchs and Israel of old, was a history of deliverances wrought out for them in answer to the prayer of faith. "We have heard with our ears, O God, our fathers have told us, what thou didst in their days, in the times of old." Psalm xliv. 1. This story of the fathers was, that God had never failed them when they called upon him. And yet the Sufferer upon the cross seems to have called upon God for help in vain. His prayers for deliverance from his enemies appear to have been unanswered. Though faith tells him that God cannot forsake any who trust in him, nevertheless, to sight and sense, to appearance and feeling, God has forsaken him! How often is the believer called to endure this conflict between faith and feeling! The history of God's dealings with others, and also his own past personal experience, forbid the thought that our God is not a prayer-hearing God. It is a thought that pierces the heart like a sword, and yet a thought of which the believer cannot always divest himself. He struggles against it, prays against it; but, at times, the conflict is so severe that he can only exclaim in tears, "Lord, I believe; help thou mine unbelief." "Save, Lord, I perish!"

VERSE 6. But I am a worm, and no man; a reproach of men, and despised of the people.

Messiah here speaks of himself as he appeared to others, and to the eye of sense. He calls himself a worm, because of the even loathing contempt with which he was treated. He was in a condition where every one, even the lowest, could and did trample him under foot. He was no longer treated as if he were a man. His enemies had denied him all the rights and privileges attaching to him as a human being. He was a reproach of men, and despised of the people. Deceiver, wine-bibber, madman, blasphemer, devil—were the names with which he was branded. It is the lot of most men, in their fall, still to retain some friends. It was otherwise with Jesus of Nazareth. He was forsaken of all men—high and low, rich and poor, bond and free. He was sold by one of his own disciples for thirty pieces of silver, the then price of a slave, (Exod. xxi. 32,) and the release of a robber and murderer demanded as a boon preferable to his release. Matt. xxvii. 21. He was insulted with a mock trial, condemned to death by a judge, acknowledging his innocence in the same breath, scourged, buffeted, spit upon, and nailed to a cross, to die between two thieves. Under such treatment, he could well say of himself, "I am a worm, and no man; a reproach of men, and despised of the people." The Hebrew word means a *scarlet* worm—so Christ's whole body was scarlet, from the lashings of the scourge, and the blood from his nail-pierced hands and feet, and thorn-perforated brows. He was indeed "a man of sorrows, and acquainted with grief." None besides have ever been able to say with the emphasis which he could say it, "Behold, and see, if there be any sorrow like unto my sorrow." If his cross had been reared in the centre of hell, it could hardly have been surrounded with fiercer, more infuriate, and more implacable spirits, than those surrounding it on Calvary. Indeed, spirits from hell did mingle in the scene.

VERSE 7. All they that see me laugh me to scorn: they shoot out the lip, they shake the head, saying,

It is one of the redeeming traits of the worst humanity, that it seldom exults over the *dying* agonies of its victim. Men will pursue an enemy with uncompromising hostility, until they get him into their power; but when he at length stands before them, pale, haggard, helpless, and dying, or about to die, the hardest heart relents, and eyes unused to weeping, fill with sympathizing tears. The soldier pities even the traitor, when he sees him kneeling on his coffin. Not one in a thousand can see his deadliest enemy die, without some touches of sympathizing sorrow. It was otherwise, however, with the enemies of the Son of God. Not one of all those witnessing his dying agonies, manifested the least feeling of sympathy for him. All they that saw him, laughed him to scorn; made his sufferings the subject of abusive merriment. They shot out the lip, to denote their contempt for him, and shook the head at him, to give him to understand that he need not look to them for sympathy; for, in their judgment, he was suffering only what he deserved, and what they rejoiced to see. The words of this and the following verse were inspired by the Divine Spirit, more than a thousand years before they were uttered on Calvary.

VERSE 8. He trusted on the Lord, that he would deliver him: let him deliver him, seeing he delighteth in him.

A thousand and seventy-seven years had these words been on record as words of prophecy in the Old Testament, before it was recorded as history in the New Testament: "And they that passed by reviled him, wagging their heads, and saying, Thou that destroyest the temple, and buildest it in three days, save thyself. If thou be the Son of God, come down from the cross. Likewise also the chief priests, mocking him, with the scribes and elders, said, He saved others, himself he cannot save. If he be the King of Israel, let him now come down from the cross, and we will believe him. He trusted in God; let him deliver him now, if he will have him: for he said, I am the Son of God. The thieves also, which were crucified with him, cast the same in his teeth." Matt. xxvii. 39–44. Here is the keenest shaft with which his enemies have yet pierced the soul of the Sufferer upon the cross—they ridicule his trust in God. With fiendish irony they bid him seek deliverance from the God whom they believe to have forsaken him. "Trust in the Lord," had been the motto of his life: "Let him act upon his motto *now*," is the taunt of his tormentors. "Faith bends omnipotence to its will, and calls it to its relief," had been

23*

the import of his teachings. His enemies, in derision, now bid him realize the truth of his teachings in his own case, by coming down from the cross, and so prove himself to be what He had often claimed to be, the Son of God. If God delighteth in him, as he hath often said he does, let him manifest it by coming to his rescue now! How keenly must this diabolic irony have pierced the soul of the Sufferer! Yet he opened not his mouth in reply, but only to say, "Father, forgive them!" How different from many of us, who resent the slightest insult with a blow, or, it may be, with blood! How fortunate for the world, that Jesus of Nazareth was not what, in modern phrase, is called a *gentleman!*—one who thinks that blood is the only thing that can extract the sting of reproach. "He saved others, himself he cannot save." His enemies meant these words as a sarcasm. They are literally true. He could not save himself, and *others too.* No; *he* must die, that *man* might live. If he had come down from the cross, human redemption would have been frustrated for ever. He knew that he was dying for the sins of the world; for the sins of the very men who were murdering him. He therefore made no appeal to Omnipotence to save him, neither any drafts upon his own Divine nature to save himself. Once only, during the six hours that he is supposed to have hung upon the cross, did he enact the God. When one of the dying thieves, ceasing to revile, said to him, "Lord, remember me when thou comest into thy kingdom," his answer was such as became him, as the Lord and Prince of life—"Verily, I say unto thee, To-day shalt thou be with me in paradise." Luke xxiii. 42, 43. This said, however, this one word of the God, henceforth, to the end of the drama, we see only the suffering *man*. Ask Jesus to save others, and he would in an instant make a draft upon his Divine nature. Ask him, however, to save himself from sufferings and death, and his only answer would be, "The cup which my Father hath given me, shall I not drink it?" John xviii. 11. However overwhelming the Saviour's sense of desertion may be, he will not believe that his Father has finally forsaken him. Hence the torture of the suggestion, that his Father had done so. A suggestion of this sort, made by his enemies, caused David to weep day and night, and was as a sword in his bones. Ps. xlii. No other thought so rends the soul of the believer, as the thought that God ever has, or ever can, finally fail to deliver one who has fled to him for refuge. This, however, is the fearful thought with which his persecutors endeavour to overwhelm the Sufferer on the cross. It is also the fearful thought with which, in seasons of spiritual desertion, the adversary endeavours to overwhelm the believer in Jesus. Jesus resisted the blasphemous thought, even unto death—his followers should resist it in the same way.

VERSES 9, 10. But thou art he that took me out of the womb: thou didst make me hope [didst keep me in safety] when I was upon my mother's breasts. I was cast upon thee from the womb: thou art my God from my mother's belly.

Here the Sufferer endeavours to stay his fainting soul by recalling the past mercies of his Father. He recalls the wonderful and divine manner in which he was brought into the world, and the extraordinary care his Father and the holy angels took of him while he was yet a child. All his life through, until now, his Father had shown himself to be *his* God, and he cannot but believe that the same relation of Father and Son, Parent and Child, still subsists. He cannot believe that his Father would kindle such lively hope by his dealings with him when he was a child, only to extinguish it in everlasting night when he came to be a man. His doing so would seem like a wanton spoiling of the work of his own hands. To such resource for comfort have Messiah's sufferings driven him. The present is dark, cheerless, almost hopeless, and he is driven back to the mercies of the past, to persuade himself that God cannot have finally forsaken him; that, having formerly cared for him with all the tenderness with which a mother cares for the child borne in her arms, and drawing its nourishment from her breasts, he cannot have finally deserted him now; and that the mystery of his sufferings will in time be removed. Thus, in spite of feeling, in spite of appearances, he *will* believe that there will be an end to the awful night now filling him, and surrounding him. The sequel proves that he did not believe in vain. And how often is the believer in Jesus driven to this same resource for comfort—driven back to the mercies of the past, whence to draw strength to sustain him under the darkness of the present. He hopes that his repentance is sincere, and that he has laboured, so far as human frailty allowed, to approve his every act and thought to Him who searches the heart. Still he is under a cloud; there is no light within him, none around him, and none before him. The past, however, is bright with the mercies of his God to him; and that fact inspires the cheering hope, that in time the future will be so too. Faith still whispers to the soul in the lowest depths, "Hope thou still in God; for thou shalt yet praise him for the help of his countenance."

VERSE 11. Be not far from me; for trouble is near; for there is none to help.

"For trouble is *near!*" near, indeed; *so* near as to touch to agony every sensibility of soul and body. His soul, as he tells us in another place, "is exceeding sorrowful, even unto death." The powers of darkness are piercing it with all their fiery darts. Their infernal suggestions beat in upon it like a storm of fire; and no other ever saw the turpitude of their suggestions as he saw it, or felt their turpitude as he felt it. Unspottedly holy as he was, they caused him an anguish of spirit such as no one else has ever experienced. The purer the mind, the more susceptible it is of being pained by an evil suggestion. How severely, then, must the holy Jesus have suffered from the temptations with which wicked spirits plied him. And yet, horrid as their temptations and suggestions were, they found an echo in the conduct of the human enemies surrounding him. What an echo of infernal malice have we exhibited to us in the protruding lip, the wagging head, the pointing finger, the defiant stare, and taunting tongue! "For there is none to help!"—no, the Saviour is *alone* in the earth. He who fed the hungry, healed the sick, raised the dead, cast out devils, and took little children in his arms and blessed them, has none to help. The Helper of all who ever applied to *Him* for help, he is now left to endure the wrath of God, of men, and of devils, *alone*. Does his faith sustain him? It does. Although he knew that, for man's sake, the wrath of God is the great element of his trouble, still he trusts in him, praying, "Be not far from me." What an illustration of the words, "Though he slay me, yet will I trust in him." Job xiii. 15. His only strength to bear up under the trouble upon him, is *faith in God.* He demeans himself here not at all as a *Divine* being, able to deliver himself and disperse his enemies in an instant; but only as a *human* being, sustained by faith in the power and grace of God to enable him to be obedient unto death, even the death of the cross. Philip. ii. 8.

VERSE 12. Many bulls have compassed me: strong bulls of Bashan have beset me round.

In these words Messiah describes his enemies as having in their treatment of him laid aside the character of human beings, and assumed that of brutes. He compares them to bulls, strong bulls of Bashan, the worst of their kind—proud, sullen, fierce, and unrelenting. So fierce and fearless are these animals, that they will at times engage in single combat against the lion himself, and they are also remarkable for uniting in immense numbers against a common enemy. "Imagine you behold," says the author of Christ on the Cross, "a fellow creature closely pursued; not only one of these enraged animals, but a whole herd fall upon him; they trample him under foot; they surround him on every side, and low against him; they strike him with their horns; they toss him to and fro; they rush upon him with one accord! What horror, what fearfulness, what helplessness, are pictured in this condition! Just so was it now with our Lord upon the cross." He was surrounded and set upon by enemies, visible and invisible, as fierce and exasperated as the brutes here named, and as eager to have a thrust at him.

VERSE 13. They gaped upon me with their mouths, as a ravening and a roaring lion.

As the lion springs upon his prey, with open mouth and a roar, so do the enemies of Christ, now that they have him in their power, gnash their teeth at him, and give utterance to the loudest expressions of delight. The comparison depicts with fearful force the pleasure that the Jews experienced in witnessing the death of the Saviour of the world. As a ravening lion they had watched and waylaid him, paid money to get him into their hands, clamoured for his blood when Pilate would have released him, and feasted their eyes upon it when they saw it flowing from his veins.

So far, in our psalm, we have had described to us the *mental* sufferings of Christ on the cross: his *physical* sufferings, and his final triumph, are set forth in the portion of the psalm yet to be explained. His mental sufferings were caused by the withdrawal of his Father's sustaining presence, and the reproaches of his enemies. The two united, pressed his spirit with a weight of wo such as none besides have ever experienced. Sustained by his Father, as he had always hitherto been, he no doubt could have endured the reproaches of men without complaint; but when his Father withdraws his sustaining presence, there bursts from his riven heart, the agonized cry, "My God, my God, why hast thou forsaken me?" Why has the Father Almighty forsaken his only begotten Son? For your sake, and mine, beloved reader. For no sin of his Son, but for our sins, the Father forsook him. It was as our surety and substitute that Messiah felt in his soul the wrath of God against sin. He had taken the sinner's place, to endure the wrath of God due to the sinner's sin; and the Father Almighty could not spare his Son, and save the sinner. One or the other must die; and God so loved the world that he gave his Son. He forsook his Son, that he might not forsake us. Sinner, think of this love of God for you and me. How can you resist it? Again, the Father Almighty forsook his Son, that the Son's victory over death and hell might be altogether his own victory—his own as *man*, sustained by simple faith in God. It was the Father's purpose to discomfit Satan by the *very same nature* over which he had triumphed in Eden. Accordingly *a holy human nature sustained by faith in God*, is the Saviour's only protection and defence in the final conflict. God the Father has left him, God the Spirit has left him, and he has also renounced all reliance on his own God-like power to aid him, so that he stands before his enemies, having, as his only weapon of defence, what Adam had in Eden, a holy human nature, to be sustained by simple trust in God. A holy human nature, sustained by faith alone, was the weapon with which the First Adam *should* have conquered Satan: a holy human nature, sustained by faith alone, was the weapon with which the Second Adam *did* conquer Satan. He used no other weapon to gain him the victory on Calvary, than that which Adam had in Eden. He withstood the onsets made upon his holy will and nature, only because his faith in God was steadfast unto the end. And God left him to himself to prove to Satan and the world, that a pure heart, sustained by an unwavering faith, is a match, and more than a match, for every assault that can be made upon it. O what a thought is this for the soul to rest upon! that it was by the power of faith alone, the faith of a pure heart, that Jesus prevailed. And this faith of a pure heart he promises to all who ask it in his name. He purchased the Divine Spirit for us, for the express purpose of making us pure within, and inspiring us with an invincible faith in the mercy of God. He endured the withdrawings of the light of his Father's face, and the cheering influences of the Divine Spirit, that we might enjoy them for ever. O then, seek those influences earnestly, unceasingly, and without delay, and then, when you come to die, it will not be with the agonized cry, "My God, my God, why hast thou forsaken me?" but with those other words, "Yea, though I walk through the valley of the shadow of death, I will fear no evil; for thou art with me; thy rod and thy staff they comfort me."

LECTURE ON PSALM XXII. 14—31.

VERSE 14. I am poured out like water, and all my bones are out of joint; my heart is like wax, it is melted in the midst of my bowels.

THE crucified One here begins to describe his physical, as blended with his mental, sufferings. Neither visible, nor invisible enemies could overcome the strength of his holy will: but they could and did overcome the strength of his sensitive body. "I am poured out like water," as incapable of rallying my wasted energies, as water poured upon the ground is of being collected together again. It is an image of utter helplessness. "All my bones are out of joint:"

when Belshazzar saw the writing hand in his banquetting hall, his countenance changed, and his thoughts were troubled, so that the joints of his loins were loosed, and his knees smote one against another. Dan. v. 6. The unloosing of Belshazzar's joints was caused by sudden terror; there was no actual dislocation, but only a relaxing of the tendons that bind the joints together, and keep them in place. There was, however, perhaps an actual dislocation of the joints of Messiah's body, especially of the wrists, elbows, and shoulders, the whole weight of his body being sustained mainly by the nails piercing his hands. He no doubt felt as if every joint in his body had been wrenched from its place, the binding tendons holding the joint in its socket having at last given way. Such was the power of the spasms with which for six hours he was visited upon the cross. What fearful spasms ensue from wounding a single nerve in the human body: and what masses of nerves had been wounded in the body of Jesus! This dislocation was, however, sometimes effected in an instant, by the violent jerk caused by *dropping* the elevated cross, the sufferer already nailed to it, into the hole excavated for its lower end in the ground. It is not surprising that he complains that his heart within him has melted like wax. A death-like faintness has come over him—he swoons, but not wholly away. It is a relief to one suffering intensely, to faint, and so to lose for a time his sense of pain in unconsciousness. But even this respite of suffering Messiah does not allow himself. He chose to be a conscious sufferer in all that his Father saw fit to lay upon him. He who had once said of the multitude who had been listening to his teachings, "I will not send them away fasting, lest they *faint* in the way," (Matt. xv. 32,) is enduring a faintness of soul, an exhaustion and sinking of the vital energies, such as none else ever experienced and survived it. Imagine yourself filled with all the sinking and death-like sickness of a fainting man, but still retaining the liveliest consciousness of your situation, and you may enter partially into the feelings of the Saviour when he says, "My heart has become like wax, it is melted in the midst of me."

VERSE 15. My strength is dried up like a potsherd; and my tongue cleaveth to my jaws; and thou hast brought me into the dust of death.

Here comes the burning fever of the last stages of death upon the cross. The blood and other humours of the body have been exhausted by his protracted sufferings. His body is as destitute of vital moisture as a potsherd, as a piece of clay that had been baked in the oven of the potter. At every moment an increasingly dry and consuming heat is kindling in his body from the crown of his head to the soles of his feet. Also a burning thirst supervenes, "his tongue cleaves to the roof of his mouth." Of the intolerableness of a burning thirst, none can conceive but those who have endured it. The wounded soldier on the field of battle can tell you what it is. The fainting traveller over the burning sands of the desert, dying for want of a cup of water, can tell you what it is. It causes a suffering that no other sensation can produce—not even hunger itself. What an agony of suffering was expressed in that one word of Christ on the cross, "I thirst!" John xix. 28. "I thirst"—it was his only physical suffering on the cross that elicited a remark from him. And yet, intolerable as his thirst was, when drink was offered him, he declined it. And is it possible that any man's thirst, even that of the maddened inebriate, can be as great as his was? His sufferings had kindled a fever in his blood and brain, and a consequent thirst, such as no other man has ever endured. Moreover, Messiah feels that his sufferings have brought him to the grave's mouth, into which his body must soon descend. And yet he acknowledges the hand of his Father in everything that has befallen him. Hence his words, "Thou hast brought me into the dust of death." It was his Father's good pleasure that he should suffer as he did, and he will not mitigate his sufferings by so much as a drop of water. He is, by his sufferings, atoning for the sins of the world, and till that be accomplished, he asks no release, no mitigation even, of his sufferings. Christ having so suffered for us, what is there which we should not be willing to do, and, if need be, suffer for him?

VERSE 16. For dogs have compassed me; the assembly of the wicked have inclosed me: they pierced my hands and my feet.

Dogs, in the East, are not the gentle, attached, and faithful creatures that they are with us. Caressed by nobody, and cared for by nobody, they there acquire no attachments, and manifest no affection for man; but are ill-natured, fierce, prowling, and marauding—haunting deserted places, where they often attack the solitary traveller, and worry him to death, and devour him dead. Nor do they always wait for one to be dead before they commence their work, but begin tearing his flesh to pieces so soon as he becomes helpless. Homeless, masterless, wild, and savage, they often exist in such multitudes in the

East as to obviate the necessity of burying the slain. The body of Jezebel was eaten by dogs in the royal city of Jezreel, and at the very sides of the palace walls. 2 Kings ix. 35–37. To these merciless and hunger-bitten creatures, Messiah compares the assembly of the wicked surrounding him on Calvary. The sight of his body sinking rapidly into the embrace of death, gave them unmingled delight. It was a feast to their greedy, ravening malice. "They pierced my hands and my feet." It would not satisfy his enemies to have Messiah die in a quick and easy way by a blow of the sword, or the thrust of a spear, or even to be broken at once upon the wheel; but their cry was, "Crucify him!—crucify him!"—selecting not only the most ignominious, but the most lingering and tormenting death that could be inflicted—a death wherein nails were driven through the hands and feet, the four great centres of the whole nervous system—centres where the whole network of nerves meet and knit together, so that any pain inflicted there is felt throughout every nerve and fibre of the body. In this way Messiah was crucified. The whole weight of his body, convulsed with dislocating spasms, and consumed besides with a burning fever, hung upon these nails for six long hours, so piercing it, till death came to his relief. What a death!—and for whom? For you and me, fellow sinner! O Lamb of God, was ever pain, was ever love like thine!

VERSE 17. I may tell all my bones: they look and stare upon me.

"I may tell all my bones."—These words describe the emaciating effect of Messiah's mental and physical sufferings. Those sufferings had consumed his flesh till little more than skin and bone remained.

"The skin and flesh," says Bishop Horne, "were so distended by the posture of his body on the cross, that his bones, as through a thin veil, became visible and might be counted." His visage, as Isaiah had predicted, "was so marred more than any man, and his form more than the sons of men." Isa. lii. 14. The form and comeliness with which he entered on his ministry had, under its labours, its watchings, its fastings, its prayers, its sorrows, its trials, and its tortures, disappeared. Isa. liii. 2. The superhuman beauty of his person had given place to the wasted form, the trembling limbs, the sunken eye, the haggard look. Sad sight! but one that delights his enemies, for he adds, "they look and stare upon me." Whichever way he turns his head, he encounters their insulting gaze—a gaze expressive of intense delight in witnessing his condition! Disfigured to a skeleton, they enjoy themselves in looking at him! No wonder that we read, as the margin renders Isaiah, "He hid as it were his face from us." Isa. liii. 3. What language can describe how acutely he must have suffered in his delicate, sensitive, shrinking feelings of modesty—the lovely companion and never-failing attendant of purity and innocence. One of the severest trials of the early Christians, and especially of Christian women, was being exposed naked to the gaze of the multitude. The thought of being so exposed, even after death, often had an effect upon their minds which nothing else could produce. They listened to the threats of the cross, of the wheel, of the stake, and of the wild beasts, undismayed; but when it was added to the sentence, that their bodies should be exposed naked to the wanton gaze of their persecutors, their hearts died within them, and, like the Saviour on the cross, they hid their faces. It was the keenest pang their pure minds had to endure.

VERSE 18. They part my garments among them, and cast lots upon my vesture.

Parting the Sufferer's garments among them, while he was yet alive, depicts with fearful force the utter indifference with which his crucifiers witnessed his sufferings. It seems to have been done, not so much for the sake of gain, as it was as a pastime—a mode of beguiling the tediousness of their watch and guard, until their prisoner should expire. The vesture for which lots were cast, was the outer garment, worn over the other clothing. These words were literally fulfilled more than a thousand years after they appeared in this psalm; for we read in the gospel of St. John, "Then the soldiers, when they had crucified Jesus, took his garments, and made four parts, to every soldier a part; and also his coat: now the coat was without seam, woven from the top throughout. They said therefore among themselves, Let us not rend it, but cast lots for it, whose it shall be: that the scripture might be fulfilled, which saith, They parted my raiment among them, and for my vesture they did cast lots. These things therefore the soldiers did." John xix. 23, 24. Who can see words so literally fulfilled, and not believe them to have been inspired; and especially when death by crucifixion, as a mode of capital punishment, was not known in Judea until ages after the prophetic words were uttered? It was, probably, an unusual thing for his executioners to cast lots for any particular part of a crucified person's clothing. If that be so, the fact makes the fulfilment of the prophecy, that they cast lots for our Lord's coat, the more remarkable.

VERSE 19. But be not thou far from me, O Lord: O my strength, haste thee to help me.

Our Lord here realizes his own precept, "that men ought always to pray, and not to faint." Luke xviii. 1. He still cries unto his Father, whom he here calls Lord, Jehovah, that is, as the name imports, *The Living One.* His own life is ebbing fast away, and he looks to him who is Life itself, infinite and eternal, to sustain him. "O my strength, haste thee to help me:" the strength of Jesus to bear up under his sufferings was not in himself, but in his Father. He had strength of his own quite adequate to sustain him—his own Divine nature—but he refused to use it. His only resource is the prayer of faith, addressed to the Father Almighty. He altogether ignores his own power, and cries to his Father, "O my strength, haste thee to help me." His mission to earth was not to glorify himself, but his Father; not his own power, but his Father's power.

VERSE 20. Deliver my soul from the sword, my darling from the power of the dog.

Soul and darling here mean the same thing—our Lord's spiritual self: so sword and dog mean the same thing—the unrelenting agents of destruction that were assaulting and piercing him. Their aim was to destroy his soul, by overpowering his faith in God. Hence his cry to God for deliverance.

VERSE 21. Save me from the lion's mouth: for thou hast heard me from the horns of the unicorns.

The lion, from whose mouth Messiah here prays to be delivered, was, no doubt, the great adversary, the Prince and leader of the powers of darkness. It is thought that he approached the Saviour, in the wilderness, as an angel of light; and that, having failed to beguile him by his subtleties there, he was his fiercest and most unrelenting assailant on the cross, inflicting torture on his soul, comparable to being crushed in the mouth of an infuriated lion. "Be not thou far from me;" "haste thee to help me;" "deliver my soul;" "save me from the lion's mouth." Brief prayers these! but issuing from a bursting heart—a heart bursting with the intensity of its desires to recover his Father's lost smile. They pierced the heavens, and brought back an answer; for the Sufferer immediately adds, in the same breath in which he had sent up his impassioned cries, "For thou hast *heard* me."

"Thou hast heard me from the horns of the unicorns." Yes! the Father has heard him at last, and delivered him even from the horns of the unicorns, an animal whose thrust and toss with its horn, the lion himself shuns, and whose thrust and toss, therefore, represent the most fearful temptations that can assault the soul. "Thou hast heard me." Now the Sufferer can say of the work which he ascended the cross to accomplish, "It is finished." John xix. 30. The spoiler of Eden's bliss is himself spoiled of his victory, the law satisfied, and man redeemed. The question, "My God, my God, why hast thou forsaken me?" is now answered. The Father forsook him till he should have made an atonement for the sins of the world. The moment that is accomplished, he restores unto him the joy of his salvation, and upholds him with his free Spirit. This the Son now *feels*, and dies satisfied. He dies not, however, until there passes before him, in bright panorama, all the glorious effects of his death—nation after nation, and kingdom after kingdom, redeemed, sanctified, and saved through his blood. His last prayer on the cross has been offered, his last cry of distress heard! Henceforth, to the end of the psalm, we hear only the voice of joy, thanksgiving, and triumph. The darkness in his soul, and the darkness shrouding the heavens, have passed away.

VERSE 22. I will declare thy name unto my brethren: in the midst of the congregation will I praise thee.

This is the beginning of the joyful transition of which we have just spoken, "I will declare thy name unto my brethren." The atoning death of Messiah reveals the name, the moral attributes, of the Father Almighty, in a brighter and more captivating light, than any in which they had ever been exhibited before. What new ideas must it have given men, of God's hatred of sin, when they saw his own Son dying to atone for it; and what new ideas of his love for the sinner, when they saw his own Son dying to redeem him! "In the midst of the congregation will I praise thee." So fervently and tenderly does Messiah love all those who take refuge in his atonement, that he identifies himself with them in praising God for the salvation *he* has purchased for them. He rejoices with them in their joy, and thanks God for it.

VERSE 23. Ye that fear the Lord, praise him: all ye the seed of Jacob glorify him; and fear him, all ye the seed of Israel.

First of all, Jesus calls upon his own people and nation to praise, glorify, and fear God, for what he has done for them. Cruelly as they had treated him, their welfare still lay near his heart. His personal ministry was wholly devoted to them, he saying, "I am not sent but unto the lost sheep of the house of Israel." Matt. xv. 24. And the direction given to his disciples, after his resurrection, and as he was about to ascend, was the same in its tone of kindness to his brethren, the Jews; that is, "that repentance and remission of sins should be preached in his name among all nations, beginning at Jerusalem." Luke xxiv. 47. The first offer of salvation, through his blood, was to be made to those who had shed it!

VERSE 24. For he hath not despised nor abhorred the affliction of the afflicted; neither hath he hid his face from him; but when he cried unto him, he heard.

Messiah here urges his own example upon his brethren, to encourage them to seek the mercy of God. He had been tried and afflicted as no other man ever was, and yet the Lord heard him when he cried unto him, sustained, and at last delivered him. And surely, says he—for such is the import of his words—he who so sustained his Son, while making an atonement for the sins of the world, will not refuse to sustain any poor sinner who seeks refuge in that atonement.

VERSE 25. My praise shall be of thee, in the great congregation: I will pay my vows before them that fear Him.

The *vows* which Messiah here pledges himself to pay, were thank-offerings due to his Father for the deliverance he had wrought out for him. Persons who had been delivered from some great danger were wont to make such offerings in the presence of the whole congregation of Israel. Most of us forget the vows we make in time of danger and of trouble: it was not so with our Surety. He remembered his vows to his Father, and performed them, publicly ascribing to God in the beginning what through his

Church he has been ascribing to him ever since, namely, that it was through him alone that he prevailed on the cross against sin, Satan, and the world.

VERSE 26. The meek shall eat and be satisfied; they shall praise the Lord that seek him: your heart shall live for ever.

Messiah's flesh is meat indeed, and his blood drink indeed, to all those who look to him for the pardon of their sins and everlasting life: the Bread from heaven, of which if a man eat, he shall never hunger; the Living Water, of which if a man drink, he shall never thirst. To this fact he refers here. The atonement he has made for their sins is, to all penitent recipients, a feast indeed. It inspires them with continual praise and thanksgiving to God. To such the Saviour says, "your heart shall live for ever." His grace in their hearts is a source of perpetual peace and joy to them. It is the water of which he elsewhere says, "whosoever shall drink of the water that I shall give him, shall never thirst; but the water that I shall give him shall be in him a well of water springing up into everlasting life." John iv. 14. The heart lives indeed when its life-principle is the love of God shed abroad in the heart by the Holy Spirit.

VERSE 27. All the ends of the world shall remember and turn unto the Lord; and all the kindreds of the nations shall worship before thee.

Here, in prophetic vision, the at last triumphant Sufferer beholds the Gentiles, as well as the Jews, sharing in the blessings of his redemption. This began to be fulfilled when the gospel was preached to Cornelius, its first Gentile convert, (Acts x. 34, 35,) and has been fulfilling ever since, in nation after nation of the heathen world casting their idols to the moles and the bats, and turning to the living God. We ourselves constitute a part of the fulfilment of this verse.

VERSE 28. For the kingdom is the Lord's; and he is the governor among the nations.

These words describe the impression made upon the mind of the heathen world, by the story of "*God manifested in the flesh.*" That story exhibited love and mercy, truth and justice, in such a light to their minds, that they were convinced that the God of Abraham was the only true God, the only God whose kingdom ruleth over all, and deserves to rule over all. Multitudes, therefore, that no man could number, became the willing and rejoicing subjects of his kingdom.

VERSE 29. All they that be fat upon earth shall eat and worship; all they that go down to the dust shall bow before him: and none can keep alive his own soul.

"All they that be fat," they that abound in every good that earth can bestow, shall find a good in Christianity that the world cannot give, and rejoice in that good. "All they that go down to the dust," they that are descending into the dust of the grave, and unable to retain the soul in the body, even they shall be strengthened, rescued, and saved, even there, by partaking in faith of the feast prepared for the soul by Messiah. It is a feast that gives strength in weakness, life in death.

VERSE 30. A seed shall serve him; and it shall be accounted to the Lord for a generation.

A prediction that the gospel of Messiah's salvation would perpetuate itself from age to age, and from generation to generation; would embrace not only the whole world, but also all time, in the circle of its blessings, and that the Lord would never want for a generation of holy ones to serve him in the gospel of his Son.

VERSE 31. They shall come, and shall declare his righteousness unto a people that shall be born, that he hath done it.

That is, the Lord Almighty, the deliverer of the Sufferer upon the cross, shall never want for witnesses to proclaim the salvation he thereby wrought out for the world. The first witnesses of the great fact were the apostles on the day of Pentecost; and other witnesses have borne the same testimony in every age since, and are bearing it now.

Here ends the bright panorama of blessings which Christ foresaw that his obedience unto death would procure for the world: blessings for all, and all-sufficient for all, in time, and in eternity. All these blessings, as flowing from his death, he foresaw when he said, "thou hast heard me:" and now, having seen them, he turns to his Father, saying, "Father, into thy hands I commend my spirit: and having said thus, he gave up the ghost." Luke xxiii. 46. His body has been wounded, torn, tormented; his soul agonized; his heart broken; little does he care for all that now. Man is redeemed, the Divine law magnified, his Father glorified, and he—dies content. The grave has no terrors for him, and he descends into it assured that his abode there will be of brief duration. His first cry on the cross was, "My God, my God, why hast thou forsaken me?" His last, "Father, into thy hands I commend my Spirit." How fearful was the first cry! how glorious the last!

And now, beloved reader, do you desire that your whole passage through the dark valley of the shadow of death may be as bright as Messiah's was from the time his Father heard him, until he gave up the ghost? Your desire can be realized. He died for the express purpose of rendering the whole passage thus bright for you. He is no longer suffering Mercy, dying Mercy, Mercy dead—but risen Mercy, ascended Mercy, Mercy at the right hand of infinite power on high, and wielding that power to secure the eternal salvation of all those who seek it in his name. Go to him in faith and prayer, and he will give you the victory—enable you at your last hour to say, in loving confidence, "Father, into thy hands I commend my spirit," and to depart hence, singing, "O death, where is thy sting? O grave, where is thy victory?"

LECTURE ON PSALM XXIII.

VERSE 1. The Lord is my Shepherd; I shall not want.

How different the opening of this psalm from that of the twenty-second! That opens with the agonizing cry, "My God, my God, why hast thou forsaken me?" That was the cry of our Surety, of the sinner's substitute, drinking off the cup of wrath against sin, and in the sinner's stead. It was the cry of the Shepherd himself, suffering the fulfilment of the words, "Awake, O sword, against my Shepherd, and against the Man that is my Fellow, saith the Lord of hosts; smite the Shepherd." Zech. xiii. 7. This psalm, however, describes the fulness of the grace and mercy which our Surety thereby purchased for us. Its whole strain, therefore, from beginning to end, is a strain of joy and triumph.

"The Lord is my Shepherd." The first thing that arrests the attention is the *name* of the Being whom David affirms to be his Shepherd. It is the Lord, Jehovah—that is, the Living One, for such is the import of the word—"the High and Lofty One that inhabiteth eternity." Isa. lvii. 15. This Living One, however, to whom eternity of existence is ascribed, is not a cold, abstract, isolated being. He has a heart, even the heart of a Shepherd. And how tender a Shepherd he is, we learn where it is said of him, "He shall feed his flock like a Shepherd; he shall gather the lambs with his arms, and carry them in his bosom, and gently lead those that are with young." Isa. xl. 11. In what captivating colouring does this one word, Shepherd, invest the character of him whose presence fills immensity! It exhibits him as one whose love for his people never tires. The affection of the eastern shepherd for his flock, and especially for the lambs of his flock, is remarkable. He treats them as tenderly as he treats his children. Hence Nathan says of the little ewe-lamb, of which the poor man had been robbed by his rich neighbour, "it grew up together with him and his children; it did eat of his own food, and drink of his own cup, and lay in his bosom, and was unto him as a daughter." 2 Sam. xii. 3. Such is the eastern shepherd; and such is David's understanding of the word, when he says, "the Lord is my shepherd." David himself had been a shepherd, and knew what it was to feel a shepherd's love for his flock, and to exercise a shepherd's care. He risked his life in rescuing a lamb from the mouth of a lion, and when the lion turned upon him, he slew him. 1 Sam. xvii. 34, 35. Our Shepherd, however, not only *risked*, but *sacrificed* his life to pluck the prey out of the mouth of the destroyer. "He gave his life for his sheep." John x. 11. Having such a Shepherd, one who, to secure his welfare, would not regard even his life dear unto himself, David could with safety say,

"I shall not want." "He that spared not his own Son, but delivered him up for us all, how shall he not with him also freely give us all things?" Rom. viii. 32. This is the believer's great argument. Having the Lord for his Shepherd, he cannot want. He may not always have everything that he thinks he wants; he will, however, certainly never want for anything that will be for his good. This is the faith of the saints: that what they have is all that would be for their good, otherwise their Shepherd would give them more.

VERSE 2. He maketh me to lie down in green pastures: he leadeth me beside the still waters.

The oriental shepherd often leads his flock hundreds of miles to secure fresh pasturage; removing them, as it fails in one place, to another, ever guarding against their coming to want. He spares no pains to make his flock lie down in green pastures. Nor is he less pains-taking to secure them an abundant supply of pure water. This is often a more difficult task than finding them pasturage, perennial streams and never-failing fountains being of rare occurrence in Judea and the neighbouring countries, especially in the wilderness portions of them. In conducting his flock from place to place, the shepherd does not drive them, but, going on before them, they follow him—led on by the sound of his voice, whose tones they readily distinguish from all others. The shepherd also gives names to his sheep, with which they in time become so familiar, that, calling any particular sheep by name, it will leave the flock, and come running to his side, with every manifestation of pleasure and recognition. Nor will it heed the call of any other person, even though another should call it by its name. All these peculiarities of the shepherd and his flock, He who calls himself the good Shepherd, applies to himself, saying, "the sheep hear his voice: and he calleth his own sheep by name, and leadeth them out. And when he putteth forth his own sheep, he goeth before them, and the sheep follow him; for they know his voice. And a stranger will they not follow, but will flee from him: for they know not the voice of strangers." John x. 3–5. How striking the parallel between the earthly and the heavenly Shepherd! "He maketh me to lie down in green pastures: he leadeth me beside the still waters." A beautiful picture this!—a picture often presented to the eye of the traveller in the East—a shepherd with his flock in a verdant, flower-enameled pasture, some cropping its tender herbage, some reposing on its soft green sward, or under the shade of its trees, and others quenching their thirst at its gushing fountains, or in its running brooks; all satisfied, all happy, and all feeling secure, seeing their guide, their protector, their friend, their shepherd, in the midst of them! Such is the imagery under which the Saviour shadows forth the endearing relations subsisting between him and his people, the strong and tender ties binding him to them, and them to him. Hearing his voice and following him, he does verily make them to lie down in green pastures, and lead them beside still waters. His love and grace in the soul are living food indeed, affording it both sustentation and repose. And what a fountain, as well as flowing stream of refreshment, are his sweet invitations and promises! Truth, descending from Sinai, is the roaring torrent, to overwhelm naked rocks, and rocks torn from their beds marking its course; but descending from Calvary, as "the waters of Shiloah that go softly," (Isa. viii. 6,) it is a stream flowing on so gently as not to move the pebble from its resting-place, so purely as to mirror the heavens in its bosom, marking its course everywhere with life, beauty, and fragrance. It is not to the voice of the trumpet, waxing louder and louder, and shaking the mountain from foot to summit, that the good Shepherd invites us to listen, but to his voice, saying, "Come unto me, all ye that are weary and heavy laden, and I will give you rest." Matt. xi. 28.

O what food for the hungry, and what drink for the thirsty soul has the Saviour prepared for us in his word! food always fresh and nourishing, drink always pure and refreshing! As food, Job says of it, "I have esteemed the words of his mouth more than my necessary food." Job xxiii. 12. So also Jeremiah, "Thy words were found, I did eat them; and thy word was unto me the joy and rejoicing of my heart." Jer. xv. 16. The Psalmist, too, "How sweet are thy words unto my taste; yea, sweeter than honey to my mouth." Ps. cxix. 103. The Divine word applied to the heart by the Divine Spirit, satisfies the soul's spiritual thirst, too, as well as its spiritual hunger. And these thirst-slaking waters God supplies wherever there is a soul panting for them. Hence his promise, "when the poor and needy seek water, and there is none, and their tongue faileth for thirst, I the Lord will hear them, I the God of Jacob will not forsake them, I will open rivers in high places, and fountains in the midst of the valleys. I will make the wilderness a pool of water, and the dry land springs of water." Isa. xli. 17, 18. He then adds, "Ho, every one that thirsteth, come ye to the waters." Isa. lv. 1. This was the voice of the Shepherd in Isaiah; and eight hundred years afterwards he closes his revelation of himself to man with the same unlimited invitation, saying, "The Spirit and the Bride say, Come. And let him that heareth say, Come. And let him that is athirst come. And whosoever *will*, let him take the water of life freely." Rev. xxii. 17.

VERSE 3. He restoreth my soul: he leadeth me in the paths of righteousness for his name's sake.

The human shepherd is careful not to lead his flock beyond their strength: he gathers the lambs with his arms, and carries them in his bosom. If any fall exhausted by the way, he does not leave it to perish, but does everything he can to revive its expiring energies. Or if it has wandered from the flock, and become exposed to perish in that way, he rests not till he has restored it to the fold. He goeth after the sheep which is lost, until he find it, and when he hath found it, he layeth it on his shoulders, rejoicing. Such, too, is the tender care of the Heavenly Shepherd. He restoreth the soul that is ready to perish. He restores it in the first instance by creating it morally anew, by infusing his grace into it as its element of a new spiritual life. And if the soul relapse into sin after being thus renewed by his grace, he restores it, if needs be, again and again. He has many ways of restoring the soul that has wandered from the fold. Sometimes he quickens conscience to reclaim us, as he quickened David's, when his heart smote him for numbering Israel. 2 Sam. xxiv. 10. Sometimes he sends some faithful minister to reclaim us, as he sent Nathan to David, to set his sin before him in all its turpitude, and then to say unto him, "Thou art the man." 2 Sam. xii. 7. Sometimes he takes the lamb of some wandering, wayward sheep, and bears it into his heavenly fold, and then the mother comes hastening after him. 2 Sam. xii. 23. A *look* only, brought Peter to his senses, and caused him to go out and weep bitterly. Luke xxii. 61, 62. The good Shepherd's eye and heart never cease to be on the soul in its wanderings, to revive the life expiring within it, and to lead it back into the green pastures and along the still waters he has chosen for it. If that life be as near to expiring as the spark on the end of the extinguished wick, he will not quench it, but kindle it into a blaze again. And how brighter than ever before does that blaze sometimes burn after having been thus rekindled! The spiritual life of David and Peter so burned, after their restoration. They followed the Shepherd more closely afterwards than they ever followed him before. The Shepherd healed them, and forgave them their wanderings, though they seem never to have forgiven themselves. Restoring love humbled them and attached them to the Shepherd of their souls, as nothing else could. It affects all true believers in the same way. "He leadeth me in the paths of righteousness." One of the principal cares of the shepherd is to conduct his flock along paths that they can travel with the least danger. He never leads them along rough and uneven paths, among thorns, and over rocks and mountains, except where their safety requires it. It is the same with the heavenly Shepherd. He always leads his flock in *right* paths; in paths along which they be may be sure that they can follow him in safety. These paths may not always be the most agreeable to our natural feelings, nevertheless they are paths in which no fatal evil can befall us. The right paths, or paths of righteousness, in which the good Shepherd leads the believer, are the ways of right conduct marked out for him in the word of God. He *puts* the believer in those ways when he creates his soul anew, and *keeps* him therein by the continual guidance of his Holy Spirit. Both the restoration and the leading here spoken of are described at length by Ezekiel. He describes the moral restoration of the soul in the words, "A new heart also will I give you, and a new spirit will I put within you; and I will take away the stony heart out of your flesh; and I will give you a heart of flesh;" and then its being led in the paths of righteousness, in the words, "And I will put my Spirit within you, and cause you to walk in my statutes, and ye shall keep my judgments, and do them." Ezek. xxxvi. 26, 27. "As many as are led by the Spirit of God, they are the sons of God." Rom. viii. 6. And that we are led by the Spirit of God, can be surely known only by our walking in the ways of God's laws and in the works of his commandments. If in any part, or in any single act of our lives, we habitually walk by any other rule, we are not led by the Spirit of God, we are not walking in the paths of righteousness intended here, we are not following in the footsteps of the Heavenly Shepherd. We may fancy ourselves walking in the green pastures and along the healing waters of the gospel. But it is all a fancy; we are mistaken. We are wandering shepherdless in the wilderness of self-delusion. The Holy Spirit leads in the paths of righteousness, and in *all* the paths of righteousness laid down in the word of God. He knows not a single requirement in the whole of God's revealed will and law that can be safely left out of our obedience—not one.

"He leadeth me in the paths of righteousness for his name's sake." "I, even I, saith the Lord, am he that blotteth out thy transgressions for mine own sake." Isa. xliii. 25. It is even so. It is for his own sake, not for mine, that the Heavenly Shepherd restoreth my soul, and leadeth me in the paths of righteousness. There is no moral excellence in me to move him to the work. It is altogether for his own sake that he saves me. He finds in himself all his reasons for saving me. He saves me because he is love, and because he would reveal himself in that character to his intelligent universe. He pardons the guilty that he may magnify his mercy. He sanctifies the polluted, that he may magnify his holiness. All his dealings with us are designed to teach us his great name—his greatness and his goodness. We have nothing in ourselves, except our great and acknowledged wretchedness, to commend us to his mercy. His own love moves him to do for us; regard for his own infinitely excellent character leads him to anticipate our wants. He finds in his own heart and character every motive that can prompt to merciful action; and he allows us to plead this with him in our prayers. Hence the inspired words, "For thy name's sake, O Lord, pardon mine iniquity, for it is great." Psalm xxv. 11. "Help us, O God of our salvation, for the glory of thy name; and deliver us, and purge away our sins, for thy name's sake." Psalm lxxix. 9. "O Lord, though our iniquities testify against us, do thou it for thy name's sake." Jer. xiv. 21. "O Lord, hear; O Lord, forgive; O Lord, hearken and do; defer not for thine own sake." Dan. ix. 19. It is not any finite excellence that the Divine Spirit teaches us to make the ground and basis of our acceptance, but to make infinite excellence that ground and basis, to plead the glory of his own name with God as the reason why he should fulfil the desires and petitions of his needy creatures. Appealing to his own name, his own character, is appealing at once to the living Fountain of infinite love and mercy. How truly then may every believer say with the author of "The Lord our Shepherd," "I recline in green pastures, but it is my Shepherd who maketh me lie down. I partake of still waters, because it is my Shepherd who leads me continually beside them! I am brought back from my wanderings, for it is his mercy alone that restoreth my soul. And I am now walking in the paths of righteousness only because my Shepherd condescends to lead me in them for his name's sake."

VERSE 4. Yea, though I walk through the valley of the shadow of death, I will fear no evil; for thou art with me; thy rod and thy staff they comfort me.

Before the flock of the good Shepherd can reach the fields that stand dressed in ever-living green, through which flows the pure river of the water of life, clear as crystal, proceeding out of the throne of God and of the Lamb (Rev. xxii. 1,) it has to pass through a dark valley. It is called the "valley of the shadow of death." It is not the valley of death itself, but only of its shadow. If you wish to see the valley of death itself, read the twenty-second psalm, and you will see in it the valley through which the sinner's Surety passed, shrieking, "My God, my God, why hast thou forsaken me!" It was through the valley of death itself that he passed. It precipitated itself upon him in its substance, veiling the heavens and the earth and his soul in darkness that was felt. He endured death in its substance. And why in its substance? To the end that all those following him as their Shepherd should henceforth endure it only in its shadow. And how often to those following him is even this shadow of death, not a dark, but a luminous shadow! More than one has exclaimed, as he entered it, "There is light in the valley!—there is light in the valley!—is this dying?—how have I dreaded as an enemy this smiling friend!" "How hard it is to die!" said one to an humble believer in his last moments. "O no, no," he replied—"easy dying, blessed dying, glorious dying! I have experienced more happiness in dying two hours this day, than in my whole life before. It is worth a whole life to have such an end as this!"

"For thy rod and thy staff they comfort me." We learn in these words the secret of the believer's passing the valley of the shadow of death, fearing no evil. His Shepherd both guides and sustains him. We read that the rod and staff of the shepherd serves a double purpose. Passing it lengthwise gently along the side of his sheep, and holding it there, he guides them in safety in paths running along the very verge of the precipice. Again, coming to rocks and ascents that they cannot surmount in their own strength, reversing the rod in his hand, he passes its crook under his panting sheep, and so helps them to surmount whatever opposes their progress, and, if needs be, even lifts them over it. The heavenly Shepherd uses his rod and staff in the same way. He guides us by his word; he sustains us by his grace; he chooses out the paths wherein we should walk—saying to us, when we would turn to the right hand or to the left, "This is the way, walk ye in it" (Isa. xxx. 21;) and when we strive to obey him, he adds, "I will strengthen thee; yea, I will help thee; yea, I will uphold thee with the right hand of my righteousness." Isa. xli. 10. In this gentle way the good Shepherd leads his flock to their final resting place; if not always in triumph, always in comfort; if not always along easy paths, always along safe ones; if not always in sight of him, yet always within sound of his voice, and that a cheering voice: "Fear not, little flock, for it is your Father's good pleasure to give you the kingdom." Luke xii. 32.

VERSE 5. Thou preparest a table before me in the presence of mine enemies; thou anointest my head with oil, my cup runneth over.

These words describe the manner in which an oriental great man welcomes the guest whom he wishes to honour. He spreads a table for him, loaded with every delicacy that can tempt the appetite; and also pours upon his head, and arms, and hands, some fragrant perfume. The host also puts a cup into the hands of his guest, and pours wine into it till it runs over. All this is done by the great man, to assure his guest that he receives him with the greatest pleasure, and that he shall enjoy under his roof every comfort in his power to bestow. David's reference to this custom in the words, "Thou preparest a table before me in the presence of mine enemies; thou anointest my head with oil, my cup runneth over," is beautiful and striking. "The Lord," says another, "had early received the Psalmist into his favour; raised him to the highest honours from a very humble condition; and, what was infinitely better, he set before him the inestimable blessings of redeeming love, prepared him by a copious unction of the Holy Spirit to enjoy them, and welcomed him in the most honourable manner by putting the cup of salvation into his hands, in the presence of all his people, and pouring into it, with unsparing liberality, the wine of heavenly consolation." This feast of redeeming love, of which we can partake in the presence of all our enemies, even of death itself—this anointing of the Divine Spirit, this cup of salvation overflowing with wine from the vineyard of the Lord, from the wine-press trodden by our Immanuel, is a feast, an anointing, a cup of salvation, prepared for all. All are invited to partake of it, for the invitation runs, Ho! every one—every one that hungereth, every one that thirsteth, and whosoever *will.*

VERSE 6. Surely goodness and mercy shall follow me all the days of my life; and I will dwell in the house of the Lord for ever.

The *surely* of this verse is better translated *only.* This then is the conclusion at which David arrives, and at what other conclusion could he arrive? Such a Shepherd as he has described could not leave him to perish at the last; nor such a host and entertainer banish him his presence at the end of his days. As only goodness and mercy had followed him in all time past, so, he was sure, goodness and mercy would follow him in all time to come. David had endured many a cross, suffered many an affliction, and tasted many a cross of bitterness, but here he speaks of all God's dealings with him as being *only* goodness and mercy. Such is the privilege of the believer, that is, to have all things work together for his good, and to reckon even death itself among his treasures.

"And I shall dwell in the house of the Lord for ever." David was persuaded that such goodness and mercy as he had experienced, could not end with his life, but that they would follow him into eternity, and be his *for ever*. This, too, is the privilege of the believer, to know that the green pastures and still waters, the feast of redeeming love, the joy in the Holy Ghost, the cup of salvation overflowing with heavenly consolations, vouchsafed him here, are an earnest of still better things in reserve for him hereafter, of joys that eye hath not seen, nor ear heard, nor has it entered into the heart of man to conceive. And need we urge any to follow such a Shepherd as this? to enter his fold and put yourselves under his care? Fear not that you will not be able to follow him. He will see to that. He giveth power to the faint, and to them that have no might, he increaseth strength. Isa. xl. 29. What though your strength should be as small and your feet as tender as the new-born lamb's?—no matter, "He gathereth the lambs with his arms, and carrieth them in his bosom." Isa. xl. 11. He will not allow the most timid child of grace, essaying to follow him, to perish by the way. Hear, too, how the Shepherd speaks of the house of the Lord, in which David was assured that he would dwell for ever. "In my Father's house are many mansions: if it were not so, I would have told you. I go to prepare a place for you. And if I go and prepare a place for you, I will come again, and receive you unto myself; that where I am, there ye may be also." John xiv. 2, 3. So it is: every one following the good Shepherd has prepared for him a house not made with hands, eternal in the heavens, a house

"Where the saints of all ages in harmony meet,
Their Saviour and brethren, transported to greet;
While the anthems of rapture unceasingly roll,
And the smile of the Lord is the feast of the soul."

May God of his infinite mercy incline us all so to follow the good Shepherd, that we may pass through the valley of the shadow of death, fearing no evil; and having so passed it, dwell in the house of the Lord for ever.

LECTURE ON PSALM XXIV.

VERSE 1. The earth is the Lord's, and the fulness thereof; the world, and they that dwell therein.

THIS psalm was composed by David, to be sung on the occasion of removing the Ark of the Covenant from the house of Obed-edom to the new tabernacle that had been prepared and pitched for it on Mount Zion at Jerusalem. So David, we read, and all the elders of Israel, and the captains over thousands, went to bring up the Ark of the Covenant of the Lord from the house of Obed-edom. 1 Chron. xv. 25. And again, "So David, and all the house of Israel brought up the Ark of the Lord with shouting, and with the sound of the trumpet." 2 Sam.

vi. 15. The procession escorting the ark was no doubt magnificent. At the head, the ark, by Divine command, 1 Chron. xv., was borne on the shoulders of Levites. While the vast multitude were thus moving in procession, with the Ark of the Covenant borne on before them, containing the golden pot of manna, Aaron's rod, and the tables of the law, this twenty-fourth psalm was chanted with music. It opens with the words, "The earth is the Lord's, and the fulness thereof; the world, and they that dwell therein." Earth here means the whole terraqueous globe—the inhabited and cultivated portions of the earth. This God, in whom all things earthly live, and move, and have their being, had chosen Israel to be his peculiar people. This distinguishing love excites their liveliest gratitude. They think of his condescending greatness and goodness, while following the symbol of his presence. The gods of the heathen were local gods;—Israel's God was the God of the whole earth. Of his God the Israelite was taught to say, "Whither shall I go from thy Spirit? or whither shall I flee from thy presence? If I ascend up into heaven, thou art there: if I make my bed in hell, behold thou art there. If I take the wings of the morning and dwell in the uttermost parts of the sea; even there shall thy hand lead me, and thy right hand hold me." Ps. cxxxix. 7–10. It is with thoughts of this sort that the Israelites solemnize and elevate their minds, as they follow the Ark of God to its new resting-place on Mount Zion at Jerusalem. The God of the whole earth was their God, and they could not but laud and magnify his name.

VERSE 2. For he hath founded it upon the seas, and established it upon the floods: [or *above* the seas, and *above* the floods.]

Here is an allusion to the words, "God said, Let the waters under the heavens be gathered together unto one place, and let the dry land appear: and it was so." Gen. i. 9. The separation of land and water so as henceforth, to the end of time, to keep each distinct from the other, is one of the most remarkable exhibitions of the Divine power. God hath set a bound to the waters that they may not pass over, to cover again the earth, Ps. civ. 9; and on reaching the bound appointed them, they hear a voice, "Hitherto shalt thou come, and no further: here shall thy proud waves be stayed." Job xxxviii. 11. For six thousand years the waters of the sea have remained where God gathered them together in the beginning. He has so held the wind in his fist, that, tossing the waves of the sea ever so high, it has never been able to force them beyond the boundaries prescribed to them at the first. Moreover, he has so regulated the temperature of the ocean, that its waters have never overflowed in that way. This is wonderful! for elevating the temperature of the waters of the whole earth a few degrees only, some say, *one* degree only, would swell them far above the tops of the highest mountains. Wonderful indeed is the manner in which God has preserved the dry land such as he made it in the beginning; and what significance does his preservation of the earth in this way give to the words, "He hath founded it above the seas, and established it above the floods." Truly, "the sea is his, and he made it; and his hands prepared the dry land." Ps. xcv. 5. Each remains where he placed it, neither rising above, nor sinking below its originally appointed level.

The rivers and the fountains too, also reckoned

parts of the sea, God confines within equally certain and established bounds. The fountain that gave out so much water six thousand years ago, gives out the same quantity to-day. He did cleave the earth with rivers, (Hab. iii. 9,) cut out channels for them among the rocks, (Job xxviii. 10;) and the channels he cut for them in the beginning are still sufficient to contain their waters, and send them onward to the ocean. His springs, too, are found alike in the hills and the valleys. Ps. civ. 10. Thus he preserveth the habitable portions of the earth always the same, ever safe for the abode of man, and fruitful in everything that can minister to his sustentation and comfort. "All the rivers run into the sea; yet the sea is not full: unto the place whence the rivers come, thither they return again," (Eccl. i. 7,) to repeat, in never-ending circuits, their fertilizing flow to the ocean. "O Lord, how manifold are thy works! in wisdom hast thou made them all: the earth is full of thy riches; so is this great and wide sea, wherein are things creeping innumerable, both small and great beasts." Ps. civ. 24, 25. Such was the God of the whole earth, the God of Israel.

VERSE 3. Who shall ascend into the hill of the Lord? or who shall stand in his holy place?

That is, what must the moral character of the man be, who would stand in the presence of God, a worthy and acceptable worshipper? The question is similar to that of Balak to Balaam: "Wherewithal shall I come before the Lord, and bow myself before the high God? Shall I come before him with burnt-offerings, with calves of a year old? Will the Lord be pleased with thousands of rams, or with ten thousands of rivers of oil? shall I give my first-born for my transgressions, the fruit of my body for the sin of my soul?" To which Balaam's answer was, "He hath showed thee, O man, what is good: and what doth the Lord require of thee, but to do justly, and to love mercy, and to walk humbly with thy God." Micah vi. 6–8. Only in holiness and pureness of living can the God of the whole earth be acceptably worshipped. This is implied in the demand, "Who shall ascend into the hill of the Lord? or who shall stand in his holy place?" A very pertinent question in the mouths of those just now beginning to ascend the mount whereon the ark was to be placed in its new tabernacle, and wherein the Lord was henceforth to be consulted, his will ascertained, his wrath deprecated, and his mercy implored. Who then is the worthy and accepted worshipper?

VERSES 4, 5. He that hath clean hands, and a pure heart; who hath not lifted up his soul unto vanity, nor sworn deceitfully: he shall receive the blessing from the Lord, and righteousness from the God of his salvation.

This is the man, and the only man, who so worships God as to obtain his blessing. "He that hath clean hands:"—the man whose life is unsullied by a single act of wrong, of which he has not repented and repaired, so far as he could. "He that hath a pure heart:"—the man whose heart is as free of every cherished wrong feeling, as his life is of indulged wrong acts. "Who hath not lifted up his soul unto vanity:"—the man who has not set his affections upon earthly things, but upon things heavenly; whose heart is in heaven, where God his treasure is. "Who hath not sworn deceitfully:"—the man who never utters a word which he does not believe to be true, nor makes a vow to God or man, which he does not do his best to perform. He, *he* is the man who shall "receive the blessing of the Lord, and righteousness from the God of his salvation." When he appears before the Lord with sacrifices, offerings, and oblations, he shall not be sent empty away. He shall return to his house justified. The moral purity of his life proves his repentance to be sincere, and his faith entire. He realizes that to obey is better than sacrifice, though he by no means neglects sacrificing.

VERSE 6. This is the generation of them that seek him, that seek thy face, O [God of] Jacob. Selah.

"This is the generation"—that is, this is the character of all those who worship God in spirit and in truth—the character of the worshipper just described. They utterly repudiate as acceptable to God that worship of him which is not connected with a just and holy life. "Selah"—this word is a call upon all persons to pause and consider this, to ponder it well, lest they be led to imagine that the form avails anything without the spirit. To imagine this has been the great error of the world from the beginning. It was the error of Cain. He imagined that his offering would obtain him the favour of God, irrespective of the feelings that prompted it. His offering was rejected. It was otherwise with Abel's offering; it was accepted, because made with a broken heart and contrite spirit. Each was treated according to the feelings that prompted him; it is always so. The Lord looketh upon the heart, and none but the pure in heart, none but those hungering and thirsting after righteousness are recognized as his friends and the welcome inmates of his house. Chanting this sentiment as they approach the holy mountain, the procession raise the cry,

VERSE 7. Lift up your heads, O ye gates; and be ye lift up, ye everlasting doors, and the King of glory shall come in.

The whole city of Jerusalem was surrounded by walls set with gates, and also, being its citadel, Mount Zion within the city, whose walls were very high, and its gates of corresponding altitude. These gates were of immense size, having large folding-doors turning upon pivots set in sockets, and having also an upper part, called the *portcullis*, that could be raised or lowered, as occasion should require. These portcullises, called also the *heads* of the gates, were never raised except upon extraordinary occasions, and when some extraordinary personage was about to enter. That was the case on the present occasion; and hence the challenge to lift them up. The King of glory was about to pass through them to the throne erected for him on the holy mountain. To this challenge of the priests advancing with the ark, the presence-symbol of Jehovah, the priests guarding the gates demand,

VERSE 8. Who is this King of glory?
The Lord strong and mighty, the Lord mighty in battle,

is the answer returned. The Personage to whom they should open wide their gates, and lift high their heads, was none other than the Lord God of Israel; he who had fought all their battles for them, and achieved all their victories. It was he who demanded to be received and welcomed as a conqueror returning to his people; hence the repetition of the challenge by his heralds—

VERSE 9. Lift up your heads, O ye gates; even lift them up, ye everlasting doors, and the King of glory shall come in.

This second challenge of the advancing priests was answered as the first was answered,

VERSE 10. Who is this King of glory?
The Lord of hosts, he is the King of glory.

Though nearly the same, nevertheless this second answer is an enlargement upon the first. Not only is he the Lord, strong and mighty, the Lord mighty in battle, but also "the Lord of hosts." This one phrase, "the Lord of hosts," shows this King of glory to be not only the God of Israel and the God of this world, but the God of all worlds. "Behold," says Moses to Israel, "the heaven and the heaven of heavens is the Lord's thy God, the earth also, with all that therein is." Deut. x. 14.

In this solemn and significant way the ark of the covenant passes through the gates, ascends the mount, to the tabernacle prepared for it, and is placed in the holy of holies, where it was overshadowed by the golden cherubim. Henceforth, when God was about to communicate his will to his people, a light of supernatural brightness shone between the cherubim overshadowing the ark, from which light there issued the voice divine. In this way did the King of glory take up his abode with men, to guide their feet in the ways of peace and everlasting life. His throne was a throne of grace; and yet, seated upon such a throne, none could approach him acceptably but those who aimed to be pure in thought, word, and deed, and were firmly resolved, God helping them, to serve him in holiness and righteousness all the days of their lives. Others might appear before him with their sacrifices and oblations, and make long prayers, but neither their persons nor their offerings would be accepted, nor their prayers heard.

A higher significance has, however, been given to this psalm, than this of representing the ascent of the ark of God to its resting-place on Mount Zion. It is believed to represent, in its highest sense, the ascent of Christ, the King of glory, to heaven, after his victories over sin, death, and hell. It therefore constitutes, in our church, a part of the special anthem for Ascension-day.* Having shown himself alive after his passion by many infallible signs, being seen of his disciples forty days, and speaking to them of things pertaining to the kingdom of God, he at last stood with them on Mount Olivet, speaking to them his last words; and while they beheld, he was taken up, and a cloud received him out of their sight. Acts i. 9. This cloud, the *shekinah* of the Divine Presence—seen first in the bush by Moses, abode on Mount Sinai, guided the Israelites in their wanderings—hovered over the tabernacle, filled the holy of holies, and the whole temple, on the day of its consecration, with a light so intense that the priests could not stand within to minister at the altar. This was the cloud which, receiving the ascending Messiah, bore him out of the sight of his disciples. It appears, too, that he was escorted to heaven by myriads of angels, who, as this psalm teaches us, as they approach the entrance to the temple on Mount Zion above, the gates of the new Jerusalem, raise the cry, "Lift up your heads, O ye gates, and be ye lift up, ye everlasting doors,

* The Protestant Episcopal Church, of which the author was a minister, observes the fortieth day after Easter as the anniversary of the ascension of Christ.

and the King of glory shall come in." "Who is this King of glory?" demand the watching angels of their advancing fellows, seeing them escorting one who seemed to them to be only a man. "The Lord strong and mighty, the Lord mighty in battle," was the startling reply. "Mighty in battle!"—mighty indeed! How mighty, let darkened heavens and the convulsions of Calvary tell! How mighty, let the great adversary of God and man, and the grave, henceforth robbed of its power to retain its victims, tell! He met in battle every enemy of God and man, and conquered all. He conquered sin; he conquered death; he conquered hell. The escorting angels, then, could well repeat their cry, "Lift up your heads, O ye gates, and be ye lifted up, ye everlasting doors, and the King of glory shall come in." They knew whom they were escorting. Perhaps some of them had ministered to Him after his temptation in the wilderness; and others of them had ministered to him in his agony in the garden. It was, however, difficult for the angels guarding the entrance to the celestial city, to realize that one approaching them in such an humble mien, to all appearance a mere man, could be what he was proclaimed to be. They therefore repeat their demand, "Who is this King of glory?" and again are answered, "The Lord of hosts." It is even so; our Messiah is the Lord of hosts! By him were all things created that are in heaven, and that are in the earth, visible and invisible. "All things were made by him; and without him was not anything made that was made." John i. 3. This is the Being whom angels escorted into heaven as our Forerunner, bearing thither our own human nature, in vital union with his own Divine nature, to the end that he might be, not only a mighty, but also a sympathizing Saviour—a Saviour understanding by experience, every feeling in the human heart. He was escorted to heaven by angels, and welcomed by the same.

And now, beloved reader, it will be all our own fault, if we are not escorted in the same way, and welcomed in the same manner. Lazarus was so escorted, and so welcomed. Following the example of the Saviour in holiness and pureness of living; being such as the man described in the fourth verse of this psalm, we shall enter heaven as the Saviour entered it. Angels, who are ministering spirits sent forth to minister to them who shall be heirs of salvation, hasten—when the soul of a believer in Jesus leaves his body—hasten with it to the celestial city, and, as they approach its entrance, raise the cry, "Lift up your heads, O ye gates, and be ye lift up, ye everlasting doors," and a ransomed soul shall come in. In this way "the ransomed of the Lord shall return, and come to Zion with songs, and everlasting joy upon their heads:" in this way they obtain joy and gladness, sorrow and sighing fleeing away. Isa. xxxv. 10. Nor are they welcomed by angels only. The King of glory himself also welcomes them to an everlasting inheritance of joys, such as eye hath not seen, nor ear heard, nor have entered into the heart of man to conceive.

LECTURE ON PSALM XXV.

VERSE 1. Unto thee, O Lord, do I lift up my soul.

THIS psalm is supposed to describe the exercises of the believer, suffering under the chastening hand of God for sin. For some open transgression, or short-coming in duty, trouble has come upon him, and his mind is filled with misgivings. He knows, however, that none but the One who has sent his troubles upon him, can remove them. Hence the cry, "Unto thee, O Lord, do I lift up my soul." It matters not how sorely the believer has sinned, nor how sorely his conscience is burthened with a sense of sin; God is still his refuge. He knows that there is help for him nowhere else, and he seeks it nowhere else. When troubles come upon the worldling, on account of his sins, and conscience worries him, he seeks relief, not in God, but in other things; often in things that make his case worse. Not so the believer—he at once lifts up his soul to God in penitence and prayer. His weakness teaches him that there is no help for him in man, nor in anything that man can do for him. His every thought of deliverance, therefore, centres in God alone.

VERSE 2. O my God, I trust in thee: let me not be ashamed; let not mine enemies triumph over me.

The psalmist's appeal to God in this verse is based upon his promises made to faith; that no one trusting in him, should fail of his help. "Let me not be ashamed"—let not the hope inspired by thy promises be disappointed: "let not mine enemies," whether external or internal, "triumph over me." There are times in the believer's history, when temptation without and corruption within, so weaken and worry him, that he needs, to sustain him, to recall all the promises made to faith. "I had fainted," says David, in another place, "unless I had believed to see the goodness of the Lord in the land of the living." Ps. xxvii. 13.

VERSE 3. Yea, let none that wait on thee be ashamed: let them be ashamed which transgress without cause.

David here pleads God's fidelity to his promises, not for himself only, but for all who wait on him in faith, and hope, and prayer. What the believer asks for himself, he desires for all. He who prays for none but himself, offers an unheard prayer. True prayer embraces the whole Israel of God in the fervour of its desires. It cannot endure the thought that any waiting upon God in the ways of his appointment should fail of his help. An ingenuous piety can desire that the hopes of none be disappointed but of those whose influence is calculated to subvert truth and righteousness in the earth—the hopes of those who transgress without cause. There are such persons in the earth—persons who mock at sin, and glory in it. David prays, as every Christian may pray, that the hopes of such may be disappointed, and they covered with shame. He thus prays that God may "discern between the righteous and the wicked, between him that serveth God, and him that serveth him not."

VERSE 4. Show me thy ways, O Lord; teach me thy paths.

The ways which David desires to be shown, and the paths to be taught, are the ways and paths of the Divine deliverance out of his present troubles. He desires to be shown the way in which God would have him go to escape the dangers and difficulties now surrounding him. His example in this respect is worthy of our imitation. When trials come upon us, we are in danger of resorting to improper modes of escaping them. Then it is that we need the intervention of infinite wisdom. There is always a best mode of meeting and overcoming evil, and God alone can show it to us. This he does by the orderings of his providence, the teachings of his word, or the operations of his Spirit. And when he has shown us what we must regard *His* mode of rescuing us, we should pursue it, regardless of earthly consequences. It is for the revelation of the *Divine* mode of rescuing him that David prays, "Show me *thy* ways, O Lord; teach me *thy* paths."

VERSE 5. Lead me in thy truth, and teach me; for thou art the God of my salvation; on thee do I wait all the day.

"Thy truth"—the truth of God manifested in the fulfilment of his promises. David desires to experience that truth at the present time, to know and feel that God had undertaken for him in the troubles now upon him. "For thou art the God of my salvation." David's only hope of deliverance was in God's faithfulness to his word of promise. The import of his conduct is, "Thou hast spoken—I believe." "On thee do I wait all the day." David's faith in God was unremitting. Its constancy is pleaded as a reason why its exercise should be rewarded. It is an exercise of faith that God never fails to reward.

VERSE 6. Remember, O Lord, thy tender mercies, and thy loving-kindnesses; for they have been ever of old.

It is well for us in seasons of trial to remember

that God's property is always to have mercy. This David does here. He pleads God to himself: asks him to remember that tender mercies and loving-kindnesses are attributes of his nature, eternal and unchangeable. Such is the privilege of the believer: to fall back, in the day of evil, upon what God is in himself—eternal love. What a thought to allay the disquietudes of the heart, and inspire it with hope. God to the believer is an infinite Fountan of mercies and kindnesses—"*tender* mercies, and loving-kindnesses," that "have been ever of old."

VERSE 7. Remember not the sins of my youth, nor my transgressions: according to thy mercy remember thou me, for thy goodness' sake, O Lord.

Still pleading his own mercy and goodness with God, as the great motive power to engage him in his deliverance, it is for the sake of his mercy that David prays God not to remember the sins of his youth. Sins of our youth are drafts for whose payment we will be called upon in after years. God alone can arrest their entailment of wo. And it is well for us that his mercy moves him to it. Otherwise there is not one of us, the follies of whose youth would not send the Divine vengeance chasing us through life, and out of life. Moreover, merciful as he is, God forgives only the *moral* penalties of our youthful follies: their physical and natural penalties are left to run their course. The Divine pardon restores to the penitent man the favour of God which the sins of his youth had lost him, but not his health and fortune. For God then not to remember the sins of our youth, is not to inflict their moral penalty.

VERSE 8. Good and upright is the Lord: therefore will he teach sinners in the way.

This David says to increase his faith and add fervour to his prayers. Though his people are still sinners, coming short in many things, God, nevertheless, commiserates their condition. He is more grieved than offended at their failures, and still teaches them, being penitent, the way wherein they should go. Thus he grieved over the apathy of the three disciples on the night of his agony in the garden, blending apology with reproof and warning, saying, "Watch and pray, that ye enter not into temptation; the spirit indeed is willing, but the flesh is weak." Matt. xxvi. 41. So good and so upright is the Lord in teaching his people the way.

VERSE 9. The meek will he guide in judgment, and the meek will he teach his way.

"The meek" of this verse shows what sort of sinners are meant in the preceding verse: that they are sinners of a broken heart and contrite spirit, such as meekly endure the chastening hand of God, conscious of suffering far less than their sins deserve. Such sinners, meekly enduring his visitations, God guides in wisdom, and, in time, to quietness and safety.

VERSE 10. All the paths of the Lord are mercy and truth unto such as keep his covenant and his testimonies.

He so administers his kingdom, both of providence and grace, that all things are made to work together for good to them that love him. Rom. viii. 28. As they identify themselves with him in promoting truth and righteousness, he identifies himself with them in causing everything that befalls them to promote their final welfare. This is the believer's solace under trials. The favour of God converts them into blessings.

VERSE 11. For thy name's sake, O Lord, pardon mine iniquity; for it is great.

It seems a strange reason to plead for the pardon of one's iniquity, that it is great. In human courts it is pleaded as the great reason why it should not be forgiven. Its magnitude renders it more unpardonable. It is otherwise with the sinner, being penitent, standing in the presence of his Judge. There the greatness of his iniquity may be pleaded as an argument for its remission. The greater the sin, if unforgiven, the greater the ruin. This seems to be David's thought in the words, "For thy name's sake, O Lord, pardon mine iniquity; for it is great." "Avert, O Lord, the awful ruin in which such iniquity as mine, if unforgiven, must involve me." It is a legitimate appeal to the Divine mercy, and one that reflects honour upon it. It is like to the appeals so often made to our Lord—the violence of the disease and sufferings being pleaded as the great reason why he should interpose to heal and save.

VERSE 12, 13. What man is he that feareth the Lord? him shall he teach in the way he shall choose: his soul shall dwell at ease, and his seed shall inherit the earth.

David here encourages himself still to hope for Divine deliverance, because of the Lord's regard for those that fear him. "For like as a father pitieth his children, so the Lord pitieth them that fear him," (Psalm ciii. 13,) and their children too, for their sakes. It is useful, in seasons of discouragement, to reflect that God can never finally forsake those who fear him. He will in due time choose out for us the way wherein he would have us go, and make it a way of peace and quietness.

VERSE 14. The secret of the Lord is with them that fear him; and he will show them his covenant.

Critics tell us that the word "secret" here means friendship; that the friendship of the Lord is with them that fear him. "Henceforth," says our Lord to his disciples, "I call you not servants, for the servant knoweth not what his lord doeth; but I have called you friends; for all things that I have heard of my Father I have made known unto you." John xv. So when about to destroy Sodom and Gomorrah, the Lord said, "shall I hide from Abraham that thing which I do?" Gen. xviii. 17. It is not as servants, but as friends, that God regards those who serve him in singleness of heart in the gospel of his Son. He has nothing to conceal from them. He will show them his covenant; manifest himself to them as a covenant-keeping God; show them, by all the orderings of his providence, that he never forgets them for a moment; that in all his dealings with them his covenant of mercy is never for a moment absent from his mind, and that he will at last make it appear so to them.

There are commentators, however, who refer this verse, not to the external orderings of the Divine providence, but to the mental assurance which God gives those that fear him, of the truth of his word, and the adequacy of the religion it reveals, to satisfy the wants of the soul. This mental assurance, wrought into the soul by God himself, is thought by some to be the secret of the Lord here intended. The Saviour is believed to refer to this secret assurance in the words, "If any man will *do* his will, he shall know of the doctrine whether it be of God." John vii. 17. The Jews had denied the Divine reality of his miracles, and also that the Messianic prophecies had been verified in him. "Very well," answers our Lord, "I propose to you another means of testing my claim to be your Messiah and Saviour. Practise the precepts of the religion I teach you, and you shall soon have revealed to you the secret whether it be of God. Do his will, and you shall know of the doctrine. In obeying the precept, all else shall become plain." I knew, and admitted to the communion of the church, a gentleman who acted upon this saying of the Saviour. He admired, as perfect, the preceptive portions of the Bible; but stumbled at some of its peculiar doctrines. He determined, therefore, to ascertain what effect obeying the precepts would have toward dissipating his difficulties in regard to the doctrines of our religion. He, therefore, at once endeavoured to live in every respect as he would have lived if he had been a Christian; reading, praying, attending public worship, and making the moral code of the Bible his only rule of action. *So* obeying the precept, in less than a twelve months' time the secret of the Lord was revealed to him, the truth of all the doctrines of God's covenant of redeeming mercy in Christ, was made plain to his understanding and grateful to his heart. Here is a cure for scepticism within the reach of every man! His mind may be filled with difficulties in regard to everything else in the Bible, in regard to its history, its miracles, its prophecies, and doctrines; still, if he will endeavour honestly and perseveringly, to practise its precepts, live according to its moral code, his difficulties will vanish one by one, till none remain. And the man who will not test the truth of our religion in this way, cannot honestly say that he desires to be satisfied of its truth and connection with his own destiny.

VERSE 15. Mine eyes are ever toward the Lord; for he shall pluck my feet out of the net.

David realizes that there is a deliverance for him in only one direction, and in that direction he keeps his eyes continually turned toward the Lord, fully believing that he would pluck his feet out of the net which his enemies had spread for them.

VERSE 16. Turn thee unto me, and have mercy upon me; for I am desolate and afflicted.

Here again he feels like one alone in the earth, desolate and afflicted. Still his faith fails not, but finds utterance in the words, "Turn thee unto me, O Lord, and have mercy upon me."

VERSE 17. The troubles of my heart are enlarged; O bring thou me out of my distresses.

How like a child pleading with his father! The Psalmist knows that nothing else goes so quickly to the heart of a parent as the sorrows of a child, and he believes the same of Him whom he has chosen as the portion of his soul.

VERSE 18. Look upon my affliction and my pain; and forgive all my sins.

Still the child's cry to his parent, appealing to his pity. Here, however, he prays for the removal of the remote and efficient, if not the immediate, cause of all troubles—his sins. "Forgive all my sins." When trouble comes on us we cannot bethink us too soon of our sins. If they are pardoned, the troubles they brought on us will depart with them, or, if the troubles still remain, can be easily borne. The sweet sense of sins forgiven renders the heaviest afflictions light.

VERSE 19. Consider mine enemies, for they are many; and they hate me with cruel hatred.

It is strange that obeying the truth should make a

man enemies. But oftentimes the closer a man walks with God, the more numerous, and the more violent his enemies are. Under such circumstances, an appeal to the God of truth to defend us, cannot be made in vain.

VERSE 20. O keep my soul, and deliver me; let me not be ashamed; for I put my trust in thee.

That we have put our trust in him is an argument that can never fail to engage the Almighty on our side. His word has passed, that no one trusting in him shall ever be confounded. Heaven and earth shall pass away, but his word of promise—never.

VERSE 21. Let integrity and uprightness preserve me; for I wait on thee.

David here prays that however unjustly men may treat him, he may not be betrayed into any sin against them. In this aspiration he is encouraged, because he waits on God, waits for him to deliver him in his own time and way.

VERSE 22. Redeem Israel, O God, out of all his troubles.

If David wrote this psalm, as some suppose, during Absalom's rebellion—a visitation upon the father, for his grievous sins in the matter of Uriah—this prayer, "Redeem Israel, O God, out of all his troubles," forms a most appropriate conclusion. To the truly generous and godly heart, there is no other thought so painful as the thought that its sins have brought trouble upon others. This was David's case. His sins had brought trouble on the nation, and he reckons his own sorrows as nothing, when compared with the sorrows of so many innocent sufferers. Hence the earnestness with which he prays God to redeem Israel out of all the troubles in which his sins had involved them. Alas, how many of us pervert others, especially in our youth, for whose restoration to purity and peace we would afterwards give worlds, if we had them to give. May God, through his infinite mercy in Christ, give us all grace so to live that we neither ruin ourselves nor others.

LECTURE ON PSALM XXVI.

At first sight no two psalms could be more antagonistic to each other in their teaching, than the twenty-fifth and twenty-sixth. Nevertheless they harmonize entirely. Each presents a view of religious experience familiar to the mind of the believer. When the believer thinks of his sins, even those of infirmity, his cry for deliverance will be the cry of the twenty-fifth psalm, a cry based altogether upon the mercy of God. When, however, he is unjustly treated by his fellow-man, and thinks of his covenant-relation to God, and of the many great and precious promises God has made to those serving him, the believer's cry will then be the cry of the twenty-sixth psalm—a cry to God for deliverance based upon the fact of *his being His servant*, obeying him from the heart. The juxtaposition of these two psalms was not without design. The believer may utter the cry of both in the same breath, just according as he thinks of God as dispensing mercy to the guilty, or as rewarding obedience. "The contents of the one psalm," says another, "supplement those of the other. In the one psalm, the suffering righteous man is directed to seek refuge in the Divine compassion, which secures forgiveness for manifold sins of infirmity: in the other, again, he is led, from a consideration of the Divine righteousness, which must make a distinction between the righteous and the wicked, to entertain the firm hope of deliverance. We have, therefore, before us a pair of psalms, which point to the *compassion* and *righteousness* of God, as the two foundations on which the Lord's people may rest a confident hope of deliverance. The two are connected, as it were, by a *bridge;* the idea which occupied a subordinate position near the conclusion of the one psalm, being brought prominently forward, and having the first place assigned to it in the other:" viz. the idea that innocency, integrity, and trust in God, can never fail to secure his favour and protection. This is the thought of our psalm, and the thought to which David gives utterance in the words,

VERSE 1. Judge me, O Lord; for I have walked in mine integrity: I have trusted also in the Lord; therefore I shall not slide.

If our heart condemn us not, then have we confidence toward God, and may appeal to him to vindicate the cause we have in hand. This was David's case. Driven into exile by the persecutions of Saul, and charged with plotting against his throne and life, he here appeals to the Searcher of hearts to vindicate his innocence. David's "Judge me, O Lord," is not a call upon God to judge him for the sins that he may have committed against Him, his God, but to judge him for the sins he was charged with having committed against Saul, his king. It would be madness in any man, however blameless his life may have been, to call upon God to enter into judgment with him for his offences against him. It is, however, often otherwise in regard to many of our fellow-men. We can safely invite the Omniscient Judge to decide between us and them. We can say in regard to them, as David does, "Judge me, O Lord; for I have walked in mine integrity." Though Saul sought David's life, and once with his own hand hurled a javelin at him to slay him, David never for a moment swerved from the conduct of a dutiful subject. He still fought Saul's battles for him, and, though Saul was pursuing him as an outlaw, spared him when it was in his power to slay him. 1 Sam. xxiv. He never raised his hand against his king, nor allowed those under his control to do so. Integrity had marked his whole conduct towards him, insomuch that Saul himself was obliged to acknowledge, in tears, "thou art more righteous than I; for thou hast rewarded me good, whereas I have rewarded thee evil." 1 Sam. xxiv. 17. So should it be with the believer always. He should never allow the injustice of others to mar his integrity, to cause him to deviate in the least from the line of conduct dictated by a divinely enlightened conscience. Principle, not passion, should be the pole-star of his course. But what was the secret of David's preserving his integrity intact, in the midst of his sore trials and temptations? He reveals it in the words, "I have trusted also in the Lord; therefore I shall not slide;" or, "that I may not slide." It was not by his own power that David expected to sustain himself in his integrity, but by faith in God. He knew that his own unaided strength would certainly fail him. He therefore looks to God to enable him to stand. He thus teaches us that moral principle and human resolve are worthless in the day of trial, where they are not animated by a fervid trust in God. Religion alone can make moral principle strong, or bring human resolve to good effect. It was the only thing that enabled David to walk in integrity towards man, and in piety towards God, and to say, "Judge me, O Lord," with the confident expectation that in judging between him and his enemies, God would vindicate him.

VERSE 2. Examine me, O Lord, and prove me; try my reins and my heart.

So conscious is David of never having even intended evil against Saul, that he calls upon the Searcher of hearts to examine, prove, and try him; and to carry the scrutiny into every thought and feeling of his heart. He was conscious of many failures in duty to God, and elsewhere deplores them, but of no failures in duty to Saul. This should be the aim of every believer, to cherish towards all men, even towards enemies, feelings such as he would not fear to have pass under the Omniscient eye. Hence David's prayer in another place, "Search me, O God, and know my heart; try me, and know my thoughts; and see if there be any wicked way in me, and lead me in the way everlasting." Psalm cxxxix. 23, 24. The believer should be willing to have the Lord see all the evil, as well as all the good that is in him, that he may strengthen the one and destroy the other.

VERSE 3. For thy loving-kindness is before mine eyes; and I have walked in thy truth.

It was by keeping his mind continually upon the

love of God, and upon his truth, the faithfulness of his promises made to faith and holy obedience, that David was emboldened to challenge the Divine decision in his case. It was his past experience of the love and faithfulness of God that made him fear no evil now. He was satisfied that, having been so loving and so true to him in all times past, he would still be to him what he had been. Under the pressure of present troubles, we are apt to forget God's former dealings with us. We lose sight of his former loving-kindnesses, and the unfailing faithfulness with which he has fulfilled his every promise of good to us. It was not so with David.

VERSE 4. I have not sat with vain persons, neither will I go in with dissemblers.

It was one of the charges preferred against David by Saul, that he had associated himself with a band of worthless and disaffected subjects, and those seeking his overthrow, while pretending to be his friends. This charge David denies—saying that he had not, and would not associate with any such persons. And his history shows that he spoke the truth. We cannot too carefully avoid the society of the vain and dissembling. We may mingle with them, as the Saviour did, to do them good, but we make companions of them at our peril. If we enjoy their society for its own sake, it is proof that we are no better than they. The truly gracious mind can have no moral sympathy with any but those who are governed by a sincere love of truth.

VERSE 5. I have hated the congregation of evil doers; and will not sit with the wicked.

David not only did not sympathize with the spirit, nor co-operate in the plans, of the treacherous and seditious, but he hated their meetings, and would have nothing to do with their secret conclaves. Saul could not point to a single act of his life where his influence over the wicked had not been for good. Although when he was driven into exile, every one that was in distress, and every one that was in debt, and every one that was discontented, gathered themselves together unto him, and he became a captain over them, (1 Sam. xxii. 2,) he never led them against his king and country, but only against their enemies; and in time changed the most reckless and turbulent of men into the best of soldiers and citizens. There is no place where the sincere Christian cannot make his influence felt for good; in the army, in the navy, in trade, at the bar, on the bench, in the halls of legislation, and everywhere; not by sacrificing, but by maintaining and exhibiting his principles in his spirit and conduct. There is a something in humble, sincere and uniform piety to which the rudest do homage.

VERSES 6, 7. I will wash my hands in innocency; so will I compass thine altar, O Lord: that I may publish with the voice of thanksgiving, and tell of all thy wondrous works.

It was not to the assemblies of the wicked, and the shedding of blood, as his enemies said of him, that David's temper of mind bore him, but to the altar of his God, there to proclaim, with thanksgiving, the many mercies and deliverances he had experienced at his hands. With pure hands too, with hands washed in innocency, he would make his offering. His conscience was at ease, his heart at rest. He was conscious of a state of mind towards God and man, utterly incompatible with the things laid to his charge. It is well for us when we can engage in the service of God with a clear conscience, accusing us of no sin habitually indulged, and of no duty habitually neglected. "The sacrifice of the wicked is an abomination to the Lord; but the prayer of the upright is his delight." Prov. xv. 8. It was this last fact, the Divine delight in the prayer of the upright, of those endeavouring to serve him in singleness and purity of heart, that enabled David to lay hold of the sin-atoning altar of God with so firm a hand, with so thankful a heart, and with a mouth so full of praise. Conscious sincerity and integrity of purpose is the only thing that will enable us to come boldly to a throne of grace, that we may obtain mercy and find grace to help in time of need.

VERSE 8. Lord, I have loved the habitation of thy house, and the place where thine honour dwelleth.

It mattered not where David was, there was one place to which, above all others, his heart still turned with longing. That place was the habitation of God's house. Wherever the tabernacle was, there was the spiritual centre of the nation, to which the heart of every devout Jew was attracted, as the needle is attracted to the pole. He there saw the glory of God as he saw it nowhere else. There was the written word, to direct him in the way wherein he should go; there was the altar, streaming with blood, and smoking with incense, proclaiming his God to be both a placable and a prayer-hearing God; there too was the mercy-seat in the holy of holies, overshadowed by the cherubim, from between whom, manifesting his presence by a luminous cloud, God still made communications of his will, in cases of doubt and difficulty. This was the place that David loved, and to which his heart turned in his exile, notwithstanding his enemies had charged him with being an enemy of God and of his religion. This was the place of which he says elsewhere, "My soul longeth, yea, even fainteth for the courts of the Lord." Ps. lxxxiv. 2. It is a most gratifying evidence of our being children of God, when we love the places hallowed by his presence—the sanctuary, the family altar, and the closet. The more of God there is in any place or thing, the more strongly the sincere believer is attracted to it. Regenerating grace can never fail to make us delight in the word and worship of God, in public and in private, and to realize his presence everywhere. David could worship him, in all the ways of his appointment, only at Jerusalem. We can worship him everywhere. The tabernacle of our worship is wherever Christ is; and where is he not? He is the substance, of which the tabernacle of David's worship was only a shadow. Unto him we can continually betake ourselves, as our altar, our sacrifice, our Priest; and also as the Divine One, whose voice issued from between the cherubim above the mercy-seat.

VERSE 9. Gather not my soul with sinners, nor my life with bloody men.

David, so far from conspiring with the wicked to dethrone his king, desires to have nothing whatever to do with them, either in this world, or in the world to come. "Gather not my soul with sinners." These words are full of startling thought. The idea of being shut up for ever with all the outcasts of earth, is a terrible one. This, however, is the doom of every man who dies without an interest in the blood of atonement. He may have been deficient in only a single thing—faith in the Son of God—still that deficiency will consign him to the everlasting companionship of all of earth's vile and worthless, from the beginning to the end of time. We can choose our society in this world, but not in the world to come. If we die in our sins, damned spirits will be our only society; nor they only, but devils also. You recollect the Saviour's words at the day of judgment, to those on his left hand, "Depart, ye cursed, into everlasting fire, prepared for the devil and his angels." How awful the thought!—if I fail to believe on Christ, my only society in the world to come will be devils and damned spirits. Who would not, in view of the possibility of such a doom, pray, with David, "Gather not my soul with sinners"? How different will be the society of the soul that has fled for refuge from the wrath to come to the cross of Christ! Its everlasting society will be angels and archangels, and the spirits of just men made perfect.

VERSE 10. In whose hands is mischief, and their right hand is full of bribes.

David describes, in these words, the character of the sinners with whom he had to do. Saul not only sought his life with his own hand, but bribed others to seek it, and betray him into his power. 1 Sam. xxii. 6–19. In this way the Jews treated the Son of David. Failing to accomplish his death themselves, they at last bribed one of his own disciples to betray him into their hands. It is strange that goodness should have always met with such treatment at the hands of the world. Many, who understand not the inveterate wickedness of the human heart, think that virtue only needs to be presented in her own beautiful colours, to be loved and embraced by all. So an eminent Scottish divine thought, when, after depicting, in terms of glowing eloquence, the moral beauty and amiability of virtue, he closed with the following apostrophe: "O virtue, if thou wert embodied, all men would love thee." His colleague, in a subsequent part of the same day, addressing the same congregation, said: "My reverend friend observed, in the morning, that if virtue were embodied, all men would love her. *Virtue has been embodied;* but how was she treated? Did all men love her? No; she was despised and rejected of men, who, after defaming, insulting, and scourging her, led her to Calvary, where they crucified her between two thieves." The world love not to have perfect virtue presented to them—it reproves their sins too much. We all have in our hearts, by nature, the wickedness that instigated Saul to persecute David, and the Jews the Son of David. "As in water face answereth to face, so by nature the heart of man to man."

VERSE 11. But as for me, I will walk in mine integrity; redeem me, and be merciful unto me.

Whatever evil may befall him at the hands of his enemies, David determines that he will not depart from his integrity; that he will still pursue toward them the line of conduct marked out for him by the law of God; that he will not return evil for evil, but contrariwise, good. We have reason to bless God when our trials strengthen our religious principles, and confirm us in our purpose to lead a life of holy obedience. "Redeem me, and be merciful to me." Strong as David's purpose is to serve God in all holiness and pureness of living, he still flees to the Divine mercy as his only hope of entering heaven. It has been objected to this psalm that it manifests a spirit of self-righteousness. It is not so. It is a simple appeal to God, as a God of righteousness, who cannot but make a difference between the righteous and the wicked. The righteousness upon which David builds his assurance of deliverance is not *self*-righteousness. All was the gift of grace, wrought into his heart by the Divine Spirit, and manifested itself in his life through the help of the same Spirit. In pleading then, his sincerity to God, his innocency, his fervid love for the service of God, and settled purpose to walk in his ways, David was only pleading God's own work of grace in him, and he could say, as heartily as St. Paul said it, "By the grace of God I am what I am." It was not the human, but the Divine in him, that David urges. He believes that God will deliver him, because he himself has made him what he is, and will not leave his work incomplete. Surely, this is not self-righteousness.

VERSE 12. My foot standeth in an even place: in the congregations will I bless the Lord.

In the first verse of our psalm David says, "I have trusted also in the Lord, therefore I shall not slide," or, therefore may I not slide; and here, in the last verse, he proclaims his prayer answered, "My foot standeth in an even place." He is no longer like to one walking over steep and slippery places, comparable to glaciers, but like to one walking in the level and unobstructed plain. God had in some way given him the assurance that the hour of his deliverance was at hand; that his enemies would not triumph over him. Nor this only—but also that he would be restored to the religious privileges from which he had been exiled. Hence his words, "In the congregations will I bless the Lord," in the midst of his worshipping people praise him again and again for his mercies to me. It is strange with what feelings of security God can inspire the hearts of his people in the midst of the greatest dangers, and with what certainty of deliverance! David had appealed to God to judge between him and his enemies, and the case has been decided, as he hoped and believed it would be, in his favour. And in all cases of unjust treatment at the hands of others, when we can point to such facts in our lives to prove the existence of grace in our hearts, we may make the same appeal with the same assurance of a final vindication. Such facts would prove us to be children of God, and as such, entitled through grace to his fatherly protection.

LECTURE ON PSALM XXVII.

VERSE 1. The Lord is my light and my salvation, whom shall I fear? the Lord is the strength of my life, of whom shall I be afraid?

HAVING his hopes stayed upon God, it is the privilege of the believer to feel secure in the midst of the greatest dangers. Nor is there anything unreasonable in this feeling of security proceeding from confidence in the protection of God. What he hath said he will do, when faith puts any saying of his to the test. It is not fanaticism, but the highest exercise of reason, to trust in God at all times with full assurance of faith. It was not the privilege of David alone to say, in seasons of trouble and peril, "The Lord is my light and my salvation, whom shall I fear? the Lord is the strength of my life, of whom shall I be afraid?" The weakest believer in Jesus is privileged to say the same. "The Lord is my light:" he shows me the way wherein I should go. He leaves me in no doubt as to the path of duty. He shows me the dangers that threaten me, and how they are to be escaped. "The Lord is my salvation." I look to no other power for safety; and I need look to no other, for if God be for me, who or what can be against me? "The Lord is the strength of my life." He not only teaches me the way wherein I should go, and protects me in that way, but he strengthens me to pursue it to the end. "I can do all things," says St. Paul, "through Christ, which strengtheneth me." Philip. iv. 13. Trusting in Christ, as he did, I can say the same. Christ then so strengthens me by his grace, that I can defy the power of any enemy earth or hell can send against me. Christ around me, with the shield of his power, and Christ within me, by the operations of his grace, surely there is no enemy of whom I need be afraid!

VERSE 2. When the wicked, even mine enemies and my foes, came upon me to eat up my flesh, they stumbled and fell.

David here encourages himself in God, by recurring to what he had experienced at his hands in times past. He had aforetime delivered him when beset with enemies as ferocious and implacable as ravening beasts. He caused them to stumble and fall, ere they could make the fatal spring. This encourages David to believe that God will treat his present enemies in the same way. It avails greatly to the strengthening of our faith, to remember, in the midst of present trials, former deliverances. How many a trial comes upon us under the pressure of which we think we shall surely sink, which is really insignificant when compared with other trials, from which our covenant-keeping God has already time and again delivered us. How seldom would any believer in Jesus despond, if he were in the habit, in the hour of darkness, of recalling God's former dealings with him! A review of those dealings would soon convince him that God's fatherly care of him had never for a moment failed, and therefore could not fail him now.

VERSE 3. Though a host should encamp against me, my heart shall not fear; though war should rise against me, in this will I be confident.

In this, that is, even in this condition of my affairs, I will still be confident of the Divine protection and deliverance. This was no idle boast on David's part of the tranquilizing power of his faith in God. There was a time in his history when war did rise against him, led on by his own son, and a hostile host were encamped against him. But "his heart did not fear." That night he retired to rest, in the midst of the perils surrounding him, without a single anxious thought in regard to the future. He says, "I laid me down and slept; I awaked: for the Lord sustained me. I will not be afraid of ten thousands of people, that have set themselves against me round about." Ps. iii. 5, 6. David found a heart's ease in his faith, that enabled him to sleep as sweetly in the midst of dangers, as a nursing child in its mother's arms. He is not, however, the only one against whom a host has encamped and war arisen. Every believer in Jesus is surrounded by hostile forces, waging war upon him to destroy him. Wicked spirits beset him on every side, seeking his ruin. They are around him, going out and coming in, rising up and sitting down, and all the more dangerous because they are invisible. If we attempt to contend with these invisible foes in our own unaided strength, we are lost; they will surely overcome us. If, however, we meet them in the strength of God, the weakest of us may be sure of victory over the utmost efforts of the powers of darkness. A child, upheld by faith in Jesus, is more than a match for Satan with all his agents. Even the child has, in its artless faith in Christ, a shield wherewith it can quench all the fiery darts of the adversary, and with the sword of the Spirit, which is the word of God, put him to flight. This certainly is one of the mysteries of faith, that it can inspire the hearts of those possessing it with supernatural heroism, a fearlessness of the utmost that finite power can do to them. Assured that God is their light and their salvation, they can, whatever threatens, smile at the thought that any evil will be allowed to overcome them.

VERSE 4. One thing have I desired of the Lord, that will I seek after; that I may dwell in the house of the Lord all the days of my life, to behold the beauty of the Lord, and to inquire in his temple.

We here learn the value David set upon the worship of God. The great object of his desires was that he might "dwell in the house of the Lord all the days of his life, to behold the beauty of the Lord, and to inquire in his temple." We understand by these words, "the beauty of the Lord," the revelation of his character contained in the laws of Moses and the rites and ceremonies of the tabernacle. Those laws and ceremonies presented the Supreme Being to the mind of the diligent inquirer in a light of transcendent moral beauty. They shadowed forth the whole gospel scheme of human salvation. Christ, more or less veiled, was in every one of its services. And it is hardly to be supposed that David did not see him there, in some measure as we see him, with the veil removed by the explanations of the New Testament. If he did, the insight must have revealed the Supreme Being to his mind as the gospel reveals him to ours, as a God of *love.* If he saw Christ in the law, and Christ in the ceremony, every part of the worship of God's house must have been to his mind luminous with mercy. Hence the fervour of his desires to engage in that worship. It is evidence of spiritual declension, when we do not hunger and thirst after communion with God in the ways of his appointment, and do not pant after a deeper insight into his character and ways. The strongest desire of David's heart, and the great effort of his life, was to learn more and more of Him.

VERSE 5. For in the time of trouble he shall hide me in his pavilion: in the secret of his tabernacle shall he hide me: he shall set me up upon a rock.

Who would not sing, as we do, in one of our metrical psalms,

"Lord, for ever at thy side
Let my place and portion be,"

when being near him ensures us such protection as David here describes? "In the time of trouble he shall hide me in his pavilion." He will treat me as an inmate of his house, and as a member of his family. "In the secret of his tabernacle shall he hide me." He shall keep me as far from all profane approach as he keeps the holy of holies, which none but the high priest dare to enter, and he only on one

29*

day in the year. God's pavilion surrounding and overshadowing the believer, is his omnipotent, omnipresent love. The secret place of his tabernacle, in which he gives the believer refuge, is his saving mercy in Christ. "He set me up upon a rock." None can feel the full force of this imagery of the rock, who are not familiar with the mountain scenery of Judea, where there are rocks towering into the skies like impregnable castles, gaining whose summit, any one can defy the power of the world to harm him. The rock, however, upon which the Lord had set David's feet was none of these, but the "Rock of Ages."

VERSE 6. And now shall my head be lifted up above mine enemies round about me: therefore will I offer in his tabernacle sacrifices of joy; I will sing, yea, I will sing praises unto the Lord.

Behold the power of unfeigned faith in God. Though David was surrounded by enemies on every side, he was as sure of deliverance as if he had already obtained it. "And now shall mine head be lifted up above mine enemies." He does not speak of his deliverance as a thing that *may* be, but as a thing that *shall* be. "Therefore will I offer in his tabernacle sacrifices of joy; I will sing, yea, I will sing praises unto the Lord." He speaks of his return to the house of God as if there was not an obstacle in his way. He who is humbly trusting for salvation to the mercy of the Lord in Christ, need not fear that he will not return and come to Zion, with songs and everlasting joy upon his head. Redeeming love, whatever creature power may oppose him, will surely bring him to his Father's house at last. His Rock will not fail him. "I am weakness itself," said a dying believer, "but I am on the Rock. I do not feel those transports which some have expressed in view of death; but my dependence is on the mercy of God in Christ; here my religion began, and here it must end." "And now, death, strike!" said another dying believer, after saying, "Christ in his person, Christ in the love of his heart, and Christ in the power of his arm, is the Rock upon which I rest." How far above all enemies, even above death itself, does it lift our heads, for God to set us up upon the rock of everlasting strength which he has provided for us in his Son!

VERSE 7. Hear, O Lord, when I cry with my voice: have mercy also upon me, and answer me.

The true believer rejoices with trembling. So long as he considers only the power of his Protector, he can use the language of the previous part of this psalm, "Whom shall I fear? of whom shall I be afraid?" The moment, however, he thinks of his own weakness and liability to fall, words of confidence and triumph are exchanged for words of prayer. Though the Lord had set David upon a rock, he felt that he was safe there only so long as the Lord kept him there.

VERSE 8. When thou saidst, Seek ye my face; my heart said unto thee, Thy face, Lord, will I seek.

David's heart here echos back God's own words. "Seek ye my face," are the words—"thy face, Lord, will I seek," their echo. It is well for us when every precept and promise of God finds a resonance in the heart. It is evidence that the same Spirit that inspired the word, has renewed the heart. We need not fear when the Spirit in the word, and the Spirit in our hearts, speak the same thing, each lovingly answering the utterances of the other.

VERSE 9. Hide not thy face far from me; put not thy servant away in anger: thou hast been my help; leave me not, neither forsake me, O God of my salvation.

David's faith is not so strong as it was. There is in this place a blending of fear with it. He fears the hiding of God's face, hastens to remind him that he is his servant, and craves his protection as such. The Lord had hitherto been his helper and the God of his salvation, and he prays that, being his servant, he would be such to him still. This making one's being the servant of the Lord a ground of prayer is well conceived. The Lord maketh a difference between him that serveth God and him that serveth him not. None can fail of the Divine protection who are humbly endeavouring to serve God in simplicity and godly sincerity. If such be the testimony of our conscience, we need have no fears that he will forsake us. He would not be himself were he to do so.

VERSE 10. When my father and my mother forsake me, then the Lord will take me up.

The love of God, it has been said, is the only love that is sure, in heaven, or on earth; the love of men disappears on the approach of misfortune, in which they recognize a dispensation to renounce love. But God shows his love to his people most tenderly when they are in affliction. He says to the soul that hopes in his mercy, and endeavours to serve him, "Can a woman forget her sucking child, that she should not have compassion on the son of her womb? yea, they may forget, yet will I not forget thee." Isa. xlix. 15. It is to this love of God, tenderer and more enduring than that of a mother, to which David refers in the words, "When my father and my mother forsake me, then the Lord will take me up." What a cordial should this be to the believer, in times of trouble—though all other loves should fail him, the love of God will not!

VERSE 11. Teach me thy way, O Lord, and lead me in a plain path, because of mine enemies.

When brought into difficulties, we cannot too soon, nor too earnestly, pray God to show us the right way out of them. This is what David does here. Hostile eyes were upon him, and he prays that he may be so guided by the Divine grace and providence, that even his enemies shall not be able to lay, except falsely, any sin to his charge. This should be the aim of every believer: "Teach me thy way, O Lord." It is not to my own strength and wisdom that I look for deliverance, but to thine. I would use no means of escape but such as are sanctioned by the teachings of thy word. God's way for the believer to walk in, is the way of his laws.

VERSE 12. Deliver me not over unto the will of mine enemies; for false witnesses are risen up against me, and such as breathe out cruelty.

False witnesses would ruin him by false accusations, and those that breathed out cruelty, by open violence. Against these two sorts of enemies, false and cruel, both David and the Son of David had to contend. And every believer's danger is like theirs. If we are not surrounded by open, avowed, and visible enemies, we are at least surrounded by invisible ones, equally powerful, and more dangerous to the soul. Satan and his hosts surround us; and, worst of all, we each have a treacherous heart within, ready to betray us into their power. We cannot pray too often, not to be delivered over to the will of such enemies, for God alone can rescue us out of their hands.

VERSE 13. I had fainted, unless I had believed to see the goodness of the Lord in the land of the living.

The only thing that kept David from despair in his troubles, was his still believing that he would yet "see the goodness of the Lord;" that the Lord would in due time deliver him. It was believing this that encouraged him to pray without ceasing. It was also believing this that enabled him at last to exclaim, "The Lord is my light and my salvation, whom shall I fear? the Lord is the strength of my life; of whom shall I be afraid?" If faith in God had not sustained him, he had been lost; but being steadfast in faith, his sorrow was in time turned into joy, his prayers into praise, and his fears of an overthrow into a song of triumph.

VERSE 14. Wait on the Lord; be of good courage, and he shall strengthen thine heart: wait, I say, on the Lord.

Here is David's grand recipe for all troubles—*waiting on the Lord*—waiting on him in faith, and prayer, and humble submission to his will. Troubled believer, let no delays discourage thee; let no apparent denials dishearten thee. Hope on, hope ever; pray on, pray ever; trust on, trust ever. Be not in haste to suppose that God has forgotten thee, because he does not come to thy relief at once. Such is the import of David's words in the last verse of our psalm. They teach us a lesson that we cannot learn too thoroughly, that we should never cease seeking the favour of God till we have obtained it. It was thus that David sought: he renewed his suit continually, till the blessing came. It was thus, too, that the Syrophenician mother, seeking relief for her poor, tormented daughter, urged her suit. At first not only denied, but apparently repulsed, she still persevered; only becoming more importunate as her case seemed more hopeless, till at last the blessing came, with the words, "O woman, great is thy faith: be it unto thee even as thou wilt." Matt. xv. 28. "Wait (then) on the Lord; be of good courage, and he shall strengthen thy heart: wait, I say, on the Lord." Wait on him in faith, and prayer, and humble submission, and he will, in his own good and best time, enable you also to say from the heart, "The Lord is my light and my salvation, whom shall I fear? the Lord is the strength of my life; of whom shall I be afraid?"

LECTURE ON PSALM XXVIII.

VERSE 1. Unto thee will I cry, O Lord, my Rock; be not silent to me: lest, if thou be silent to me, I become like them that go down into the pit.

THIS psalm so nearly resembles the twenty-seventh, that it was, as many think, probably written on the same occasion. Both contain the same complaints of enemies seeking the writer's destruction by force and fraud, violence and treachery. Both contain also the same earnest cries to God for deliverance, the same confident expectation that it will be granted, and the same praise and thanksgiving for the blessing vouchsafed. Each seems very much like an echo and resonance of the other, and the latter to have been written to deepen the impression supposed to have been made by the former. The words,

"Unto thee will I cry, O Lord, my Rock," indicate the stability of the strength upon which David relied. It was not in human strength, not in angelic strength he trusted, but in the Lord. Jehovah was his rock of hope. The rock continues the same from generation to generation; what it was thousands of years ago, the same it is to-day. It is the same with the Lord in the strength and immutability of his purpose to save those hoping in his mercy. He is of one mind, and changes not in his eternal purpose to make a difference between the righteous and the wicked. It is this upon which David bases his hope and prayer. The thought of this eternal purpose inspires the prayer, "be not silent to me; lest if thou be silent to me, I become like them that go down into the pit." It is an easy matter to move God to do for us, when we can plead his own attributes and purposes as the basis of our prayers. Himself righteous, he cannot fail to deliver those who hunger and thirst after righteousness. He may, for the trial of their faith and the purification of their hearts, leave them to contend with their enemies, visible and invisible, till they seem to themselves ready to perish; but at the right time the long silence will be broken, and a saving answer returned to their cry.

VERSE 2. Hear the voice of my supplications, when I cry unto thee; when I lift up my hands toward thy holy oracle.

Lifting up the hands as an attitude of prayer, was at one time general, perhaps universal, throughout the world, and symbolized the lifting up of the heart to God. The lifting up of holy hands indicates the worshipping God with a pure heart fervently. This is what David does here. Every movement of his body is instinct with the intensity of his desires.

He lifts up his hands toward God's holy oracle—toward the mercy-seat in the holy of holies. He expects mercy only upon the terms dictated by the Voice speaking there from between the cherubim. There he approached Deity enshrined in the luminous cloud, and placable through the blood of atonement. Deity did there, as it were, embody himself, so that his worshippers could not only hear his voice, but actually see the source whence it came. But how dim an embodiment of Deity was the *shekinah* in the holy of holies, when compared with his embodiment of himself in Christ! Dazzlingly bright as the *shekinah* in the holy of holies was, it was but the shadow of God as he has revealed himself to us in Christ! Christ is God's holy oracle indeed, in whom, having taken up his abode, he manifests all his attributes, and through whom we can lift up our hands to God with full assurance of faith. How delightful the voice proceeding from God in Christ, "Come unto me, all ye that labour and are are heavy laden, and I will give you rest!" If it were a joy to the Israelite to lift up his hands to God enshrined in the holy of holies, how much greater joy should it be to us to lift up our hands to him enshrined in Christ, and rendered for ever placable by an atonement that cleanseth us from all sin, and exalts us to everlasting life!

VERSE 3. Draw me not away with the wicked and with the workers of iniquity, which speak peace to their neighbours, but mischief is in their hearts.

"Draw me not away." These words refer to the practice in the East of dragging away to execution those who have been condemned to capital punishment. David prays that their lot and doom may not be his. Conscious of no fellowship with the wicked and the workers of iniquity, he deprecates being made a partaker of their punishment. Happy the man who can appeal to the Searcher of hearts to bear witness that he has no sympathy with evil and evil-doers. Many countenance the wickedness in which they will not openly engage. They love the sin, and are deterred from its commission only by the fear of the accruing penalty. It was not so with David. He hated sin in every form, and would have avoided it if there had been no punishment attached to its commission. The temper of his mind was morally averse to it.

"Which speak peace to their neighbours, but mischief is in their hearts." These words describe the sort of wicked workers of iniquity with whom David had to do. They were wretched dissemblers, men who, while making loud professions of friendship, were at the same time secretly plotting his ruin. There were fair words on their lips, but mischief was in their hearts. Conscious of no such duplicity and insincerity towards them as they were practising towards him, David prays that the blow of Divine vengeance, which would in time reach them, might not reach him. The argument of his prayer is this, namely, that as there was no identity of character between himself and the wicked of whom he speaks, so there should be no identity of doom. On this same ground we too may pray not to be identified with the wicked in their doom. We cannot, however, be too careful not to utter with our lips what we do not feel in our hearts. Insincerity is the most detestable of vices, and the dissembler the most detestable of characters. He flatters, only to destroy.

VERSE 4. Give them according to their deeds, and according to the wickedness of their endeavours; give them after the work of their hands; render to them their desert.

This is strict justice that David here prays for his enemies; that they should be judged not only for their deeds, but also for their endeavours; not only for what they had actually *done*, but also for what they had only *attempted* to do. It is even so. As a man thinketh in his heart, so is he. Prov. xxiii. 7. The evil purpose, the wicked attempt, even where it fails, is punishable in the sight of God. There is many a murderer who never gave a blow. It is the *heart* that commits the sin, not the hand. Whoever gains his own consent to do an evil deed, if opportunity offers, has, in the sight of God, already involved himself in the guilt of it. God will judge us for the thoughts of the heart as well as for our deeds; for our endeavours, as well as for our wicked purposes accomplished. David then prayed for what is consonant with the known will and purpose of God, when he prayed that the incorrigibly wicked might be dealt with according to their deeds, and according to their endeavours. But some over-critical readers of the Bible profess to dislike David's praying for the destruction of his enemies. They forget that he does not pray for their destruction as his own *personal* enemies, but only as the enemies of truth and order in the earth, for the defence of which he had been set by the God of truth and order. No other man, except the man Christ Jesus, was so forgiving of his personal enemies as David was. It was for the destruction of the enemies of his country and of his God that he prayed, and justly too, as we may do, and should do, if such were to come against us to cast us down. There, is however, another answer to this objection to David's prayer. The structure of the language in which it was originally written does not necessarily require David's words to be understood as a prayer, but only as a *prediction*, a prediction that God will not let the wicked go unpunished. And what can be more certain than this, that God does give the incorrigibly wicked according to their deeds, and according to the wickedness of their endeavours? The meting out to them their desert may be long delayed, but it is sure to come at last. God so administers the moral government of the world, that every unrighteous blow aimed at another, sooner or later recoils on him who gave it.

VERSE 5. Because they regard not the works of the Lord, nor the operations of his hands, he shall destroy them, and not build them up.

We have here as a simple prediction, what seems in the preceding verse to be a prayer, namely, that God *will* destroy the wicked, and not build them up. And here, moreover, we have the reason assigned for his destroying them, "Because they regard not the works of the Lord, nor the operations of his hands." David prayed in the preceding verse, then, if pray he did, and not simply predict, that God would do only that which he will do, and must do, as the righteous Governor of the world; that is, destroy all those who are not deterred from sin by the teachings of his providence. It needs not the voice of revelation to teach us that the way of the transgressor is hard, that the sinner's sin will surely find him out. The history of individuals and of nations shows that no one can sin with impunity. If men disregard this great fact, they precipitate themselves upon destruction.

They are crushed before the movements of the Divine Providence, because they throw themselves in the way of those movements. They are blind to the fact, which a moment's reflection would teach them, that none can contend against the Almighty and not perish. To illustrate the truth of this remark we need not refer to the extreme case of the royal butcher of thirty thousand Huguenots, Charles the Ninth of France, who, bathed in his own blood, which burst from his veins, died, exclaiming, "What blood!—what murders!—I know not where I am!—how will all this end?—what shall I do?—I am lost for ever!—I know it!" It requires no such extreme case as this to prove that God visits the opposers of his truth with his vengeance. His vengeance overtakes not only those who oppose, but also those who do not embrace his truth in the love of it, and do all they can to promote a dissemination of it among the destitute of the earth. He that is not with Christ, is against him.

VERSE 6. Blessed be the Lord, because he hath heard the voice of my supplications.

It was not in vain that David cried, "Hear the voice of my supplications when I cry unto thee, when I lift up my hands toward thy holy oracle." The Lord has heard the voice of his supplications, and here he blesses him for it. It is strange how suddenly God can turn the darkest night into the brightest day, the deepest sorrow into the highest joy, the saddest notes of despondency into songs of triumph. He speaks, and it is done!—light and joy and full assurance of victory flood the soul. Thus it happened to one of our English martyrs. For several days previous to his execution, he was overwhelmed with the prospect of martyrdom, and continued so overwhelmed until he came within sight of the stake where he was to be burned, when, all of a sudden, his whole soul was so filled with light and heavenly consolation, that he could not forbear clasping his hands, and crying out, "He is come, he is come!" In some such way as this, and quite as suddenly, perhaps, light and consolation seem to have been poured into the soul of the psalmist. One moment we hear his impassioned cry for help; the next, "Blessed be the Lord, for he hath heard the voice of my supplications." He feels assured that his enemies shall not triumph over him, and that the cause of truth and righteousness will prevail.

VERSE 7. The Lord is my strength and my shield; my heart trusted in him, and I am helped: therefore my heart greatly rejoiceth; and with my song will I praise him.

His whole nation and his own son are supposed to have been arrayed against David at this time, while he was surrounded by a mere handful of weak and weeping followers; nevertheless, his heart did not fear: on the contrary, he says, "My heart greatly rejoiceth; and with my song will I praise the Lord." David reveals the secret of his joy and singing—the Lord was his strength and his shield. He was assured that the everlasting arms were round him. He knew that such faith, and hope, and confidence as he felt throbbing in his heart, God alone could have inspired, and that he had not inspired them to disappoint them. O what songs God can put into the mouth of the believer in the night, if he steadfastly trusts in him! The human heart can experience no sorrow which he cannot cure, and fill it with a joy unspeakable and full of glory.

VERSE 8. The Lord is their strength, and he is the saving strength of his anointed.

The help vouchsafed to David was vouchsafed also to his few faithful followers. The Lord was their strength also. God had poured the same spirit of confident and joyous faith into the heart of his still loyal subjects, that he had poured into the heart of his anointed, into the heart of David their king. They were few in number, but strong in faith; they feared not the world in arms against them. What a prodigy of courage and heroism can faith in God make of weak and timid man! Once Peter cowered before the browbeating of a silly maid, and was driven by it to deny his Master, with oaths and execrations; but afterwards, when the Divine Spirit had poured into his heart that most excellent gift, Divine faith, he did not fear to stand up, and charge his whole nation with having murdered the Holy One of Israel. And the same most excellent gift wrought the same transformations in all the apostles. Once they all forsook their Master, and fled; but no sooner had power descended into their souls from on high, than they no longer knew what fear was. They smiled at what man could do to them; they feared nothing but sin. Let us all pray earnestly, and without ceasing, that this same power from on high may descend into our souls, that we too may fear nothing but sin.

VERSE 9. Save thy people, and bless thine inheritance: feed them also, and lift them up for ever.

The believer never prays only for himself. What he craves for himself, he craves for the whole Israel of God. The spirit of true prayer is not a selfish spirit, but embraces all, in the fervour of its desires.

It is a spirit that identifies the individual with the mass, and causes him to sympathize with the whole. Hence David's prayer, "Save thy people, and bless thine inheritance: feed them also, and lift them up for ever." He was not satisfied with being blessed himself, unless the whole family were blessed with him. Indeed, David seems to have desired life for himself, only that he might be useful to the Church of God; as we read elsewhere, "If I forget thee, O Jerusalem, let my right hand forget her cunning. If I do not remember thee, let my tongue cleave to the roof of my mouth; if I prefer not Jerusalem above my chief joy." Ps. cxxxvii. 5, 6.

Do we love the Church of God more than we love all things else? Do we reckon life valuable, and to be desired, only as a means of promoting the glory of God in the salvation of others? Is it our prayer, as we lie down at night, and again as we rise in the morning, "Thy kingdom come"? And do we embody this prayer into our lives? Do we pursue even our secular callings altogether in subserviency to this great end? In short, is the glory of God in the salvation of the world, the governing motive of everything we do? It should be, it will be, if our hearts are in the right place. It is vain to think ourselves Christians, if we do not prefer the service of God above our chief joy. "Save thy people, and bless thine heritage; govern them, and lift them up for ever," comes as words of mockery from our lips, when we do not co-operate with God in accomplishing the work which we pray him to do. Our very profession makes us co-workers with God in establishing his kingdom in the earth. He works through human agents and human agencies, and no man alive is exempt from doing his best to advance the cause of truth and righteousness. May God give us all grace to love his cause as he loves it, with the whole heart. So he loves it, so his Son loves it, and so we should love it.

LECTURE ON PSALM XXIX.

THIS twenty-ninth psalm describes all the phenomena of a violent thunder-storm. It gives us the storm in all its parts, and in the order in which they naturally occur. It is worthy of remark, too, that the psalm is strictly *geographical* in its structure. The region of country over which the storm passes, is described with the utmost accuracy. It rises in the Mediterranean, away to the north of Judea, and sweeps, in its course, along the mountains lying on either side the Jordan, until it reaches Jerusalem and the regions south of it. We may, therefore, conceive of the writer of this majestic ode, as standing, with an awe-stricken multitude, on the mount where the temple afterwards stood, and watching the storm as it rises, and every step of its onward progress, until, having passed over the sacred mountain without doing it any harm, it passes on to regions farther south. "Rightly to appreciate the feelings of David on such an occasion, one ought," Tholuck writes, "to realize an oriental storm, especially in the mountainous regions of Palestine, which, accompanied by the terrific echoes of the encircling mountains, by torrents of rain like water-spouts, often scatters terror on man and beast, destruction on cities and fields." "I was overtaken," writes a traveller in the holy land, "by a storm, as if the flood-gates of heaven had burst: it came on in a moment, and raged with a power which suggested the end of the world. Solemn darkness covered the earth: the rain descended in torrents, and sweeping down the mountain side, became by the fearful power of the storm, transmuted into thick clouds of fog." It was a storm of this sort, whose winds and floods beat upon and swept away the foolish man's house that had been built upon the sand. On witnessing then a storm so grand, so sublime, and so awful, as the one he here describes, and so indicative of the irresistible might of Him who sent and directed it, David could with propriety open this psalm only as he does, saying,

VERSE 1. Give unto the Lord, O ye mighty, give unto the Lord glory and strength.

The thought that this God, whose power is so conspicuous in the thunder-storm, is his God, and therefore his Guardian and Protector, so fills his soul with love and holy enthusiasm, that he is not satisfied with his own solitary praise of him, but calls upon the mighty, the sons of Elohim, to join him in his song. He makes a similar call in the one hundred and third psalm, where, after calling upon his soul and all that is within him to bless the Lord for all his mercies to him, he breaks forth, "Bless the Lord, ye his angels, that excel in strength, that do his commandments, hearkening unto the voice of his word. Bless the Lord, all ye his hosts; ye ministers of his that do his pleasure." The believer whose heart is a-glow with the love of God, a love kindled by a vivid perception of his greatness and power, longs to see everything that hath breath praisng the Lord; and especially to see higher and holier natures doing it. If there be a creature in the universe higher than any other, that creature he would engage in His praise, that creature the believer would invoke to raise its song of praise and adoration in heaven itself. This longing of the loving and adoring soul to have angels join it in its song and swell its strains, proves that the family in heaven and the family on earth are indeed but one. It is a beautiful illustration of what we in part mean by "the communion of saints," that every holy being in the universe sympathizes with every other holy being, and would make it a sharer in its joys and praises of God.

VERSE 2. Give unto the Lord the glory due unto his name: worship the Lord in the beauty of holiness.

To give unto the Lord the glory due unto his name, is to render him the homage and worship that his character demands: a character glorious in holiness, fearful in praises. For his infinite power, under the guidance of his infinite love and wisdom, the angels are exhorted to worship the Lord in the beauty of holiness; with reverence and godly fear. "In the beauty of holiness;" or, in holy attire, for so the original may be rendered. There is an allusion to the law requiring the priests of the earthly temple to clothe themselves in *holy garments*, before engaging in the worship of God. So, too, the worshippers in the heavenly temple, when they come before the Lord, to adore him for the glorious manifestations of his omnipotence, should do it with no ordinary thoughts and feelings, but only with those of the profoundest reverence and holy awe. This they should do, because his omnipotence can invest his holiness, his justice, and his truth, with the whole of its power, and is therefore to be feared, as well as adored. Nor is David's appeal to the celestial choir to join him in rendering unto the Lord the glory due unto his name, unauthorized by the word of God. It assures us that the angels in heaven feel a lively interest in all the manifestations of the Divine power upon the earth. They watch every movement of his here below, with an interest that never flags. Isaiah tells us that the seraphim standing around the throne of God, cry one to another, in never-ending chorus, "Holy, holy, holy, is the Lord of hosts: the whole earth is full of his glory." Isa. vi. 3. It is not in the manifestations of his glory in the heavens only, that cherubim and seraphim, angel and archangel rejoice, but they rejoice also in the manifestations of his glory upon the earth. They are deeply interested in every movement of the Divine power.

VERSE 3. The voice of the Lord is upon the waters: the God of glory thundereth; the Lord is upon many waters.

Here is the beginning of the storm, whose power and sublimity David invocates the heavenly host to join him in celebrating. "The voice of the Lord is (heard) upon the waters:" afar off over the sea, the storm-cloud is reverberating with his thunders. Distant thunder is in some respects more sublime than thunder that is crashing around us. Distance so blends its separate peals, that they strike the ear as almost one continued sound; comparatively low, it may be, but with a power that makes the very earth under our feet, as well as the atmosphere around us, tremble, as if shuddering in conscious terror at its approach. It seems indeed as the voice of Omnipotence sounding from afar; and David's words, "the God of glory thundereth; the Lord is upon many waters," are words that would spring spontaneously to the lips of every intelligent listener. It would require no great force of imagination to conceive of a storm thus shaking, even while afar off, earth and air, also the waters above the firmament, and the waters below it, as being the voice of an approaching God.

VERSE 4. The voice of the Lord is powerful; the voice of the Lord is full of majesty.

Here the psalmist is supposed to describe the deafening roar and din of elements, as the storm advances, increasing in strength and fury more and more, as it spreads over the heavens. Its peals of thunder are no longer blended as into one, but, however rapidly they succeed each other, each peal is heard by itself, and fills the mind of the listener with overwhelming thoughts of the power and majesty of Him who gave it its voice. Louder and yet louder at every moment, as the storm-cloud, with its many waters, advances upon the wings of the wind, it gives the beholder an idea of the strength of God, that no other words than David's own can describe, "The voice of the Lord is in power; the voice of the Lord is full of majesty."

VERSE 5. The voice of the Lord breaketh the cedars; yea, the Lord breaketh the cedars of Lebanon.

The storm, having hitherto manifested itself only over the sea and in the skies, here, in this verse, descends to the earth, sweeping first the mountains in its course. It sweeps, first of all, Mount Lebanon, situated at the head-waters of the Jordan, and evinces its irresistible power in the trees it prostrates, even "the cedars of Lebanon." There is an emphasis in mentioning the cedars of Lebanon as the trees that the storm prostrated. Their size, and strength, and towering height, are almost incredible to one who has not seen them. Travellers tell us that there are cedars still standing, whose girth around the trunk, a few feet above the ground, is twenty, thirty, and even forty feet. A traveller mentions one, whose circumference he found, upon measurement, four feet above the ground, to be forty-seven feet. A single branch of this tree was ninety feet in length. He also writes that the trunks of five of the largest trees consisted of three or four divisions, or, as we call them, forks, each of which equalled in circumference the stem of our largest oaks. Indeed, there are accounts of cedars of Lebanon still larger—of one, forty-nine, and of another sixty-three feet in circumference. This was the kind of tree that bent and broke before the fury of the storm. Its blast brought the stateliest of them to the ground, broken in pieces. Such, in the Hebrew, is the import of the second "breaketh" of our translation. It is a stronger word than the first "breaketh." The second "breaketh" is also, in the original, not in the *present*, but in the *past* tense, as if there were no appreciable interval of time between the beginning and the end of the complete destruction wrought by the storm. Rendered literally, the verse reads, "He is breaking—he hath *broken*, the cedars of Lebanon."

VERSE 6. He maketh them also to skip like a calf; Lebanon and Sirion like a young unicorn.

To one standing, during the storm, in the valley between them, the mountains, Lebanon and Sirion, seem to be alive, and under the most rapid onward motion. Inanimate things are fleeing before the storm, sweeping them, like the fleetest of living creatures. Lebanon and Sirion, called also Libanus and Anti-Libanus, are two parallel ranges of mountains, east of the Mediterranean, extending from their northern extremities some sixty miles south, to the northern boundary of Palestine. From north to south, along these two parallel ranges of mountains, separated from each other by only a narrow valley, the storm here described rages in terrific power and majesty; the trees broken, or torn up and prostrated by its violence, are seen whirling onward, as if fleeing in fright before it, like wild, affrighted animals, running for their lives. The animals to whose flight the rapid movements of the trees are compared, are among the fleetest known—supposed to be the antelope and the unicorn.

VERSE 7. The voice of the Lord divideth the flames of fire.

Here another element is introduced, to add to the power and terror of the storm: the voice of the Lord is armed with forked lightnings. He divideth the flames, the electric fires with which his clouds are everywhere charged, so that they seem as myriads of burning arrows shot from a bow that never misses its mark. They smite, rive, prostrate, and consume what the winds had spared. They light up the whole scene, too, with a light that is truly appaling; now here, now there, now gone, and now flashing upon us again with overwhelming and blinding effulgence.

VERSE 8. The voice of the Lord shaketh the wilderness; the Lord shaketh the wilderness of Kadesh.

Having traversed the whole length of the Libanus and Anti-Libanus ranges of mountains to the borders of Palestine—indeed, the whole length of the valley of the Jordan, from its northern to its southern extremity, including the Dead Sea, and regions south of it, but seeming, in its passage through the holy land, and over the holy mountain, to have done *them* no harm, the storm here in this verse is described as shaking the wilderness of Kadesh. This wilderness, the northern portion of the great Arabian desert, and the southern boundary of the holy land, is one of the wildest in the world. Moses speaks of it as the great and terrible wilderness, where were serpents, and scorpions, and drought—a desert land, and a waste howling wilderness. Here, in this wilderness, the storm is now manifesting its power; its naked rocks, stinted growths, and barren wastes, shake and tremble as the storm passes over them. This is the wilderness to which Elijah fled to escape the wrath of Jezebel, and while there, standing upon one of its mountains, "Behold, the Lord passed by, and a great and strong wind rent the mountains, and brake in pieces the rocks before the Lord." 1 Kings xix. 11. A violent thunder-storm at sea, or in a wilderness, where all is waste, is perhaps more terrific than in any other place. The absence of everything but that which is as wild as its own turmoil, renders it appaling indeed.

VERSE 9. The voice of the Lord maketh the hinds to calve, and discovereth the forests: and in his temple doth every one speak of his glory.

Here the scene of the storm is changed from the mountains and wilderness to the densely and heavily wooded forests, the abode of gentle deer, which become so affrighted at its din, and roar, and desolation, that they cast their young before the time. That man, having a guilty conscience, should fear and

and tremble at the voice of God in the storm, is not at all surprising. But that innocent, irrational creatures should fear and tremble—relax in every nerve and muscle that binds their bodies together, is certainly a thing to excite our wonder. Knowing no sin, no judgment, no second death, why should they tremble and be in pain? Their doing so bespeaks the power of the voice of God in the storm as hardly anything else can. That voice, we also read, "discovereth the forests"—that is, strips them of their attire, leaves them destitute of limbs and foliage, and makes their darkest recesses bright as day. Strange! He that tempers the wind to the shorn lamb, sends also the tempest and the tornado, the lightning and the storm, before which the strongest things of even inanimate nature cannot stand for an instant!

"And in his temple doth every one speak of his glory!" This is spoken of God's upper temple; beholding such manifestations of his power on earth, every one there ejaculates, Glory! David, in the first and second verses of our psalm, had invoked the angelic hosts, the mighty ones of God, standing around his throne in heaven, to join him in his song of praise; and this is their universal answer—Glory! Glory! they ejaculated as the storm commenced—Glory! as it advanced—and Glory! rising no doubt to a higher note and a more swelling chorus, when it had ceased, and the earth smiled again in renewed beauty beneath unclouded skies and a beaming sun! David, however, carries the mind beyond the power of God as manifested in the storm, for he adds,

VERSE 10. The Lord sitteth upon the flood; yea, the Lord sitteth King for ever.

The verb *sitteth* in the first clause of this verse,

is, in the original, not in the present but in the past tense—"the Lord *sat* upon the flood." The allusion is to his presiding over the storms and agitations of the deluge. The deluge was not a storm of a few hours' continuance only, and of limited extent, but a storm that raged over the whole earth for a twelve month. Nevertheless, its winds, and waters, and electric fires were at every moment under the Divine control. He still and always held its winds in his fist, its waters in the hollow of his hand, and so directed its lightnings that none but his enemies perished, while his friends escaped unharmed. It was seeing him continually ruling in the storm, but most of all, seeing him ruling over the deluge, that convinced David that the Lord sitteth King for ever; that he presideth always, everywhere, and over all things with a power which none can resist, and not perish; and yet a power in which none can trust, and not be safe. This is still more clearly expressed in the next and last verse of our psalm, which reads,

VERSE 11. The Lord will give strength unto his people; the Lord will bless his people with peace.

Why, it may be asked, did David write this psalm—this magnificent description of a thunder-storm? Not to display his poetical powers, although in all that belongs to descriptive poetry it surpasses everything of the kind ever sketched by human pen—how vivid its painting, how vigorous its conceptions, how rapid its transitions!—yet David did not write it to display his poetical powers, but to depict the irresistible power of God, and thereby to show us how vain a thing it is for man to oppose him, and how safe to trust in him. This is the golden thread that runs through the whole; the one great thought with which he would deter us from sin, and bind us to the throne of God. "The Lord is strong, and he will give strength to his people." The Lord is strong, and he will use his strength to protect and bless his people for ever. That is the thought that pervades the whole. The voice that "breaketh the cedars of Lebanon; that maketh the mountains to skip like a young unicorn; that shaketh the wilderness of Kadesh;" that maketh irrational creatures labour with premature pains; that strippeth the forests of their attire, and sendeth forked lightnings to every part of the heavens and of the earth in an instant—*that* voice is only the voice of a Father to all those who have forsaken their sins, and taken refuge in the mercy of the Lord in Christ. All *His* power is *theirs*, theirs to protect and bless them for ever. The great question then for us to settle is, the relation in which we stand to this great Being whose voice is so powerful. Are we his, and is he ours? Is his law written in our hearts, and exemplified in our lives? The time is coming when his voice will shake, not Lebanon only, and Sirion, and the wilderness of Kadesh, but the whole heavens and the whole earth, removing them out of their places as he descends to judgment. Does his Spirit bear testimony with and to our spirits that we shall then meet him in peace?—meet him as our God and Friend?

It has been mentioned, that though the storm passed through the holy land and over the holy mount, it seemed to have done them no harm. And what, do you suppose, robbed it of all its power to do any harm on the holy mountain? *The blood of atonement flowing there!* And that blood alone, beloved reader, can save you or me. Moreover, there is but one place in the universe where that blood has flowed, consequently but one place in the universe where you can be safe—and that is upon Calvary—sin-atoning, wrath-averting Calvary. There only is there any safety for you from the storm of final wrath. But standing upon that mount, dyed in blood that flowed from Immanuel's veins, you, and all standing there with you, will escape unscathed a storm that will sweep away the whole word beside, and never end!

LECTURE ON PSALM XXX.

The title of this psalm reads, "A psalm and song of the dedication of the house of David." This is evidently an incorrect reading. It should read, "A psalm of David: a song of the dedication of the house." The house at whose dedication this song was sung, was not any house of David's, but Mount Moriah, the piece of ground divinely selected as the place whereon the temple, *the house of God*, should be subsequently built. Of this ground David himself says, having erected thereon only an altar unto the Lord, "This is the house of the Lord God, and this is the altar of the burnt-offering for Israel." 1 Chron. xxii. 1. It was an open space, yet David speaks of it as the house of the Lord God. Jacob, too, in speaking of a place—though it had no covering but the skies—where God had made special manifestation of his character to him, says of it,

"This is none other but the house of God, and this is the gate of heaven." Gen. xxviii. 17. The history of our psalm will, however, make it plain to every one, at the consecration of what house this song was sung. Its history is recorded in the twenty-fourth chapter of the second book of Samuel; also in the twenty-first chapter of the first book of Chronicles, and the first verse of the twenty-second chapter. David had fallen into a state of great spiritual declension during the long prosperity with which he had been blessed. He had, in a great measure, forgotten that the Lord was his strength, and was looking to the multitude of his people as his great reliance and defence. He had evidently become proud and vainglorious in spirit, and, being in this mood, Satan was permitted, in order to punish him for his own sin and his people for theirs, (see 2 Sam. xxiv. 1,) to move him to take the census of his people, in order to ascertain his military strength, how many soldiers he could upon an emergency bring into the field. This was distrusting the power of Him who is able to save by few as well as by many, and was, besides, virtually rejecting him as being specially the God and protector of Israel. No sooner, therefore, had the census been taken, than David was made conscious of his sin; his heart smote him for what he had done, and the prophet Gad was sent to give him, in the name of God, the choice of one of three modes of being punished; three years' famine; three months' flight before his enemies; or, three days' pestilence. David chose the pestilence, saying, "Let me now fall into the hand of the Lord; for very great are his mercies: but let me not fall into the hand of man. Having made this choice, the pestilence prevailed throughout all the coasts of Israel, and seventy thousand had already perished, when "God sent an angel unto Jerusalem to destroy it; and as he was destroying, the Lord beheld, and he repented him of the evil, and said to the angel that destroyed, It is enough, stay now thine hand. And the angel of the Lord stood over the threshing-floor of Ornan the Jebusite. And David lifted up his eyes, and saw the angel of the Lord stand between the earth and the heaven, having a drawn sword in his hand, stretched out over Jerusalem; then David and the elders of Israel, being clothed in sackcloth, fell upon their faces. And David said unto God, Is it not I that commanded the people to be numbered? even I it is that have sinned and done evil indeed: but as for these sheep, what have they done? Let thine hand, I pray thee, O Lord my God, be on me, and on my father's house: but not on thy people, that *they* should be plagued. Then the angel of the Lord commanded the prophet to say to David, that David should go up, and set up an altar unto the Lord in the threshing-floor of Ornan the Jebusite, on Mount Moriah. . . . . And David builded there an altar unto the Lord, and offered burnt-offerings and peace-offerings, and called upon the Lord; and the Lord answered him from heaven by fire upon the altar of burnt-offering. And the Lord commanded the angel; and he put up his sword again into the sheath thereof. And when David saw that the Lord had answered him in the threshing-floor of Ornan the Jebusite, then he sacrificed there;" and said, "This is the house of the Lord God; and this is the altar of burnt-offering for Israel." Such is the history of the psalm now before us: a history which explains the title as referring to the selection and consecration of the ground upon which the temple was subsequently built, and gives us also a key to the better understanding of the whole. The pestilence having been so suddenly stayed, and he himself spared, after the sword of the destroying angel was stretched out over him, David could well open the psalm as he does,

VERSE 1. I will extol thee, O Lord; for thou hast lifted me up, and hast not made my foes to rejoice over me.

It certainly becomes us to exalt God when he exalts us, and to let our songs of praise and thanksgiving to him, be proportionate to the greatness of his mercies to us. This is what David does here. His theme is the mercy of God, not following but arresting wrath. Just now the pestilence that walketh in darkness, and the destruction that wasteth at noon-day, was doing its worst. Its work, however, is now ended, and his people, whom his pride and vainglory had caused to be so sorely visited, rejoice in the salvation of the Lord. He had grieved over them as a father grieves over the sufferings of children, of whose sufferings he himself had been the guilty cause. What language then can adequately express the greatness of his gratitude when the Divine wrath was in an instant turned both from himself and them; God, at the same moment, putting an end to the rejoicing of his enemies, and the sorrows of himself and friends. David's enemies had hoped to have seen him and his kingdom utterly consumed: but behold, though brought so low, they have risen and stand upright! So shall it ever be with all, however grievously they have sinned, who sincerely repent them of their sins.

VERSE 2. O Lord my God, I cried unto thee, and thou hast healed me.

David still speaks of the Lord as *his* God, though he had sinned so against him. It is well for us when our sins do not drive us away from God in despair, but only send us back to him in haste, with importunate cries for mercy. "Thou hast healed me." We have no evidence that David had been touched by the power of the pestilence. The healing, then, of which he here speaks, must have been the healing of the wounds inflicted upon his soul by sin. Sin diseases the soul, and infuses spiritual sickness into its every faculty. This sin-sickness of the soul, in David's case, God healed when he forgave him the sin that had induced it. God is the soul's physician, as well as its lawgiver and Judge; and where he pardons sin as a crime, he cures the soul of it as a disease, and restores it to spiritual health.

VERSE 3. O Lord, thou hast brought up my soul from the grave: thou hast kept me alive, that I should not go down to the pit.

So great were David's sorrow and remorse at the recollection of his misconduct, and grief at the sight of the evil it had brought upon his people, that it seemed to him that he could not bear up under them, that he must die. His words are like those of the Saviour, when he began to taste, in all its bitterness, the cup of our sins: "My soul is exceeding sorrowful, even unto death." Matt. xxvi. 38. So David felt here: he felt as if he could not survive the weight of grief pressing upon his soul; he seemed to himself to be descending into the grave. Nevertheless, the Lord sustained him, and kept him alive. Nor did he keep him simply alive, but brought him up from the pit's yawning mouth, full of joy and gladness. When

God speaks peace to the soul, he does it effectually. It is a happy thing for us that he does so, otherwise the sight of our sins, in all their evil consequences to ourselves and others, would overwhelm us.

VERSE 4. Sing unto the Lord, O ye saints of his, and give thanks at the remembrance of his holiness.

God's grace and mercy are all the outgoings of "his holiness;" and all those who have been made the recipients of his grace and mercy, are here called upon to "sing and give thanks at the remembrance of his holiness." God's holiness is the eternal and immutable rectitude of his nature, a rectitude of nature that raises him infinitely above being moved by anything like to human passion, and makes him infinitely intent upon promoting the everlasting welfare of his creatures. His holiness is therefore, in one sense, his creatures' only hope. It harmonizes all his other attributes, and gives them direction, force, and efficiency. It permeates the whole as their great element of life. His love is a holy love, his justice a holy justice, his mercy a holy mercy. It is, however, as connected with his forgiving mercy as one of its effluxes, that David here calls upon his saints to sing and give thanks to God "at the remembrance of his holiness"—

VERSE 5. For his anger endureth but a moment; in his favour is life: weeping may endure for a night, but joy cometh in the morning.

Such is the lot of the people of God: their sorrows, as compared with their joys, are but as a moment to the whole life; and even if their whole earthly life were a life of sorrow, it would still be but as a moment, when compared with the joys before them in eternity: "For our light affliction," writes St. Paul, "which is but for a moment, worketh for us a far more exceeding and eternal weight of glory." 2 Cor. iv. 17. "Weeping may endure for a night, but joy cometh in the morning." This is the great consolation of the children of God: no night can ever come upon them, which shall not have its morning, if not in this world, yet certainly in the world to come. How different from the night which will at last close in on those who are not children of God! a night without a morning, and where joy never follows weeping! May God save us all from being shrouded in that night!

VERSE 6. And in my prosperity I said, I shall never be moved.

"I shall never be moved." This David said, not because his faith was strong in God, but because he was prosperous. His prosperity had induced a feeling of inordinate self-reliance. The very abundance of the blessings with which God had blessed him, had caused him to forget where, and where only, his strength lay. He now sees and deplores the impiety of this thought of his heart. He sees in it the real and sufficient cause of the calamity with which he had been visited. If, trusting in God, he had said, "I shall never be moved," he would have been right; but trusting in his prosperity to give stability to his affairs, David was guilty of the sin of idolatry.

VERSE 7. Lord, by thy favour thou hast made my mountain to stand strong: thou didst hide thy face, and I was troubled.

The mountain of which David speaks, was his kingdom: this, God had made to stand strong; had enriched with every element of strength and stability. This, David had virtually forgotten, and was thinking of the greatness and power of his kingdom as the result of his own prowess, and skill, and wise management. And how soon did God bring a change over the spirit of his dream! "Thou, Lord, didst hide thy face, and I was troubled." This hiding of God's face was evinced by the pestilence destroying seventy thousand of the people in a few hours' time. It was to have prevailed throughout three entire days, but it was stayed after it had ravaged through only nine of the seventy-two hours. It was the multitude of his people that tempted David to say in his heart, "I shall never be moved:" it was in diminishing this multitude that he was punished; and if the pestilence had ravaged for the whole seventy-two hours, as it did the nine, David would have found that his kingdom could be not only moved, but swept away. Few of us realize the perils of prosperity. It induces a forgetfulness of our dependence upon the grace and providence of God, and leaves us to think, and plan, and act only for this life. Then it is that God, if he wills to bring us to our senses, sends the rod, and often in the most sudden and overwhelming manner, takes away from us that which had drawn our hearts away from him.

VERSES 8, 9. I cried to thee, O Lord; and unto the Lord I made supplication. What profit is there in my blood, when I go down to the pit? Shall the dust praise thee? shall it declare thy truth?

The sentiment of David's heart was like to that of Job, "though He slay me, yet will I trust in him." He addresses his prayer to Him who was chastening him, and while he was chastening him. Even then did he cry and make supplication unto the Lord. He repeats, too, some of the words that he used in his prayer. He deprecates death because it could in nowise *profit* God—his dust could not praise him and declare his truth. It is the same argument for sparing mercy that Hezekiah used in his prayer unto the Lord, when he was thought to be sick unto death, saying, "The grave cannot praise thee; death cannot celebrate thee; they that go down into the pit cannot hope for thy truth. The living, the living, he shall praise thee, as I do this day: the father to the children shall make known thy truth." Isa. xxxviii. 18, 19. If we desire to live only that we may glorify God in our lives; only that we may declare and make known his truth to the world, we may with propriety ask God to spare us. It is asking life for the highest possible purpose for which it can be given.

VERSE 10. Hear, O Lord, and have mercy upon me: Lord, be thou my helper.

This is substantially the same prayer as the cry and supplication of the last verse. Intense emotion seldom multiplies words. As there are but few words that can give it adequate utterance, it necessarily repeats them. Of this fact we have an illustration in the Saviour when praying in an agony in the garden. Three times he prayed, offering up prayers and supplications with strong crying and tears, and three times even he used the same words. Matt. xxvi. 44.

VERSE 11. Thou hast turned for me my mourning into dancing: thou hast put off my sackcloth and girded me with gladness.

David and the elders of Israel, when they saw the angel of pestilence stretching out his sword over Jerusalem, being clothed in sackcloth, the robe of penitence, fell upon their faces before the Lord. But David, being moved thereto by the word of the angel, built, on the mountain over which the angel stood in the air, an altar unto the Lord, and offered thereon burnt-offerings and peace-offerings, and called upon the Lord; and the Lord answered him from heaven by fire upon the altar of burnt-offering. 1 Chron. xx. 15–26. This descent of fire from heaven was visible and palpable evidence to David's mind that his prayers had been heard, his offerings accepted, and the plague stayed. The sight of it, therefore, instantaneously turned his mourning into dancing, his sorrow into joy and gladness, his robe of penitence into garments of praise. His sacrifices and offerings had been consumed in the same way in which those placed upon the altar of the tabernacle had been consumed at the beginning of its services in the wilderness. Lev. ix. 24. David knew, therefore, that God was reconciled, and his wrath turned away. And now, what improvement of God's sparing and forgiving mercy, thus signally manifested to himself and people, does David propose to make? The best improvement possible: that is, that henceforth he will set no limits to his praise of God, and this he will do, because God had spared him for this very end—

VERSE 12. To the end that my glory may sing praise to thee, and not be silent. O Lord my God, I will give thanks unto thee for ever.

Having prayed in the ninth verse that he might be spared to praise God, and having had his prayer signally answered, David here promises that his praises and thanksgivings to God shall be perpetual.

His glory, that is to say, his tongue that gives utterance to the emotions of a soul made in the image of God, shall not be silent, but be continually sounding forth the praises of God's grace and mercy, truth and goodness. Nor was this a vain promise on David's part. Henceforth to the end of his life, his walk with God was closer than it had ever been before. Moreover, having selected and consecrated a site for the temple, the place where the angel of the pestilence had stayed its ravages, and returned its sword to its scabbard, David employed the greater part of the remainder of his days in collecting together the vast and costly materials to be used in the construction of the sacred edifice. He laboured to make it sure that the temple should stand upon Mount Moriah, where his altar stood and the pestilence ceased, as a monument and memorial to all generations of the forgiving mercy of God to his people. And now, beloved reader, can we recall no instances of God's sparing and forgiving mercy to us, which should move us, as it moved David, to a holier walk and a more useful life? Can we recall no instances in which, if God had dealt with us in justice rather than in mercy, we must have perished? Depend upon it, that all time not spent in the service of God is time misspent, and worse than lost. Time not so spent will meet us at the judgment, terrible as the ghost of a murdered friend, and haunt us through eternity with ceaseless upbraidings.

LECTURE ON PSALM XXXI.

VERSE 1. In thee, O Lord, do I put my trust; let me never be ashamed: deliver me in thy righteousness.

DAVID'S prayer for deliverance in this verse is based upon the assumption that it is a righteous thing in God to deliver those who have put their trust in him. He takes it for granted that the righteousness of God will not allow such to be put to shame, to be disappointed in their hopes of his mercy. This is a feeling that cannot be dislodged from the believer's heart. However unworthy he may feel himself to be, and however imperfectly—though he hopes with sincere endeavour—he may have served him, the believer cannot but feel that a righteous God must and will make a difference between the righteous and the wicked; between him that serveth God, and him that serveth him not. This is evidently the feeling that pervades and animates David's cry for deliverance in the verse before us. It springs, not from any sense of worthiness in himself, but from the feeling that God cannot fail to help those who fear him, and hope in his mercy. It is a feeling justified by the teachings of God's word everywhere.

VERSE 2. Bow down thine ear to me: deliver me speedily: be thou my strong rock, for an house of defence to save me.

David's danger here is imminent; it presses hard upon him; and unless help comes speedily, he feels that all will be over with him. There was many a time in his history when there seemed to be but a step between him and death. At such times his prayer was no doubt the prayer of the verse before us: "Bow down thine ear to me; hear me speedily:

be thou my strong rock, for an house of defence to save me." When dangers press upon the soul, and threaten it with destruction, God is the only rock upon which it can stand secure; his omnipotent love the only house of defence in which it can take refuge and be safe.

VERSE 3. For thou art my rock and my fortress: therefore, for thy name's sake, lead me and guide me.

What David prays in the preceding verse that the Lord would be to him, he here declares that he is—namely, his Rock and Fortress. On this relation between himself and God he grounds the prayer, "therefore, for thy name's sake, lead me and guide me." God had certainly glorified his name, and especially his attributes of truth and mercy, in the many deliverances he had wrought for David; and David prays that he would still glorify it by adding another to His many deliverances of him. "For thy name's sake lead me, and guide me!" A thought how full of comfort and encouragement do we find in these words!—that God will, for his name's sake—moved to it merely by the regard that he has for his own character and glory, "lead us and guide us in the way wherein we should go."

VERSE 4. Pull me out of the net that they have laid privily for me: for thou art my strength.

It was through the strength of God alone that David could escape being caught in the net privily spread everywhere to ensnare him. The case is not otherwise with any of us. We can escape the snares of evil spread everywhere in this world, only as we escape them in the strength of God. His grace alone is sufficient for us.

VERSE 5. Into thy hand I commit my spirit: thou hast redeemed me, O Lord God of truth.

It was his knowledge of God as the God of truth that emboldened David to commit his life and soul to his keeping. He was confident that God could never falsify any promise of help that he made to his people; and that, having promised to deliver the righteous man out of all his troubles, he would make his promise good. He therefore casts himself upon this promise, and commits his spirit into God's hand. These words are found elsewhere. David's Divine Son repeated them on the cross the moment before he bowed his head and gave up the ghost, saying, "Father, into thy hands I commend my spirit." Luke xxiii. 46. This is the glorious privilege of the believer—to commit his soul—when heart and flesh are failing him—to commit his soul into the hands of the God of truth, the God who will never disappoint any hope excited in the minds of his creatures by any of his great and precious promises.

VERSE 6. I have hated them that regard lying vanities: but I trust in the Lord.

David here contrasts the God in whom he trusts with the gods in whom the heathen trust. The God in whom he trusts is the God of truth; the gods in whom they trust are lying vanities. The object of his trust is the Lord, the great I AM; the Fountain of all being and all bliss. The object of their trust is—nothing—senseless idols, in which their votaries trust only to be deceived and disappointed in their hopes. And there is still the same contrast between the Christian's trust and the worldling's trust now, that there was in David's day. The Christian, trusting in the Lord as his fountain of good, is never disappointed; the wordling, trusting in earthly things as his fountain of good, never fails to be disappointed; so entirely so, that after the world has given him everything that it has in its power to bestow, he is obliged to inscribe on the whole, "vanity and vexation of spirit."

VERSES 7, 8. I will be glad and rejoice in thy mercy: for thou hast considered my trouble; thou hast known my soul in adversities; and hast not shut me up into the hand of the enemy; thou hast set my feet in a large room.

David has many reasons for being glad and rejoicing in the mercy of the Lord. His eye of love had been upon him in adversities; he had been a present help to him in trouble; he had not left him to be overcome by the enemy that he most feared, but had made his feet to stand in a place where he could move freely and in safety. He is supposed to refer here to the deliverances wrought out for him by the Lord from the hand of Saul. And let us all remember that every one of us has his Saul—Satan, with his myriads of emissaries, seeking our destruction. If God delivers us not out of his hand, we perish. If He be not with us when trouble and adversities come on us, we shall be overcome.

VERSE 9. Have mercy upon me, O Lord, for I am in trouble mine eye is consumed with grief, yea, my soul and my belly.

How sore David's trouble, from which he prays to be delivered, was, we may infer from its effects upon his body. His "eye was consumed by the grief" that it had caused him; indeed, his whole mental and physical nature seemed to be sinking under the weight of it. There is no sorrow like to spiritual sorrow in its depressing effects on mind and body.

VERSE 10. For my life is spent with grief, and my years with sighing: my strength faileth because of mine iniquity, and my bones are consumed.

The thought and sentiment of this verse are nearly the same as that of the last, only that we have added here a new element to David's sufferings—his own iniquity. "My strength," says he, "faileth me because of mine iniquity." He may have been innocent and righteous in regard to the enemies of whom he complains, still he had his infirmities, requiring, for their correction, chastening from the hand of God. The consciousness of both needing and deserving this chastening, adds greatly to his grief. His example here teaches us that, in making complaints to God of the sins of others, we should never fail to acknowledge and deplore our own. "To recognize," writes another, "in our sufferings a righteous retribution, is the only sure foundation on which the hope of deliverance can be made to rest; he only who can say with the heart, 'my strength is broken because of my guilt,' will be able to utter with inward truth the prayer, 'deliver me for *thy* righteousness' sake.' It is only as we cast off all righteousness of our own, that we are clothed with the righteousness of God, which is by faith in Jesus Christ."

VERSE 11. I was a reproach among all mine enemies, but especially among my neighbours, and a fear to mine acquaintance: they that did see me without fled from me.

During the persecutions that he experienced at the hands of Saul, when he was outlawed and a price set upon his head, David's enemies reproached him as a rebel; his neighbours as one whose presence among them would involve them in his ruin. He was a fear to his acquaintances—that is, to the members of his own family—lest they should be punished for harbouring him; and even they who were about to meet him on the street, fled from him, to avoid suspicion of being implicated in his guilt! How keenly must David, sensitive as his mind was, have felt this abandonment of him by every one! There is perhaps hardly any earthly suffering greater than that of a generous mind under universal abandonment and public reproach. This was David's case, and also the case of the Divine Son of David. And their case has been the case of many a good man since, meriting nothing but good, and experiencing nothing but evil at the hands of their fellow-men.

VERSE 12. I am forgotten as a dead man out of mind; I am like a broken vessel.

Driven alike from the abode of friend and of foe, and avoided by all, David here speaks of himself as a dead man, for whom nobody cared; out of sight, out of mind; a broken vessel, worthless, and to be cast away. This oblivious contempt of all who knew him seemed to David quite as hard to be borne as their hatred and persecution. David is not the only good man whose deeds of kindness to others have been forgotten by them when he was no longer to be seen.

VERSE 13. For I have heard the slander of many: fear was on every side: while they took counsel together against me, they devised to take away my life.

What excites David's fears is the slander of the many. They do their worst to defame him with the people, that, having the populace on their side, they can safely make an onset upon his life. This is precisely the course that the Jews pursued toward the Son of David. The rulers dared not to lay their hands upon him to take away his life, till they had first of all, by the tongue of slander, depicted him to the people as one who deserved to die.

Such is David's description of his deplorable condition, and surely it is a condition of his affairs that justifies his prayer to God in the second verse of our psalm, saying, "Deliver me speedily!" Situated as he was, it seemed that if help did not come soon, it would come too late. And yet his faith in God did not fail, for he adds, in the next verse in course:

VERSE 14. But I trusted in thee, O Lord: I said, Thou art my God.

However sorely pressed by his enemies, and by the consciousness of his own weakness and unworthiness, David had not wholly despaired. "Thou art my God," was a feeling that never altogether left his heart. He sighs, and groans, and weeps, and complains, not because his trust in God had failed him, but that his sighs, and groans, and tears, and complaints might be heard by Him who alone could turn them into songs of joy.

VERSE 15. My times are in thy hand: deliver me from the hand of mine enemies, and from them that persecute me.

"My times are in thy hands," David said in his trouble. He whose times, whose fortunes, are in the hand of God, need not fear what man can do unto him. God will surely be present at every crisis in his history, to turn—even when all seems to be lost—the tide in his favour.

VERSE 16. Make thy face to shine upon thy servant: save me for thy mercies' sake.

Because he is his servant, and for his mercies' sake, David prays God to save him. God can never be asked in vain to magnify his mercy in helping one who is truly his servant. It is a name as dear to his heart as that of child. David knew this, and pleads the relation in his prayer.

VERSE 17. Let me not be ashamed, O Lord: for I have called upon thee: let the wicked be ashamed, and let them be silent in the grave.

God has promised to hear all who call on him with heart-felt confidence. Of this promise David here reminds him. God loves to have his promises plead to him. His pleasure is to see his creatures take him at his word. Their doing so never fails to obtain his blessing. "Let the wicked be ashamed, and let them be silent in the grave:" *i. e.*, be overwhelmed with the doom with which they were endeavouring to overwhelm him; and this, not because they were his enemies, but because they were the enemies of God and righteousness. As such, and only as such, does he pray that they may descend into the silence of the grave.

VERSE 18. Let the lying lips be put to silence, which speak grievous things proudly and contemptuously against the righteous.

This petition is one that every good man may reiterate; that all lying lips may be put to silence, all lips that proudly and contemptuously utter falsehoods against the righteous. Such persons, if they should realize their hearts' desire, would make heaven a fable, and earth a hell. Such has been the tendency of all the sayings and writings of those who have opposed the religion of the Son of David.

VERSE 19. O how great is thy goodness, which thou hast laid up for them that fear thee: which thou hast wrought for them that trust in thee before the sons of men!

Here prayer has turned to praise. He has been heard, and the full assurance of faith has glided into the soul, that it will be answered. He sees that God has, as it were, hoarded his goodness for them that fear him; and manifests it toward them, before the sons of men, and in such a way that their very enemies cannot but see that God is with them.

VERSE 20. Thou shalt hide them in the secret of thy presence from the pride of man; thou shalt keep them secretly in a pavilion from the strife of tongues.

The pride of man can never reach, to do them harm, those who have put their trust in God; nor the strife of tongues, to destroy their fair fame. The invisible, yet real, presence of God around them, is as a hiding-place that effectually conceals them, and as a pavilion that surrounds, overshadows, and shelters them.

VERSE 21. Blessed be the Lord; for he hath showed me his marvellous kindness in a strong city.

What David says in the two preceding verses of the goodness of God to all who fear him and trust in him, he here affirms to have been verified by his own personal experience. David's "strong city" was God himself, surrounding him on every side as a wall of brass against his enemies. Though he stood alone in the world, and with every man's hand against him, God enabled him to feel as secure under his protection as he would have felt in an impregnable fortress.

VERSE 22. For I said in my haste, I am cut off from before thine eyes; nevertheless thou heardest the voice of my supplications when I cried unto thee.

"For I said in my haste, I am cut off from before thine eyes:"—yes, the same man who is now so strong in faith and confident in the protection of God, once was so overcome by his fears that he thought himself lost, cast out of God's sight, and forgotten by him. This is a phase of faith by no means uncommon. The strongest believer is not without his seasons when fear and trembling seize on him. Such seasons with him, however, will be of brief duration. He will soon be enabled to say with David, "Nevertheless thou heardest the voice of my supplications when I cried unto thee."

VERSE 23. O love the Lord, all ye his saints: for the Lord preserveth the faithful, and plentifully rewardeth the proud doer.

The difference that God makes between the righteous and the wicked, between the humble believer and the proud evil-doer, is certainly cause for the most ardent love to God on the part of his people. It is a difference that proclaims him to be indeed the righteous Governor of the universe, and that the soul can therefore safely entrust itself in his hands for time and for eternity.

VERSE 24. Be of good courage, and he shall strengthen your heart, all ye that hope in the Lord.

Such is the improvement which David exhorts all those who hope in the Lord, to make of the history of his trials and triumphs, sorrows and joys, as that history is given to us in the psalm before us. However dark the cloud that overshadows us, he teaches us to think of God as seeing through it. However sorely we may be oppressed with guilt, he teaches us still to think of God as being, through the merits of his Son infinitely more merciful than we can possibly be sinful. However bitterly men may persecute us, and cast out our name as evil, he teaches us to think of God as able to deliver from the strife of tongues. The import of the whole is, that the word *despair* should never be found in the vocabulary of those who hope in the Lord. He has given us the history of his trials in order to show us what trials the Lord can and will carry the believer through. And surely, the Lord having carried him triumphantly through such trials as are described in this psalm, David could well close it only as he does, "Be of good courage, and he shall strengthen your heart, all ye that hope in the Lord."

LECTURE ON PSALM XXXII.

THE occasion of the writing of this psalm was, no doubt, the same as that of the fifty-first. David did that which was right in the eyes of the Lord, and turned not aside from anything that he commanded him, all the days of his life, save only in the matter of Uriah the Hittite. 1 Kings xv. 5. In that matter he sinned sadly. In an evil hour he had yielded to the solicitations of lust, and, to conceal his crime, had added to his guilt by slaying the man whose wife he had robbed of her innocence. David knew too well the turpitude of his crimes to leave his conscience at ease. For a long time, however, he seems not to have made a full, unqualified, and hearty confession of them to God. The consequence was, that there was not a more miserable man on earth than David. If you would ascertain the mind in which the pangs of remorse are keenest and most insufferable, go not to the man hardened in sin, but to the sincere believer, who, in an evil hour, has yielded to temptation and sinned. He suffers an anguish of spirit that no other can. He has sinned against light and grace, and that fact exhibits his sin to him in an aspect that is truly appalling. It makes an impression upon his mind that it makes upon none beside; it fills him with terrors with which it fills none beside; for he sees his sin as no other can see it—with eyes that have been enlightened from above. He knows that sin is no trifle; he realizes it to be what God himself has pronounced it to be, "an evil and a bitter thing." How evil, and how bitter, David tells us in portions of the psalm now before us. Soul and body felt its consuming power. An accusing conscience tied his tongue, so that he could not pray. The awful conviction of Cain seems for a time to have fastened upon his soul, that his sin was too great to be forgiven. At length, however, he is brought to repentance and a better mind. The fearful crisis in his moral history is passed, and the peace of God again flows into his soul with a sweetness and power to which he gives utterance in the words,

VERSE 1. Blessed is he whose transgression is forgiven, whose sin is covered.

"Thy sins are forgiven thee; go in peace," are words which have at length been spoken, and he feels their magic power in every faculty of his soul. He is another man! God has restored unto him the joy of his salvation, and is upholding him with his free Spirit. The darkness that filled his soul is gone; the conscience that so tortured him is at ease. The heavens that so frowned upon him are again radiant with smiles. The abyss that yawned at his feet is closed. He breathes free again, and realizes the truth of God's description of Himself as given to Moses: "The Lord, the Lord God, merciful and gracious, long-suffering, and abundant in goodness and truth, keeping mercy for thousands, forgiving iniquity, transgression, and sin." Exod. xxxiv. 6, 7. Only those who have at length realized some great hope long deferred, can fully enter into David's feelings when he uttered the words, "Blessed is he whose transgression is forgiven, whose sin is covered." What a weight had been lifted from his soul! what a sight had been hidden from his eyes! His transgression was forgiven, his sin was covered! Justice, with flaming sword, no longer stood between him and the tree of life. Guilty, indeed, he knows himself to be—that he does not deny, but confesses; but where sin abounded, grace did much more abound. The recollection of his sin now remains, not to terrify, torment, and consume him, but only to excite the intensest gratitude to Him who has forgiven it. David has been forgiven much, and he loves much.

VERSE 2. Blessed is the man unto whom the Lord imputeth not iniquity, and in whose spirit there is no guile.

"Imputeth not iniquity." When the Lord forgives, he no longer takes account of sins; he deals with us as if we had never been guilty of them. "I," he says, "even I am he that blotteth out thy transgressions for mine own sake, and will not remember thy sins." Isa. xliii. 25. "I have blotted out, as a thick cloud, thy transgressions, and, as a cloud, thy sins." Isa. xliv. 22. He makes no mental reservation to call our sins to remembrance at some future time. But who is the man to whom the Lord imputeth not iniquity? The man "in whose spirit there is no guile;" the man who makes no subtle palliations of his sins in his confession of them to his conscience, to his fellow-men, or to God; the man who is willing and anxious to see his sins in all the magnitude of their guilt, and to confess them all, and especially the sins of which his conscience is most afraid. No general confession of sin will satisfy the man in whose spirit there is no guile. He wishes to see his sins as God himself sees them, both as to their number and vileness. He shudders at the thought of the least deceit, of the least hypocrisy, in his approaches to God in prayer. His constant prayer therefore is, "Search me, O God, and know my heart; try me, and know my thoughts; and see if there be any wicked way in me, and lead me in the way everlasting." Psalm cxxxix. 23, 24. We do not understand by the man "in whose spirit there is no guile," a man who has no faults, but only a man who seeks not to conceal nor to extenuate his faults—any of his faults—when confessing his sins to God. Of this concealment, or at least extenuation, of some of his faults, David had been guilty, and he begins in the next verse to describe the sufferings it cost him.

VERSE 3. When I kept silence, my bones waxed old through my roaring all the day long.

"When I kept silence:"—so long as David did not declare his sin, so long he had no peace. Unacknowledged and unconfessed with sincere contrition, it nestled in his very heart of hearts like a scorpion of a thousand stings. Its torments consumed his strength as if premature age had stolen upon him. All the day long he felt its depressing power. However absorbing the cares of his kingdom, they sufficed to give him no respite from his pain. His mental anguish still continued. Business brings relief for the time to ordinary sorrow; it brought none to David's. His, in the midst of the most engrossing cares of business, still gnawed at his heart. This picture of David's mental disquietude is not without its parallel in the history of others. Others have experienced the same in the midst of all that is gay and dazzling. Corroding sorrow makes them wretched in the full possession of every means of happiness that the world has to bestow. And if remorse be an element in their sorrow, then is it intense indeed! The tears that the soul then weeps are not as balmy dews of heaven, descending to soothe and heal, but as the deadly droppings of the upas, falling upon the soul, to agonize and poison it. This was David's case. He wept—his tears, however, were not yet the tears of penitence, but of remorse. He felt his wretchedness, and knew the cause of it, but could not bring himself to go to God, confessing its cause to him, in its enormity, and imploring his forgiveness. There is no other bosom in which remorse so ravages as it does in the bosom which was once the abode of joy and peace in the Holy Ghost. If he has fallen into some great sin which an angry and accusing conscience deters him from humbly confessing, remorse clutches the Christian's heart, as it clutches the heart of none beside.

VERSE 4. For day and night thy hand was heavy upon me: my moisture is turned into the drought of summer. *Selah.*

It cannot be doubted that the wrath of God is felt in the inflictions of conscience, when it torments us as David's tormented him. It is his wrath against sin that arms it with its desolating power over the soul. David is not, however, the only man who has felt its fiery lashings day and night, consuming even bodily strength, as the burning suns of the torrid zone scorch and consume every green thing with the intensity of their heat. Men have sweat blood under the scourgings of a guilty conscience—they have died under its scourging, there being no other ascertainable cause of death. Yea more, men have sought death as a relief from its scourgings, voluntarily giving themselves up to the demands of public justice, and asking death as a boon. This has been signally the case with those whose conscience has been burdened with blood-guiltiness, as David's was. Have you ever passed a night with a duelist? If you have not, listen to a description of his nightly terrors. Acknowledging to a friend that he was afraid to sleep alone, his friend consented to pass the night with him; and what followed? After long tossing on his unquiet pillow, and repeated half-stifled groans, that revealed the inward pangs of the murderer, the duelist sunk into slumber, and as he rolled from side to side, the name of his victim was often uttered, with broken words, that discovered the keen remorse that preyed like fire on his conscience. Suddenly he would start up in his bed, with the terrible impression that the avenger of blood was pursuing him; or hide himself under the covering, as if he would escape the burning eye of an angry God, that gleamed in the darkness over him, like lightning from a thunder-cloud. For him there was "no rest, day nor night." Conscience, armed with terrors, lashed him unceasingly, and who could sleep? And this was not the restlessness of disease, the ravings of a disordered intellect, the anguish of a maniac struggling in chains. It was a man of intelligence, education, health, and affluence, given up to himself

—not delivered over to the avenger of blood, to be tormented before his time, but left to the power of his own *conscience*, suffering only what every one may suffer who is abandoned of God. David's description of the unrestrained inflictions of a guilty conscience is none too strong, when he says of them in his own case, "Day and night thy hand was heavy upon me: my moisture was turned into the drought of summer. *Selah.*" Alas! the stoutest heart cannot but wither and become dried up under the inflictions of conscience, impregnated with the wrath of God!

VERSE 5. I acknowledged my sin unto thee, and mine iniquity have I not hid. I said, I will confess my transgressions unto the Lord; and thou forgavest the iniquity of my sin. *Selah.*

These words describe the great turning point in David's moral history. The ingenuous confession of his great fault has at last been made. He has seen it in all its turpitude, and acknowledged it to God. That which had pressed so heavily upon his heart, and which, it is probable, he had never before mentioned, even in his general devotions, he has now confessed, with its aggravated circumstances of baseness and guilt. His adultery and murder he now calls adultery and murder, with the feelings of self-loathing and self-condemnation which they should excite. He attempts no concealment, neither palliation of his two great sins. He no longer pleads that the temptation to the first was strong; that the second was committed to conceal the first; nor that Uriah might have fallen, if he had not had him placed in the forefront of the hottest of the battle. The reason why we do not obtain peace of conscience, after the commission of some great sin, is because we do not bring ourselves to confess it by itself alone, and in its naked and terrible deformity. There is no reason why the sin of blood-shedding should not, on sincere repentance, be pardoned as readily as any other. The blood of Christ cleanseth us from all sin. There is no exception, except the sin against the Holy Ghost. With this one excepted sin, we cannot charge the man who has slain his fellow-man. He therefore fails of the Divine pardon, and its consequent peace of conscience, because he generally attempts to extenuate his crime, at least to himself. The common murderer may think that the wrongs he suffered should in some measure justify his act. The duelist may plead the force of public opinion; that this opinion did, as it were, compel him to do as he did, or be disgraced. So of every other transgression of the Divine law, which we may seek to extenuate by something in the circumstances attending it. But peace of conscience can never enter the guilty breast, so long as the least spirit of self-justification or self-exculpation lingers there. That spirit must be wholly ejected, and substituted by the spirit that takes all the blame of faults home to one's self alone. It was thus that David at last took the blame of his faults home to himself alone; and no sooner had he done that, than the peace of God again filled his soul. This is both briefly and beautifully expressed in the metrical psalm:

"No sooner I my wound disclosed,
The guilt that tortured me within,
But thy forgiveness interposed,
And mercy's healing balm poured in."

There was not a moment's interval between the full and unqualified acknowledgment of his guilt and the Divine forgiveness. Hence his words, "I said, I will confess my transgressions unto the Lord; and thou forgavest the iniquity of my sin. Selah." Mark that; no sooner was the purpose formed, than the blessing came.

VERSE 6. For this shall every one that is godly pray unto thee in a time when thou mayest be found: surely in the floods of great waters they shall not come nigh unto him.

"For this," that is, for this reason, because thou dost forgive the sins of thy people the moment they ingenuously confess them to thee, therefore "shall every one that is godly pray unto thee in a time when thou mayest be found." Having experienced in his own person the truth of both propositions, "He that covereth his sins shall not prosper: but whoso confesseth and forsaketh them shall have mercy," (Prov. xxviii. 13,) David trusts that from his case others will learn to make confession of their sins at once, and not to sin, and suffer by delay, as he had done. He sees that he might long ago have enjoyed the peace he now enjoys, if he had only brought himself to an unqualified acknowledgment of guilt. For this reason he trusts others will pray unto God while he may be found. The time of finding God is while he is still waiting to be gracious; and that is every moment of our lives, till he gives us up to final hardness of heart and blindness of mind. Until then, there is not a moment of our lives in which we may not take refuge in his mercy, by an humble confession of our sins; and of every one thus sheltered by the Divine mercy, we can say, with David, "Surely in the floods of great waters they shall not come nigh unto him." The believer having sinned, and truly repented him of his sin, may not escape all its natural and temporal evil consequences: on the contrary, those consequences he may be made, as David was,

34

(2 Sam. xii. 9–13,) to feel in such ways as to remind him continually of his sin. Nevertheless, sincere repentance saves the believer from all eternal evil consequences of his sin. Having taken refuge in the Divine mercy, "the floods of great waters," the desolating judgments of everlasting woe that will overwhelm the finally impenitent, will not reach him. He will outride the deluge of fire that shall consume the world at last, as surely and safely as Noah, and those with him in the ark, outrode the deluge of waters that overwhelmed every living thing beside. Only with his eyes shall the penitent believer behold and see the reward of the wicked. This is one of the most astonishing things in the mercy of God. The forgiving arms that were opened so wide to receive us when we first repented, are opened still again and again, even so often as, having sinned, we truly repent us of our sin!

VERSE 7. Thou art my hiding-place; thou shalt preserve me from trouble: thou shalt compass me about with songs of deliverance. Selah.

For twelve months and more, sin had deprived David of his hiding-place in God; but having at last recovered it again by sincere repentance, he rejoices in it as the prodigal rejoiced in his father's smile, and embrace, and welcome, on his return from the far-off country, in which he was perishing with hunger. Just now the hand of God was heavy upon him; now he is his deliverer from trouble. Just now God was surrounding him with a circle of sorrows; now he is compassing him "about with songs of deliverance." He feels that the sweet relations once subsisting between him and God have been renewed, and he is restored to the Divine favour.

VERSE 8. I will instruct thee, and teach thee in the way which thou shalt go: I will guide thee with mine eye.

Some suppose these words to be the voice of God himself sounding in David's heart; the Spirit itself bearing witness to his spirit that God would henceforth guide him in the ways of truth and righteousness. No earnest believer can for a moment doubt that the Divine Spirit does sometimes thus speak in our hearts, and guide us by gentle intimations in his ways. Most commentators, however, regard the words as David's own, and as being addressed to every fellow believer who may have been, like himself, overtaken by a fault; and designed to point out to him the way of recovery, illustrating and enforcing his instructions by his own personal experience and example. This interpretation is certainly rendered highly probable by his words elsewhere, (Psalm li. 12, 13,) where, in deploring the sin confessed in this psalm, he says, "Restore unto me the joy of thy salvation, and uphold me with thy free Spirit: then will I teach transgressors thy ways, and sinners shall be converted unto thee." No other believer can so effectually teach a fallen brother how to return to God, as the believer who has himself fallen and been restored. He understands the sorrows and trials of such a brother as no believer else can, and will restore him in a spirit of meekness, considering himself. Gal. vi. 1. It is a sad way of acquiring skill to raise the fallen and elevate the downcast. It is, however, a way in which many an eminent servant of God has been made specially useful to his fellow members in Christ. The story of his own sins, told with tears of grief, and the story of God's free pardon, told with tears of joy, have brought light and consolation to many a heart, which otherwise would have been consumed by despair. It was thus that David encouraged every erring brother still to hope in the mercy of God, from the fact of *his* having obtained mercy. It was in a similar way that our Lord required Peter to improve his mortifying personal experience, saying to him, after predicting his deplorable lapse, "when thou art converted—i. e., recovered from thy fall, strengthen thy brethren." Luke xxii. 32. Having himself fallen, Peter would know best how to restore the fallen.

VERSE 9. Be ye not as the horse, or as the mule, which have no understanding; whose mouth must be held in with bit and bridle, lest they come near unto thee, [or, that they *may* come near unto thee.]

The allusion is to the necessity of bitting and bridling the horse and mule before they can be subdued to your will. David exhorts those whom he counsels here, not to resist doing the will of God till he shall be obliged to bit and bridle them, to lead them per force where reason alone should guide us with willing feet. This comparison of the wicked to the most obstinate of brutes, depicts, in the most humiliating light, the degradation to which sin has subjected man's rational nature. The sinner verily acts as if he had no understanding; his highest manifestations of mind are seen in defeating all the efforts of the Divine mercy to guide his feet into the paths of truth and peace. It is amazing that a creature made in the image of God, with thoughts that wander through eternity, should be wise only to do evil. But so it is. If he walks in the ways of God at all, it is only by compulsion. The very obedience he renders is not a willing obedience; he is kept within bounds only by restraint. God, however, never uses the bit and bridle to guide us the way we should go, till all his gentler means of reclaiming us have failed of accomplishing their end. His first and favourite means are the persuasions of love and wisdom, addressed to the reason and the heart. To these David exhorts his friends to yield, and not wait for sterner means.

VERSE 10. Many sorrows shall be to the wicked: but he that trusteth in the Lord, mercy shall compass him about.

There are, indeed, many sorrows to the wicked; they are their own tormentors. Their sin is a fire in their bones, and a poison in their veins. It corrodes both mind and heart, soul and body. "There is no peace, saith my God, to the wicked." They work in the fire, and every sin they commit adds intensity to the flames which consume them. Passion and appetite gain power by indulgence, till they feel themselves to be slaves indeed working in chains. They lose all power of self-control, and float on helplessly to ruin, knowing all the while whither they are bound. What a lot is that of the wicked! Out of harmony with God's moral government, their hurrying on from sin to sin, is a hurrying on from sorrow to sorrow too. Every succeeding transgression inflicts a deeper wound; and every succeeding transgression makes it more certain that still another will be added to the list. How then can it be otherwise than that "many sorrows shall be to the wicked; but he that trusteth in the Lord, mercy shall compass him about"? Here is the contrast between the righteous and the wicked, between the believer and the unbeliever. Trusting in the Lord brings the soul into moral harmony with God. An element of love surrounds and fills him. He is in God, and God is in him, and—God is love. The righteous man, as well as the wicked, has his sorrows, but his faith in God transmutes them into blessings. All things are made to work together for good to them that love God.

VERSE 11. Be glad in the Lord, and rejoice, ye righteous: and shout for joy all ye that are upright in heart.

"Be glad—rejoice—shout for joy." These are the only words that can adequately express David's feelings in view of the character given us of the Lord our God in this psalm. His hatred of sin, how intense! And yet his pardoning mercy, how full, how free, the moment we repent! David had felt in his own soul the truth of both of these characteristics of the Divine Being, and rejoiced in both, in his hatred of sin, and in his delight in mercy, and calls upon the righteous and the upright to rejoice with him. The righteous man of whom David here speaks is not one absolutely righteous, one without spot or blemish in his moral character, but only one who is upright in heart; one whose repentance is sincere; one whose confession of his sins has been without reserve. Such a confession, in the name of Christ, will make us all evangelically righteous and upright in heart, and bring peace to bosoms to which peace has long been a stranger. If any of us have sinned against our fellow-men, let the confession of our faults to them be immediate, unqualified, and without reserve. It is the only way in which darkness can be banished from the heart. So too, if there is any particular sin against God that clouds our hopes, let us not conceal it from our consciences, and leave it out of our prayers, but confess it, unmitigated by a self-exculpating thought, by itself alone, by name, and by its right name. Then how soon will God, for the sake of his Son Jesus Christ, enable us to say, with all the joyousness with which David said it, "Blessed is the man whose transgression is forgiven, whose sin is covered!"

LECTURE ON PSALM XXXIII.

VERSE 1. Rejoice in the Lord, O ye righteous: for praise is comely for the upright.

THE last psalm closes with a call upon the righteous and the upright in heart, to praise God for his forgiving mercy; this opens with a call upon the same class of persons to praise him for his almighty power, and providential goodness manifested in the preservation of his people. To praise God for his preservation of them in the midst of the greatest dangers, is comely in the upright. It is the only return they can make to him for his goodness to them, and is suitable and becoming. The righteous and the upright in heart of our psalm, are not persons without moral defect, but persons without hypocrisy in their service of God—Israelites, indeed, in whom there is no guile.

VERSE 2. Praise the Lord with harp: sing unto him with the psaltery, and an instrument of ten strings.

The melody of voice and heart seems insufficient to David's mind in his ovation of praise and thanksgiving, unless it is accompanied by the melody of sweet sounds, to augment its fervour and heighten its glow. To what instruments of music reference is here made in the harp, the psaltery, and an instrument of ten strings, it is not easy to determine. And if we could decide the question, it would be of little practical importance to us. They were, no doubt, instruments whose tones were of the joyous and jubilant sort, in order to be in keeping with the spirit of the psalm.

VERSE 3. Sing unto him a new song: play skilfully with a loud noise.

Not a new song in its theme—the greatness of God's power and goodness to his people—but a new celebration of his power and goodness. It is a *new* song only as being a new outpouring of praise and adoration excited by augmented displays of the Divine. mercies; mercies never ceasing, calling for ceaseless songs of praise, and for songs of praise ever new.

VERSE 4. For the word of the Lord is right; and all his works are done in truth.

The "word of the Lord" here intended, is his word of promise: his "works done in truth," the perpetual fulfilment of his promises to his people. He never falsifies his word. What he promises, he performs. "God is not a man, that he should lie; neither the son of man, that he should repent: hath he said, and shall he not do it? or, hath he spoken, and shall he not make it good?" Num. xxiii. 19. This is the character of the God of Israel, given by the wicked Balaam; given unwillingly, but given truly.

VERSE 5. He loveth righteousness and judgment: the earth is full of the goodness of the Lord.

Here is another source of confidence and joy in God. He loveth righteousness and judgment, universal justice, so that all who have right on their side may be sure of ultimate deliverance. God's love of justice, and his so ordering all things as to accomplish its ends, is the good man's strongest stay in all his conflicts with oppression and wrong. It nerves his heart with strength in the hour of trial. And God is as mercy-loving as he is justice-loving. "The earth is full of the goodness of the Lord." We see on every side manifestations of the Divine benevolence as numerous as the manifestations of the Divine justice. They walk hand in hand; one, avenging the good man's wrongs; the other, pardoning his offences, and crowning his life with loving-kindnesses.

VERSE 6. By the word of the Lord were the heavens made; and all the host of them by the breath of his mouth.

Already described as being faithful, just, and good, God has here ascribed to him another attribute that should be cause for joy to the believer—omnipotence. This is the *arm* of his other attributes, and gives infinite ability to them all. It is no labour whatever for him to accomplish the greatest things. "By his word were the heavens made; and all the host of them by the breath of his mouth." There is omnipotent power in his very breath. It brought into existence every visible thing with which immensity teems—the earth beneath our feet, and the star whose distance from us no numbers can express.

VERSE 7. He gathereth the waters of the sea together as a heap: he layeth up the depth in storehouses.

There is here a descent from the general to the particular, from the manifestations of Divine power in the illimitable heavens, to the manifestations of the same power in a single instance on the earth, God's gathering the waters of the sea together and retaining them in their places as if they were solid substances, when, left to themselves, they might again overflow the earth. They are as secure in the places God has assigned them as they would be locked up in storehouses constructed for that very purpose. They cannot pass their barriers, except at his bidding. His hand is upon their every wave, though tossing itself mountain high, repressing its fury until it sinks quietly to rest again—the wildest storm being always succeeded by a calm, leaving the waters of the great deep still where they were, and the earth where it was.

VERSES 8, 9. Let all the earth fear the Lord: let all the inhabitants of the world stand in awe of him: for he spake, and it was done; he commanded and it stood fast.

These words compose one of the many passages in the word of God where any attempt at expansion and explanation only mars their force. Standing alone by themselves, they speak to the imagination and the heart with a power which no other words can augment. "He spake, and it was done; he commanded, and it stood fast." Who would not fear and stand in awe of such a Being as this, who called a universe into existence out of nothing, by a word; and by the same word, it stood fast, impressed with laws from which it has never deviated, except at his behest? Man requires means to accomplish ends. God requires them not. He has in his mere will all that he needs to accomplish infinite ends. Man's most finished works may be still improved, and soon perish. God's works are perfect from the beginning, and continue what he made them, till he bids them change. What a God is this to have for one's enemy! and yet, what a God to have for one's friend!

VERSES 10, 11. The Lord bringeth the counsel of the heathen to nought; he maketh the devices of the people of none effect. The counsel of the Lord standeth for ever, the thoughts of his heart to all generations.

This was said to encourage God's Israel of old not to fear what man could do unto them. He who made all creatures so easily, could control them as easily. He who called them into being out of nothing, could certainly bring their counsel to nought, and their devices to none effect—defeat all their plans and purposes of evil. It was not so, however, with the counsel of the Lord; it would stand, and the thoughts of his heart to all generations. His purposes of mercy toward his people, he would certainly accomplish. These words were spoken for the encouragement of the Israel of God now, as well as for his Israel of old.

VERSE 12. Blessed is the nation whose God is the Lord; and the people whom he hath chosen for his own inheritance.

The history of the world is a verification of these words. Only those nations whose God was the Lord, have been eminently blessed. Knowing and worshipping the God of revelation, has been their only enduring bond of union, strength, and peace. Their choosing him for their inheritance, leading him to choose them for his, has thrown around every such nation the shield of his omnipotent wisdom and immeasurable love. Their undertaking the defence and promotion of his cause has invariably enlisted him to undertake the defence and promotion of theirs. In whatever nation this has not been the case, there anarchy, falsehood, and oppression have in time carried the day against order, truth, and justice. Of this fact all the nations now on the earth are illustrations; each is distinguished and prosperous, or degraded and downcast, just in proportion as the love of God's revealed truth does, or does not, rule in the minds of the people.

VERSES 13, 14. The Lord looketh from heaven; he beholdeth all the sons of men. From the place of his habitation he looketh upon all the inhabitants of the earth.

Notwithstanding the heaven is his throne, the eyes of the Lord are everywhere, beholding the evil and the good. Prov. xv. 3. "He looketh upon all the inhabitants of the earth." Not one of all the sons of men is hid from his view. He observes them with a watchfulness that never wearies, and with an eye that never slumbers. His interest in his creatures did not cease, as some have taught, as soon as he had launched them into being. The workmanship of his hand is never for a moment out of his sight, or out of his mind. Men can envelope themselves and plans in no covering through which his eye does not penetrate. This the wicked man forgets when he would sin; and the righteous man when he would despair. We can conceive of no greater preventive of vice, or encouragement to virtue, than fully realizing that the eye of God is at every moment upon us.

VERSE 15. He fashioneth their hearts alike: he considereth all their works.

"He fashioneth their hearts alike"—that is, the hearts of all the inhabitants of the earth. The words refer, either to God's originally fashioning the hearts of all men alike, instinct with the same general passions, impulses, and aspirations; or to his still moulding and turning them as he lists to the accomplishment of his own wise and gracious purposes. Either interpretation yields substantially the same sense.

Each teaches that God's looking from heaven has to do with the hearts of men. The Father of the spirits of all flesh, he scans all their thoughts, and watches whither they tend—whether to himself as their centre, or to sin. If they tend to himself, he fashioneth them more and more to himself; if, however, they tend to sin, he still so overrules their working as to subserve his own glory and the good of his people. "He considereth all their works;" these too, seated on his throne in heaven, God sees—all the works of all men. He sees them too, as he sees the thoughts and intents of their hearts, as matters for which he will deal with them as their King and Judge. It is not an idle seat that God occupies in the place of his habitation, the abode of his undisturbed glory in the heavens. He beholds from thence, to punish or reward it, every thought of every heart, and every deed of every hand, upon the face of the whole earth. This omniscient judgment of God is another reason why the righteous and the upright should not fear what man can do unto them.

VERSES 16, 17. There is no king saved by the multitude of a host: a mighty man is not delivered by much strength. A horse is a vain thing for safety; neither shall he deliver any by his great strength.

That there is no king saved by the multitude of a host, was verified in Sennacherib, when, having taken all the fenced cities of Israel, he sat down before Jerusalem with what he thought to be an invincible host, defying Israel and Israel's God. That night the angel of the Lord went forth, and smote in the camp of the Assyrian an hundred and four score and five thousand, (2 Kings xix. 35,) sending the vaunting king back to his kingdom, leaving his mighty host behind him, dead. And that "a mighty man is not delivered by much strength," was verified in Goliath of Gath, when, for defying Israel and Israel's God, a smooth stone from a sling in the hands of a youth, felled the giant to the ground. 1 Sam. xvii. 35. "A horse is a vain thing for safety;" this Pharaoh learned to his cost, when, pursuing the Israelites into the midst of the Red Sea, with all his horses, his chariots, and his horsemen; his horses, chariots, and horsemen were overwhelmed in the waves; there remained not so much as one of them. Exod. xiv. 28. So long as they are willing and obedient, and look to him in faith, and prayer, no human power, however great, can prevail against the people of God. He can bring to nought, both as and when he will, his enemies and theirs; and cause that in which they trusted most, and thought invincible, to be a vain thing to them. The horse is prepared for the day of battle, but victory is of the Lord. Prov. xxi. 31.

VERSES 18, 19. Behold, the eye of the Lord is upon them that fear him, upon them that hope in his mercy; to deliver their soul from death, and to keep them alive in famine.

They who truly fear the Lord need no material strength to ensure their safety. Trusting in his mercy makes his strength theirs; enlists his omnipotence upon their side. His eye is ever on them for their good. "He delivereth their soul from death:" the last enemy never invades them till he permits: he can preserve them unharmed in the lions' den, and in the seven times heated furnace; and when at length their dust returns unto the earth as it was, and the spirit unto him who gave it. "He keepeth them alive in famine:" if it be better for them to live than to die, his people can never lack the means of subsistence. He will command the ravens to feed them, or cause that those who undertake to give them daily bread, shall have barrels of meal that waste not, and cruses of oil that fail not. 1 Kings xvii. 1–16. God's care of those who endeavour to please him is unceasing. No want of theirs can be too insignificant for him to notice and relieve. His loving care of them extends from the greatest to the least thing concerning them, from the eternal welfare of the soul to the numbering the hairs of the head.

VERSES 20, 21. Our soul waiteth for the Lord; he is our help and our shield. For our heart shall rejoice in him; because we have trusted in his holy name.

This waiting for the Lord is not an idle waiting on the part of his people: it is a waiting in faith, and hope, and prayer. It is a waiting in patience, too, while using all the means of preparing ourselves for a due appreciation and improvement of the blessing when it comes. It is a doing all we can to help ourselves, while realizing that success can come from God alone. It is only this sort of waiting for the Lord, that makes him our help and shield. God never does for men what they can do for themselves. He who was about to raise Lazarus from the dead, said, "Take ye away the stone" from the grave's mouth; and, having raised him from the dead, said again, "Loose him," free him from his grave clothes, "and let him go." John xi. 39, 44. It is idle for us to suppose that we are truly waiting for the Lord, while we are not doing all that our human power can accomplish. Man's extremity is God's opportunity. He interposes with his power, only where human power can no longer avail. At that point, however, he always does interpose in behalf of those fearing him and hoping in his mercy. They may travel on in their own strength to the last sand of the sea shore, and if it be his will that they go still forward, he opens a way for them through the deep on dry ground. Exod. xiv. 15, 22. It is this fact that brings joy to the heart of all those who fear the Lord and have trusted in his holy name. Their experience teaches them that he never fails them in extremity: that when human power can no longer avail them, he is present to help and shield them with his own Divine power. What a thought is this to bring quiet to the mind and peace to the heart, that whatever the people of God lack in themselves, they have in him, to infinity!

VERSE 22. Let thy mercy, O Lord, be upon us, according as we hope in thee.

To the blind men seeking the restoration of their sight, and professing their belief that he could grant what they asked, our Lord, touching their eyes, said, "According to your faith, be it unto you; and their eyes were opened." Matt. ix. 29–30. He said also to the centurion, whose faith had uttered itself in the words, "Speak the word only, and my servant shall be healed. . . . Go thy way: and as thou hast believed, so be it done unto thee. And his servant was healed in the self-same hour." Matt. viii. 8–13. God has ordained an immutable connection between faith and mercy, between our hoping for his salvation, and obtaining it. It is the one indispensable condition upon which he will interpose to save us. It is a condition, however, which being fulfilled by us, secures us his help in the self-same hour, in the self-same moment. If then we are conscious of exercising faith in him, we can with safety offer up the prayer of the last verse of our psalm, "Let thy mercy, O Lord, be upon us, according as we hope in thee:" trust in thee, wait for thee. The prayer is just a reminding God, that having through his grace fulfilled the condition on which he has promised to show mercy, we hope for the fulfilment of his promise so made. It is claiming no merit for our faith —that also being the gift of God, (Eph. ii. 8)—but only that, having himself inspired the hope that is in our hearts, he would realize it, according to the strength he has given it. This then being the connection between the exercise of faith on our part, and the exercise of mercy on his part, how earnestly and incessantly should we put up the prayer of the apostles, "Lord, increase our faith." Luke xvii. 5. It enlists on our side at once the great I AM; him who is true, and just, and merciful, omniscient and omnipresent; him who called the universe into being by a word: who spake, and it was done; who commanded, and it stood fast. And surely, if we have him on our side, him, as he was manifested in Christ, we need not fear what man can do unto us. Our safety and our happiness are in hands where no created power can reach them.

LECTURE ON PSALM XXXIV.

The heading of this psalm reads, "A Psalm of David, when he changed his behaviour before Abimelech; who drove him away, and he departed." The reason for this caption is given us in the history to which it refers, 1 Sam. xxi. 10–15. Being so sorely persecuted by Saul, that he could no longer remain with safety in any part of the land of Israel, David betook himself to the court of Achish, the king of Gath, who is called in our title also Abimelech, the general name of the kings of the Philistines, as Pharaoh was for a long time the general name of the kings of Egypt, and Cæsar, of the emperors of Rome. Whether or not David visited Achish at his solicitation, we cannot tell. Some suppose that he did, Achish hoping to find him useful in his wars against Saul. It seems, however, that the captains and chief men of Achish were not pleased with David's presence at the court of their king. They seem to have in some way ascertained his true relation to the throne of Israel, as its future occupant; for they say to Achish, "Is not this David the king of the land? did they not sing one to another of him in dances, saying, Saul hath slain his thousands, and David his ten thousands? And David laid up these words in his heart, and was sore afraid of Achish the king of Gath. And he changed his behaviour before them, and feigned himself mad in their hands; and scrabbled on the doors of the gate, and let his spittle fall down upon his beard. Then said Achish, unto his servants, Lo, ye see the man is mad: wherefore have ye brought him to me? Have

I need of madmen, that ye have brought this fellow to play the madman in my presence? shall this fellow come into my house?" Thus dismissed by Achish, David escaped the dangers threatening him. His conduct, however, on this occasion has been the subject of a great diversity of comment. Some have defended it; more have condemned it; while others have so explained it as to free it of all just censure. If David's madness was really feigned, the propriety of his conduct is certainly to be questioned; and it was a deception unworthy of him, both as a man and as a believer: unworthy of him as a man, because the true man will no more act an untruth, than he will utter one; and still more unworthy of him as a believer, because it was, for the time-being at least, a distrusting of the power of God to deliver him. It was, in short, doing evil that good might come, and that, too, when the prayer of faith, ascending from his heart at the moment, would have secured him the Divine interposition and protection. The man whose trust in God continues steadfast, will never be left to be tempted beyond his strength. He therefore, to escape from danger, need resort to no mode of questionable morality. There are, however, some few persons who think that David's conduct on the present occasion was not feigned; that the change in his behaviour was caused by a sudden attack of sickness, which, for the time, did actually deprive him of his reason—epilepsy. The persons holding this opinion, think they discover the unmistakable symptoms of that spasmodic and delirious sickness in David's scrabbling, or rather, *falling* upon the posts of the gate, and foaming at the mouth. If this was so, the fact exculpates David of all blame: if, however, the more common opinion be true, that his madness was feigned, his conduct is without excuse. The man who saves his life by a falsehood, pays more for it than it is worth. When told that he might save his life by telling a falsehood, by denying his handwriting, Algernon Sidney replied, "When God has brought me into a dilemma in which I must assert a lie or lose my life, he gives me a clear intimation of my duty, which is, to prefer death to falsehood." But whether David effected it by means justifiable or unjustifiable, he was equally bound to thank God for the mercy of his escape; and he does this in this psalm, and also improves the occasion to teach, as another has said, his fellow-believers "the art of leading a quiet life, and of being secure against enemies. This art consists in the fear of God, in keeping watch on the lips, in doing no evil, and in following after peace: the consequences of which are, prayer heard, deliverance out of all danger, the gracious presence of God, communion with him, consolation from him, and the protection of person and life."

VERSE 1. I will bless the Lord at all times; his praise shall continually be in my mouth.

Great and special deliverances excite the mind, as nothing else can, to praise God without ceasing. Such deliverances not only recall to our minds similar deliverances, but they also excite within us a more vivid and abiding sense of God's common mercies to us, and the recollection of the two, so revived in the memory, keeps his praise continually upon our lips. This was the case with David here. He had been delivered when, throughout all Israel, there was hardly a man whose hand was not against him to take away his life; and for mercy so vouchsafed him, he resolves that he will render unto the Lord the tribute of continual thanksgiving. This is all the return that God asks of us for any of his mercies to us; and yet how few of us make him the return, so easy, so natural, and so becoming to dependent creatures!

VERSE 2. My soul shall make her boast in the Lord: the humble shall hear thereof, and be glad.

What causes David specially to exult in the Lord is this—the encouragement which his deliverance would give to others similarly situated, not to despair of the Divine mercy. "The humble shall hear thereof, and be glad." Other tried and tempted believers shall learn, from my experience, that God will never leave them nor forsake them. This we are too apt to forget, and to think, when trouble and sorrow come upon us, that no one else ever had trouble or sorrow like ours. In this we are mistaken; and herein consists the great advantage of being familiar with the spiritual exercises and experiences of other Christians. Their religious history soon teaches us that we have not a trouble which they had not, nor a trial which they had not, nor a temptation which they had not, nor a weakness which they had not, and did not overcome in the strength of the Lord. We hear thereof, and are glad; their experience of the sufficiency and certainty of the grace of God leads us to hope and believe that we too may conquer. Thus the victorious faith of every believer in the whole Church becomes a heritage of hope, and strength, and comfort to every other believer; they hear thereof, and are glad.

VERSES 3, 4. O magnify the Lord with me, and let us exalt his name together. I sought the Lord, and he heard me, and delivered me from all my fears.

It is difficult for the soul that has been delivered out of great dangers, not to call upon others to join it in its ovation of praise and thanksgiving; and especially difficult for it not to call upon those who have experienced similar mercy. It cannot refrain from calling upon them to join it in magnifying the Lord, to join it in proclaiming the greatness of his mercy, the immutability of his promises, and his readiness to hear the prayer of every one who calls on him for help. "O magnify the Lord with me, and let us exalt his name together," is the spontaneous language of the soul that has experienced the salvation of God, and tasted the sweets of redeeming, regenerating, and sanctifying love.

VERSE 5. They looked unto him, and were lightened; and their faces were not ashamed.

David here changes his nominatives and verbs from the first person singular to the third person plural, to teach us that what he says of himself, as a beneficiary of the Divine mercy, is equally true of all believers; that the experience of every one who trusts in the Lord is what he describes his own to have been, where he says: "I sought the Lord, and he heard me, and delivered me from all my fears." It is one of the subtle devices of Satan to insinuate into our minds the thought that the experience of eminent believers can never be ours. "Yes, it can," David answers; God's dealings with *me* are only a specimen of what he is ready to do for *all* who look to him; no burning blush of shame at hope disappointed, but the beaming light of hope realized, shall play over every face that is turned to him. God is no respecter of persons; he is alike rich unto all who call upon him.

VERSE 6. This poor man cried, and the Lord heard him, and saved him out of all his troubles.

Here again, speaking of himself in the third person, David turns to God's dealings with him individually, still giving his own experience, however, as an encouragement to others. "This poor man cried." David was poor indeed when he offered up the prayer to which he here alludes. He had not where to lay his head; no man dared to call him friend, or to show himself friendly to him, and Ahimelech, the priest, for giving him a morsel of bread, was slain, with four-score and five other persons that did wear the ephod. 1 Sam. xxii. 18. Nevertheless, although he was disowned of all, and marked for slaughter, when this poor man cried, the Lord heard him, and saved him out of all his troubles. "Whose situation," David seems to say, "could be more hopeless or more helpless than mine was?—and yet the Lord delivered me."

VERSE 7. The angel of the Lord encampeth round about them that fear him, and delivereth them.

This encamping of the angel of the Lord round about them that fear him, may mean either the actual encamping of the angelic hosts round them that shall be heirs of salvation, or it may mean the girdings of the Divine Omnipotence surrounding all those who have taken refuge in his mercy. Perhaps, in the fulness of its import, it comprehends both meanings. Certain it is, that God delights to share with the angelic host his great work of saving man. It was they who first announced the birth of a Saviour, and shouted in glad accents, "Glory to God in the highest; and on earth peace, good-will toward men." We also read that there is joy in the presence of the angels of God over every sinner that repenteth. How cheering a thought should this be to the children of God; not only is God himself round about them to protect them, but also his holy angels. "Fear not," said Elisha to the young man intimidated by the numbers and power of the enemy surrounding them—"fear not; for they that be with us are more than they that be with them." And when he prayed the Lord to open the young man's eyes, he saw, and behold the mountain was full of horses and chariots of fire round about Elisha. 2 Kings vi. 14–17. These horses and chariots of fire were guardian angels. It was such angels that, having watched over him during his life, bore the soul of Lazarus, when it was released from his diseased body, to the bosom of Abraham. The extreme care with which the angels watch over those committed to their charge, is indicated in the words that they bear them up in their hands, lest they should at any time so much as strike their foot against a stone.

VERSE 8. O taste and see that the Lord is good: blessed is the man that trusteth in him.

It is not to meagre, evanescent joys, that the Lord admits the man whose trust is in him: he admits him to an everlasting feast of joys such as eye hath not seen, nor ear heard, nor have entered into the heart of man to conceive. The soul no sooner gets a foretaste of these joys than it feels that it is in the way to the good for which it was made, and the good whose full possession will make it perfectly and eternally happy.

VERSES 9, 10. O fear the Lord, ye his saints: for there is no want to them that fear him. The young lions do lack and suffer hunger: but they that seek the Lord shall not want any good thing.

The young lions that do lack and suffer hunger, may mean persons who seek enjoyment with ardent, impetuous, and headlong feeling, but seek it only in things temporal. Such persons, however vehemently they may seek happiness there, still suffer the hunger of desires unsatisfied. They enjoy no substantial peace, no abiding happiness. In the midst of every blessing that earth can bestow, there is still with them a hungering of the heart, and a thirsting of the spirit, after a bliss not yet attained. They are, too, generally quite as far removed from real happiness in prosperity as they are in adversity. It is otherwise with those who fear the Lord, seeking their happiness in him. They shall not want any good thing. If their God crowns their lives with mercies and loving kindnesses, he will look to it that their prosperity shall not injure them. If he visits them with the rod, and strips them of their earthly comforts, he will still so order the providence that affliction shall be better for them than prosperity would have been. God will allow those who fear him to lack nothing which will be really a good to them.

VERSE 11. Come, ye children, hearken unto me: I will teach you the fear of the Lord.

That is, I will teach you *how* God should be feared, and *why* he should be feared. This seems to be David's thought here, which thought he draws out, illustrates, and expands in the remaining verses of the psalm.

VERSE 12. What man is he that desireth life, and loveth many days, that he may see good?

That is, who desires to live a long and happy life, to have many days allotted to him wherein to enjoy life as a blessing and a joy. Whoever of you, says David, covets this blessing, give heed to the following directions, and he shall obtain the desire of his heart.

VERSE 13. Keep thy tongue from evil, and thy lips from speaking guile.

This is David's first lesson in teaching the fear of the Lord: to avoid all sins of the tongue. While it is only a negative virtue, to utter no injurious and no false word, it nevertheless contributes as much toward a happy life as any other that can be named. How rare the excellence to be blameless in one's speech! Hence the saying of St. James, "If any man offend not in word, the same is a perfect man, and able also to bridle his whole body." James iii. 2. He who has so gained the mastery of his tongue that no unkind, unjust, or insincere word escapes his lips, certainly cannot be other than a happy man. He must enjoy a mental quietude peculiarly his own. If he suffer evil, it will not be in return for evil, and it can therefore be easily borne. If he suffer reproaches, he knows that they are not the echo of his own words, and he can therefore care as little for them as he cares for the idle wind. The grace of silence is a grace that we do not sufficiently seek and cultivate. We reflect too little how much the happiness of life is in the power of the tongue, and how much we need the fear of God in our hearts to control it. It is, therefore, the first lesson which the Divine Spirit strives to teach us, when he infuses the principles of the Divine life into our minds. He would have us, as our very first step in the fear of the Lord, govern our tongues by the laws of truth and love.

VERSE 14. Depart from evil, and do good; seek peace, and pursue it.

"Depart from evil, and do good." Another part of the fear of the Lord is a ceasing to do evil, and a learning to do well. He whose soul is filled with the fear of the Lord, loving him as his Father, and fearing him as his God, will not be satisfied with the merely negative character of doing no harm in the world. He will aim and labour to do good, and to leave the world better and happier for his having been in it. "Seek peace, and pursue it." He, whose soul is filled with the fear of the Lord, will have his heart set on peace. He will *seek* it, he will *pursue* it with an energy that never abates, and a patience that never tires. The sentiment of his heart and the words of his lips are, "On earth peace: good will toward men." As much as it lieth in him, he will live peaceably with all men, and do all he can to persuade all men to live peaceably with each other. This is what David calls the fear of the Lord: "keep thy tongue from evil, and thy lips from guile: depart from evil, and do good; seek peace and pursue it." And now come his reasons for our fearing the Lord in this way.

VERSE 15. The eyes of the Lord are upon the righteous, and his ears are open unto their cry.

The righteous then should not hesitate to undertake to "keep the tongue from evil, and the lips from speaking guile; to depart from evil, and do good; to seek peace, and pursue it." While thus endeavouring to serve him in holiness and pureness of living, God is all eye to watch over them, and all ear to hear their cry to him for help. He regards with lively sympathy their struggles to overcome sin in themselves and its spread over the earth. How much should this fact encourage us never to despair of perfecting ourselves in any virtue required of us by our religion!

VERSE 16. The face of the Lord is against them that do evil, to cut off the remembrance of them from the earth.

God's eyes are on evil-doers as fixedly as they are on the righteous, but for a very different purpose; not to deliver them, but to cut off the remembrance of them from the earth. It is as impossible for God not to hate and punish sin, as it is for him not to love and favour holiness. His nature, therefore, impels him as strongly to overwhelm and destroy the wicked, as it does to deliver and save the righteous. This is a fact full of hope to the righteous, but one that should be full of fear to those who persevere in their wickedness. The same eye that beams upon one in light and love, flashes down upon the other as a consuming fire.

VERSE 17. The righteous cry, and the Lord heareth, and delivereth them out of all their troubles.

It matters not how many troubles the righteous may have, the Lord delivereth them out of all. He may not deliver them at once, but, for a time, only give them grace to bear their troubles, until they have wrought out for them all the spiritual good they can work, and then the final deliverance comes. St. Paul besought the Lord many times to remove his thorn in the flesh; and if it would have been for his spiritual good, no doubt it would have been removed at once: but it was needful to the perfecting of his Christian character. The Lord, therefore instead of removing it, gave him grace still to bear it. 2 Cor. xii. 7–9. In this way God often makes the troubles of the righteous man his most precious blessings.

VERSE 18. The Lord is nigh unto them that are of a broken heart; and saveth such as be of a contrite spirit.

God regards the penitent soul with tenderest sympathy. The sighs of its contrition go direct to his heart. Its broken moanings over its sinfulness move him as nothing else can. "For thus saith the high and lofty One that inhabiteth eternity, whose name is Holy; I dwell in the high and holy place, with him also that is of a contrite and humble spirit, to revive the spirit of the humble, and to revive the heart of the contrite ones." Isa. lvii. 15. What a balm should such words as these be to the heart of all those who are truly grieving over their sins, to whom the remembrance of them is grievous, the burden of them intolerable.

VERSES 19, 20. Many are the afflictions of the righteous: but the Lord delivereth him out of them all. He keepeth all his bones; not one of them is broken.

It is only entire ultimate deliverance from all his afflictions that God promises the righteous man. He necessarily suffers so long as he sins; and the most thoroughly righteous man will sin, more or less, to the last. The most thoroughly righteous man, then, will suffer more or less to the last. Sin, even in the righteous man, is indissolubly connected with suffering. God, however, will take care that none of his sufferings shall overcome him; he will deliver him before they reach that point. "He keepeth all his bones; not one of them is broken." He thus kept his own Son; not one of his bones was broken. No evil can befall those who trust in God, except as he permits or directs. The smallest thing connected with the believer is under His perpetual care. He has numbered the very hairs of his head, and not a hair can perish without his consent. Matt. x. 30. Who would be without such a Guardian, Protector, and God as this? and who, having such a Guardian, Protector, and God, should ever allow his heart to be oppressed by a single anxious care?

VERSE 21. Evil shall slay the wicked; and they that hate the righteous shall be desolate.

"The wicked, and they that hate the righteous," are the same—the same ungodly characters. Their doom is that they "shall be desolate," that evil shall slay them. God allows no evil befalling the righteous ultimately to injure them, but, on the contrary, in the end overrules it for their good. It is otherwise with the ills of life which befall the wicked; these do them only harm. There being in the ills they suffer no hand of God to lighten, and, at last, to remove them, their trials come upon the wicked with a force that overwhelms them. They are slain by them, and perish without hope, as they have lived without happiness. There is no other fate for those who make not the Lord their trust.

VERSE 22. The Lord redeemeth the soul of his servants; and none of them that trust in him shall be desolate.

This last verse contains substantially the teaching of the whole psalm; that is, God's never-failing care of those who endeavour to serve him in holiness and righteousness. He guides them by his wisdom, strengthens them by his grace, protects them by his power, and redeems their soul from death. Such is the God of the believer as he revealed himself to

David. How like the God who afterwards revealed himself to the world in the man Christ Jesus! He is not another, but the same God! Let us all then place ourselves under his protection by trusting in his mercy and obeying his laws. Doing this, let none of us fear that he will ever leave us or forsake us; for "He that spared not his own Son, but delivered him up for us all, how shall he not with him also freely give us all things?" Rom. viii. 32.

LECTURE ON PSALM XXXV.

VERSES 1, 2. Plead my cause, O Lord, with them that strive with me: fight against them that fight against me. Take hold of shield and buckler, and stand up for my help.

THIS psalm was composed by David while suffering every kind of persecution at the hands of Saul and of his servants. They were not only seeking to take away his life, but left no slander unuttered that could cover his name and memory with infamy. Thus situated, and speaking not merely as an individual, but as the representative of persecuted righteousness, he prays for deliverance for himself, and for confusion to his enemies. In fact, the contest here waged between David and his enemies, represents the contest that has ever been going on in the world between truth and error, holiness and sin. Portions of the psalm, therefore, carry the mind beyond David to David's Son—to him who was Righteousness itself. "Plead thou my cause, O Lord." The man persecuted for righteousness' sake can never call in vain upon God to plead his cause. He may call, assuredly believing that God will obtain for him all his rights. The God of truth and justice, he will not suffer one who loves truth and justice to be cast in a judicial contest with his enemies. He will be in court when the trial comes on, to see that justice is done his client. This we might infer from what we know of his attributes, and is certainly the testimony of his providence.

"Take hold of shield and buckler." Having in the first verse invoked God to his help as his Judge and Advocate, David here invokes him to come as a warrior, with shield and buckler. God's protecting power is the shield and buckler with which he comes to the help of his people; a shield and buckler which no weapon formed by man can penetrate to reach those sheltered by it.

VERSE 3. Draw out also the spear, and stop the way against them that persecute me: say unto my soul, I am thy salvation.

It is not defensive armour only, but also offensive, that David prays the Lord to use against his enemies—the spear, to oppose its point to them, while they are yet on their march against him. So it is, God not only protects us against the evils immediately about us, but goes out to stop the way against others that are only approaching us. "Say unto my soul, I am thy salvation:" let me not only have thy saving protection, but let me be conscious of having it; let me, as it were, hear thee saying to "my soul, I am thy salvation." When God takes us under his covenant protection, he makes us aware of it: his Spirit in some way bears witness to our spirits, that such is the fact. Rom. viii. 16.

VERSES 4—6. Let them be confounded and put to shame that seek after my soul: let them be turned back and brought to confusion that devise my hurt. Let them be as chaff before the wind; and let the angel of the Lord chase them. Let their way be dark and slippery; and let the angel of the Lord persecute them.

To be confounded, to be put to shame, to be as chaff before the wind, to have their way dark and slippery, and to be chased by the angel of the Lord, that is, to be pursued by an avenging and retributive providence, has certainly been the fate of all who have arrayed themselves against the Church and people of God, to destroy them. David's words, then, taken as an imprecation or as a prophesy, only indicate the immutable connection between wicked men's opposing the truth, and their being destroyed. That there is this immutable connection between opposition and destruction, no one will deny, who is familiar with history.

VERSE 7. For without cause have they hid for me their net in a pit, which without cause they have digged for my soul.

Here we have the reason assigned for the imprecations or denunciations of the three preceding verses. The hostility of the wicked there denounced was without cause, without any provocation, proceeding from sheer malice, and hearts incurably intent on evil.

VERSE 8. Let destruction come upon him unawares; and let his net that he hath hid catch himself: into that very destruction let him fall.

It has been the fate of more than Haman to perish upon his own gallows, to be caught in the net hid for another, to fall into the very destruction sought for the innocent. It was thus with Saul. The evil he sought to do David came upon himself, leaving David free to ascend, unmolested, the throne which Saul had striven so hard to retain and perpetuate in his own family. It was thus too with the Jews. They crucified Christ, lest the Romans should come and take away their place and nation, John xi. 48–50; and their doing so precipitated upon them the very evil they aimed to avoid. This recoiling of the wickedness of the wicked upon themselves, an ordering of the Divine Providence, has been signally illustrated in regard to all opposers of the religion of the Son of David.

VERSES 9, 10. And my soul shall rejoice in the Lord: it shall rejoice in his salvation. All my bones shall say, Lord, who is like unto thee, which deliverest the poor from him that is too strong for him, yea, the poor and the needy from him that spoileth him?

"My soul shall rejoice—all my bones shall say:" that is, with soul and body, with every power of his whole nature, David promises to praise God for the deliverance for which he has been praying. There is beauty in this reference to his body joining the soul in its thanksgiving. The deliverance of David from all his human enemies, and especially from his great enemy, Saul, may represent our deliverance from all our spiritual enemies, and especially from our great enemy and spoiler, Death. Accordingly, in the redemption wrought out for us by our Lord, the body shares as largely as the soul, and should therefore rejoice with the soul. "It is sown in corruption; it is raised in incorruption: it is sown in dishonour; it is raised in glory: it is sown in weakness; it is raised in power: it is sown a natural body; it is raised a spiritual body." Verily, who is a deliverer like to thee, O Lord?

VERSES 11, 12. False witnesses did rise up: they laid to my charge things that I knew not. They rewarded me evil for good, to the spoiling of my soul.

It was the lot of David, and of the Son of David, to suffer from the tongue of calumny. Both were charged with being deceivers of the people, exciters of sedition, the enemies and subverters of religion. Both laboured to do their nation only good, and yet both experienced in return only evil—David, till he came to the throne; Christ, to the end of his life. This treatment of them was to the spoiling of their souls, and filled their hearts with a grief harder to be borne than any other. It was a blow for a kiss, curses for blessings. These are things hard to bear; and the more loving the heart upon which they fall, the more deeply they wound it.

VERSES 13, 14. But as for me, when they were sick, my clothing was sackcloth: I humbled my soul with fasting; and my prayer returned into mine own bosom. I behaved myself as though he had been my friend or brother; I bowed down heavily, as one that mourneth for his mother.

How certainly Divine must that religion be, which leads one not to rejoice, but grieve over the misfortunes of its worst enemies! David shed tears of as sincere grief over the death of Saul, as any other subject of his kingdom. He put on sackcloth, fasted, and prayed; and his head was so bowed down with sorrow, that his prayer passed from his lips into his bosom. 2 Sam. i. 11, 12. It was the same with the Son of David. He, too, grieved over the calamities befalling his worst enemies, as if each had been a friend or brother. His spirit was oppressed with sorrow for them. It is said of Him, that he was never known to smile, though he was often seen in tears; and certainly his tears could not have been for himself, nor any holy being. You recollect his weeping lament over Jerusalem, out of which it was impossible that a prophet should perish—"O Jerusalem, Jerusalem, how often would I have gathered thy children together as a hen gathereth her chickens under her wings, and ye would not." Matt. xxiii. 37. You recollect, too, his prayer upon the cross, for his murderers—"Father, forgive them; for they know not what they do." Luke xxiii. 34. We ask no stronger proof of the divinity of our holy religion, than its awakening grief for the misfortunes of enemies—its pitying the hand that smites, and praying for the hand that crucifies.

VERSES 15, 16. But in mine adversity they rejoiced and gathered themselves together: yea, the abjects gathered themselves together against me, and I knew it not: they did tear me, and ceased not: with hypocritical mockers in feasts, they gnashed upon me with their teeth.

Behold in these words the contrast between the Spirit of Christ, and the spirit of the world: between the spirit of the truly regenerate man, and the spirit of every one of us as we are born into the world. The misfortunes of his enemies were a grief to David: to them his misfortunes were a joy. They delighted in his adversity, and gathered themselves together to aggravate it in every way that malice could suggest. Abjects, the veriest dregs of society, men of whose existence, or, certainly, of whose hostility he knew not, until the time of his adversity, were among his most vociferous defamers; they did tear, and ceased not. Hypocritical mockers in feasts, gnashed upon him with their teeth, like hounds hissed on by the masters who had fed them. This is certainly a dark picture that David draws of his enemies. Was it not, however, realized, and more than realized, in the enemies of the Son of David? What abject, or what man willing to do the work of even perjured detraction for his bread, did the rulers of the Jews not retain and use to accomplish their murderous designs against Messiah? What insult did they not offer him before he breathed his last upon the cross? Who was there among them too high, or too low, not to mock at his calamity? Did the high priest, the highest of the nation, revile him as an impostor? So did, at least, one of the thieves crucified with him, cast the same in his teeth. Matt. xxvii. 4. And that, too, while there were sounding in their ears, those wonderful words, "Father, forgive them; for they know not what they do!" O the wickedness of the human heart when left to itself! The depths of its depravity God alone can sound, and his Spirit alone light up with the light of life.

VERSE 17. Lord, how long wilt thou look on? rescue my soul from their destructions, my darling from the lions.

"Lord, how long wilt thou look on" as an unconcerned spectator of my situation? I am surrounded by dangers from which thou alone canst rescue me: come thou to my help: save my soul from them who would destroy it: my darling* from enemies as active, powerful, and relentless as young lions. These words express an urgency of desire amounting almost to impatience. They remind one of the nobleman's words, seeking relief for his sick son. Coming to our Lord and entreating him to go down to Capernaum with him, to heal his son, but thinking that he lingered, he cried out, "Sir, come down ere my child

* Darling here means soul.

die." Without farther delay our Lord replied, "Go thy way; thy son liveth." John iv. 49, 50. When some great grief oppresses the heart, God is not displeased if the cry for help is vehement. His own Son, in the days of his flesh, offered up prayers and supplications, with strong crying and tears, and was heard. Heb. v. 7.

VERSE 18. I will give thee thanks in the great congregation: I will praise thee among much people.

To praise God with grateful hearts is the only return any of his creatures can make him for his mercies to them. This David promises here. In the great congregation, among much people, he will thank and praise God, if he vouchsafe him the deliverance he sought. He will proclaim to his whole church how great a Deliverer and Saviour the Lord is. This will be the employment of the redeemed in heaven, and throughout eternity; their anthem of praise to Him that loved them and washed them from their sins in his own blood, evermore increasing in fervour and heightened gratitude.

VERSE 19. Let not them that are mine enemies wrongfully rejoice over me; neither let them wink with the eye that hate me without a cause.

One greater than David quoted the last words of this verse as spoken of himself. Christ says of his enemies, "They hated me without a cause." John xv. 25. We must reckon many things that David says of himself and his enemies in this psalm, as being said in a still higher sense of Christ and his enemies. This is the case with many of the psalms: we give them the full extent of their meaning, not until we apply them to Christ as well as to David. He, more than any other, was hated without a cause.

His betrayer was obliged to acknowledge that he was innocent; and Pilate when he gave him up to be crucified, that he had found no fault in him. Surely his enemies rejoiced over him wrongfully. Their rejoicing, however, was of short duration. When God brought him again from the dead, their rejoicing was at an end. How careful should we be, if hated, that it shall be without cause: then may we with confidence look to God for deliverance. The cry of innocence can never ascend to him in vain.

VERSE 20. For they speak not peace; but they devise deceitful matters against them that are quiet in the land.

David would gladly have remained quiet in the holy land under the government of Saul, and our Lord under the government of the Romans; but their enemies were not for peace; they devised deceitful matters against them; so misled the people in regard to their purposes, motives, and conduct, as to oblige them, at times, to flee the land to save their lives. Nor has this treatment been experienced only by David and the Son of David. Many a follower of Christ, to escape the fury of enemies whose good was the sole aim of his life, has had to flee the home where he would gladly have remained quiet.

VERSE 21. Yea, they opened their mouth wide against me, and said, Aha, aha! our eye hath seen it.

That is, our eye hath at length seen what it has long desired to see, the downfall of our hated enemy! He is snared at last, and we enjoy the sight, no one can tell how much! Such is the spirit of the "Aha, aha! our eye hath seen it." It indicates the most malicious and mocking exultation; such as that in which the Jews indulged, when they at last beheld Christ upon the cross, wagging the head and saying,

"Ah, thou that destroyest the temple, and buildest it again in three days, save thyself. If thou be the Son of God, come down from the cross. He trusted in God; let him deliver him now if he will have him. He saved others, himself he cannot save. If he be the King of Israel, let him now come down from the cross, and we will believe on him." Matt. xxvii. 39–43. How fearful an exhibition of human depravity and hatred of righteousness! Fearful indeed! and yet who among us, if we had been there, can say that we would not have joined in the frantic exultation? Not one. If any of us are at all better than the crucifiers of our Lord, we are so altogether by the restraining or regenerating grace of God.

VERSES 22–24. This thou hast seen, O Lord; keep not silence: O Lord, be not far from me. Stir up thyself, and awake to my judgment, even unto my cause, my God and my Lord. Judge me, O Lord my God, according to thy righteousness: and let them not rejoice over me.

These several phrases, "keep not silence—be not far from me—stir up thyself, and awake to my judgment, my cause—judge me—let them not rejoice over me," are all the utterances of a heart which feels that it cannot be denied its requests; that its petitions must be granted, and that, too, soon. These accumulated petitions indicate the state of desire in which we may suppose Jacob to have been, when, though he had already wrestled with the angel of the covenant in prayer, from evening till the dawn of day, he still persevered, saying, "I will not let thee go, except thou bless me." Gen. xxxii. 26. "This thou hast seen, O Lord"—thou hast seen all of which I have complained, the number, power, and cruel hatred of my enemies. Lord, save me; I perish without thy help. Delay thine aid no longer. It was thus, no doubt, that David prayed in some great moral crisis of his life; and thus, too, that the Son of David prayed in the garden and upon the cross. There is many a crisis in the believer's history when the strong, oft-reiterated cry for help is the only form of prayer that can adequately express his sense of danger and desire for deliverance.

VERSE 25. Let them not say in their hearts, Ah! so would we have it: let them not say, We have swallowed him up.

The exclamation, "Ah, so would we have it!" indicates the extreme pleasure with which the enemies of the righteous would witness any overwhelming calamity befalling him. They would hail it as the realization of the most cherished desire of their hearts, and be ready to add, "we have swallowed him up," "we have utterly overthrown him." So the Jews thought and expressed themselves when they had crucified our Lord, and consigned him to the grave. But they were mistaken; as all others have been who have fancied that they had accomplished the overthrow of one for whom God cares.

VERSE 26. Let them be ashamed and brought to confusion together that rejoice at mine hurt: let them be clothed with shame and dishonour that magnify themselves against me."

Here again David prays for the shame, confusion, and dishonour of his enemies; but only, we are allowed to believe, upon the supposition of their continuing implacable. God delighteth not in the death, but in the repentance of the sinner, and David, speaking as the representative of "God manifested in the flesh," could not pray for the unconditional destruction of his worst enemies. He could, however, without any violation of charity, pray that, if they would not desist from their course, they might be covered with the shame, confusion, and dishonour with which they were seeking to cover him. And such has, in fact, always been the doom of all those who have rejoiced at the hurt of the King of Israel, and magnified themselves against him.

VERSE 27. Let them shout for joy, and be glad, that favour my righteous cause; yea, let them say continually, Let the Lord be magnified, which hath pleasure in the prosperity of his servant.

It is not because they are his friends, otherwise than as they are the friends of righteousness, that David here prays that they who favour his cause may shout for joy and be glad. He desires that they may be jubilant only as the Lord gives them occasion to be so, by the favour he shows him, his servant. Of course, the principle applies to all like cases.

VERSE 28. And my tongue shall speak of thy righteousness and of thy praise, all the day long.

If the deliverance sought is vouchsafed him, David here promises the only return he could make for it, to proclaim the fact with unceasing praise. "My tongue shall speak of thy righteousness," of thy vindication and justification of me against the accusations of mine enemies. There is a higher justification for which all Christians are bound to thank God with praise unceasing—his justification of them, though guilty, against all the accusations of the Divine law, Satan, and their own consciences; his treating them, for Christ's sake, as if they were both innocent and righteous.

It has often been remarked as a great beauty of the psalms, that there is not a phase either of personal or national experience, which they do not describe. This thirty-fifth psalm has for us Americans a historical association of peculiar interest. It is the opening psalm in the psalter for the seventh day of the month. On that day, September 7, 1774, the third day after its members had convened in Philadelphia, the proceedings of the first American Congress were opened by prayer and other devotional exercises. The officiating clergyman was an Episcopalian. He used the psalter for the day; and how—excited as the delegates must have been by the rumour of the cannonade of Boston by the British, which rumour had reached the city only the day before—how must their hearts have thrilled at the words, "Plead my cause, O Lord, with them that strive with me: fight against them that fight against me. Take hold of shield and buckler, and stand up for mine help. Draw out, also, the spear, and stop the way against them that persecute me: say unto my soul, I am thy salvation." These imploring words spoke the feelings of all hearts present. One of the most eminent of the delegates has written, "I never saw a greater effect upon an audience. It seemed as if Heaven had ordained that psalm to be read on that morning." Whether or not Heaven ordained the psalm to be read on that morning, we cannot say: we no more doubt, however, that God was with us in achieving our political liberties, than we doubt that he was with David and the Son of David in achieving our spiritual liberties, our redemption from hell and the grave. May he give us all grace to make a wise use of both the bright heritages with which he has blessed us.

LECTURE ON PSALM XXXVI.

To the Chief Musician. A Psalm of David, the servant of the Lord.

COMMENTATORS are not agreed as to the occasion on which this psalm was written. The more common opinion among them is, that it was written by David about the beginning of his persecution by Saul; at the time when Saul, though still professing friendship and conferring honours upon him, had his heart set upon his ruin, and was secretly plotting it. If he allude to Saul, it is to Saul as *representing in the spirit and temper of his mind* the ungodly world. What, therefore, he says of Saul, we may apply to every ungodly man: and what he says of himself, we may also apply to one whose moral nature has been renewed from heaven. Saul stands here as the representative of the wicked; David, as the representative of the righteous. Each is a *representative* man. In the title of the psalm, David is called "the servant of the Lord," an intimation that he spoke by inspiration, and therefore that what he says of the wicked man, of the righteous man, and of the Lord, must be true. He depicts in vivid contrast the wickedness of man, and the goodness of God, and prays that the Divine mercy may never be wanting to him in time of need.

VERSE 1. The transgression of the wicked saith within my heart, that there is no fear of God before his eyes.

The first part of this verse is obscure: it would not be so, however, if the Hebrew word rendered "saith" had been rendered, the *oracle*, the *Divine voice* within my heart. If the original had been so translated into English, the whole verse would read, The oracle, the divine voice in my heart, respecting the transgression of the wicked, is, that there is no fear of God before his eyes. The voice in David's heart was the voice of God testifying to the wickedness of man. Its testimony is, that there is no fear of God before his eyes. He lives and acts without any reference to God as the righteous Governor of the universe. We read elsewhere, that "the fear of the Lord is the beginning of wisdom," the principle whence proceeds everything that is holy, just and good; the absence of his fear is the beginning of folly, the principle whence proceeds every evil that can be named. If men fear not the Divine Majesty, there is nothing for them to fear; if they fear not his holiness, justice, and power, there is nothing to restrain them from attempting any evil thing they may set their hearts upon. And yet this is the sad moral condition of us all by nature; we come into the world, having in our hearts no reverence, no regard for even Infinite Excellence: and from this sad moral condition none of us escape till our hearts are changed by the Spirit of God. Till then there is no true fear of God before our eyes.

VERSE 2. For he flattereth himself in his own eyes, until his iniquity be found to be hateful.

Having shut out from his mind all thoughts of God as the avenger of evil, the sinner flatters himself that he will escape the punishment due his sins. As he fancies that God will not find out his iniquity, to hate it, and punish for it, he recklessly adds sin to sin, and transgression to transgression. So secure does he become in his thoughts, that, when God's curse against iniquity is sounding in his ears, even then he blesses "himself in his heart, saying, I shall have peace, though I walk in the imagination of my heart." Deut. xxix. 19. So confident is he of impunity in sinning, that he is prepared to say, with the ungodly in Isaiah, "I have made a covenant with death, and with hell am I at agreement: when the overflowing scourge shall pass through, it shall not come unto me." Isa. xxviii. 15. He imagines that, whatever evils befall others, he will escape. Even God's threatened final wrath causes him no alarm. He beguiles himself into the fancy that it will not reach him.

VERSE 3. The words of his mouth are iniquity and deceit: he hath left off to be wise, and to do good.

In the preceding verse we have had described what the wicked man is in the thoughts of his heart: in this verse we have the thoughts of his heart embodying themselves in his words and actions. His words "are iniquity and deceit:" "out of the abundance of his heart his mouth speaketh." And as to his actions, he has "left off to be wise, and to do good;" to act wisely, to act well. He is governed in his conduct by no wise and just rules of action. He does not care to maintain even the appearance of well-doing. To such recklessness in sinning, every man who casts off the fear of God is liable to be brought.

VERSE 4. He deviseth mischief upon his bed; he setteth himself in a way that is not good; he abhorreth not evil.

"He deviseth mischief upon his bed:" evil is sweeter to him than his sleep. His love of it keeps him waking, to concoct plans for accomplishing it. "He setteth himself in a way that is not good:" there is no wavering in his career. He presses on with ever-strengthing resolution to the accomplishment of the sinful desires of his heart. "He abhorreth not evil:" no, he loves it. Evil is his good; the delight of his heart, and the employment of his life. "There is no fear of God before his eyes. For he flattereth himself in his own eyes, until his iniquity be found to be hateful. The words of his mouth are iniquity and deceit: he hath left off to be wise, and to do good. He deviseth mischief upon his bed; he setteth himself in a way that is not good; he abhorreth not evil." But who is this man, whose moral character is here so darkly drawn? Unconverted reader, "thou art the man." And so is every man of the whole world of mankind, who still retains, unchanged, the moral nature with which he was born into the world. Every such man is more or less the wicked man here described, and capable of becoming, and liable to become as completely given up to the love and service of sin as he was. And what can the righteous man—surrounded by a world of such wicked men, loving sin and hating righteousness, and the righteous man, because of his righteousness—what can the righteous man expect at their hands? Certainly nothing good. His only hope, therefore, is to look to the Lord, saying,

VERSE 5. Thy mercy, O Lord, is in the heavens; and thy faithfulness reacheth unto the clouds.

Here begins the contrast between the wickedness of man and the goodness of God. All the thoughts and doings of man are evil, and only evil, continually: all the thoughts and doings of God are true and righteous altogether. God's fidelity to his word, his never failing to realize any promise of good to his people, loomed up before David's mind, like the pillar of cloud before the eyes of the Israelites in the wilderness. It was his shade by day, his light by night. Man would make promises of good, and not keep them—not so the God of Israel. His promises are as certain to be fulfilled as they are made.

VERSE 6. Thy righteousness is like the great mountains; thy judgments are a great deep: O Lord, thou preservest man and beast.

God's righteousness is as unlimited as his faithfulness and mercy—that is, his righteousness in dispensing to every man according to his works. It is as conspicuous in his administration of the affairs of the world, as the great mountains. It is in stern and lofty majesty that the retributive righteousness of God stands out before the eyes of men, in the history of the race. "Thy judgments are a great deep;" or, a mighty flood. There is thought to be an allusion here to the avenging righteousness of God, as it was seen in the deluge—his judgments sweeping away those against whom they are directed, as the waters of the deluge swept away the wicked of Noah's day. Why, then, should the righteous fear lest the wicked gain and retain the ascendency in the earth? "O Lord, thou preservest man and beast:" in the ark he preserved them, when the waters of the deluge drowned the whole world beside. This fact encouraged David to believe that, however overwhelming and wide-spread they might be, he would never be harmed by any judgments that God might send upon the wicked; that, in the midst of the most desolating of such judgments, God would keep him still alive and safe. He preserved the beast of the field and the bird of air alive in the ark, and surely he cannot take less care of a creature made in his own image, and hoping in his mercy. Yes, believer, if God care for the sparrow, think you that he can ever fail to care for thee?

VERSE 7. How excellent is thy loving-kindness, O God! therefore the children of men put their trust under the shadow of thy wings.

God's loving-kindness to his creatures is manifest in the exercise of all his attributes. Its excellency, however, is most conspicuous in the manifestations of his mercy to those who have taken refuge in it. It is the tenderness with which he treats them that most surely persuades the children of men to put their trust under the shadow of his wings. When we hear Him who was "God manifested in the flesh," saying to the most wicked of the wicked, "How often would I have gathered thy children together, even as a hen gathereth her chickens under her wings!" (Matt. xxiii. 37,) we cannot but realize that there is a depth of love in the Divine heart that has never been fathomed, and never can be. Even they who have experienced most of it, and been drawn by it to become the servants of God, cannot describe it fully; they can only say with David, "How excellent is thy loving-kindness, O God!"

VERSE 8. They shall be abundantly satisfied with the fatness of thy house; and thou shalt make them drink of the river of thy pleasures.

To be abundantly satisfied with the fatness of God's house, is to be made partakers of the rich blessings and pure pleasures of his holy religion—its love, its joy, its peace, and indwelling of the Holy Spirit, in the fulness of their power to bring rest to the soul. This shall be the blessed lot of all the children of men who put their trust in the shadow of the Divine mercy. "Thou shalt make them drink of the river of thy pleasures;" the river of thy *edens*, of thy delights. *Eden* means delight, and there is thought to be an allusion here to the river that went out from Eden to water the garden. Gen. ii. 10. If this be so, how full and abounding does it represent the flow of God's grace to those who have taken refuge in his mercy. It is not as a rill, but as a river, that he pours it into their hearts. Many a believer has said in his dying hour, "My peace is as a river;" and every believer will say it with even greater emphasis when he shall at length drink of the pure river of the waters of life, clear as crystal, proceeding out of the throne of God and of the Lamb.

VERSE 9. For with thee is the fountain of life; in thy light shall we see light.

"The fountain of life." God has within himself not only the power to give and sustain life, but also the power to crown it with every good that can render it desirable. When he speaks peace to the soul, no created power can disturb its serenity; the river of its pleasures flows on for ever full, and inexhaustible as its fountain, God himself.

"In thy light shall we see light." When God smiles upon us, it is impossible for us not to be happy. If he but lift up the light of his countenance upon us, a joy fills the heart that is unspeakable and full of glory. We can then rejoice, even though men should destroy the body; we know that they can do no more; that the soul escapes their hands, and ascends, unharmed, to its great Fountain of life and light.

VERSE 10. O continue thy loving-kindness unto them that know thee; and thy righteousness to the upright in heart.

Still be to them what thou hast ever been, their life, their light, and their salvation. "Unto them that know thee." The knowledge of God here intended, is not a mere intellectual knowledge. It is knowledge instinct with love. It is such a knowledge of God as none but those who have been made upright in heart can have. It is a knowledge of God which we can have only by having our affections purified by Divine grace, and his love shed abroad in our hearts by the Holy Ghost. "He that loveth not, knoweth not God; for God is love." 1 John iv. 8. To all, however, who know him in love, God's loving-kindness will be continued, both here and ever.

VERSE 11. Let not the foot of pride come against me, and let not the hand of the wicked remove me.

It is sometimes well for us, in our general devotions, to bring our own individual cases specially before the Lord. David does this here. The heart knoweth its own bitterness as it can know the bitterness of none beside. Who has not felt it? who has not had sorrows that made him wish to leave the crowd, to go away and be alone while breathing them in the ear of God? Alas, how little does he know of true Christian experience, whose sense of weakness and unworthiness is not at times so great as to cause him to forget all others, and to think only of his own need of help, and to cry out, "Lord, have mercy upon me! Lord, save me, I perish!"

VERSE 12. There are the workers of iniquity fallen; they are cast down, and shall not be able to rise!

Behold the power of faith! It enables the believer to speak of things future as if they were already past. David had been praying his God, "Bring the wickedness of the wicked to an end; but establish thou the just," and here, in this last verse, he speaks of the workers of iniquity as already fallen, cast down, and unable to rise. *There!* they are fallen! and *there*, too, in that very place and assault where they thought to have triumphed! It was also in the past tense that our Lord spoke of the downfall of Satan, saying, "I beheld Satan as lightning *fall* from heaven," (Luke x. 18,) though Satan's complete overthrow was then, and is now, prospective. It is, however, the privilege of every believer, having asked anything agreeable to the will and purposes of God, to think and speak of his prayer as granted. This, says St. John, "is the confidence we have in him, that if we ask anything according to his will, he heareth us." 1 John v. 14. Let us all strive for the attainment of this faith, the faith that sees its victory over all spiritual foes to be so certain, that it can think and speak of it as a victory already won; the faith that utters itself in the words, "the Lord is my light, and my salvation; whom shall I fear? The Lord is the strength of my life; of whom shall I be afraid?"

LECTURE ON PSALM XXXVII.

As the Mosaic dispensation abounded in promises of great temporal prosperity to the righteous, the so often seeing the wicked prosperous, while the righteous were afflicted, was a sore trial to the faith of many an ancient believer. It appeared to them an inconsistency between the word and the providence of God. To the solution of this difficulty David addresses himself in the psalm before us, assuring us that what God has promised the righteous can never fail them; that he will, in his own good time, and at a time the best for them, crown them with every blessing he has promised them, and bring the wicked with all their schemes and successes to nought. He therefore counsels the righteous to wait patiently for the issue God is sure to bring about.

VERSES 1, 2. Fret not thyself because of evil-doers, neither be thou envious against the workers of iniquity. For they shall soon be cut down as the grass, and wither as the green herb.

Why then allow the successes of the ungodly to irritate you, as if God had been unkind to you in being kind to them? or, why envy them for what you have not? There is nothing durable in their prosperity—neither they nor their treasures of wickedness can last. As the scythe in the hand of the mower upon the grass and green herb, such is the hand of God upon the workers of iniquity. The righteous man having God for his portion, what reason has he to envy the wicked man his prosperity? The thought of these first two verses, the thought of how unreasonable it is for a righteous man to envy the wicked their short lived prosperity, is a thought which David has woven into every other verse of the whole psalm. It has accordingly been said of this psalm, "that one and the same subject is handled in it under the most diversified applications and manifold variations, which all lead nearly to one point, although every one of them possesses its own proper force; so that they are not otherwise connected together than as so many precious stones or pearls are strung together upon one thread to form a necklace." That one thread, connecting all the parts of this psalm together, each with every other, is the thought just mentioned—the unreasonableness of the good man's envying the ungodly their prosperity. We, therefore, find this thought in the next verse, and in every succeeding verse to the end of the psalm.

VERSE 3. Trust in the Lord, and do good; so shalt thou dwell in the land, and verily thou shalt be fed.

Let not your own sufferings and the prosperity of the wicked shake your confidence in God as the righteous Governor of his creatures, nor turn you aside from doing good: still press on doing what is known to be right; "so shalt thou dwell in the land, and verily thou shalt be fed." If you do not become rich, and great, and powerful, as the wicked do, by wicked ways and means, you shall at least have a home and bread, and with them a clear conscience and the favour of God. And what earthly good can be reasonably compared with these?

VERSE 4. Delight thyself also in the Lord; and he shall give thee the desires of thine heart.

It is not delighting in earthly things that will give you the desires of your heart: the best of earthly things cannot bring peace to the troubled breast, nor fill the void within. I show you a more excellent way of attaining the bliss you desire: "Delight thyself in the Lord." Seek your happiness in loving and serving him, and living according to his laws, and you will not miss your aim. He will satisfy every longing, the satisfying of which would not work your injury.

VERSES 5, 6. Commit thy way unto the Lord; trust also in him; and he shall bring it to pass. And he shall bring forth thy righteousness as the light, and thy judgment as the noon-day.

If others have wronged you, oppose not wrong to wrong; but commit your cause to God. He will bring it to pass that your wrong shall be righted. He will exhibit both your cause and your character in their true light to the world, to your justification, and your enemies' condemnation. God will allow no good man's character to remain for ever under an eclipse. True, "the promise here delivered will find its complete fulfilment in the day when the saints of God shall shine as the sun, and as the stars for ever and ever. But vain would be the hope of that, if it were not realized also in the present state; what has no place on this side, can have none on that. There nothing will begin, everything is only perfected." But here or there, the good man's character will certainly be vindicated.

VERSE 7. Rest in the Lord, and wait patiently for him; fret not thyself because of him who prospereth in his way, because of the man who bringeth wicked devices to pass.

Having committed your cause to God, rest in him, wait for him till he accomplish the desire of your heart: let no success of your enemy over you tempt you to think hard of God, or to take the work of retributive justice out of his hands. Cheerfully leave yourself and all your interests in the hands where you have placed them, not allowing yourself to be tempted for a moment to take them into your own again.

VERSES 8, 9. Cease from anger, and forsake wrath: fret not thyself in any wise to do evil. For evil-doers shall be cut off: but those that wait upon the Lord, they shall inherit the earth.

You cannot indulge anger and wrath without becoming yourself an evil-doer. You must, therefore, repress their first and feeblest risings in your soul, or you will precipitate yourself among those whose doom is to be cut off, to be destroyed. You cannot, while any resentful or vindictive passion is glowing in your bosom, wait on the Lord in a way to please him; and none but those who do so wait upon the Lord, shall inherit the earth, shall dwell in the good land he hath provided for his people.

VERSES 10, 11. For yet a little while and the wicked shall not be; yea, thou shalt diligently consider his place, and it shall not be. But the meek shall inherit the earth, and shall delight themselves in the abundance of peace.

What a waste of feeling, to spend anger and wrath upon one who, after a little, will not be; and whose very place will not be; himself and every memorial of him having disappeared from the earth. O when the wicked destroys himself by the wickedness in which he indulges against us, why should we not rather pity him? Let us pity him, and we at once become the meek, the patient, and forgiving, who shall inherit the earth, and delight themselves in the abundance of the peace with which the Lord will bless their lives.

VERSES 12, 13. The wicked plotteth against the just, and gnasheth upon him with his teeth. The Lord shall laugh at him; for he seeth that his day is coming.

The just man has no occasion to undertake the punishment of one who plots against him, and, with brute malignity, gnashes upon him with his teeth. The Lord laughs at him, derides his utmost ire as impotent to injure one whom he has taken under his protection. He laugheth at him, for he seeth that his day is coming—the day of his calamity—the day when his rage against the righteous will be repressed for ever, and he be reserved in everlasting chains under darkness unto the judgment of the great day.

VERSES 14, 15. The wicked have drawn out the sword, and have bent their bow, to cast down the poor and needy, and to slay such as be of upright conversation. Their sword shall enter into their own heart, and their bows shall be broken.

So it is. No weapon that is drawn against the good man shall prosper. The sword that the wicked draw against him shall enter their own hearts; and the bow, wherewith they would pierce him with their arrows, shall be broken in their hands. They can make suicides of themselves, but nothing more. Why then should the righteous raise his hand to destroy his enemies when every blow they aim at him recoils upon themselves? Indeed, if they were to take away the good man's life, why should he not even then pity them, knowing that the blow that destroys his body murders their own souls?

VERSES 16, 17. A little that a righteous man hath is better than the riches of many wicked. For the arms of the wicked shall be broken: but the Lord upholdeth the righteous.

A clear conscience, the blessing of God, and a contented mind, make the "little that a righteous man hath better than the riches of many wicked." There is connected with the history of his *little*, no remorseful recollection, no anxious thought how to increase it, nor anxious fear lest he should lose it. "The Lord upholdeth the righteous." His wants will be supplied as they arise. It is not so with the riches of the wicked; connected with their history there is many a remorseful recollection, many an anxious care, many a secret misgiving, and many a foreboding fear lest they lose what they have, and have, besides, their "arms broken"—that is, be deprived of all power to acquire more. Their abundance brings no content with it—only cares and fears.

VERSES 18, 19. The Lord knoweth the days of the upright; and their inheritance shall be for ever. They shall not be ashamed in the evil time; and in the days of famine they shall be satisfied.

The upright remain secure in their inheritance; are not "ashamed in the evil time;" and in the days of famine still have bread, because the Lord knoweth their days—their whole life is before him as an object of loving care; every day with its wants, to be by him supplied; every day with its dangers, to be by him averted. This is the general lot of the upright, even in this life; it will be their universal lot in the life to come, when they enter upon the inheritance that is incorruptible, undefiled, and that fadeth not away. Why, then, should they envy the wicked who may seem to be more prospered in this life than they are?

VERSE 20. But the wicked shall perish, and the enemies of the Lord be as the fat of lambs: they shall consume; into smoke shall they consume away.

As the fat of lambs, laid on the altar of sacrifice,

was quickly consumed, and vanished away in smoke, so shall the wicked and the enemies of the Lord be consumed; not a vestige of them being left behind. Why envy such their short-lived prosperity, or think that it militates against the Divine righteousness? Their prosperity is but for a moment, and then—nothing remains to them. The afflictions of the righteous are but for a moment, and then—everything is theirs!

VERSES 21, 22. The wicked borroweth, and payeth not again: but the righteous showeth mercy and giveth. For such as be blessed of him shall inherit the earth; and they that be cursed of him shall be cut off.

Such as "be cursed of him." It is the Divine curse upon the wicked that obliges him to borrow, and so impoverishes him that he is not able to pay again. "Such as be blessed of him." It is the Divine blessing upon the righteous that so enriches him that he is able to show mercy and to give. God's general providence towards the righteous and the wicked, is that here described. He generally maketh a difference between them in their external condition corresponding with their internal character.

VERSES 23, 24. The steps of a good man are ordered by the Lord; and he delighteth in his way. Though he fall, he shall not be utterly cast down: for the Lord upholdeth him with his hand.

This is the good man's comfort; his steps, the whole course of his life, are ordered by the Lord; and when his doings please the Lord, he delighteth in his way, and enables him to accomplish his desires. If he fail in some of his undertakings, he shall not be utterly cast down; he shall rise again, for the Lord upholdeth him with his hand. However much the good man may suffer, the Lord will not allow him to perish. In this respect his lot is in complete contrast with that of the wicked. When they fall, there is no Divine hand to lift them up and set them on their feet again. Luther's comment on the second of these two verses is excellent. "Thus," says he, "the Spirit comforts and answers the secret thoughts which every one might have, saying with himself, 'I have, however, seen it happen that the righteous is oppressed, and his cause trodden in the dust by the wicked.' 'Nay,' the Spirit replies, 'dear child, let it be so, that he falls; he still cannot remain lying thus, and be a cast-away; he must be up again, although all the world doubts of it. For God catches him by the hand, and raises him again.'"

VERSES 25, 26. I have been young, and now am old; yet have I not seen the righteous forsaken, nor his seed begging bread. He is ever merciful, and lendeth; and his seed is blessed.

This second verse gives us the character of the righteous man whom David had never seen forsaken, nor his seed begging bread. "He is ever merciful, and lendeth:" his life is one of uniform kindness and charity to the poor and needy. Many think that they will impoverish themselves and children by being always thus liberal. No, it is the surest way to prevent you and your children from coming to want. Those whom you befriend in their straits, will befriend you in yours, and the kindness of the father they will remember also to his children. And besides all this, God will move upon other hearts to minister to you and yours, in your necessities. He will also secretly increase your substance. It cannot be doubted, that God provides for the righteous man, and the righteous man's seed, following in his footsteps, as he provides for none beside. There are indeed exceptions to the rule, but not enough to prevent our regarding it as a general feature of the Divine Providence. It is conceded, however, that temporal prosperity followed obedience under the Old Testament dispensation, more unvaryingly than it follows it under that of the New; and for this reason, perhaps, the ancient believer had not the same clear views of the glories of the life to come, that we have, to encourage his faith, and therefore needed, more than we do, the stimulus of temporal and visible mercies, to keep him still walking on in the ways of the Lord.

VERSES 27–29. Depart from evil, and do good; and dwell for evermore. For the Lord loveth judgment, and forsaketh not his saints; they are preserved for ever: but the seed of the wicked shall be cut off. The righteous shall inherit the land, and dwell therein for ever.

As the well-doing of the righteous preserves both him and his seed, and secures them, as a general thing, a permanent inheritance of peace, so the evil-doing of the wicked destroys him and his seed: "his seed shall be cut off." As God can never fail finally to bless those who serve him, so he can never fail finally to punish those who serve him not. "This is deeply grounded in the Divine righteousness, imprinted thence upon the hearts of men, and as with terrible griffins guarded, that no wickedness can remain unpunished, and that the ungodly shall infallibly come to a miserable end. If such perdition does not always meet the bodily eye or sense, still everything is only contributing to their deeper ruin. For the destruction of their poor souls is certainly much more dreadful before God."

VERSES 30, 31. The mouth of the righteous speaketh wisdom, and his tongue talketh of judgment. The law of his God is in his heart; none of his steps shall slide.

David here distinguishes the righteous from the wicked by a new test—by his words—words of wisdom and sound judgment perpetually flowing from his mouth and tongue; all, however, coming from a heart in which is the law of his God. It is out of the abundance of his heart that his mouth speaketh. His words savour of the divine and heavenly. How unlike the words of the wicked! Moreover, actuated by the law of God in his heart, he not only speaks, but also acts aright: "none of his steps slide;" he walks steadily on in all the ways of holiness and pureness of living. He is not satisfied with having the law of his God in his heart and upon his tongue, unless he also embodies it in his life.

VERSES 32, 33. The wicked watcheth the righteous, and seeketh to slay him. The Lord will not leave him in his hand, nor condemn him when he is judged.

How many has man condemned to the flames of the stake, and to the flames of hell, whom God did not condemn at all. He justified them; and though he left their bodies for a time in the hands of their enemies, he received their souls unto himself. This is the consolation of the good, that God never joins the world in their condemnation of his people; and if we escape his condemnation, what need we care who else condemns? If unjustly condemned by others, we can afford to wait patiently till he sees fit to vindicate us.

VERSE 34. Wait on the Lord, and keep his way, and he shall exalt thee to inherit the land: when the wicked are cut off, thou shalt see it.

Still wait upon God, as an obedient servant and

loving child; "and keep his way:" walk only by the rules that he has prescribed you, and he will exalt you "to inherit the land;" he will crown you with the blessings of his covenant of salvation. "When the wicked are cut off, you shall see it;" you shall see all those enemies, whether visible or invisible, who would have accomplished your ruin, utterly and for ever overthrown.

VERSES 35, 36. I have seen the wicked in great power, and spreading himself like a green bay-tree: yet he passed away, and, lo, he was not; yea, I sought him, but he could not be found.

It matters not how deeply the roots of the wicked man's tree of prosperity have buried themselves in the earth, nor how far it has spread its branches abroad, it is the work of but a moment for Divine Providence to pluck it up, root and branch, so that not a vestige of it, though sought after, can be found in the place where it once stood. This image of sudden and complete destruction, can be applied to nations as well as to individuals. How many a nation that once persecuted the people of God, has now no existence but in history? It is under this same image of a vigorously growing tree, towering to the heavens, and stretching out its branches unto the ends of the earth, that Daniel represents the persecuting Babylonish monarchy, and that tree at last passed away in a single night! Dan. v. 30, 31.

VERSES 37, 38. Mark the perfect man, and behold the upright; for the end of that man is peace. But the transgressors shall be destroyed together: the end of the wicked shall be cut off.

If nothing else can reconcile the suffering believer to his trials, and the unmerited prosperity of the wicked, surely the contrast between the last moments of the upright and the wicked should do it. The end of one is peace; the end of the other, total and everlasting destruction. Who would regret any amount of suffering endured, to die as the good man dies, full of hope, peace, and joy, springing from the sweet assurance that he is going direct to the bosom of his God? Or who would regard any amount of prosperity enjoyed, as a compensation for dying as the bad man dies, launching away, hopeless, helpless, and alone, into outer and eternal darkness?

VERSES 39, 40. But the salvation of the righteous is of the Lord; he is their strength in time of trouble. And the Lord shall help them and deliver them: he shall deliver them from the wicked, and save them, because they trust in him.

The sentiment of these verses is like to that with which the twenty-seventh psalm opens, "The Lord is my light and my salvation; whom shall I fear? the Lord is the strength of my life; of whom shall I be afraid?" The Lord being the light, the strength, and the salvation of all who trust in him, David, in this psalm, counsels such not to quarrel with any dispensation of his that may seem dark to them; not to be angry against the wicked either, on account of their unmerited prosperity, or of the wrongs they may have inflicted upon them. He teaches us that innocence, quietness, and trust in the Lord, are the surest path to victory. He gives this as, no doubt, the conviction of his own personal experience—"Trust in the Lord, and do good, and he shall give thee the desires of thy heart:" seek to obtain them in no other way, is the import of all that he says. Let us all endeavour to realize the lesson in our lives, looking to One greater than David, even the Son of David, to gird us with strength for the battle, and to crown us with victory!

LECTURE ON PSALM XXXVIII.

THIS psalm was composed by David while suffering some severe affliction both of mind and body. What his bodily affliction was, or what his peculiar mental affliction, each seeming to aggravate the severity of the other, it is difficult to tell. He acknowledges, however, that all his sufferings are but the due reward of his sins; and to be traced directly to them. Still he prays most earnestly for the removal of the penalty so justly their due. The cause of his sufferings, *sin*, being removed by the Divine forgiveness, he hopes that his sufferings also will be removed. This idea, that all suffering is punishment direct from the hand of God for our sins, is an idea that readily suggests itself to our minds, when afflictions come upon us. We then begin to realize the truth of the saying, that God distributeth sorrows in his anger. Job xxi. 17. The title of this psalm reads, "A Psalm of David, to bring to remembrance:" that is, a psalm composed by David, either to bring to his own remembrance, for future use and improvement, his mental experiences and exercises when he was suffering so severely under the hand of God; or, as God seemed to have forgotten him, in so far at least as any manifestation of his mercy toward him was a remembrance of him—a psalm composed by David to remind God of the intensity of his sufferings, the cruelty of his enemies, the patience with which he endured the whole, and the steadfastness of faith with which he still looked to him for help: in the midst of all, still trusting in him, and doing good.

This second meaning of the words, *to bring to remembrance*, is probably their true meaning. It is the meaning sustained and required by the phraseology of the whole psalm. It is from the beginning to the end a vehement and reiterated calling upon God to notice, regard, and relieve, the great sufferings of the petitioner; to give his mind an efficient attention to them at once.

VERSE 1. O Lord, rebuke me not in thy wrath; neither chasten me in thy hot displeasure.

Some think that David here prays only for an abatement of his sufferings. That, however, can hardly be. He was no doubt willing to suffer more and longer, if such were the will of God: but what he here desires is evidently entire deliverance, a deliverance as complete as the pardon of the sins that brought his sufferings upon him. Regarding sin as the sole producing cause of his sorrows, he could not regard himself fully pardoned, till he was fully delivered. It was thus that the Saviour prayed under the mighty sorrows overwhelming him, not for an abatement, but for an entire removal of them, saying, "Father, if it be possible, let this cup pass from me." Matt. xxvi. 39. He, however, as no doubt David did, prayed with entire submission to the will of God in the matter.

VERSE 2. For thine arrows stick fast in me, and thy hand presseth me sore.

God's arrows, and his sorely pressing hand, mean the same thing here: they are sharp, piercing, and oppressive afflictions. When God visits us with these for our sins, he rebukes us in anger, and chastens us in hot displeasure. It was of such afflictions that Job speaks, where he says, "The arrows of the Almighty are within me, the poison whereof drinketh up my spirit: the terrors of God do set themselves in array against me." Job vi. 4. It was not of his merely bodily sickness that Job here speaks, but also of his grief at the loss of his children and property, the alienation of friends, and the hidings of the Divine presence. These were the arrows of the Almighty, these the terrors of God.

VERSES 3, 4. There is no soundness in my flesh because of thine anger; neither is there rest in my bones because of my sin. For mine iniquities are gone over my head: as a heavy burden they are too heavy for me.

David never for a moment disconnects the anger of God from his sins, as its provoking cause. If his whole body wither under the inflictions of that wrath, it is because of his sin. It is even so, and always so. The soul cannot sin without involving the body in the payment of the penalty: nor can the body sin without involving the soul. Each is made to feel the anger of God excited by the other's sin. David's iniquities, or rather, the punishments visited upon him for his iniquities, went over his head like rolling billows; and were, also, a burthen that he was unable to bear. Alas, how soon all human strength, both of mind and of body, sinks, crushed and overwhelmed, when God rebukes us in wrath, and chastens us in hot displeasure.

VERSE 5. My wounds stink, and are corrupt because of my foolishness.

Or, as an eminent critic has translated this verse, "They are corrupt, my sores fester because of my folly." David's sufferings for his sins had not only weakened and prostrated the strength of his body, but here, in this verse, the body is represented as actually *perishing* by the decomposition of its vital parts, corrupting and festering into running sores. And if sin thus disease the body, how much more must it disease the soul! It would seem, indeed, that the desolating effects of sin upon the body are so graphically described in this psalm, only to suggest to our minds its necessarily still more desolating effects upon the soul.

VERSES 6, 7. I am troubled; I am bowed down greatly; I go mourning all the day long. For my loins are filled with a loathsome disease; and there is no soundness in my flesh.

David is still describing the effects of sin upon his body. A loathsome disease has invaded his loins; that portion of the spinal column where the greatest strength in man centres and resides. To weaken that part of the body, is to weaken the whole. An injury inflicted there not only bows the head and causes the hands to hang down, but also the knees to tremble under us. How both forcibly and fearfully does this fact, or illustration, teach us the power of sin to invade, disease, and destroy the strongest parts of the human soul! It subdues the iron will to its wishes, and then the whole soul is indeed troubled, crazed, and bowed down greatly, and may well go mourning all the day long!

VERSE 8. I am feeble and sore broken: I have roared by reason of the disquietness of my heart.

It was not so much his external and bodily sufferings that caused David to utter such loud and bitter lamentations, as the disquietness of his heart. His mental and spiritual suffering was greater than any pain, however great it might be, that he felt in body. It was his sense of sin that made his burden too heavy for him. But for that, it could have been easily borne. With a clear conscience, and God on our side, how comparatively light are the heaviest afflictions of earth; but with an accusing conscience and God against us, how soon do even light afflictions overcome us, and we "roar by reason of the disquietness of our hearts. The spirit of a man will sustain his infirmity; but a wounded *spirit*, who can bear? Prov. xviii. 14. It is a wounded spirit, wounded by a vivid sense of sin unforgiven, that makes the soul exceeding sorrowful, even unto death. How many, that they might not endure a wounded spirit, an accusing conscience, have fled to the flames of the stake as a grateful alternative and pleasant refuge!

VERSE 9. Lord, all my desire is before thee: and my groaning is not hid from thee.

David here appeals to his omniscient God to bear witness that he has neither exaggerated his desires nor his miseries; that his desires were as intense as his language would indicate them to be, and his miseries as great. It has been well remarked on this verse, that it suggests a caution to all those who seek God in prayer, not to express with their lips what they do not feel in their hearts, nor to seek to move God by strong language rather than by strong desires, and a heart-felt sense of need. It is not the strength of our language, but the strength of our desires that brings God to our help.

VERSE 10. My heart panteth, my strength faileth me: as for the sight of mine eyes, it also is gone from me.

These words describe one whose sufferings are so great that he is at the point to die. The palpitating heart, the fast-failing strength, and the dimmed sight, all betoken that the sufferer's last moment is at hand. To this extreme of prostration had David's grief brought him. He felt as if he could not survive them—indeed, that he was literally expiring! There is no grief that so prostrates the whole man as spiritual grief; it cuts the sinews of both soul and body. Our Lord hungered, and thirsted, and grew weary, but we nowhere read that he was afflicted with any bodily sickness; and yet what ravages spiritual grief made upon his physical nature! It brought him prone to the ground, and caused him to sweat blood. He was but thirty-three years old when he died, and had spent only three of those thirty-three in public contact with the world; and yet we read of him that "his visage was marred more than any man, and his form more than the sons of men." Isa. lii. 14. And how so marred, except by spiritual grief?

VERSE 11. My lovers and my friends stand aloof from my sore; and my kinsmen stand afar off.

Sore, in this place, means *stroke*—the stroke of God—the Divine visitation under which David was suffering. His lovers and friends, those who should have been the first to sympathize with him in his affliction, and prompt to do it, come not near him. They stand aloof; they seem afraid to join him, lest, he being smitten of God, they should be made to feel a part of the stroke in their own persons. His kinsmen, or rather his neighbours, also stand afar off. To be deserted in the hour of trial by those we have loved most, and trusted most, is a grief hard to bear. It was, however, a grief that David had to bear, and also the Son of David. He too was deserted by his lovers and friends. When he was arrested, "all his disciples forsook him and fled." Matt. xxvi. 56. And while enduring the stroke of God upon Calvary, all his acquaintances, and the women who followed him from Galilee, stood afar off, gazing at his crucifixion. Luke xxiii. 49. They left him alone to his enemies, lest his enemies should become theirs, and involve them in his sore. How forlorn, the most forlorn of earth, is the feeling that comes over the heart when, in the evil day, one is unjustly deserted by his friends! When forsaken by all others, what pathos was there not in the interrogation addressed by our Lord to his twelve disciples, saying to them, "Will ye also go away?" John vi. 67.

VERSE 12. They also that seek after my life lay snares for me: and they that seek my hurt speak mischievous things, and imagine deceits all the day long.

It was not alone by the desertion of lovers, friends, and neighbours, that David was pained, but also by cruel and unscrupulous enemies, who sought after his life, spoke mischievous things and imagined deceits all the day long. They would take away his life, if they could; but, failing in that, they load him with calumnies. How accurately this verse describes the treatment that the Son of David experienced at the hands of his enemies! Their seeking after his life, and loading him with calumnies, went hand in hand; and they loaded him with calumnies in order to justify their murderous act to the misguided people, when they should, as they hoped, have at last accomplished it.

VERSES 13, 14. But I, as a deaf man, heard not; and I was as a dumb man that openeth not his mouth. Thus I was as a man that heareth not, and in whose mouth are no reproofs.

David sets us an example here eminently worthy of our imitation; that is, never to attempt to reason with an angry man, nor to reply to his reproaches. It is, indeed, often a severe trial of one's patience to do this; still it is the surest way ultimately to silence an enemy, and obtain the Divine interposition. Shimei cursed and cast stones at David, when he was fleeing before Absalom, and one of David's faithful followers would have slain him on the spot: but David restrained him, saying, "Let him alone, let him curse; for the Lord hath bidden him. It may be the Lord will look upon mine affliction, and that the Lord will requite me good for his cursing this day." 2 Sam. xv. 5–13. The Son of David also heard the reproaches of his enemies as if he heard them not, and was as silent under them as if he had nothing to reply to them. "He was oppressed, and he was afflicted, yet he opened not his mouth." Isa. lxviii. 7. "To all the evil things attempted to be proved against him at his trial, he held his peace." Matt. xxvi. 62. "Herod, too, interrogated him, but Jesus gave him no answer." John xix. 9. Both David and our Lord had to do with enemies with whom to reason would be worse than vain, and therefore they were silent.

VERSE 15. For in thee, O Lord, do I hope: thou wilt hear, O Lord my God.

David here assigns the reason for his silence under reproach: it was the effect of his faith, of his trust in God, of his waiting for the Lord to vindicate him. I was "as a deaf man that heareth not; and as a dumb man, that openeth not his mouth, for in thee, O Lord, do I hope;" I feel assured that thou wilt answer for me. David's patient silence was the offspring of his faith and hope. This same patient and confiding waiting for God to do for him, also characterized the Saviour, "who, when he was reviled, reviled not again; when he suffered, he threatened not; but committed himself to him that judgeth righteously." 1 Pet. ii. 23. And in this he has left us an example that we "should follow in his steps." 1 Pet. ii. 21–23.

VERSE 16. For I said, Hear me; lest otherwise they should rejoice over me: when my foot slippeth, they magnify themselves against me.

And if David's enemies magnified themselves against him, at the least calamity befalling him, such as the slipping of his foot, a trip, or stumble, how greatly would they rejoice were he to fall? It is this utter downfall that David dreads, and prays God to save him from. We cannot pray God too earnestly to preserve us from apostasy. The fall of believers, and especially of eminent believers, fills the enemies of religion with the most exultant hopes and expectations of soon seeing an end of it.

VERSE 17. For I am ready to halt, and my sorrow is continually before me.

"I am ready to halt:" I am conscious of my weakness and liability to fall; and that my enemies will certainly rejoice over my fall, unless thou, God, hear me. "My sorrow is continually before me:" I see without ceasing the full extent of my danger, and the distress that is ready to come upon me, and which will come upon me, unless thou avert it.

VERSE 18. For I will declare mine iniquity; I will be sorry for my sin.

David does not pray God for deliverance from his enemies, as one without sin himself. On the contrary, the sense of his own sins presses heavily upon his heart, and aggravates all his other afflictions. He knows that his own sins have brought all his other afflictions upon him, and that he cannot hope for entire relief till his own sins are forgiven. He therefore makes for himself the confession that secures forgiveness and leads to God's cleansing us from all unrighteousness, "I will declare mine iniquity; I will be sorry for my sin." 1 John i. 8, 9. But beside the depressing sense of his own sins, David is also distressed by numerous, powerful, and implacable enemies, hating and persecuting him on account of his very virtues.

VERSES 19, 20. But mine enemies are lively, and they are strong; and they that hate me wrongfully are multiplied. They also that render evil for good, are mine adversaries; because I follow the thing that good is.

One of the darkest traits of our fallen human nature is its hating the good that reproves its evil. It hates not only the word that reproves its evil, but also the silent life that reproves it. When the Athenians were about to ostracise Aristides, who had acquired for himself the appellation of the *Just*, a peasant approaching him, asked him to write a vote for him, condemning Aristides to exile. The statesman, without betraying who he was, asked him what harm Aristides had done him? "None," the man replied, "but I am tired with hearing him called the *Just*." It was for no better reason that the enemies of David and of the Saviour hated them. It was their purity and well-doing that offended their enemies most, because that purity and well-doing reproved their wickedness. It is not alone by the world, however, that the believer is opposed in doing good. He finds his old nature opposing him, so that when he would do good, evil is present with him.

He finds a law in his members warring against the law of his mind, and evermore threatening to bring him into captivity to the law of sin in his members. These unholy impulses of our old nature are lively and strong indeed, and hinder us when we would do good: and except for these enemies within us, the enemies without could do no harm.

VERSES 21, 22. Forsake me not, O Lord; O my God, be not far from me. Make haste to help me, O Lord, my salvation.

Having made known his wants and misery to God, and having also confessed and been sorry for his sins, David here flees to God as his only Saviour and salvation. He thus teaches us to whom we should flee when calamity comes upon us from any source whatever. Are our souls diseased and festering with the wounds inflicted upon them by a guilty conscience? God alone can heal those burning wounds. Are we reviled and our names cast out as evil? Let us not revile again, meeting taunt with taunt, reproach with reproach, wickedness with wickedness; but endure all in patient silence, till God sees fit to vindicate us. So doing, he will not forsake us, nor be far from us, but make haste to help us, for the sake of Him who is able to save unto the uttermost all that come unto God by him.

LECTURE ON PSALM XXXIX.

THE first six and remaining seven verses of this psalm, though expressly the religious exercises of the same mind, are in strong contrast with each other. The previous part of the psalm describes a mind honestly, yet ineffectually, struggling to repress and conceal its vexation and hard thoughts of God, at his prospering the wicked and afflicting the righteous. The latter part of the psalm is in altogether another tone, justifying God in all his dealings and severity with the righteous man, by acknowledging that all his sufferings are a merited punishment for his own individual sins. The first part should not be read without keeping continually in mind the thought that it was written under only the light of the Old Testament dispensation, where a withholding of the temporal prosperity, therein so largely promised to the righteous, seemed, at least to the weak and afflicted believer, hard. How much more favoured are we, when affliction comes on us, who have, to sustain our faith, the words of Him who spake as never man spake, and who assures us, "that our light affliction, which is but for a moment, worketh for us a far more exceeding and eternal weight of glory; while we look not at the things which are seen, but at the things which are not seen." 2 Cor. iv. 17, 18.

VERSE 1. I said, I will take heed to my ways, that I sin not with my tongue: I will keep my mouth with a bridle, while the wicked is before me.

Whatever might be the thoughts of his heart, David here resolved that he would not give them utterance. He would take heed to his ways, that he sinned not with his tongue, if he did with his heart. It is not always possible to keep repining thoughts out of our minds; it is, however, possible for us to keep them from leaping to the tongue. Sorely tried and sorely tempted, while humbly endeavouring to do the will of God, David might feel the providence to be a hard one, but he would not say so. Not to offend in speech is a virtue that has few superior to it—hence the inspired saying, "If any man offend not in word, the same is a perfect man, and able also to bridle the whole body." James iii. 2. In speech, at least, David resolved to be without fault: "I will keep my mouth with a bridle, while the wicked is before me." He was specially resolved, however much and mysteriously he might suffer, not to let fall, in the presence of the wicked, of those who prospered in iniquity, any word that could be construed to disparage the providence of God. This would subject both him and his trust in God to their ridicule. When Christians become restive under the orderings of Divine Providence, and complain of them, they give the world an opportunity to disparage their religion, which it does not fail to improve. The words, however, "while the wicked are before," probably refer, not to their bodily presence, but only to their presence to David's thoughts. It is thus that he uses the words elsewhere, saying, "My sin is ever before me." Ps. li. 3. That is, his sin was ever present to his mind. Accordingly, David here promises, that when thoughts of the prosperity of the wicked are present to his mind, exciting discontent and envious resentment, he will put a guard upon his lips, a muzzle upon his mouth, to prevent all expression of his unhappy feelings. Christians cannot be too guarded in giving utterance to expressions of envious discontent at the prosperity of others.

VERSE 2. I was dumb with silence: I held my peace, even from good; and my sorrow was stirred.

David was so anxious not to offend in word, that he abstained from all comment whatever upon God's dealings with him. He was so fearful, if he spoke at all, of saying something amiss, that he held his peace from speaking the good that he might, and no doubt should have spoken, of the Divine providence. The darkest providence that overshadows us, has still some blendings of mercy and goodness in it; and upon these relieving features of an afflictive dispensation, we should willingly dwell and freely speak. Because of his not doing this, David's grief found no abatement. On the contrary, his sorrow was stirred, roused, and excited into greater intensity, by his silence. His pent-up feelings of discontent were exasperated by it.

VERSE 3. My heart was hot within me; while I was musing the fire burned: then spake I with my tongue.

David's musing silence at last set his heart on fire; his feelings of repining discontent reached the point of glowing heat, and he was weary of longer forbearing, and could not do it. His long coerced silence could be no longer kept, and he did what he, in the first verse, had so resolutely determined that he would not do—he sinned against God with his tongue. And in the next three verses we have, it is generally believed, the very words he uttered when he at last spake with his tongue.

VERSE 4. Lord, make me to know mine end, and the measure of my days, what it is; that I may know how frail I am.

Or, that I may know when I shall cease; when the measure of my days will come to its end. It was, perhaps, not in the spirit of true prayer, but of impatient desire, that David prayed thus. Despairing of any escape from his sufferings, except in death, he is anxious to know how far it is removed from him. He evidently hopes that it is near, and will soon be upon him. This desire for death, now looked upon as the only termination of his sufferings, we see also in Job. He too, like David, for a long time sinned not with his lips; at last, however, he opened his mouth and cursed his day, and desired to die, saying, "O that I might have my request; and that God would grant me the thing that I long for! Even that it would please God to destroy me; that he would let loose his hand, and cut me off!" Job vi. 8, 9. Though wise and good men have, under sore afflictions, indulged in this extreme of impatience, it cannot be justified. It is quarreling with God; it is the remains of indwelling sin gaining the ascendency, for the time being, over the believer's better nature. Such weariness of life, and desire to be relieved of it as an insupportable load, may not indicate the utter extinction of the Divine life in the soul, but they do certainly indicate that our faith is suffering an eclipse.

VERSE 5. Behold, thou hast made my days as an hand-breadth; and my age is as nothing before thee; verily every man at his best estate, is altogether vanity. Selah.

How sad, how grievous, that anything so brief, so fleeting, so evanescent, so vain and empty in its best estate, as human life is, should be embittered by so many sorrows! This is evidently David's thought here; to which he adds a Selah, that we may ponder it. This is also the thought of Job, where he says: "Man that is born of a woman is of few days, and full of trouble. He cometh forth like a flower, and is cut down: he fleeth also as a shadow, and continueth not. And dost thou open thine eyes upon such an one, and bringest me into judgment with thee?" Job xiv. 1–3. It seemed to Job's mind hard that a creature, so short-lived, should be dealt with so severely as God was dealing with him. This same thought has found its way into other human hearts. It has seemed a mystery to them that life should be so full of suffering and sorrow. It is indeed a mystery, which nothing but the entrance of sin into the world can solve. Its entrance "brought death into the world and all our wo."

Verse 6. Surely every man walketh in a vain show; surely they are disquieted in vain: he heapeth up riches, and knoweth not who shall gather them.

"What shadows we are, and what shadows we pursue!" is the thought of this verse. Shadows indeed, and pursuing shadows, if in this life only we have hope; and David, under the obscuration of his faith caused by the intensity of his sufferings, seems to have forgotten that there is in reserve for the believer a something better than temporal prosperity. Man, he says, busies and disquiets himself in vain; he rises early, toils late, and eats the bread of carefulness, but cannot tell who shall enjoy the fruit of his labours. He heapeth up riches, and cannot tell who shall gather them, whether his own seed and offspring, or a stranger. Even while he is saying to his soul, "Soul, thou hast much goods laid up for many years; take thine ease," God may be saying to him, "Thou fool! this night shall thy soul be required of thee; then whose shall those things be which thou hast provided?" Luke xii. 19, 20.

We have now given what we believe to be the true interpretation of the words that David uttered, when, having at length broken his long silence, he spake with his tongue. His words are not to be commended; they indicate an impatient and repining spirit, a spirit dissatisfied with its lot, and envious at what it conceives to be the more desirable lot of others. At this point, however, David comes to himself; his faith in God revives, saying,

VERSE 7. And now, Lord, what wait I for? my hope is in thee.

David is perplexed, but not in despair. His hope is still in God. He has suffered greatly under the chastenings of his hand; nevertheless, the language of his heart now is, "though he slay me, yet will I trust in him." Much as he had complained, both of the sorrows of life and of the nothingness of its joys, he now seems to forget them all in the treasure that he has in the Lord. "Lord, what wait I for? my hope is in thee." He had been fondly thinking that temporal prosperity was essential to his happiness; he now acknowledges his error, and confidingly waits for God to solve the mysteries of his providence in his own time and way. David's long and painful struggle with his hard thoughts of the Divine providence has resulted in a renewal, in greatly augmented strength, of his faith in God as his only hope and all-sufficient treasure. And a blessed thing it is for the believer, when his very aberrations are overruled to bring him into a closer walk with God.

VERSE 8. Deliver me from all my transgressions; make me not the reproach of the foolish.

David here goes to the root of all that he had suffered at the hand of God and of his enemies—his own transgressions—and among them, no doubt, were numbered his complaints of the Divine providence. It was these things that brought down the rod of God upon him, and made him to be reproached by the foolish; and if these were but pardoned and removed, he knew that the judgments they had provoked would be removed with them. When in trouble, we cannot too soon inquire what sin or sins of our own have brought it upon us, and pray to be forgiven. We should, till the contrary appears, take it for granted that the cause of all our troubles is in ourselves.

VERSE 9. I was dumb, I opened not my mouth; because thou didst it.

The silence of the Psalmist here is very different from that of which he spoke in the second verse. His silence there was constrained, his heart was not in it; though silent, his spirit was still swelling with feelings of envious discontent. It is otherwise here. Silence here is the effect of his entire and cheerful acquiescence in the Divine dealings with him. It proceeded not from compulsion, but from filial love. "I opened not my mouth, because *thou* didst it." Tracing all his afflictions directly or indirectly to the hand of God, he was not at all disposed to repine at them, but to receive them as the chastenings of a Father, administered in love. O for the spirit of David to enable us all to say, when afflictions come upon us, "I was dumb, I opened not my mouth, because thou didst it."

VERSE 10. Remove thy stroke away from me: I am consumed by the blow of thine hand.

Though filially submissive to the Divine correction, he still prays that the stroke may be removed. His silence extended only to his not murmuring against God, and not to his still addressing him in prayer. Indeed, the most acceptable and effectual prayer that ascends to the Majesty on high, is that which ascends thither from a submissive, uncomplaining, unmurmuring heart.

VERSE 11. When thou with rebukes dost correct man for iniquity, thou makest his beauty to consume away like a moth: surely every man is vanity. Selah.

God's blows are not wanton blows, but rebukes to correct us for our sins; and yet his corrective rebukes sometimes consume the soul as a moth consumes a garment—lays its whole texture waste. This is an appeal to the Divine compassion to forbear punishment, since it so consumes the beauty of man, so lays waste all that he most loves and most desires. That is thought to be the import of the word *beauty* in this place. Man's most precious things are made to appear worthless when God visits him with severity for his sins. "Surely, every man is vanity, Selah." This is not said in the spirit and meaning with which it was said in a previous part of the psalm. It is here said to move the compassionate God to help one so helpless; not to deal with him in severity, but in tender mercy. How delightful is the thought thus presented to our minds, that we may plead our very weaknesses with God as an argument why he should help us, and not plead them in vain.

VERSE 12. Hear my prayer, O Lord, and give ear unto my cry; hold not thy peace at my tears; for I am a stranger with thee, and a sojourner, as all my fathers were.

It is not with querulous complaints that David now seeks to move God, but by prayers and tears, and by representing himself as a stranger in the earth, and a sojourner, without a home, and without refuge, except in him, the Lord his God. And here again David pleads his need of help, as his great argument to move God to grant it. He urges God to have compassion on him, for, if he do not, he must perish.

VERSE 13. O spare me, that I may recover strength, before I go hence, and be no more.

This is a much more appropriate prayer than that of the fourth verse, where David prays to know the measure of his days, evidently hoping that the end was near. He there felt life to be a burthen of which he would gladly be rid—not, indeed, by his own hands, but by the providence of God. He still had grace enough to deter him from suicide. Here, however, having been brought to repentance and a better mind, he prays that his life may be prolonged. He realizes that he needs to be strengthened before he can depart hence in peace. And this, no doubt, will be the experience even of those of us who have the most earnestly desired to escape life and its sorrows. When the time approaches in which we perceive that we must soon depart hence, we shall see that we are not so well prepared to take the journey as we, in our impatience, thought we were; and we may then desire, as earnestly as David desired it, to be spared till we have gained strength for what is before us. You need not to be told whence alone this strength can be obtained; that He who died on Calvary, that He alone, can enable you to pass the valley of the shadow of death, fearing no evil.

LECTURE ON PSALM XL.

SOME eminent critics suppose that David, throughout the whole of this psalm, speaks in the name of Christ. Others, however, equally learned and judicious—while admitting that all that David says *may* be applied to Christ in his humiliation and work of redeeming love—suppose that he speaks of Christ, primarily and exclusively, only in the verses, reading, "Sacrifice and offering thou didst not desire; mine ears hast thou opened: burnt-offering and sin-offering hast thou not required. Then said I, Lo, I come: in the volume of the book it is written of me, I delight to do thy will, O my God: yea, thy law is within my heart." It would be difficult to determine which of these two classes of critics comes the nearer to the true interpretation:—we, however, incline to the interpretation that makes the psalm refer for the most part to Christ. It seems to me that we do not attain to the full meaning of the psalm without so understanding it.

VERSES 1, 2. I waited patiently for the Lord; and he inclined unto me, and heard my cry. He brought me up also out of an horrible pit, and out of the miry clay, and set my feet upon a rock, and established my goings.

To be in an horrible pit, whose bottom is nothing but miry clay, describes as helpless and disagreeable a situation as can well be conceived. It is a situation in which the being obliged to wait long for help and deliverance would be extremely irksome. But situated as he was, and suffering as he must have been, David waited patiently for the Lord to deliver him: and his patient waiting was not in vain. The

Lord inclined unto him, and heard his cry, and brought him up out of the pit in which he was sinking, supposed to be a deep religious melancholy, and set his feet upon a rock, and established his steps, quieted all his mental anxieties, and strengthened him with might by his Spirit in the inner man to go on his way rejoicing. Out of how many such pits does God lift the believer in the course of his religious history!

VERSE 3. And he hath put a new song in my mouth, even praise unto our God: many shall see it, and fear, and shall trust in the Lord.

Every new token of the Divine mercy should be celebrated with a new song: if not always new in words, yet always new at least in the fervour with which old words of praise and thanksgiving are chanted. New fervour will make a new song out of old words and an old theme. And the fervour of our song should be specially glowing when we celebrate, as David does here, some great and signal mercy. So celebrated, it will have a blessed effect also upon others: they will see and fear, and trust in the Lord: hearing how great both the power and the mercy were that God manifested on our behalf, they will stand in awe of the power, and hope in the mercy, and so be led to take refuge in the Lord as their Helper.

VERSE 4. Blessed is that man that maketh the Lord his trust, and respecteth not the proud, nor such as turn aside to lies.

Blessed, because, having made the Lord his trust, he has a Refuge that can never fail him; a Friend that will never forsake him; a Fountain of bliss that can never be exhausted. In his hour of need he has no occasion to respect the proud, to look to the great and mighty of the earth for help; nor to such as seek their happiness in things that cannot confer it, in things that flatter only to deceive, promise only to disappoint, and hence are said to "turn aside to lies." All their hopes and expectations of happiness in the things in which they place it, are belied at last. Not so the hopes and expectations of the man who hath made the Lord his trust.

VERSE 5. Many, O Lord my God, are thy wonderful works which thou hast done, and thy thoughts which are to us-ward: they cannot be reckoned up in order unto thee: if I would declare and speak of them, they are more than can be numbered.

The signal mercy of having been delivered from the noisome pit into which he had fallen and was sinking, excites David's memory into the utmost activity. It revives in his mind the recollection of all other mercies that he and his nation had received at the hands of their covenant-keeping God. His works of mercy and thoughts of mercy towards them, had been more than could be numbered. It is a gratifying evidence of grace alive and operative in our hearts, when every new mercy revives and deepens the impression of former mercies to us and ours. Stinted as we may sometimes think our mercies to have been, if we let memory tell its story, we soon find that they have been more than can be numbered.

VERSE 6. Sacrifice and offering thou didst not desire; mine ears hast thou opened; burnt-offering and sin-offering hast thou not required.

Behold a greater than David here! These are Messiah's words: the very words that St. Paul represents him as using when he at last came into the world; only, instead of saying, "mine ears hast thou opened," he says, "a body hast thou prepared me." Heb. x. 5. The words proclaim the great fact that ritual sacrifices could not put away sin. For that purpose God neither desired them, nor required them. He instituted them not to atone for sin, but to symbolize the necessity for an atonement, and to keep perpetually alive in the heart and conscience of the offerer, a vivid consciousness of that fact. Offered as if they were in themselves efficacious to remove human guilt and desert of punishment, they were not acceptable. It was as a sin-remembrancer, and not as a sin-remover, that sacrifices were instituted. It was the mind of the offerer, and not his offering, that the Lord regarded in the sacrifice. The offering was as nothing to him, if it was not made with a willing and obedient mind. "Hath the Lord as great delight in burnt-offerings and sacrifies as in obeying the voice of the Lord? Behold, to obey is better than sacrifice." 1 Sam. xv. 22. The sacrifice was nothing worth, unless the offerer therein sacrificed his own will to the will of God. This important fact is indicated in the words "mine ears hast thou bored." In this boring of the ears there is an allusion to a servant who, when he might have been free, his term of service having expired, voluntarily and from love made himself a servant for life to his former master, the master, in token of the life-long relation, *boring his ears.* Exod. xxi. 6. This was by Divine direction. This submitting to have his ears bored, was an acknowledgment on the part of the servant that, henceforth to the end of his days, he would know no will but the will of his master, always sacrificing his own to it. In this allusion, then, our Lord intimates his entire devotion to doing the will of God; that, in working out human redemption, he would know no will but the will of his Father, always sacrificing his own to it. This was the obedience that is better than sacrifice. It was an obedience even unto death, on the part of our Lord, in the body that God had prepared him. And it was this willing, voluntary obedience that gave his death all its value as an atoning sacrifice. Heb. x. 10.

VERSES 7, 8. Then said I, Lo, I come: in the volume of the book it is written of me, I delight to do thy will, O my God; yea, thy law is within my heart.

"Then said I, Lo, I come." When did Messiah say this? When he saw the utter insufficiency of ritual sacrifices to atone for sin, and redeem man to God—when he saw that man was utterly hopeless and helpless in himself—then it was that he said, "Lo, I come:" I come to offer a sacrifice that will atone for sin, and redeem man to God, even the *sacrifice of myself.* This, no doubt, is the import of the words. This is the meaning given to them by St. Paul, in his epistle to the Hebrews, (x. 5–10.) Nor did Messiah make this sacrifice of himself reluctantly, but with delight. Hence he adds, "In the volume of the book it is written of me, I delight to do thy will, O my God." To obey his Father's will, even unto death, was a pleasure to him. As St. Paul represents Christ coming into the world with these words on his lips, Heb. x. 5–7, "the volume of the book," of which he here speaks, is thought by some to comprise all that is said of Christ in the law of Moses, in the prophets, and in the Psalms, Luke xxiv. 44; he speaking of the whole prophetic record in regard to himself, as if it were already complete. If this be the meaning of the words, "the volume of the book," in how many places shall we find it written of Christ, that he delighted in doing his Father's will! "Yea, thy law is within my heart." This is the reason why Messiah delighted to do the will of his Father, even his will in regard to his own most fearful death. His law was in his heart. He loved it, and obeyed it from love.

VERSES 9, 10. I have preached righteousness in the great congregation: lo, I have not refrained my lips, O Lord, thou knowest. I have not hid thy righteousness in my heart; I have declared thy faithfulness and thy salvation: I have not concealed thy loving-kindness and thy truth from the great congregation.

Our Lord came into the world as our Prophet, to teach us the way of salvation, as well as our Priest, to atone for our sins by the sacrifice of himself. And here, in the verses just recited, he speaks as the teaching prophet. He calls upon God to witness, that he has not refrained to proclaim the whole truth: "I have preached righteousness in the great congregation—I have not hid thy righteousness in my heart." The righteousness of God, of which our Lord here speaks, is, no doubt, at least three-fold—his righteousness in exacting full satisfaction for the dishonour done his law; his righteousness in rendering to every man his due; and also his righteousness in justifying every one that believeth in his Son. He exhibited this attribute of Divinity to the world, as it had never been exhibited before; not as an abstraction, but as an active principle, modifying, directing, and controlling all his other attributes: "I have declared thy faithfulness and thy salvation: I have not concealed thy loving-kindness and thy truth." The God whom Messiah declared unto the world, is not a God of righteousness only, but also of faithfulness and truth. What he promises, he performs. He never belies his word. Moreover, he is also a God of salvation and loving-kindness:—of salvation, in giving his only begotten Son to die for our redemption; of loving-kindness, in bearing with our infirmities, and crowning our lives with his mercies. The Lord our God was, comparatively, an unknown God, until Messiah declared him to the world. But how bold is the relief in which he brings out the Divine character in his teachings, exhibiting each particular attribute as perfect, and the whole as operating together in infinite harmony—mercy and truth meeting together, righteousness and peace kissing each other! Ps. lxxxv. 10.

VERSE 11. Withhold not thou thy tender mercies from me, O Lord: let thy loving-kindness and thy truth continually preserve me.

David is thought to be speaking here, no longer in Messiah's name, but in his own, and seeking for himself the grace and mercy proclaimed in the preceding verses. It is not, however, to the righteousness of God that he looks for help, but to "his tender mercies, loving-kindness, and truth." And he asks that he may experience these, not once only, nor at intervals only, but continually. Nothing but continual grace and mercy can preserve us. If God withhold his loving-kindness from us but for a moment, we fall. In a spiritual, as well as in a physical sense, in him we live, and move, and have our being.

VERSE 12. For innumerable evils have compassed me about; mine iniquities have taken hold upon me, so that I am not able to look up: they are more than the hairs of mine head; therefore my heart faileth me.

Here is the reason why the psalmist prayed God not to withhold his tender mercies from him: he is compassed about with innumerable evils. He sees danger on every side. His sins, either in his conviction of them, or punishment for them, have found him out. They have laid hold of him like so many ministers of justice, and have him under arrest. Moroever, they seem to him more numerous than the hairs of his head. O, when God's Spirit, quickening memory and conscience, recalls our sins to our minds, how numerous and appalling they are made to appear! Whose heart, at such times, has not, like David's, failed him? And how often does it happen with us, as it did here with David, that the most vivid sense of our sinfulness springs up in our hearts along with the clearest perceptions of Christ as the only, and yet all-sufficient Saviour of sinners! It is mercy indeed, that the Divine Spirit thus connects the two—that while he makes us so painfully conscious of our danger, he suggests the refuge; that while he makes us so conscious of our disease, he reminds us also of the only Physician. A sight of our sins, without a sight of the Saviour, would drive us to despair.

VERSE 13. Be pleased, O Lord, to deliver me: O Lord, make haste to help me.

This cry for help is very like an emphatic "Lord, save! I perish!" When a sense of our sins lays hold of us, as David's laid hold of him, we feel that deliverance cannot come too soon; as if delay would be perdition; and the prayer, "O Lord, make haste to help me," seems the only appropriate one to be offered up. But while we thus pray God to make haste to help us, we should not be impatient, or despair, if he should not vouchsafe an answer at once. If he answered us at once, he might make too great haste for our good. He might grant us the pardon of our sins before we had sufficiently felt the burthen and intolerableness of them, and consequently before we had sufficiently realized the preciousness of Christ as our Deliverer.

VERSES 14, 15. Let them be ashamed and confounded together that seek after my soul to destroy it; let them be driven backward and put to shame that wish me evil. Let them be desolate for a reward of their shame that say unto me, Aha, aha!

The verbs in these verses being translated in the imperative mood, appear to contain a prayer—appear as if David really desired the destruction of his enemies. It is an unfortunate translation. The verbs should have been translated in the future tense, and thus made to contain merely a prediction of what would, in the orderings of the Divine providence, inevitably befall David's enemies; and, indeed, all persecutors of the people of God. David expects, but can hardly be said to desire—and certainly not from any personal feeling in the matter—that his enemies would be put to shame, confounded, and made desolate. And he was justified in the expectation, for both the word and providence of God taught him that such would be the case. A precious thought it is, too, to the troubled believer, that God will, in his own good time, put to shame all enemies of his peace and safety, whether visible or invisible, human or infernal. It is a joy to him to know that there is a place where the "wicked cease from troubling, and the weary are at rest; a new heavens and a new earth, wherein dwelleth righteousness only." 2 Pet. iii. 13.

VERSE 16. Let all those that seek thee rejoice and be glad in thee: let such as love thy salvation say continually, The Lord be magnified.

Here again the several verbs of the verse should have been translated in the future, so as to read, "All they that seek thee *shall* rejoice and be glad in thee; those that love thy salvation *shall* say continually, The Lord be magnified." So read, the words do not express a desire, but declare a *fact*—namely, that God causes all those who seek him to rejoice and be glad in him; and those who love his salvation, to say continually, "the Lord be magnified." There is thought to be an emphasis in the words, *thy* salvation. They are thought to refer back to Messiah's words, "Lo, I come," uttered by him after he had declared the utter insufficiency of all animal sacrifices to atone for human guilt. If this be the meaning of the words, the salvation here intended, the salvation purchased for us by Christ, is indeed a fountain of joy and gladness in the hearts of all those who love and embrace it. They know by happy experience, that his blood is, indeed,

"Of sin the double cure,
Saves from wrath and makes us pure."

And this experimental knowledge of God's great salvation constrains them continually to say, "the Lord be magnified"—let the greatness of his mercy be unceasingly proclaimed, till all men shall experience its saving power.

VERSE 17. But I am poor and needy; yet the Lord thinketh upon me: thou art my Help and my Deliverer; make no tarrying, O my God.

"I am poor and needy." Poor and needy indeed we all are by nature; sin has emptied the soul of moral good, and filled it with moral evil. We are not sufficient of ourselves to think a good thought; the holy of holies once existing in the soul has been polluted; and the Divine light once shining there extinguished. Nor are we at a stand-still in this our deplorable moral degradation by nature. Till a Divine power arrests our descent, we are at every moment sinking still deeper in the mire of our corruptions. What have we? what element of goodness and happiness do we not want? Yet, poor and needy as we are, the Lord thinketh upon us. And this psalm shows us how much his thoughts were upon us. We here learn *how* he brought us up out of the horrible pit of miry clay into which our sins had sunk us; brought us up by giving his own Son to die for us. We learn, too, that the Son was as ready to die as the Father was to give him up to die for our redemption. Was it the will of the Father that the Son should die for us men and for our salvation? The Son answers, "Lo, I come: I delight to do thy will, O my God." O what tender light do these things shed over the words, "yet the Lord thinketh upon me"? Did he ever think upon any other of his creatures with thoughts of such tenderness and love? Never. When angels sinned, he cast them down at once, and reserved them in everlasting chains under darkness. Not one of that once bright angelic host has been permitted to say to him, "thou art my Help and my Deliverer." This has been permitted to none of his sinning creatures except to man. Why the Lord should have thought upon man with such distinguishing tenderness, we cannot tell. We should none the less receive the peculiar mercy with peculiar gratitude; and pray God without ceasing, if he has not already done so, to lift us out of the pit, set our feet upon the Rock of Ages, establish our goings, and carry us on in triumph to the end of our course.

Poor and needy though we be, the Lord thinketh upon us, and will, for the sake of Him who came to redeem us from death, by dying himself, hear our prayers, whether for regenerating or sanctifying grace; and, in so doing, make no undue tarrying.

LECTURE ON PSALM XLI.

THIS psalm is thought, not without reason, to have been composed by David when he was old and stricken in years, and about to go the way of all the earth. It was his lot to have had two rebellions during his reign, each headed by a son; the first, by Absalom; the second by Adonijah. The account of Adonijah's rebellion is recorded in the first chapter of the first book of Kings. Adonijah was older than Solomon, and presuming, no doubt on the right of primogeniture, regarded the throne of Israel as his birth-right, ignoring the will of his father in the matter, and the fact that Solomon had been divinely designated to the place. Absalom, in his rebellion, succeeded in gaining over to his side, Ahithophel, David's prime minister and chief counsellor of state; Adonijah, in his rebellion, in gaining over Joab, the captain of the hosts of Israel, and also Abiathar, the high-priest. Tidings of these things came to David confined to his bed with age and sickness. In the midst of such high-handed and impious treachery, he knew not whom to trust, nor which way to turn himself, except to the Lord. And turning to him, he cannot but hope that the Lord will show him in his troubles the same mercy that he, David, has shown to others in theirs.

VERSE 1. Blessed is he that considereth the poor: the Lord will deliver him in time of trouble.

"Blessed are the merciful: for they shall obtain mercy," (Matt. v. 7,) is the thought pervading this whole psalm. It is the basis upon which David grounds his prayer for deliverance. Not that the being kind to the poor and needy, and relieving the wretched, enables one to claim mercy for himself as a thing of right and merit, but only as a thing of Divine promise. Whatsoever a man soweth, that shall he also reap: if he soweth mercy, he shall reap mercy. He who has endeavoured to imitate his Father Almighty in showing kindness to others, will not be forsaken of him when his time comes to be tried and suffer. The Lord will preserve him when he in his turn is called to mourn. He shall then learn that his tender sympathy for the afflicted has not been in vain: for

VERSE 2. The Lord will preserve him, and keep him alive; and he shall be blessed upon the earth: and thou wilt not deliver him unto the will of his enemies.

It is not to be denied that there are instances of good men devoting themselves, their time and substance, to relieving the necessities of the needy, who have nevertheless not been long-lived, nor escaped the tongue of calumny. Such instances, however, are only exceptional cases. The general rule of the Divine Providence has been to deal with man as he has dealt with his fellow-man. Mercy has been requited with mercy, liberality with prosperity. Indeed thousands have attested that their prosperity began with, and was proportionate to, their liberality to the needy and the cause of Christian benevolence; that, the more they gave, the more they were enabled to give; that, the more they endeavoured to make themselves a blessing to others, the more they were blessed in their secular undertakings. Hence the words of one who had made this subject his special study and investigation, "that the most marked interpositions and signal blessings of even earthly prosperity have attended the practice of Christian benevolence in every age. Volumes might be filled with well attested instances of the remarkable manner in which God has honoured those who in faith and obedience have devoted their property to him." Keep what you have, and get all you can, is the motto of the man of the world. God, however, shows the good man another road to affluence, which is, "Honour the Lord with thy substance, and the first fruits of all thine increase; so shall thy barns be filled with plenty, and thy presses shall burst out with new wine." Prov. iii. 8, 9. "He that hath pity upon the poor, lendeth unto the Lord; and that which he hath given will the Lord pay him again." Prov. xix. 17. "Give, and it shall be given unto you; good measure, pressed down, shaken together, and running over, shall men give into your bosom. For with the same measure that ye mete withal, it shall be measured to you again." Luke vi. 38. "The liberal deviseth liberal things, and by liberal things he shall stand." Isa. xxxii. 8. "The selfish, self-seeking man defeats his own aims: the blessing of a benevolent God cannot continue to rest upon him. His aims and those of a benevolent God are too antagonistic for that. "There is that scattereth, and yet increaseth; and there is that withholdeth more than is meet, but it tendeth to poverty." Prov. xi. 24. Nor is it only in the continuance of the good man's life and prosperity that God interests himself.

VERSE 3. The Lord will strengthen him upon the bed of languishing: thou wilt make all his bed in his sickness.

He who has ministered to the sick, shall not want for tender care when he is sick. The Lord will be in his sick-chamber to sustain his languishing head, and, like a tender mother, to turn his bed and make it soft to give him repose. If he do not give him physical strength to rise and walk at once, he will at least strengthen him with might by his Spirit in the inner man. The kindness he has shown to others under similar circumstances, the Lord will show to him. He will then remember kindnesses to others which perhaps the sufferer himself had forgotten. In the comforts which the Lord will pour into the sufferer's soul, not even the cup of cold water shall go without its reward. The cheering word, the kind look, and even the kind wish too, will all be remembered, and all rewarded. Such was David's conception of the benevolent character of the Lord our God; and it led him to believe that with tenderness only he would deal with him in his trouble.

VERSE 4. I said, Lord, be merciful unto me: heal my soul; for I have sinned against thee.

The *me* and the *my* of this verse are thought to be emphatic, and to be equivalent to saying, "Lord, have mercy upon me," as one who has considered the poor: "heal my soul," as one who has ministered to the needy. I, who have been merciful to the suffering, am now myself a sufferer, and ask of thee the mercy thou hast promised the merciful in my situation. This, as already remarked, David asks, not as a thing of right, but only as a thing of Divine promise; for, in the same breath in which he prays for the mercy and healing pledged to the merciful, he confesses, "I have sinned against thee." He thus teaches us, that even when asking blessings, a claim to which we have acquired by having fulfilled the conditions upon which God has graciously promised to grant them, we should still urge our suit with an humble confession of the sins that render us altogether unworthy of what we ask. When David's enemies were suffering, he tells us elsewhere how he felt and acted. "As for me," says he, "when they were sick, my clothing was sackcloth: I humbled my soul with fasting; and my prayer returned into mine own bosom. I behaved myself as if he had been my friend, or brother: I bowed down heavily, as one that mourneth for his mother." Ps. xxxv. 13, 14. But with what feelings did David's enemies regard him, when he was sick and in trouble? He answers:

VERSE 5. Mine enemies speak evil of me: When shall he die, and his name perish?

Here, certainly, is a striking contrast between David and his enemies. When they were in trouble, he was full of tender sympathy for them: when he is in trouble, they are full of spite and malice against him. He was merciful to them: they are merciless to him; wish him dead, and his very name obliterated from the records of earth. He prayed for them: they speak only evil of him. We may suppose these words to express the feelings of Adonijah and his partizans in treason, while impatiently waiting David's death, as an event that would enable them to set Solomon aside as his successor to the throne, and accomplish their own ambitious designs.

The words of this verse may also be applied to the enemies of the Son of David. His enemies, too, spake only evil of him, wishing him dead, and that his very name might perish; and in return for his prayers, they loaded him with execrations.

VERSE 6. And if he come to see me, he speaketh vanity: his heart gathereth iniquity to itself; when he goeth abroad, he telleth it.

If, at any time, Adonijah visited his aged and afflicted father, as if to condole with him, it was all vanity, all pretence: his show of love and filial affection was all feigned; there was no unison between his words and the feelings of his heart; his heart was all the while gathering iniquity, that is, material for detraction, that when he went abroad, he might publish it to his fellow-conspirators. All this David at last saw to be true of his son Adonijah, that he had visited him in his affliction, only to act the spy upon him. And what David relates as his experience, was also the experience of his Divine Son. His enemies, too, did all they could to entangle him in his talk: they watched him, and sent forth spies, who should feign themselves just men, that they might take hold of his words, and so deliver him into the power and authority of the Roman governor. Luke xx. 20. You recollect how he escaped the snare of the Roman coin, by answering them, "Render unto Cæsar the things which are Cæsar's; and unto God the things that are God's." Judas also, at last, watched his words, with the same eager desire to turn them to his disadvantage abroad.

VERSE 7. All that hate me, whisper together against me: against me do they devise my hurt.

It was not alone against the outspoken calumnies

of Adonijah and his fellow conspirators that David had to contend: they plotted against him secretly also. They uttered in whispers what they dared not utter aloud. Of all enemies in the world, a whispering enemy is most to be dreaded. Subtle as the serpent, he hisses out his poison so silently, that, ere he is aware of danger, his victim is ruined. We do one of the serpent kind wrong in comparing it to the whisperer—we mean the rattlesnake—it always sounds its rattles before injecting its poison. The whisperer, on the contrary, gives us no warning of his presence, nor of the work in which he is engaged. It was in this silent way that their enemies sought to ruin both David and the Son of David.

VERSE 8. An evil disease, say they, cleaveth fast unto him: and now that he lieth, he shall rise up no more.

Yes, "an evil disease"—and they mean, by an evil disease, not only a mortal disease, but a Divine judgment sent upon him in wrath, for his destruction, and not a fatherly chastening of him for his good. Maliciously supposing him thus divinely afflicted for his sins, they exult in the thought that he will never rise from his bed again; that he will soon be out of their way, and the realization of their heart's desire. It is thus that the wicked often turn the Divine chastenings of the righteous, chastenings designed only for their good, into proofs that they are sinners above all others, because they suffer such things. It was in this way that the Jews, in their malice, construed the sufferings of Christ.

VERSE 9. Yea, mine own familiar friend, in whom I trusted, which did eat of my bread, hath lifted up his heel against me.

This verse was realized in the history of David, first, in Ahithophel, his chief counsellor of state;

then in Joab, the captain of his hosts; and also in Abiathar, the high priest—with each of whom he was, from their relations to him, necessarily on terms of the utmost intimacy and confidence, but each of whom betrayed him. The verse was realized also in the history of Christ, when Judas betrayed him—although our Lord, in quoting the verse as applicable to himself and Judas, only says, "He that eateth bread with me, hath lifted up his heel against me," (John xiii. 18,) leaving out the words "mine own familiar friend," as inapplicable to Judas, and the words "in whom I trusted," as inapplicable to himself. Our Lord never trusted in Judas: he knew from the beginning that Judas was not a friend, but a devil, John vi. 70, and would betray him. John vi. 64. But applied, as it may be in all its parts, to David, this verse shows that his situation was deplorable indeed. He cannot, however, but believe that the Lord will deliver him out of it; for resuming and repeating the first part of the prayer begun in the fourth verse, he adds:

VERSE 10. But thou, O Lord, be merciful unto me, and raise me up, that I may requite them.

The requital here intended cannot mean personal revenge—for of any such feeling toward his enemies no mere man was ever more free than David was. The requital, then, which he prays that he may be raised up to make his enemies, must mean his being enabled to defeat all the plans of his enemies to subvert his kingdom by transferring the crown from Solomon to Adonijah. And the sequel shows that his prayer to be enabled thus to requite his enemies was answered; for, on hearing of the rebellion of

Adonijah, he rallied from the low and prostrated condition in which he seemed to be fast sinking into the arms of death, and survived long enough to see Solomon consecrated, crowned, and proclaimed king of Israel. This, of course, brought shame and confusion upon all those who had been labouring to defeat it.

VERSE 11. By this I know that thou favourest me, because mine enemy doth not triumph over me.

It is even so. When a man's ways please the Lord, he maketh even his enemies to be at peace with him. Prov. xvi. 7. This assurance David has received, that his ways have pleased the Lord. Formidable as the conspiracy was that had been formed against his throne and successor, God inspired him with a few last words so potent as to scatter the whole to the winds, and inaugurate the most peaceful and glorious reign that distinguishes the history of Israel—the reign of Solomon. May God, as our last hour approaches, give us the same glorious assurance, that none of our enemies, whether visible or invisible, have triumphed over us, and that he has endowed us with a kingdom that cannot be subverted.

VERSE 12. And as for me, thou upholdest me in mine integrity, and settest me before thy face for ever.

What David means here by his integrity, was his blameless and charitable life; not so blameless and charitable, however, that he does not confess, "I have sinned against thee." Strange! that for an integrity so imperfect—and when, too, that integrity itself is inspired by his own blessed Spirit—strange that God should set one continually before his face as an object of his unceasing protection, love, and care! Yet so it is! Such is his mercy toward the merciful. So greatly doth he love even imperfect goodness in his creatures! "A bruised reed will he not break, and smoking flax will he not quench, till he bring forth judgment unto victory." Matt. xii. 20. God grant that at our last review of life, conscience may bear as favourable testimony in our cases as it bore in David's—that we were the friends of the poor and needy, and did good unto all men as we had opportunity. We shall then learn that he who did most for others, did most for himself; and that he who did nothing for others, did nothing for himself.

VERSE 13. Blessed be the Lord God of Israel from everlasting, and to everlasting. Amen, and Amen.

A most suitable doxology with which to close a psalm setting forth in such glowing colours the mercy of God to those showing mercy to others, and endeavouring to serve him in holiness and pureness of living. If such be the mercy of the Lord God of Israel from everlasting, and to everlasting, who would not join in the anthem, and add thereto its fervid Amen, and Amen? May the spirit of this psalm—its spirit of benevolence, faith, and holy fear—fill the hearts of us all. It is none other than the spirit of Christ, of him who went about doing good, and who could not doom even implacable enemies to destruction, without, in the same breath, weeping over them.

LECTURE ON PSALMS XLII. AND XLIII.

To be cut off from communion with God in the services of his sanctuary, was regarded by every devout Israelite as an unmistakable token of the Divine displeasure, and a great calamity. This was David's situation when he composed these two psalms. From his beloved sanctuary, with its sensible communion with God in its sacrifices and oracular responses, he was now an exile, fleeing in the wilderness beyond Jordan before his rebellious Absalom. He might have kept up communion with God by taking the ark of the covenant with him in his flight; but when the priests and the Levites brought it forth, to bear it with them, he said to Zadoc, "Carry back the ark of God into the city; if I shall find favour in the eyes of the Lord, he will bring me again, and show me both it and his habitation: but if he thus say, I have no pleasure in thee; behold, here am I, let him do to me as seemeth good unto him." 2 Sam. xv. 26, 27. Nevertheless, David's heart, in his exile, was still drawn towards the sacred place where the presence of the ark proclaimed the peculiar presence of God; hence his words,

VERSES 1, 2. As the hart panteth after the water-brooks, so panteth my soul after thee, O God. My soul thirsteth for God, for the living God: when shall I come and appear before God?

No perishing hind, or deer, ever longed more earnestly to reach the cooling streams where it could quench its thirst, than David longed to stand in the presence of God on Mount Zion. It may seem strange to us, who know that in every place incense can be offered unto his name and a pure offering, (Mal. i. 11,) that so much importance should have been attached by the Israelite to worshipping God in his sanctuary. It would not, however, seem strange to us, if we reflected that in the sanctuary alone the Israelite could offer up the bleeding victim, whose blood told him of pardon, peace, and acceptance with God—that in the sanctuary alone he could lay his sins upon the head of the scape-goat, and have them borne away (Lev. xvi. 21, 22)—that it was in the sanctuary alone that he could consult God in cases of difficulty, and have them solved by an answer from the oracle in the holy of holies. In this respect, the Levitical form of religion was peculiar; it had but *one* place where God could be duly worshipped, and all the blessings promised his people obtained. Consequently, to be excluded by the providence of God from that one place, seemed to the Israelite equivalent to a Divine excommunication. This accounts for David's vehement longing to return to Jerusalem, and Zion. He could think of himself as being inwardly near to God, only as he was outwardly near to him. It is otherwise with us. Since the great Sacrifice has been offered, and his atonement accepted, God's sanctuary is everywhere; and nothing but our sins can exclude us from communion with him in any place in which we may be. And when our sins have excluded us from spiritual communion with him, we should pant as vehemently after restoration to that communion, as David to be restored to his special local presence in his sanctuary on Mount Zion.

VERSE 3. My tears have been my meat day and night, while they continually say unto me, Where is thy God?

David's grief was so intense that it took away the desire for food. He wept, and ate not. He knew that he was deservedly suffering the hidings of the Divine favour and the consciousness of this made the unceasing taunt, "Where is thy God?" all the harder to bear. The taunt struck upon a wounded spirit, and the words, as insinuating Divine desertion, found too faithful an echo in the fears of his heart. How often the adversary thus deals with the believing soul when God is visiting it for its sins to bring it to repentance. "Ah!" he sneeringly demands, "where now is thy God? where now is the God in whom you always trusted as a very present help in time of trouble? Your trust was a delusion; there never were any such endearing relations between you and him as you imagined." These infernal suggestions to the believing soul under the hidings of God's favour on account of its sins, are fiery darts indeed! They are designed to drive the contrite to despair, and we deal with despairing thoughts in the right way then, only when we treat them as Satanic suggestions. Mercy's cry to the soul truly grieving over its sins is, "Hope on, hope ever."

VERSE 4. When I remember these things I pour out my soul in me: for I had gone with the multitude to the house of God, with the voice of joy and praise, with a multitude that kept holy day.

The joys of the past add pungency to the sorrows of the present. The contrast between David's for mer and present condition melts his soul within him. How blest his former, how miserable his present state! and how the recollection swells the fountain of his grief, already overflowing freely! How different his situation in the wilderness, cut off from communion with God, and mocked by enemies, from what it was when he went up to the house of God with a multitude to keep holy day, with the voice of joy and praise! *There* was everything to fill the heart with hope and joy—*here*, there was everything to fill it with sorrow and misgivings. How sad, and yet how frequent, are these contrasts in the believer's experience! How often is he constrained to say,

> "Where is the blessedness I knew
> When first I saw the Lord?
> Where is the roul refreshing view
> Of Jesus and his word?
> What peaceful hours I then enjoyed,
> How sweet their memory still:
> But *now* I feel an aching void
> The world can never fill."

VERSE 5. Why art thou cast down, O my soul? and why art thou disquieted within me? Hope thou in God, for I shall yet praise him for the help of his countenance.

The thought of this verse is,

> "Judge not the Lord by feeble sense,
> But trust him for his grace:
> Behind a frowning providence
> He hides a smiling face."

It is faith, still strong in God, that here demands of the soul, "Why art thou cast down? why art thou disquieted within me?" as if it had no good reason for its fears. The demand is a *reproof* of the soul for its despondency. Governed by faith, the believer utters only the language of hope, and wears the same calm, self-possessed look in the storm as in the sunshine. But yielding to feeling, the moment clouds and darkness gather around him, he speaks as if God had forgotten him, ceased to care for him, and there were an impassable gulf between him and the heaven of his hopes. And where is the earnest believer who has not in times of trouble been more or less conscious of this desponding state of feeling, and reproved himself for it as disparaging to the Divine goodness? Duly considering what God is in himself, what he has promised us, and what he has done for us, would soon lead the most desponding of us to say to our souls, Why art thou cast down? why art thou disquieted? hope thou in God, for I shall yet praise him for his help.

VERSE 6. O my God, my soul is cast down within me: therefore will I remember thee from the land of Jordan, and of the Hermonites, from the hill Mizar.

Persecuted, but not forsaken; perplexed, but not in despair, David still encourages himself in the Lord. Though his soul is still cast down within him, notwithstanding his expostulations with it for its fears, he is looking in the right direction for help. He promises to remember God in every place to which his feet may bear him, in fleeing before his rebellious son. If he cannot do what he *would*, meet Him face to face in his sanctuary, he will do what he *can*, still *remember* him. Alas, how many cease even to remember God, when they can no longer meet him in the regular services of his house!

VERSE 7. Deep calleth unto deep at the noise of thy water-spouts: all thy waves and thy billows are gone over me.

Water-spouts seldom occur singly, but generally in pairs, the whirlwind that forms the spout in the clouds, forcing up a second from the body of waters beneath, that meets the descending spout in the air, when both descend together with appalling force and noise into the waters below, and thus the roar and din of the ocean below calleth back to the roar and din of the clouds above—"Deep" literally "calleth unto deep at the noise of God's water-spouts." To this turmoil in the elements David compares the turmoil in his feelings and fortunes. Troubles were descending upon him from above, and rising up from beneath; his son had risen up against him, and the chastening hand of God also was upon him; "all thy waves and thy billows are gone over me." David seems to himself like a shipwrecked sailor buffeted about by waves. Trouble follows trouble, as wave follows wave in a storm at sea. Others beside David have had sorrows come upon them like meeting water-spouts, and been buffeted by sorrows, like as angry billows buffet one in a storm. This has been the experience of many a believer, eminent both for piety and usefulness. Distressing, however, as the verse now explained depicts David's condition, he is not in despair, for he adds,

VERSE 8. Yet the Lord will command his loving-kindness in the day-time, and in the night his song shall be with me, and my prayer unto the God of my life.

How strange and mysterious a thing is Divine faith!—how inextinguishable when it has once been lighted up in the heart! Many waters cannot quench it, nor floods drown it. It still lives even a vigorous life, while God himself is filling the heart with griefs. Such is the teaching of David's words here. He knew that he was suffering under the hand of God—still he adds, "the Lord will command his loving-kindness." However fast and heavily the blows fell upon him, they could not for a moment shake his confidence in the Divine mercy. God's loving-kindness would be his in the day-time, and he would also furnish him with an occasion for a song in the night. Nor would the Lord put it into his heart only to sing, but also to pray unto him as the God of his life, as the God who had hitherto preserved him, and would still keep him alive with covenant fidelity. In all the afflictions wherewith he afflicts them, God never fails to give his people a heart to sing and pray. Paul and Silas had many stripes laid upon them, and were thrust into the inner prison, and had their feet made fast in the stocks; but at midnight they prayed, and sang praises unto God. Acts xvi. 23–25.

VERSES 9, 10. I will say unto God my Rock, Why hast thou forgotten me? why go I mourning because of the oppression of the enemy? As with a sword in my bones, mine enemies reproach me; while they say daily unto me, Where is thy God?

David still affirms God to be his Rock, his confidence; we therefore understand his words, "Why hast thou forsaken me?—why go I mourning?" not as words of murmuring impatience, but as words of hope that God, being his Rock, would deliver him. It is the consciousness of the endearing relations subsisting between him and God, that suggests the *whys.* They are the *whys* of a loving child, who knows that his Father loves him, asking that Father why he delays granting him what he has it in his heart to grant. His enemies ridiculing this filial and paternal relation between him and his God, was like a sword in David's bones. "Where now is thy God?" they demand. "He has forsaken you; he has cast you off—your sufferings prove it. He is not chastening you in love, but punishing you in wrath."

All this is implied in the words, "where now is thy God?" How often do Satan and our unbelieving heart taunt us in the same way when we are in trouble, suggesting to our anxious minds the fearful thought that God has forsaken us, because he is afflicting us.

VERSE 11. Why art thou cast down, O my soul? and why art thou disquieted within me? Hope thou in God: for I shall yet praise him, who is the health of my countenance, and my God.

"The health of my countenance." He who, by restoring unto me the joy of his salvation, will light up my hitherto dejection-clouded face with the light of joy and peace. "And my God"—this he says in answer to the taunt, "where is thy God?" and it is equivalent to saying that he would soon be to him everything that he had ever been, and everything that he had ever said he would be. How rapid in this psalm have been the transitions of faith and fear, hope and despondency! It is, however, the voice of triumphant faith alone with which it closes, "Hope thou in God, O my soul; for I shall praise him." Happy triumph of faith over all the trembling fears of the flesh, and the malicious reproaches of enemies! May our faith triumph over all our fears and foes, as David's triumphed over his.

PSALM XLIII.

We now pass on to explain the forty-third psalm, which so closely resembles the forty-second, that eminent critics have held that the two originally constituted but one. Though evidently written on the same occasion, the rebellion of Absalom, the more common opinion is, that the forty-third was originally distinct and complete by itself. Its first verse reads,

VERSE 1. Judge me, O God, and plead my cause against an ungodly nation: O deliver me from the deceitful and unjust man.

This psalm differs from the last in at least two observable particulars. David there speaks, not of the number of his enemies, nor of their distinguishing character, except that they were taunting enemies, constantly ringing in his ears the tormenting demand, "Where is thy God?" It is not improbable that during the time in which the scene of the forty-second psalm is laid, cursing and upbraiding Shimeis were crossing David's path at every turn in his wanderings. 2 Sam. xvi. 5–13. Here, however, he speaks not of a few individuals, but of an ungodly nation, being engaged in the strife against him, and prays specially to be delivered from the deceitful and unjust man. This deceitful and unjust man may have been either Absalom or Ahithophel, for both had deceived and treated David with great injustice. This explanation would seem to justify the belief that the forty-second psalm was composed at the beginning of the rebellion, when David may have thought his insurgent subjects few in number, and this forty-third when, to his amazement, he learned that nearly all Israel, under the lead of Absalom and Ahithophel, were in arms against him. He accordingly here prays to be delivered, not from a few taunting and cursing enemies immediately around him, but from a nation of merciless foes. "Judge me, O God, and plead my cause against an ungodly nation," is therefore praying God to interpose between him and his rebellious subjects, and, by restoring him to his throne, prove to them that he, as their king, had done them no wrong.

VERSE 2. For thou art the God of my strength: why dost thou cast me off? why go I mourning because of the oppression of the enemy?

The Lord being the God of his strength, or, as the words have been rendered, his Guardian-God, David puts these questions as in the ninth verse of the last psalm, as if there were an inconsistency between the Lord's treatment of him and his relations to him. Being his Guardian-God, and so by covenant engagement, David speaks as if he could both expect and claim his protection. This much the questions, "Why dost thou cast me off?" "why go I mourning?" seem to imply; and also wonder that his Guardian-God does not at once come to his relief. The questions, then, do not indicate absence of faith, but its presence in the heart in active, yet longing exercise.

VERSE 3. O send out thy light and thy truth: let them lead me; let them bring me unto thy holy hill, and to thy tabernacles.

Light here means favour; and *truth*, fidelity in the keeping of one's promises. David's words then, "Send out thy light and thy truth: let them lead me; let them bring me," is a prayer that God would show him the favour pledged to him in his promises, and manifest that favour in *act*, in bringing him again to meet him in his sanctuary. And we, when we are in spiritual exile, away from God in our thoughts and feelings, cannot pray him too soon, nor too earnestly, nor too incessantly, to bring us into his presence again, by restoring us the joy of his salvation, and upholding us with his free Spirit. Such restoring and upholding is the only thing that can prove to us that our exile is not an eternal one.

VERSE 4. Then will I go unto the altar of God, unto God my exceeding joy; yea, upon the harp will I praise thee, O God, my God.

Sacrifices of praise and thanksgiving should always follow signal mercies. And when God becomes again the life and joy of our hearts, by visiting us with the light of his favour, we should be willing to proclaim the fact in his house, and before the world. We should be prepared to say, with David, "Yea, upon the harp will I praise thee, O God, my God." It is not enough for David to call his friend and protector God, the one perfect Being, but he must repeat the name with the possessive pronoun *my*, before it—"*my* God"—thus intimating that this one perfect Being, acknowledged by the wiser portion of the heathen themselves to be supreme, was his God in a peculiar and endearing sense. O what a glorious moment is that in the moral history of the soul, when, all its doubts having been removed, it can exclaim, "My Lord and my God!" John xx. 28; that moment, when, the Divine Spirit having inspired the feeling, the soul can say, "My beloved is mine, and I am his." Cant. ii. 16.

VERSE 5. Why art thou cast down, O my soul? and why art thou disquieted within me? Hope in God; for I shall yet praise him, who is the health of my countenance, and my God.

Thus this psalm ends, word for word, as the last ended—faith still reproving the flesh for its fears, the heart for its misgivings, and bidding the soul to hope in God, as one from whom deliverance was sure to come. The sequel shows that David's faith was not disappointed. The impious and unnatural rebellion, before whose fury he was fleeing when he wrote this and the preceding psalm, was speedily suppressed, and he restored to his throne, and to the sanctuary-services, whose loss he felt so keenly, and laments so pathetically. 2 Sam. xix. 9, 10, &c. His faith had not apprehended more than it had realized. All that he had longed and prayed for in his exile, God had granted to him in his restoration. May such be the final result of all our contests with evil within us and around us! And if truly penitent for our sins, while looking to Christ to deliver and cleanse us from them, let us address our souls—however sorely our hearts may at times misgive us—let each of us still address our soul, as David addressed his, "Hope thou in God; for I shall yet praise him, who is the health of my countenance, and my God." Who does not see in this psalm the contest between faith and fear, the spirit and the flesh, so graphically described by St. Paul, the flesh crying out continually, "O wretched man that I am! who shall deliver me?" and the spirit as continually rejoining, "Thanks be to God, which giveth us the victory, through our Lord Jesus Christ."

LECTURE ON PSALM XLIV.

THE historical occasion of this psalm was probably the same as that of the sixtieth. The caption of that psalm reads, "To the chief Musician upon Shushan-eduth, Michtam of David, to teach; when he strove with Aram-naharaim and with Aram-zobah, when Joab returned, and smote of Edom in the valley of Salt twelve thousand." The Edomites, as the descendants of Esau, owed the Israelites, as the descendants of Jacob, an implacable grudge. They could not but remember with resentment how Jacob inveigled his brother Esau out of his birthright, as the first-born. Gen. xxvii. They therefore availed themselves of every opportunity to make the Israelites feel their resentment at having been thus deprived of the pre-eminence as the favoured people. They accordingly took advantage of David's absence, in carrying on war in Arabia and Syria, to make an irruption into his kingdom, slay a great number of his subjects, make captives of others, and load themselves with spoil. But before they could reach, and plunder Jerusalem, David's wars in Syria taking a favourable turn, he sent Joab, the captain of his hosts, in pursuit of the Edomites, of whom, overtaking them in the region of country south of the Dead Sea, he slew twelve thousand, and took possession of their country. 2 Sam. viii. 13; 1 Kings xi. 15, 16. It was while his people were, in his absence, slain, made captives, and pillaged by the Edomites, that David is supposed to have composed this psalm. It seemed strange to him, that, while he and his faithful soldiers were fighting the battles of the Lord abroad, his people should be so severely tried at home. God had been the help of Israel in all time past, and was under covenant obligations to be their helper still, so long as they continued faithful in their allegiance to him. And yet the present posture of their affairs looked as if he had forgotten them, though Israel had not forgotten him, neither dealt falsely in his covenant. (See verse 17.) David, however, notwithstanding a state of things so calculated to shake his faith, cannot but believe that God will still be the helper of his people, as he ever had been in time of need, when they sought him with their whole heart. It is only by a review of the past, that he is enabled to dissipate the dark clouds of the present.

VERSES 1, 2. We have heard with our ears, O God, our fathers have told us, what work thou didst in their days, in the times of old. How thou didst drive out the heathen with thy hand, and plantedst them; how thou didst afflict the people, and cast them out.

As the Lord our God is of one mind, and changes not—the same yesterday, to-day, and for ever—what he has done once, we may expect him, under similar circumstances, to do again, always. What, therefore, "we have heard with our ears," we may expect to see with our eyes. Hence the testimony of God's Church elsewhere is, "As we have heard, so have we seen." Ps. xlviii. 8. Experience has always confirmed the testimony of the past. And yet an earnest faith will speak just as positively of the future—as we have heard, so shall we see. It is this anticipative faith that sustains David here. However calamitous the evils may be under which he and his people may be suffering, he cannot but believe that they would be delivered as their fathers had been—that He who had wrought so powerfully for the fathers, would not allow the children to perish out of the land which he himself had given. It is well for us to remember in seasons of trial what God has done for others under like circumstances; for what he has done for others, we may expect him under the same circumstances to do for us.

VERSE 3. For they got not the land in possession by their own sword, neither did their own arm save them; but thy right hand, and thine arm, and the light of thy countenance, because thou hadst a favour unto them.

It was not by military prowess, but by the favour of God, that Israel of old prevailed. It was his favour, vouchsafed to faith, that enabled five of them to chase an hundred of their enemies, and an hundred to put ten thousand to flight. Lev. xxvi. 8. When God strengthens us, no creature-power can overcome us, or do us harm. We need no other hand than God's right hand, no other arm than his, to ensure us the victory over every enemy. This was the experience of God's Israel of old; David hoped that it would be the experience of the Israel of his day.

VERSE 4. Thou art my King, O God: command deliverances for Jacob.

As the Lord's being the King of ancient Israel secured them deliverance, so David here virtually pleads the same relation as a reason why he should deliver the Israel of his day. The Lord was their King too. They had stood firm in their allegiance to him, and could therefore expect the favour always vouchsafed to faithful subjects. They, as truly as the Israel in the wilderness and in the conquest of Canaan, were the elect of God. Here, and again in the sixth verse, David speaks in the first person singular; not, however, as an individual, but as one giving utterance to the feelings of the entire national heart. It was not as David, but as the leader of Israel that he speaks.

VERSES 5—8. Through thee will we push down our enemies: through thy name will we tread them under that rise up against us. For I will not trust in my bow, neither shall my sword save me. But thou hast saved us from our enemies, and hast put them to shame that hated us. In God we boast all the day long, and praise thy name for ever. *Selah.*

In each of these four verses there is a silent parallel run between the Israel of old and the Israel of David's day. Did the former trust in God alone to thrust down and trample their enemies under their feet? so did the latter. Did the former renounce all reliance on their bow and sword to save them? so did the latter. Did the former experience continual deliverance out of the hands of those that hated them? so did the latter, until the present sore calamity overtook them. Did the former boast themselves in God all the day long, and praise him continually as their Help and Deliverer? the latter did the same. But notwithstanding these parallels between the faith and practice of the two Israels, which would lead one to expect a parallelism in the treatment of the two, he goes on to say:

VERSES 9, 10. But thou hast cast off and put us to shame, and goest not forth with our armies. Thou makest us turn back from the enemy; and they which hate us spoil for themselves.

In these and the six following verses we have represented the contrast between God's dealings with his people in the conquest of Canaan, and his dealings with them at the date of our psalm. In their conquest of Canaan he cast down every enemy that rose up against them; at the date of our psalm he seems to have forgotten them, though Israel had not forgotten him. He went not forth with their armies: and the consequence was that their enemies not only routed them in the field, but took possession of their homes and *spoiled* them of their goods. The few soldiers that David left at home to defend the kingdom during his wars in Syria, fled before the invading hosts of Edom, like sheep before ravening wolves. An appalling spectacle to those whose ancestors, having God as their leader and ally, had conquered by few as easily as by many! Even a slight discomfiture in battle with the heathen was a sore affliction to Israel: for such discomfiture was proof to them that God was not with them, waging the battle for them. A slight discomfiture, therefore, as indicating the absence of their Almighty ally, afflicted Israel sorely. Hence the bitterness with which they mourned the loss of only thirty-six men in an assault upon Ai. The hearts of the people melted, and became as water: and Joshua rent his clothes, and fell to the earth upon his face before the ark of the Lord, he and the elders of Israel, and put dust upon their heads. Josh. vii. 5, 6. They thus mourned the loss because, small though it was, it was proof to their minds that He by whose help alone they conquered was not taking part with them in the battle. It would be well for the soldier of the cross to regard his slightest discomfitures in the same way, and to mourn over them as bitterly. The smallest failure in his warfare with the world, the flesh, and the devil, is evidence that there was something wrong in him, because of which, He by whom alone he conquers, had for the time given him up to himself.

VERSES 11, 12. Thou hast given us like sheep appointed for meat; and hast scattered us among the heathen. Thou sellest thy people for nought, and dost not increase thy wealth by their price.

How many of the Israelites were slain in the Edomitish invasion we are unable to say. The number seems to have been great, so great that the Edomites left them unburied. 1 Kings xi. 15. Nor can we tell how many were scattered among the heathen, led away captive by the Edomites. The number was doubtless large, for, as descendants of Esau, the Edomites delighted in making captives of the descendants of Jacob, since, to their minds, the possession of *Israelitish* slaves was "a matter-of-fact" counter proof of the decree, "the elder shall serve the younger." Gen. xxv. 23. We may also infer the number of captives to have been great, from the words, "Thou sellest thy people for nought, and dost not increase thy wealth by their price." The words sound as if God seemed to the Israelites to have given them up to the heathen without an effort to retain them, parted with them as if he were glad to get rid of them, and regarded their removal out of his holy land, not as a loss, but as a boon.

VERSES 13, 14. Thou makest us a reproach to our neighbours, a scorn and derision to them that are round about us. Thou makest us a by-word among the heathen, a shaking of the head among the people.

"Miserable as a Jew," was once a by-word to designate the most wretched and pitiable of human beings. It was generally uttered in derision, and, as the shaking of the head indicates, contemptuous pity. In such light, and with such feelings, their captors regarded Israel at this time. They mocked at their sufferings, and ridiculed their claim to be the peculiar people of God. "Ah!" we imagine we hear them say, "if your God be so powerful as ye say he is, why did he deliver you into our hands? why are ye thus cast down? or why doth he not now come and save you?" To be thus reproached and taunted by those who have us wholly in their power, is hard to bear. It is one of Satan's most burning arrows to goad the soul to madness.

VERSES 15, 16. My confusion is continually before me, and the shame of my face hath covered me, for the voice of him that reproacheth and blasphemeth; by reason of the enemy and avenger.

There was no cessation of the kind of persecution just described. The voice of reproach and of blasphemy was dinned in the ears of the captive people, and was continually crimsoning their faces with the blush of shame. Their enemies gave them no rest. They would not allow them to forget their condition. It was not enough to discomfit them in battle, to spoil them of their goods, to make them captives, to slaughter them in cold blood as sheep are slaughtered for the butcher's stall, and to sell them for nought, but to all this they must add, Israel being now powerless in their hands, the lowest and most odious of persecution, taunting the helpless. Such has always been the way of the world toward the Church of God when she was in affliction. And does it not tell a startling story of the profound depravity of the human heart as we find it by nature?

VERSES 17–19. All this is come upon us; yet have we not forgotten thee, neither have we dealt falsely in thy covenant. Our heart is not turned back, neither have our steps declined from thy way; though thou hast sore broken us in the place of dragons, and covered us with the shadow of death.

What David here claims for Israel—that they had

not dealt falsely in the covenant of the Lord, either in thought or act—is not that they had served the Lord in all things, without fault and without defect, but only that they had not been guilty of the sin of apostatizing from God into idolatry. This their very sufferings proved. They were suffering at that very time for their adherence to the service of Jehovah. The heathen hated and persecuted them because they would not join them in, nor tolerate their idolatries. It was for this that they had "sore broken them in the place of dragons;" converted so large a portion of their beautiful land into a waste for wild beasts and beasts of prey, and covered them with the shadow of death—filled them, that is, with deep despondency by the destruction of so many of their friends. Not on the ground of their being sinless, then, but only on the ground of their not having apostatized from Jehovah as their God, Israel hopes he will come to their relief.

VERSES 20, 21. If we have forgotten the name of our God, or stretched out our hands to a strange God; shall not God search this out? for he knoweth the secrets of the heart.

Happy the believer who can appeal to the Searcher of hearts to attest the truth of his allegiance to him. It was such an appeal that Peter made, when, our Lord having said to him the third time, "Lovest thou me?" he answered, "Lord, thou knowest all things; thou knowest that I love thee." John xxi. 17. He had been guilty of other and great sins, yet his heart told him that he had not been guilty of apostatizing from his Lord. May such, however guilty and unworthy we may feel ourselves to be in other things, ever be the testimony of our hearts.

VERSE 22. Yea, for thy sake are we killed all the day long; we are accounted as sheep for the slaughter.

So far were Israel from having apostatized from God, this verse declares that they were continually suffering for their very fidelity to him. As the religion they professed tolerated no rival, and allowed no fellowship with any other, it arrayed against them the religions of the world beside. If it would only have been willing to compromise the matter, and been content to occupy its niche in some common pantheon, the heathen would have tolerated the religion of the Hebrews as they tolerated the religion of each other. But Israel's religion being the only true religion, teaching that all others were a delusion, it was alike antagonistic to all others, and excited alike the hostility of them all. It was for affirming this exclusive claim to a Divine religion, that every infidel and pagan hand was against the Israel of God in David's days, and from David's days till now. Thus, for their very fidelity to God, and loyalty to his truth, the people of God have always had to suffer. There has never been a time when some portion of his Church could not say, "Yea, for thy sake are we killed all the day long." St. Paul applies this very verse to the Church in his day. Rom. viii. 36. I cannot forbear introducing here the remarks of another on this description of God's people suffering for his sake, for their very fidelity to the cause of truth and righteousness:

"The first feeling that arises in our minds on reading these verses is, Does God ever permit his children, his true Israel, to be thus visited and oppressed? Does he ever himself bring them into such heavy and sore calamities? Yes! even so—'whom the Lord loveth he chasteneth, and whom the Lord intendeth to honour he trieth.' It is very different culture that is required for the fruits and flowers of grace from that which is requisite in our conservatories and gardens; there they are cherished and watched over with assiduous eye and care, that no frost should check, no insect devour or injure. The gardener riseth early, and late taketh rest, to tend and protect alike from the summer's sun or winter's cold; and in many an instance brings them to an earlier bloom by forced appliances of heat and cultivation. Not so, in many a case, with the trees of God's planting; they are rocked by the wind and storm, and grow amid the drought of summer and the frost of winter; they are oftentimes left exposed to all the assaults and inroads of fierce and unremitting enemies; their hedges and fences are so broken down that all that pass by the way pluck at them, and the wild beast of the field doth devour them; and the traveller, as he passes by and sees them in their desolation, may well deem them injured of man, and forsaken of God. But it is not so—it has been God's mode of cultivation with many of the choicest fruit-bearers of his garden through every age. The wilderness church is the most flourishing, and sends forth the choicest and strongest saplings. And one can well believe what precious seed was sown, and what abundant harvest reaped, to the praise and glory of God, in such times of persecution, oppression and terror, as are described in this psalm."—*Rev. B. Bouchier, A.M.*

We come now to the prayer with which our psalm concludes; a prayer, notwithstanding the great sufferings of the petitioners, expressive of strong faith, and of love still fervid.

VERSES 23–26. Awake, why sleepest thou, O Lord? arise, cast us not off for ever. Wherefore hidest thou thy face, and forgettest our afflictions and our oppression? For our soul is bowed down to the dust; our belly cleaveth unto the earth. Arise for our help, and redeem us for thy mercies' sake.

Why God suffers his people to be persecuted for his sake, for their very fidelity to him and his truth, is a mystery of his providence that we do not undertake to solve. It is, however, a mystery which no suffering believer should permit for a moment to shake his confidence in the Divine rectitude and mercy. If conscious to himself that the love of God governs him, it would be blasphemy in him to believe that God will not in time, and at the *best* time for his good and his own glory, come to his relief. He will not always be to the believer prostrate upon the earth, and glued, as it were, to it—as if he were asleep, or had forgotten him, or turned his face away from him in anger; but he will at length surely arise for his help, lift him up, and save him for his mercy's sake. Let none of us despair, then, however much we may suffer at the hands of our enemies, whether visible or invisible, if we are conscious of suffering for our love to Christ and his truth. So suffering, he will not leave us to perish. It was when he was situated precisely as the suffering believers described in this psalm were situated, that St. Paul demands, "What shall we then say to these things? If God be for us, who can be against us?

He that spared not his own Son, but delivered him up for us all, how shall he not with him also freely give us all things? Who shall lay anything to the charge of God's elect? It is God that justifieth. Who is he that condemneth? It is Christ that died, yea rather, that is risen again, who is ever at the right hand of God, who also maketh intercession for us. Who shall separate us from the love of Christ? Shall tribulation, or distress, or persecution, or famine, or nakedness, or peril, or sword? As it is written, For thy sake are we killed all the day long; we are accounted as sheep for the slaughter. Nay, in all these things we are more than conquerors, through him that loved us. For I am persuaded that neither death, nor life, nor angels, nor principalities, nor powers, nor things present, nor things to come, nor height, nor depth, nor any other creature, shall be able to separate us from the love of God, which is in Christ Jesus our Lord." Rom. viii. 31–39. Such is the song of triumph which the believer is enabled to raise under the severest afflictions with which man can be visited. May this song be ours in every season of temptation and trial; and especially in that day when, the vital cord being loosed, the body returns unto the earth as it was, and the spirit unto God who gave it.

LECTURE ON PSALM XLV.

THIS psalm sets forth, under the imagery of a marriage ceremony, observed in oriental style and magnificence, the tender and endearing relations subsisting between Christ and his people. In the title it is called "A Song of loves," because it celebrates the ardent attachment that each has for the other. It is also called "Maschil"—a song designed to instruct—and is dedicated "to the chief musician upon Shoshannim." *Shoshannim* means *The Lilies*, and is generally supposed to refer to a tune of that name, to which the psalm was to be sung. Some, however, think that "Shoshannim" is designed to describe the persons herein represented as being spiritually united to Christ: that, as he is elsewhere called the "Lily of the valleys," (Cant. ii. 1,) so those resembling him in beauty and fragrance of moral character, are called by the same name. Christ's removing his sanctified ones from the Church on earth to the Church in heaven, is described as coming down into his garden—*to gather lilies.* This both ingenious and pleasing interpretation of "Shoshannim," as those spiritually resembling Christ as the Lily of the valleys, may apply, and have been intended to apply in this place, where the praises of the bride and of the Bridegroom are so largely blended. It cannot, however, be so applied in the titles of other psalms—Ps. lx. lxix. lxxx. Shoshannim, or the lilies, must there mean the tune, or style of vocal and instrumental music, to which the words of the song were to be sung.

VERSE 1. My heart is inditing a good matter: I speak of the things which I have made touching the King; my tongue is the pen of a ready writer.

The "good matter" which the heart of the psalmist "was inditing," the goodly theme with which it was running over like the waters of a bubbling spring or heated vessel, was the glory of the King, Messiah. That glory had been so revealed to him, that his tongue could not but be as "the pen of a ready writer," in describing it. In what panoramic vividness he paints each scene, you will see as we pass on. The Spirit had enriched him not only with all knowledge, but with all utterance. 1 Cor. i. 5. Where the Spirit of the Lord is, there is freedom, and the most stammering tongue is taught to speak of the glory of the Redeemer in words of more than human eloquence.

VERSE 2. Thou art fairer than the children of men: grace is poured into thy lips; therefore God hath blessed thee for ever.

Of our Lord's personal appearance, we have no reliable description. It is difficult, however, for us to conceive of it as being other than the perfection of human beauty and comeliness. It is difficult, because we almost intuitively conceive of high moral and intellectual endowments as existing in connection with a physical organization of corresponding excellence. Hence the feeling of disappointment that comes over us, when, on meeting one whose rare moral and intellectual qualities we have long admired, we find them in union with a personal appearance by no means prepossessing. If, therefore, we conceive of infinite excellence embodied, we naturally conceive of it as embodied in the mould of form. Hence the facility with which we conceive of our Lord's outer man being as perfect in form and beauty as the inner man of his heart. Whether or not this was the case, we have no means of ascertaining. Nor is it needful; for it is not in a physical, but in a moral sense, that the Divine Spirit says of Messiah, "Thou art fairer than the children of men." It is in his *soul* that the excelling fairness here ascribed to him is to be found. And in that he was indeed "fairer than the children of men:" there he was all beauty, all attractiveness, the One altogether lovely! Grace was poured into his lips: the law of kindness was in his heart, and its words evermore upon his tongue. And such words, too! Listen to some of them: "The Spirit of the Lord is upon me, because he hath anointed me to preach the gospel to the poor: he hath sent me to heal the broken-hearted, to preach deliverance to the captives, and recovering of sight to the blind; to set at liberty them that are bruised, to preach the acceptable year of the Lord." Luke iv. 18, 19. "Come unto me, all ye that labour and are heavy laden, and I will give you rest. Take my yoke upon you, and learn of me: for I am meek and lowly in heart; and ye shall find rest unto your souls." Matt. xi. 28, 29. "Suffer the little children to come unto me, and forbid them not: for of such is the kingdom of heaven." Mark x. 14. Son, daughter, be of good cheer; thy sins are forgiven thee: go in peace. Matt. ix. 2. "I will; be thou clean." Matt. viii. 3. "Verily, I say unto thee, To-day shalt thou be with me in paradise." Luke xxiii. 43. "Surely, never man spake like this man." John vii. 46. We wonder not that all they that heard him, "wondered at the gracious words which proceeded out of his mouth." Luke iv. 22. Grace was indeed poured into his lips, and poured itself forth in streams of mercy to the guilty, of truth to the benighted, and of encouragement to the downcast. "Therefore God hath blessed thee for ever:" yes, because of the unrivalled majesty, and yet loveliness of Messiah's moral character, God hath blessed him for ever. Of the glory with which he crowned himself, in redeeming man from death, there shall be no end. God will see to it, that eternity shall only develop it in ever more brightening hues, and more captivating colours.

VERSE 3. Gird thy sword upon thy thigh, O most Mighty, with thy glory and thy majesty.

Here the glorious and gracious One of the preceding verse, appears before us as a hero, a mighty warrior exhorted to gird on his sword for the battle, to buckle on his panoply of glory and of majesty. Messiah's only sword, his only panoply of glory and of majesty, is "the sword of the Spirit, which is the word of God." Eph. vi. 17. He asks for no other weapon, wherewith to wage the war. Girded with it, quick and powerful, and two-edged, piercing to the heart, (Heb. iv. 12,) undaunted he takes the field against the world. It was with it alone, that, using the simple words, "It is written," he repelled every assault made upon him by him who overthrew the bliss of Eden.

VERSE 4. And in thy majesty ride prosperously, because of truth, and meekness, and righteousness: and thy right hand shall teach thee terrible things.

"Terrible things," indeed, to all those who oppose their breasts to the point of His sword, and attempt to arrest the progress of his chariot! No man ever yet opposed Messiah and prospered. "Terrible things," however, is not the better translation of the

Hebrew word; but "wonderful things—astonishing achievements." And what more wonderful thing, or astonishing achievement can be imagined, than that accomplished by the simple story of the cross! Messiah's *right hand*, indeed! As told by his disciples, how quickly it subdued nations before him! Hearing it, they cast their idols to the moles and the bats, forsook their oracles, beat their swords into ploughshares, and their spears into pruning-hooks, and walked abroad in all the dignity and purity of sons and daughters of the Most High. If there was anything *terrible* in these mighty changes, this march of Messiah for the vindication "of truth, and meekness, and righteousness," it was so only to those who opposed the truth, oppressed the meek, and hated righteousness.

VERSE 5. Thine arrows are sharp in the heart of the King's enemies; whereby the people fall under thee.

As the sword is for hand to hand conflict, the arrow is for that waged at a distance. Now the word of God may be either a sword to slay one at a single blow, as it slew Saul of Tarsus—or as an arrow to pierce the heart, again and again, from a distance. And where is the Christian man, or Christian woman, who will not tell you that the King's arrows, pungent convictions of sin and of ill desert, were once sharp indeed in their hearts, and gave them no peace till they fell under him, when he extracted the arrows and healed their wounds?

VERSES 6, 7. Thy throne, O God, is for ever and ever: the sceptre of thy kingdom is a right sceptre. Thou lovest righteousness and hatest wickedness: therefore God, thy God, hath anointed thee with the oil of gladness above thy fellows.

St. Paul quotes these verses, (Heb. i. 8, 9,) to

prove both the Godhead and the manhood, the Divinity and the humanity of our Lord. As God, his throne is for ever and ever. As man, the Holy Spirit filled his heart with a joy greater than that experienced by any of those whom, by uniting their human with his Divine nature, he thereby, in one sense, made his fellows. This superior joy is ascribed to his love of righteousness and hatred of wickedness. Therefore, "God hath anointed thee." There may be also another meaning to the words, "oil of gladness above thy fellows." They may mean that the joy of Messiah's heart at the sight of those whom he has redeemed, is greater than that which, unspeakable as it must be, fills the heart of the redeemed themselves. Seeing the travail of his soul, (Isa. liii. 11,) fills him with a joy to which every bosom but his own is a stranger. Such is the reward of the man Christ Jesus for having redeemed us from death by the sacrifice of himself. In how captivating a light it exhibits our Immanuel! Who would not rejoice that His throne is for ever and ever, and the sceptre of the universe in his hands?

VERSE 8. All thy garments smell of myrrh, aloes, and cassia, out of the ivory palaces, whereby they have made thee glad.

Anointing the person with fragrant perfumes, and sprinkling the dress with fragrant waters, has always prevailed in the East, and especially with persons of regal dignity; which dignity is here indicated by their palaces being palaces of ivory. That is, palaces whose inside work, chambers, and furniture, were ornamented with inlayings of that material. Ahab had an ivory palace, 1 Kings xxii. 39; and Amos speaks of others. Amos iii. 15. Of course one coming forth from such a palace as a king to ascend his throne, or as a bridegroom to welcome a young bride to his home, would come forth with all his garments redolent with the most precious and exquisite perfumes. No cost would be counted to give the perfumes a richness and delicacy of fragrance that would ravish the senses of all who should come within the circle of their power. So, too, our Lord; he, with garments thus redolent with every spiritual perfume, comes forth to meet his spiritual bride, the Church he purchased with his blood, and sanctifies by his Spirit. For he, too, has received an anointing that gladdens his heart more than the anointing of the dwellers in ivory palaces gladdened theirs, even the anointing by the Holy Ghost to be our Prophet, Priest, and King. And how fragrant is the moral atmosphere that floats around his name in all these his threefold relations to his Church! As our Prophet to teach us the truth—"Never man spake like this man!" As our Priest to gain us access to God—"He put away our sins by the sacrifice of himself, and now ever liveth to make intercession for us!" As our King to rule over us—where is the king who ever enacted laws so perfect for the government of his subjects, or administered his laws so impartially? Under whatever aspect we view our Lord in his great work of redeeming love, "all his garments smell of myrrh, aloes, and cassia." An unrivalled moral aroma invests his character on whatever side we approach it. His name is indeed as ointment poured out. His whole life, everything he said, everything he did, exhaled the air of heaven, and bespoke his breast the abode of its purity, love, and peace.

VERSE 9. Kings' daughters were among thy honourable women; upon thy right hand did stand the queen in gold of Ophir.

Kings' daughters are, in Scripture phrase, their kingdoms. The kings' daughters then in attendance on Messiah are the gentile nations that were to be gathered into his Church. They were gathered in largely in the beginning—they will come in still more numerously in the ages to come. The queen at Messiah's right hand in gold of Ophir is believed to represent the Hebrew Church. Her being clothed in gold of Ophir is probably designed to represent her as being at last completely clothed "in the truth as it is in Jesus." This, of course, is a looking forward to the time when the veil that is now upon her heart shall have been taken away, the fulness of the Gentiles having been gathered in. When that shall have come to pass, then shall the Hebrew Church, as Messiah's first love, stand in the place of honour on his right hand. Of this restoration of the Hebrew Church to the first place in the affections of her former Lord, there are clear intimations in the word of God. "He will surely betroth the Church of Israel unto himself again, and for ever." Hosea ii. 19, 20.

VERSES 10, 11. Hearken, O daughter, and consider, and incline thine ear: forget also thine own people, and thy father's house; so shall the King greatly desire thy beauty: for he is thy Lord; and worship thou him.

The psalmist, or rather the Divine Spirit, here admonishes the queen bride, and so, virtually, all the Gentile brides, as a father would admonish a daughter, to identify herself entirely in thought, feeling, and purpose, with Him to whom she was about to be united for life—admonishes her to forget her own people, and her father's house, to bring into the kingdom of Messiah no previous prejudice, no previous preposession, no habit, no custom, that would in any way interfere with her worshipping and serving him with supreme affection as her Lord. So coming to him, in all the beauty of pure evangelical holiness, "the King would greatly desire her beauty;" would look upon her with all the tender complacency with which the bridegroom looks upon his blooming bride, in whose face he sees depicted nothing but love and devotion to himself. Alas, how few of us consider how entire our devotion to Christ must be to ensure his complacency; how entirely every thought, word, and deed, that might interfere with supreme love to him must be omitted and forgotten!

VERSE 12. And the daughter of Tyre shall be there with a gift; even the rich among the people shall entreat thy favour.

"The daughter of Tyre" means the city of Tyre, at the time these words were uttered the richest among the nations, the mart of the world, and her merchants, princes. Isa. xxiii. 3, 8. Her entreating the favour of the queen-consort *with a gift*, a mode of expressing homage still common in the East, indicates that in time to come the trade and commerce, the arts and science, of the wealthiest portions of the world would reckon it an honour and a privilege to pay tribute to the Church of God. And is it not a fact confirmed by the history of missions, that as these have spread, missions have spread with them? Where is there another nation that has so excelled in trade and commerce, art and science, as England? and where is there another nation that has done so much to honour the Church of our Redeemer—so much to speed its messages of salvation to the isles of the sea and the remotest parts of the earth? In every such nation we see a

Tyre seeking the favour of Messiah's queen with a gift. The more they excel in trade and commerce, the more they do to honour and advance the Church of Him whose throne is for ever and ever.

VERSE 13. The King's daughter is all glorious within: her clothing is of wrought gold.

It is to be remarked here that the Spirit of inspiration denominates the Church of Messiah in one place as his wife, in another as his daughter, and in still another, as his sister, thus varying the name and relation the more vividly to impress upon our minds the thought that the ties that bind him to his people are the strongest and purest that can be conceived: that a husband cannot love his wife, a father love his daughter, nor a brother love his sister, more tenderly than Messiah loves his Church, and every member of his Church. "The King's daughter is all glorious within"—that is, in spiritual graces and endowments. And what are some of them? "Love, joy, peace, long-suffering, gentleness, goodness, faith, meekness, temperance." Eph. v. 22. These are the fruits of the Spirit, and constitute "the King's daughter all glorious within" in the temper of her mind, being of the same mind with her Lord. "Her clothing is of wrought gold:" is made up of "whatsoever things are true, of whatsoever things are honest, of whatsoever things are just, of whatsoever things are pure, of whatsoever things are lovely, of whatsoever things are of good report." Philip. iv. 8. She adds to her "faith virtue; and to virtue, knowledge; and to knowledge, temperance; and to temperance, patience; and to patience, godliness; and to godliness, brotherly kindness; and to brotherly kindness, charity." 2 Pet. i. 5, 6, 7. A drapery of "wrought gold" indeed! a life of active virtues as bright as her catalogue of inward graces! as glorious without as she is within, in act as she is in thought.

VERSES 14, 15. She shall be brought unto the King in raiment of needlework; the virgins her companions that follow her shall be brought unto thee: with gladness and rejoicing shall they be brought unto thee: they shall enter into the King's palace.

They shall enter into His spiritual palace here on earth; they shall enter into his palace on high, the house not made with hands, eternal in the heavens. The daughter's "raiment of needlework" must needs mean substantially the same as her "clothing of wrought gold," already explained. We must also conceive of her bridal attendants as equally glorious within and similarly attired. They follow the Hebrew bride as her equals, though joyfully giving her the precedence as the King's first, and, for a long time, only love.

VERSE 16. Instead of thy fathers shall be thy children, whom thou mayest make princes in all the earth.

Addressing the King again, the psalmist here promises him as the fruit of the espousals now represented as consummated, a royal progeny more numerous than his ancestors, children of his own, whom he may "make princes," not in Judea only, but "in all the earth." These children are, of course, Messiah's spiritual children, kings and rulers with his image impressed upon their hearts and ruling in his fear. This prophecy has been already partially fulfilled, nation after nation, and kingdom after kingdom, having already joined the marriage procession herein before described. Its complete fulfilment is, however, yet to be realized—to be realized when the seventh angel of the Apocalyptic vision sounds, and great voices are heard in heaven, saying, "The kingdoms of this world have become the kingdoms of our Lord, and of his Christ; and he shall reign for ever and ever." Rev. xi. 15. Till then Messiah's sword must remain girt upon his thigh. His arrows set to the string upon his bow, and he go on from conquering to conquer.

VERSE 17. I will make thy name to be remembered in all generations: therefore shall the people praise thee for ever and ever.

It is thought that the psalmist speaks here as a representative character, as one in a succession of evangelists whose business it should be to preach Christ always, even unto the end of the world; to make his "name to be remembered in all generations;" and, in so doing, cause perpetual praise of him among the people. If this be the meaning of these inspired words, they have been in process of fulfilment ever since they were uttered. The name of Messiah, proclaimed from generation to generation by the ministers of his word, has awakened among the nations of the earth higher, holier, and more fervid songs of praise than any other name given under heaven among men. It was his name, as a Deliverer to come, that kindled in the heart of the pious Jew its liveliest and most abiding joy. It is his name, as a Deliverer who has come, that kindles the same joy in our hearts. And how captivating the insight this forty-fifth psalm gives us into the deep and tender meaning of "His name!"—the majesty and loveliness of his character! First, he appears as our Champion, waging the battle for us; then, as the God whose throne is for ever and ever; and then, as welcoming us unto abodes of everlasting bliss, with all the love and tenderness with which the bridegroom welcomes the loveliest and most beloved of brides to his heart and home. "Behold, the Bridegroom cometh; go ye out to meet him:" delay not to join the procession at once, lest, when you present yourselves at his palace for admission, you find the door shut. Matt. xxv. 6, 10.

LECTURE ON PSALM XLVI.

Louder notes of triumphant confidence in God as an ever-present and almighty Help are nowhere to be found, than we find in this forty-sixth psalm. It was composed on the occasion of God's deliverance of Israel out of the hand of Sennacherib, king of Assyria. It was to be sung upon Alamoth—that is, to a tune suited to the clear shrill voice of female minstrels, *al-amoth* meaning virgin-manner. The history of Sennacherib's invasion of Israel is recorded in the eighteenth and nineteenth chapters of the second book of Kings, in the thirty-second chapter of the second book of Chronicles, and also in the thirty-sixth and thirty-seventh chapters of Isaiah. Having already subdued all the surrounding nations to his sway, and also taken all the other fortified towns of Judah, the inflated conqueror sat down with his vast veteran armies before Jerusalem, to take it also. The king of Judah at the time was Hezekiah, who excelled in his simple trust in God and zeal against idolatry. 2 Kings xviii. 3–7. But before making what he no doubt thought would be a successful assault upon the holy city, Sennacherib sent an insulting message to those shut up in Jerusalem, bidding them not regard Hezekiah, if he should say to them, "the Lord will surely deliver us, and this city shall not be delivered into the hand of the king of Assyria: for who," demands Sennacherib, "who among all the gods of the countries, have delivered their country out of my hand, that the Lord should deliver Jerusalem out of mine hand?" 2 Kings xviii. 30, 35. Hezekiah's only reply was prayer, saying, "O Lord God of Israel, which dwellest between the cherubims, thou art the God, even thou alone, of all the kingdoms of the earth: thou hast made heaven and earth. Lord, now bow down thine ear, and hear: open, Lord, thine eyes, and see; and hear the words of Sennacherib which he hath sent by his messenger to reproach the living God. Of a truth, Lord, the kings of Assyria have destroyed the nations and their lands, and have cast their gods into the fire: for they were no gods, but the work of men's hands, wood and stone: therefore have they destroyed them. Now therefore, O Lord our God, I beseech thee, save thou us out of his hand, that all the kingdoms of the earth may know that thou art the God, even thou alone." 2 Kings xix. 15–19. Then Isaiah answered Hezekiah, "Thus saith the Lord God of Israel, That which thou hast prayed to me against Sennacherib, king of Assyria, I have heard. This is the word that the Lord hath spoken concerning him: The virgin, the daughter of Zion, hath despised thee, and laughed thee to scorn; the daughter of Jerusalem hath shaken her head at thee. Whom hast thou reproached and blasphemed, and against whom hast thou exalted thy voice, and lifted up thine eyes on high? Even against the Holy One of Israel. Because thy rage against me, and thy tumult is come up into mine ears, therefore will I put my hook in thy nose, and my bridle in thy lips, and I will turn thee back by the way thou camest. Thus saith the Lord concerning the king of Assyria: He shall not come into this city, nor shoot an arrow there, nor come before it with shield, nor cast up a trench against it. For I will defend this city, to save it for mine own sake, and for my servant David's sake. And it came to pass that night, that the angel of the Lord went forth, and smote in the camp of the Assyrians an hundred and four-score and five thousand men." 2 Kings xix. 20–35. So Sennacherib, king of Assyria, returned with shame to his own land.

When they saw the hosts of Sennacherib threatening Jerusalem itself, Hezekiah said to the people, "Be strong and courageous, be not afraid nor dismayed for the king of Assyria, nor for all the multitude that is with him; for there be more with us than with him. With him is an arm of flesh; but with us is the Lord our God, to help us, and to fight our battles." 2 Chron. xxxii. 7, 8. Such were the words of Hezekiah, and such their fulfilment! The angel of the Lord breathed on the hosts of Sennacherib, and they were not; and he, a fugitive for his life, fled to his own country. And now, having been thus delivered, how could the liberated inhabitants of Jerusalem commemorate their deliverance with other words than those with which our psalm opens?

VERSE 1. God is our refuge and strength, a very present help in trouble.

"A very present Help," indeed! The sun went down on Israel's enemies, boasting what they would do on the morrow: the morrow's sun dawned on them—*dead!* A wind from the desert passed over them—they breathed it once, to breathe no more! It was the Lord's doing, and the people saw that it was. The watchers upon the walls of the holy city in the morning looked out in vain to discover a vestige of any living remains of their so formidable enemies of the night before. It had happened to them as it happened to the hosts of Pharaoh, pursuing Israel into the midst of the Red Sea, not one of whom remained alive to tell the story of the disaster that befell them there. Exod. xiv. 13, 14. In both instances, the people of God experienced the salvation of the Lord, when he alone could save them, without their raising a hand to achieve it for themselves. God was their refuge, and strength, and help. When the time came for punishing their enemies, and delivering them, he spake, and it was done: he commanded, and it stood fast. They stood still, and saw the salvation of God.

VERSES 2, 3. Therefore will not we fear, though the earth be removed, and though the mountains be carried into the midst of the sea; though the waters thereof roar and be troubled, though the mountains shake with the swelling thereof. *Selah.*

For the earth to be removed—understanding by *the earth*, its inhabitants—is supposing all the bonds that unite mankind in civil society, to be sundered, law and order to be at an end, and anarchy reigning in their stead. Nevertheless, so secure does the Church of God feel under his protection, that she declares she could witness even such a scene of lawlessness and confusion, without fear; satisfied that there was still a Divine hand at the helm, which would in time bring back the ship of human destiny to its bearings. The sea, and the waters of the sea—are thought to represent the masses of mankind, not in their multitudinous, but in their national aspects, as men confined within certain metes and bounds, and living under established governments. These established governments are also "the mountains" in the midst of the sea, and are, as every one knows, often shaken by the swelling of its waters—indeed, the tide of human passion not only shaking them, but often sweeping them away. Maddened popular feeling is truly a sea whose waters cannot rest, but still roar and are troubled. If, however, we choose to regard these mountains separately—each as some powerful state or empire, with its subjects and rulers, citizens and sovereign acting together as an organized, closely cemented, and energetic whole—when such a mountain is "carried into the midst of the sea," makes war upon the other nations of the earth, how fearful are the commotions that ensue! Such a mountain was each of the four great monarchies—the Chaldean, Medo-Persian, Macedonian, and Roman—and France, too, revolutionary France!—the burning mountain of the Apocalypse, which, being cast *into the sea*, a third part of the waters thereof became blood. Rev. viii. 8. Even in the midst of such scenes as these, scenes of the wildest commotion of the powers of the earth, it is the duty and privilege of the people of God, having him as their refuge, and strength, and help, still to say, "we will not fear." There is a *Selah* added at the end of these verses, that we may pause, to consider the thought they contain.

VERSE 4. There is a river, the streams whereof shall make glad the city of God, the holy place of the tabernacles of the Most High.

It is as a sea whose waves roar and waters cast up mire and dirt, that the world is represented to our moral vision. All the influences proceeding thence work disastrously. Not so the influences that proceed from the Church of the living God—they are "a river, the streams whereof" gladden wherever they flow. They gladden the understanding, enlightening its darkness; they gladden the heart, chasing away its sorrow; they gladden the conscience, giving it peace. The sea contains in its dark depths the washings of the whole earth: the river of Divine influences, gladdening "the city of God, the holy place of the tabernacles of the Most High," is clear as crystal, and flows with streams so numerous, that its waters reach and refresh every attribute of human character that can ennoble man.

VERSE 5. God is in the midst of her; she shall not be moved: God shall help her, and that right early.

It is vain to assault the city that has God in the midst of it, as its defender. Such a city cannot be moved. Its strength is Omnipotence. We can say the same of the soul in which God has taken up his abode, through his Spirit—it "shall not be moved." Dangers may threaten it, but "God will help it, and that right early." The Hebrew, rendered "right early," means the turning of the morning, the dawning of day; and may therefore have a literal reference to the suddenness with which the Lord destroyed the hosts of Sennacherib. Flushed with hope, and confident of victory, they lighted their camp-fires at night; but when the inhabitants of Jerusalem "arose early in the morning, behold," their besieging enemy "were all dead corpses." Isa. xxxvii. 36. At eventide there was trouble for Israel; before the morning, it was no more. How well this accords with the experience of many a believer—the interval between the greatest distress and the greatest relief, the deepest sorrow and the highest joy, often being the interval of an instant only!

VERSE 6. The heathen raged, the kingdoms were moved: he uttered his voice, the earth melted.

That is, they raged, and were moved against Jerusalem, the city of God, to destroy it: not one heathen nation only, but kingdoms that Sennacherib had subjected to his sway, and whose chosen troops were, no doubt, marching under his banner. "He uttered his voice, the earth melted." These words describe the effect, upon the heathen world, of the fearful judgment inflicted upon the hosts of Sennacherib before Jerusalem. That judgment caused them to stand aghast, and their hearts melted within them. Its greatness and suddenness filled them with dismay. They could not but acknowledge the voice of God, even of the God of the whole earth, in it.

VERSE 7. The Lord of hosts is with us; the God of Jacob is our refuge. *Selah.*

Having experienced such deliverance as they had, Israel could well say this. No human power could have overcome the formidable host that had come up against them: none but the Lord of hosts. It was a case worthy of his interposition, and he had interposed in a way to leave his people no room to doubt his presence. As he had delivered Jacob, so had he delivered them, and thereby manifested that he had not forgotten his covenant with Jacob to be a *God to his seed after him.* This covenant fidelity of their father's God enhances the joy of their deliverance. How glorious a sight it is to see the grace of God continuing in the same family from generation to generation! the God of the fathers being the God of the children, and of the children's children.

VERSE 8. Come, behold the works of the Lord, what desolations he hath made in the earth.

The devastations of the conqueror are permitted by Him whose kingdom ruleth over all. He says, "I will show wonders in heaven and in earth, blood, and fire, and pillars of smoke." Joel xx. 30. The wicked are his sword wherewith to punish the wicked, and sometimes his own people, to reclaim them. The people then, no doubt, include in the desolations here spoken of, the desolations of their own land, every portion of which had been desolated, except Jerusalem. All these desolations the Lord had made. He maketh the wrath of man promote the great benevolent ends of his moral government of the world; the remainder he restrains.

VERSE 9. He maketh wars to cease unto the end of the earth; he breaketh the bow, and cutteth the spear in sunder; he burneth the chariot in the fire.

"He maketh wars to cease" at one time, by cutting off the power, and at another, the life of him who had caused them. He brought Sennacherib's wars to a close in both ways. First, the pestilence swept away in a single night the myriad hosts on whose prowess he relied; and then, on his return home, two of his sons smote him with the sword, that he died. Isa. xxxvii. 38. Wars then ceased unto the ends of the earth. The many nations that Sennacherib had subjugated to his iron yoke, once more had peace; beat their swords into ploughshares and their spears into pruning-hooks. God had dealt with him as he had said he would, saying, "I will put my hook in thy nose, and my bridle in thy lips, and I will turn thee back by the way by which thou camest." Isa. xxxvii. 29. So God has always controlled as he listed, all the mighty conquerors of history. As long as the use of the bow, the spear, and the chariot, can be overruled to promote his wise and benevolent purposes of good to his Church, he endures their use: when, however, he cannot so overrule their use, "he breaketh the bow, cutteth the spear in sunder, and burneth the chariot in the fire." When the tide of war would sweep away his Church, he turns it, and lulls its agitated waves to rest.

VERSE 10. Be still, and know that I am God: I will be exalted among the heathen, I will be exalted in the earth.

This is a direct address to the whole heathen world by God himself, bidding them learn from Sennacherib's overthrow, the mightiest king, as well as conqueror of them all, that it is vain to contend against his people, that their help and champion must be Divine. He also adds, "I will be exalted among the heathen, I will be exalted in the earth:" and the history informs us that his dealings with the king of Assyria did "exalt him among the heathen:" many, we read, brought gifts unto the Lord to Jerusalem, when they heard how the Lord had saved Israel, and also presents to Hezekiah, so that he was magnified in the sight of all nations from henceforth." 2 Chron. xxxii. 23. The wonderful manner in which he had delivered his people out of the hand of Sennacherib, convinced even the heathen world, for the time being, that the God of the Hebrews was the true God.

VERSE 11. The Lord of hosts is with us: the God of Jacob is our refuge. *Selah.*

To no other conclusion can the Israelites come, in no other words can they close their anthem of praise for the deliverance wrought out for them! And yet cannot we, as Christians, say, with even greater emphasis and significance than God's Israel of old said it, "The Lord of hosts is with us; the God of Jacob is our Refuge"? This Lord of hosts has since revealed himself to us in Christ. We know who he is, for he visited us in our human nature! We know the kindness of his heart, that he wept with those that wept, and shed tears over those whom his love could not reclaim. We know the greatness of his power, that he said to the angry winds and waves, "Peace! be still!" and they obeyed; to the dead Lazarus, "Come forth!" and he that was dead came forth and took his place among the living! We know his readiness to comfort the disconsolate! How sweet were his words to such, "Come unto me, all ye that labour and are heavy laden, and I will give you rest." He is not one who cannot be touched with sympathy for our infirmities. He became man that he might enter into every feeling of the human heart. The lowly, and the lofty! a Man of sorrows, and yet the Lord Almighty! No Sennacherib can encamp against us with a host so formidable that He cannot destroy them and set us free. Nor earth, nor hell, can do us harm, having him as our Help.

"The soul that to Jesus has fled for repose,
I will not, I will not desert to his foes;
That soul, though all hell shall endeavour to shake,
I'll never—no never—no never forsake."

Let us all, then, take refuge in Him who died on Calvary, and then shall we be able to say, in all time of our tribulation, in all time of our prosperity, in the hour of death, and in the day of judgment, "the Lord of hosts is with us; the God of Jacob is our Refuge. Selah."

LECTURE ON PSALM XLVII.

THE historical basis of this psalm is the confederate invasion of Judah by the children of Ammon, Moab, and Mount Seir, for the purpose of dispossessing Israel of their land. 2 Chron. xx. 1–30. Aware of this hostile purpose, and knowing, too, that he had no military force sufficient to meet the invading enemy, Jehoshaphat, then reigning at Jerusalem, addressing himself to seeking Divine aid, proclaimed a fast throughout all Judah. The people's response to their sovereign's call to fasting and prayer was with one mind and one heart. And Jehoshaphat, standing in the midst of the congregation assembled in the house of the Lord, prayed thus, "O Lord God of our fathers, art not thou God in heaven? and rulest not thou over all the kingdoms of the heathen? and in thine hand is there not power and might, so that none is able to withstand thee? Art not thou our God, who didst drive out the inhabitants of this land before thy people Israel, and gavest it to the seed of Abraham, thy friend, for ever? And they built therein, and have built thee a sanctuary therein for thy name, saying, If, when evil cometh upon us, as the sword, judgment, or pestilence, or famine, we stand before this house, and in thy presence cry unto thee in our affliction, then thou wilt hear and help. And now, Lord, behold, the children of Ammon, and Moab, and Mount Seir, whom thou wouldest not let Israel invade, when they came out of the land of Egypt, but they turned aside from them and destroyed them not: behold, I say, how they reward us, to come and cast us out of thy possession, which thou hast given unto us to inherit. O our God, wilt thou not judge them? for we have no might against this great company that cometh against us; neither know we what to do: but our eyes are upon thee."

This humble appeal to God's covenant fidelity as the God of Israel was not in vain; for he immediately answered, "Be not afraid, nor dismayed, by reason of this great multitude; for the battle is not yours, but God's. To-morrow go ye down against them: behold, they come up by the cliff of Ziz; and ye shall find them at the end of the brook, before the wilderness of Jeruel. Ye shall not need to fight in this battle; set yourselves [in battle array,] but stand ye still in your places, and see the salvation of the Lord with you, O Judah and Jerusalem: fear not, nor be dismayed; to-morrow go out against them; for the Lord will be with you. And Jehoshaphat bowed his head, with his face to the ground: and all Judah and the inhabitants of Jerusalem fell before the Lord, worshipping the Lord. And the Levites of the children of the Kohathites, and of the children of the Korhites, stood up to praise the Lord God of Israel with a loud voice on high. And they rose early in the morning, and went forth into the wilderness of Tekoa: and as they went forth, Jehoshaphat stood and said, Hear me, O Judah, and ye inhabitants of Jerusalem; believe in the Lord your God, so shall ye be established; believe his prophets, so shall ye prosper." He also appointed singers that should go before the army, and say, "Praise the Lord; for his mercy endureth for ever." Thus they approached the camp of the enemy with songs; "and when they began to sing and to praise, the Lord sent ambushments against the children of Ammon, Moab, and Mount Seir, which were come against Judah; and they were smitten [that is, by each other.] For the children of Ammon and Moab stood up against the inhabitants of Mount Seir, utterly to slay and destroy them; and when they had made an end of the inhabitants of Seir, every one helped to destroy another."

The confederates being divinely bewildered, the ambushes which they had laid for Israel turned their swords against each other, till not a man of them remained. The victory had been achieved for Israel without their raising a hand. All that they had to do was to enrich themselves with the spoil of their self-slaughtered enemies; spoil of riches and precious jewels so great that they were three days gathering it. This signal deliverance of Israel out of the hands of their enemies is supposed to have been the occasion of the singing of this forty-seventh psalm. It seems to have been sung for the first time in the very place where the deliverance was vouchsafed them, for on the fourth day, (2 Chron. xx. 26,) three having been consumed in gathering the spoil, the men of Judah assembled themselves in the Valley of Berachah—the Valley of Blessing—so called because there they blessed the Lord, offered up to him an ovation of homage, praise, and thanksgiving; which ovation was, no doubt, this very psalm, opening with the words,

VERSE 1. O clap your hands, all ye people; shout unto God with the voice of triumph.

It may seem strange to some that the Spirit of God should call upon all people to laud him for what he had done for Israel. It would certainly be difficult for the nations whom he had just stricken, to respond to the call. And yet what God had done for Israel was really cause for joy to the whole Gentile world. For what he had done for Israel was a proclamation of what he would do for all nations who should take refuge in him as Israel had done. God is no respecter of persons, but in every nation he that feareth him, and worketh righteousness, is accepted with him. Acts x. 34, 35. Elsewhere, (Psalm xcvi. 1; cxvii. 1,) all the earth, all nations, all people, are called on to rejoice in God's mercies to Israel; to rejoice in them as illustrations of the mercies he had in reserve for all who should turn to him. Viewing God's mercies to them in this light, Israel could with propriety call on all people to clap their hands, and shout unto God with the voice of triumph.

VERSE 2. For the Lord Most High is terrible; he is a great King over all the earth.

And therefore King of the heathen, as well as of his own chosen people. Not a local, but a universal King, who would rule over the heathen as tenderly as he ruled over Israel, when they too should seek him as their Refuge. This fact, then, should be cause of joy to them, even while suffering under his hand, "The Lord Most High is terrible"—terrible indeed! but only to his enemies and the enemies of his people; only to those, who, if they were to realize the wickedness of their hearts, would turn earth into a pandemonium, and the universe into a hell. He does indeed look down with stern and awful majesty upon the wicked going on still in his wickedness, but with ineffable tenderness upon him who hath turned away from his wickedness, and is seeking that which is lawful and right.

VERSE 3. He shall subdue the people under us, and the nations under our feet.

Every new victory that God vouchsafes his people is the earnest of still another. His past and present dealings with them will project themselves into the future. Hence the great victory just given his people over the children of Ammon, Moab, and Mount Seir, inspires them to speak of other victories which the Lord their God has in reserve for them. It is the property of an earnest faith to anticipate with increasing assurance, victory after victory over its enemies, till all shall at length be vanquished, and God reigns supreme in his soul. May God give this faith to us all; the faith that presses on with a step of always increasing strength.

VERSE 4. He shall choose our inheritance for us, the excellency of Jacob whom he loved. *Selah.*

Having defeated the purpose of their invading enemy to dispossess them of their beautiful land, (2 Chron. xx. 11,) God here leads his people to speak of the deliverance as a choosing their inheritance anew for them by the Lord. We are thus taught to regard the preservation of our blessings in the light of a continual first bestowment. It is even so; if God keep not continually alive in our souls the grace of life given us in regeneration, we cannot retain it a moment. If he choose not at every moment our inheritance for us, watch over it, guard it, and protect it as a thing dear to his heart, alas for us! the enemy enters and takes possession. There is no help for us for a moment, except as we find it in God. If, however, we are sincere in our efforts to serve him, we need not fear. He will both choose our inheritance for us, and keep it for us. He is in that case saying to us what he said to Jehoshaphat and the inhabitants of Jerusalem, "Be not afraid nor dismayed by reason of the great multitude arrayed against you; the battle is not yours, but God's." 2 Chron. xx. 15.

VERSE 5. God is gone up with a shout, the Lord with the sound of a trumpet.

Like as a king, having achieved some great victory for his people, returns in triumph to the throne he had left for the occasion, so God, having won the victory for his people in the valley of Ziz, is here represented as ascending to his throne on high with a shout, and the voice of a trumpet. This triumphal procession, escorting Israel's Leader from the field of victory to heaven, is of course altogether ideal; nevertheless, a scene which an excited imagination could have readily conceived. The idea has since, however, been realized in the history of our Lord. In his return to heaven after his great victory over death and hell, it was not an ideal, but a real triumphal procession that escorted him thither. We accordingly read that, as he ascended in the presence of his disciples, "a cloud received him out of their sight."

Acts i. 9. That cloud, luminous above the light of the sun, was doubtless an angelic host. This is confirmed by the exposition generally given of the twenty-fourth psalm. As the angelic host, there represented as escorting Messiah back to his throne, approach the golden city, they raise the cry, "Lift up your heads, O ye gates; and be ye lift up, ye everlasting doors, and the King of Glory shall come in;" and, in answer to the demand of the angels standing upon the watch-towers of the city, "Who is this King of Glory?" they reply, "the Lord strong and mighty, the Lord mighty in battle: the Lord of hosts, he is the King of glory." Applied then—as this verse may be, and was doubtless meant to be—to Christ and his ascension to heaven, there is no exaggeration in the words, "God is gone up with a shout, the Lord with the sound of a trumpet." He was attended to the skies by such a triumphal and lauding procession as the universe had never seen before, and will never see again till the same Jesus shall so come in like manner as he was seen to go into heaven. Acts. i. 11.

VERSE 6. Sing praises to God, sing praises: sing praises to our King, sing praises.

If we apply, as the Spirit of inspiration evidently designed that we should apply them, the words, "God is gone up with a shout, the Lord with the sound of a trumpet," to Christ, these repeated calls to praise Israel's King are beautifully in place. We cannot praise him too often, nor too long. If for the victory achieved for Jehoshaphat and his people over their enemies in the valley of Ziz, they returned to Jerusalem praising the Lord all the way with psalteries, and harps, and trumpets, (2 Chron. xx. 27, 28,) how much more fervid should our praises be of him for the victory which he hath achieved for us—a victory wherein he spoiled the spoiler of all, and opened the kingdom of heaven to all believers. To praise our King for such a victory as this, eternity, eternity will be none too long, and the tongue of Cherubim none too fervid. Then "sing ye praises to God, sing praises; sing praises to our King, sing praises."

VERSES 7, 8. For God is the King of all the earth: sing ye praises with understanding. God reigneth over the heathen: God sitteth upon the throne of his holiness.

In these verses we have the reasons assigned why all men, every one that hath understanding, should praise our King. They should praise him because he is the King of all men, reigneth over the heathen as well as over the Israelite, over the uttermost parts of the earth as well as over the Holy Land. That he ruleth over the heathen, he had just shown by the fearful manner he had just punished them. God's rule extends to all creatures and to all events—not one is excepted. "God sitteth upon the throne of his holiness." The Divine rule is as pure as it is universal. The Judge of all the earth never fails to do right. His throne is a great white throne. No stain of injustice has ever sullied its brightness. These things should excite every mind to praise God. How glorious the thought that we and all belonging to us are under the protection, not only of an omnipotent and universal, but also of a holy government, a government as infinitely incapable of doing us wrong, as it is infinitely able and willing to help us. And with what an increase of interest should this government be invested to our minds, who know that it is presided over by Him who became man and dwelt among us, and died for us on Calvary! Surely we need not fear infinite power in his hands. He who took little children in his arms and blessed them, saying, "of such is the kingdom of heaven:" and said to a dying thief, "to-day shalt thou be with me in paradise," surely He can administer the government of the universe only in love!

VERSE 9. The princes of the people are gathered together, even the people of the God of Abraham: for the shields of the earth belong unto God: he is greatly exalted.

"The shields of the earth" are its rulers, so called because they should be to their people what his shield is to the soldier, his safety and defence. These shields, these ruling ones of the world, God declares to belong to him, that he has as absolute a right to their service as he has to the service of their subjects. "The princes of the people gathered together, even as the people of the God of Abraham," were princes of Gentile nations, who should profess the faith of the gospel, and thus become partakers with Abraham of the great salvation. Their conversion would necessarily result from the King of Zion being the God and King of the whole earth, and ruling in holiness. "He is greatly exalted." Greatly exalted indeed in the gospel of his Son, "the brightness of his glory, and the express image of his person." Heb. i. 3. Philip said, "Lord, show us the Father, and it sufficeth us." Jesus answered him, "Have I been so long time with you and yet hast thou not known me, Philip? he that hath seen me, hath seen the Father, and how sayest thou then, Show us the Father?" John xiv. 8, 9. I want no other words than these to charm away the disquietudes of my guilty breast and lead me to trust implicitly in the mercy of the Lord our God. He such as Jesus was! His heart as tender, his love as large? O yes, he that hath seen Jesus, hath seen the Father. This is the thought that hath exalted him in heaven and in earth, as he was never exalted before. This is the thought that hath subdued the nations under him, and will subdue them under him, "till the kingdoms of this world are become the kingdoms of our Lord and of his Christ; and he shall reign for ever and ever." Rev. xi. 15. May we all become the loving subjects of him who "ascended on high, leading captivity captive." Ps. lxviii. 18.

LECTURE ON PSALM XLVIII.

As the preceding psalm seems to have been first sung in the wilderness of Tekoa, in the very place where God had achieved a signal victory for his people over the children of Ammon, Moab, and Mount Seir, (2 Chron. xx. 23–26,) so this psalm—evidently commemorative of the same event—seems to have been first sung in the temple at Jerusalem. We accordingly read that the Israelites having blessed the Lord in the valley of Berachah, then returned, every man of Judah and Jerusalem, and Jehoshaphat in the fore-front of them, to go again to Jerusalem with joy; for the Lord had made them to rejoice over their enemies. "And they came to Jerusalem with psalteries, and harps, and trumpets, unto the house of the Lord." 2 Chron. xx. 27, 28. If we are right in what we have supposed the occasion on which this psalm was composed and sung, no words could be more suitable to such an occasion than the words with which it opens.

VERSE 1. Great is the Lord, and greatly to be praised in the city of our God, in the mountain of his holiness.

God's greatness is visible everywhere. We can penetrate to no part of his universe where we will not discover tokens of his infinite power, wisdom, and goodness. It is, however, in his Church, "in the mountain of his holiness," they are most conspicuously seen, and excite to the highest praise. There alone he is made to appear the glorious Being that he truly is! There every attribute of his infinite nature is made to harmonize with every other, and the whole combine to proclaim him perfect. How sublime the idea we acquire of his greatness in the revelation of his character given in the Church planted with his own hand, and watered with his own blood! "An idea," says Robert Hall, "which has this peculiar property; that as it admits of no substitute, so, from the first moment it is formed, it is capable of continual growth and enlargement. God himself is immutable; but our conception of his character is continually receiving fresh accessions, is continually growing more extended and refulgent, by having transferred to it some new element of beauty and goodness, by attracting to itself, as a centre, whatever bears the impress of dignity, order, or happiness. It borrows splendour from all that is fair, subordinates to itself all that is great, and "sits enthroned on the riches of the universe." God alone is great! the God of revelation and of redeeming love!

VERSE 2. Beautiful for situation, the joy of the whole earth, is mount Zion, on the sides of the north, the city of the great King.

"Jerusalem," says a writer, who saw it a few centuries before the Christian era, "is situated in the midst of mountains, on a lofty hill, whose summit is crowned with the magnificent temple, girt with three walls seventy cubits high, of proportionate thickness, and length corresponding to the extent of the building." Approached from the south, as it was by Jehoshaphat and his returning soldiers, it must have been to them a sight, beautiful indeed! How different from what they feared, only four days before, it would have been at this time! Then the foot of pride was advancing against it, and the hand of violence, to cast it down. But there—high and lifted up on its mountain foundation of everlasting rock, and appearing as if stretching far away into the regions of the north—it still stands! "the joy of the whole earth:" the city whence at length should go forth the religion that would gladden all lands—for salvation is of the Jews, (John iv. 22)—and guide their feet into the ways of truth and peace. "The city of the great King." These words disclose the secret of its preservation. It still stood in all its strength and beauty, because it was the royal abode of the Most High. His presence in it was at once its defence and glory. Glorious as the temple was in itself—more glorious than anything the world ever saw beside—its chief glory was not in its external splendour, but in the glory of the Lord, in the divine *Shechinah*, shining in its holy of holies. It was this thought, the presence of God in it as its King, that made Jerusalem appear so beautiful to the eye of the devout Israelite. And it is this same thought that should make our Christian Jerusalem equally beautiful in our eyes. It is "the city of the great King," of him whom God himself enthroned on his holy hill of Zion. Ps. ii. 6.

VERSE 3. God is known in her palaces for a refuge.

To the truth of this, every one can bear witness, who has placed himself under the protection of the King of Zion. Once in "the city of the great King," through repentance toward God, and faith toward our Lord Jesus Christ, he is made continually to feel that he is in a city of refuge, where no evil can overtake him, where no avenger of blood can come to slay him. "God is known in" his Church, by all those who seek him with their whole heart as a sure refuge. They have the witness of the fact in their hearts.

VERSES 4–6. For, lo, the kings were assembled, they passed by together. They saw it, and so they marvelled; they were troubled, and hasted away. Fear took hold upon them there, and pain, as of a woman in travail.

These verses illustrate the manner in which God sometimes makes himself known as the protector of his people. Now he appals their enemies with his judgments; and now fills them with supernatural fear and astonishment of heart. "I came, I saw, I conquered," is a military dispatch, celebrated the world over. Here, however, is the record of a victory even more speedily won. The first sight of the city of the great King put its enemies to flight: "Fear took hold upon them there." "They saw it, marvelled, were troubled, and hasted away." The sight of the city, "beautiful for situation," recalling the fearful power of its King, filled them with supernatural dread; and no doubt the voice of the great

King himself was also sounding in their hearts, "Flee for your lives!" The hearts of all men are in the hand of the Lord, and he turneth them whithersoever he listeth; yet always so that not a soul of his true Israel shall perish. He so turned the heart of the Roman governor, Cestius Gallus, who marched against Jerusalem with a force abundantly sufficient, if he had pressed the siege at once, to have taken the city. But, contrary to the expectations of all, he suddenly raised the siege, and drew off his troops. He could give no reason for his sudden retreat, except this only, that there was an impression on his mind that he should retreat. Whence came that impression? Doubtless, from God; and to the end that no followers of his Son should perish in the destruction of Jerusalem, as thousands of them would have done, if the siege had been pressed, and the city taken at that time. Meantime, acting upon the advice of their Lord, given forty years before, to flee to the mountains, when they should see the Romans about to besiege the city, all that believed in Jesus left the city; so that at the last, when Titus Vespasian took it, causing the death of more than a million Jews, "we do not anywhere read that so much as one Christian perished in the siege of Jerusalem." Verily, God is known as a refuge for his people! At one time he saves us by overwhelming our enemies with his judgments; at another, by so moving upon their fears, that they come not near us, turn from us, and pass away.

VERSE 7. Thou breakest the ships of Tarshish with an east wind.

Ships of Tarshish were of a stronger build, could sail rougher seas, and outride heavier storms, than any other: nevertheless, "with an east wind" the Lord could break them in pieces in an instant, and submerge them in the deep. In the same way can he also break in pieces and overwhelm the most powerful of his enemies. If he breathe upon them with the breath of his anger, they disappear, to be seen no more. Who should not fear such power arrayed against him? Or who should not feel safe under its protection?

VERSE 8. As we have heard, so have we seen in the city of the Lord of hosts, in the city of our God: God will establish it for ever. *Selah.*

It was not merely as a God of history and of hearsay, that the Israel of the date of our psalm knew the Lord their God. All that their fathers had told them of him, they had realized in their own personal experience. He still manifested the same love for his Church, that he had manifested in times of old. He was still the same "very present help in time of trouble." More signal deliverances he had not wrought for Israel, in the days of other years, than that which he had wrought for them now. They could with truth say, "As we have heard, so have we seen, in the city of the Lord of hosts." The mercy just vouchsafed to them was equal to any that he had ever vouchsafed to his people at any time. The past in no wise excelled the present; on the contrary, the past seemed to be repeated in the present, radiant with all its pristine glory of the Divine favour. This was proof to Israel that the Lord was their God in as dear, and intimate, and tender a sense as he was the God of their fathers. "God shall establish it for ever"—that is, the city of the Lord of hosts. His love, care, and protection of his

Church, shall never cease. He will make it for ever a sure refuge for all who shall seek refuge in it. These words comprehend, in the fulness of their meaning, a city greater than that erected on Mount Zion, even the Church of God throughout the whole world, and also the heavenly Jerusalem. Literally then, "God will establish it for ever;" eternity alone will measure the glory and duration of "the city of our God."

VERSE 9. We have thought of thy loving-kindness, O God, in the midst of thy temple.

Not that Israel had thought of God's loving-kindness in the temple only; they had first thought of it in a song of praise in the very place where it had been shown them. 2 Chron. xx. 26–28. This was as it should always be. Our first song of praise should be in that place, wherever it may be, where God speaks us delivered from all our transgressions; then should we return singing, as Israel did, unto the house of the Lord, there to repeat our thanksgiving in a song that shall never end, its notes on earth being at last renewed and perpetuated in heaven. In commemorating the same mercy in his temple as that already commemorated in the place where it was vouchsafed them, it was the purpose of grateful Israel to make the commemoration national and perpetual; to cause that their children, and their children's children, to the latest generation, should chaunt the greatness of their God. We cannot too soon, nor too publicly, nor too constantly, praise him who hath saved us from destruction. Special mercies demand special returns of praise and thanksgiving, and where else can they be so fittingly rendered as in the house of God, where we laud and magnify him for all his mercies?

VERSE 10. According to thy name, O God, so is thy praise unto the ends of the earth: thy right hand is full of righteousness.

The *name* of God, as the word is here used, evidently means the *character* he has developed in his moral government of the world. The character thus developed constitutes his name—that whereby we know him. To history then, as well as to revelation, we must go to learn the name of God. And what does history, not of his own people only, but the history of all nations prove him to be? A God of power and righteousness!—a God who can do whatsoever he pleaseth, and yet a God who doeth all things well! Powerful as his right hand is, it is full of righteousness. No stain of injustice has ever disfigured any act of his power. Wherever this idea of the name of God—an idea specially developed in his dealings with his own people—prevails, it cannot but make him an object of praise even unto the ends of the earth. If all men do not render unto his name, as thus learned, the homage of their hearts, they will at least render unto it the homage of their intellects; stand in awe of it, if they do not love it. The fear of God was on all the kingdoms of those countries surrounding Israel, when they had heard that the Lord fought against their enemies. 2 Chron. xx. 29. Heathen as they were, they rendered a heart-felt homage to the power, if not to the righteousness of God. Just in proportion as they learned his name, understood his character, just in that proportion they stood in awe of him. It is therefore undoubtedly true, as a general proposition, that according as God's name is known among any people, so will their praise of him be. This fact should teach us the great importance of a correct and extended knowledge of God.

VERSE 11. Let mount Zion rejoice, let the daughters of Judah be glad, because of thy judgments.

Mount Zion, here stands for Jerusalem; and the "daughters of Judah" for the other towns of the kingdom, all of whom would have suffered equally with Jerusalem, if God had not, by his judgments, prevented the enemy from coming against them. All, therefore, are exhorted to rejoice with the holy city, still standing in all its integrity and beauty. If our hearts are right, we will rejoice in the mercy shown to any part of the Church of God.

VERSES 12, 13. Walk about Zion, and go round about her: tell the towers thereof. Mark ye well her bulwarks, consider her palaces; that ye may tell it to the generation following.

Jerusalem was one of the most strongly fortified places in the world. High and lifted up on its mountain site, it was surrounded on three sides by deep precipitous valleys. But besides these naturally all but impassable trenches, there sprung from their precipitous sides a wall of circumvallation, here called *bulwarks*, of extraordinary height and thickness; and upon this wall, at a short distance from each other, and rising high above it at their base, were towers of surprising size and strength. The palaces which we are called on to consider, were the temple, with the buildings surrounding it and belonging to it, standing on Mount Moriah, and forming together the most magnificent group of buildings upon which the sun ever shone; and so elevated as to be visible from every part of the city and surrounding country.

This was the strong and glorious city in whose preservation Jerusalem, and all the daughters of Judah, were called on to rejoice and be glad. Not a stone in the ramparts environing it, nor one of its towers, nor one of its sacred edifices, bore the mark of a hostile hand. This was Jerusalem, while the first temple was yet standing; the city during the continuance of the second temple, though vastly inferior to its predecessor, was nevertheless remarkable for the beauty of its sacred edifices, and especially for the strength of its fortifications. For when Titus, the Roman General—God having at last forsaken it—took the city, he was amazed at his success, exclaiming, as he gazed upon its defences, "Surely, we have had God for our help in the war; for what could human hands, or human engines, do against these towers? It is no other than God who has expelled the Jews from their fortifications." Of course, all that is here said of the great external strength and beauty of Jerusalem in Judea, may be applied mystically to another city—the heavenly Jerusalem—the Church of him who in the beginning was with God, and was God, but became flesh, and dwelt among us. And applying the words to the Church of Christ, we say, "Walk about Zion, and go round about her: tell the towers thereof. Mark ye well her bulwarks, consider her palaces." And what are the bulwarks, the ramparts, the impregnable wall of circumvallation around our Zion?—The Divinity of her King, the Godhead of Him who redeemed her. And what are some of her towers?—Prophecy—miracles—a perfect rule of faith and practice—the character of Jesus—a divinely instituted ministry, to whom the promise reads, "Lo, I am with you alway, even unto the end of the world," Matt. xxviii. 20; and also, higher than all the other towers, and shedding celestial effulgence over them all, the tower of Divine influences. These are some of the towers builded upon the encircling wall of our Zion; and what have human hands, or human engines, done against them to do them harm? Nothing—literally nothing. They stand now as they stood thousands of years ago; and as they will stand thousands hence, even to the end of the world. May we not also consider the palaces of our Zion as embracing all the great and precious promises of pardon, peace, and everlasting life, which God has given us in the gospel of his Son?—promises, each of which is indeed as a beautiful house of refuge, a palace of mercy, a sanctuary of the Lord, to a soul weary of its sins, and anxious to escape from them to a place of safety. O how spiritually homeless and houseless would we be in this world without the precious promises of the gospel in which to take shelter from fear of the wrath to come. But in these, as in sacred refuges, we may dwell until we are transferred to our Father's house of many palaces.

VERSE 14. For this God is our God for ever and ever: he will be our guide even unto death.

And certainly He who so cares for us all our lives through, "even unto death," will at death receive us unto himself, that "where he is, there we may be also." Not for time only is he our God, but "our God for ever and ever." The earthly Jerusalem which he so long and tenderly cherished, was long ago a heap of ruins: but the heavenly Jerusalem, which the earthly but prefigured, remains with all its walls and towers and palaces still standing, and to stand for ever. Its walls of gold and precious stones, and gates of pearl, and its streets paved with pure gold, and its river of the waters of life flowing through the midst of it, will never pass away. Rev. xxi. 10, 11, &c. To that Mount Zion the ransomed of the Lord return, and come with songs and everlasting joy upon their heads: they obtain joy and gladness, and sorrow and sighing flee away. And then they begin to learn, as they gaze upon the face of Him who redeemed us, the full import of the words, "this God is our God for ever and ever."

LECTURE ON PSALM XLIX.

VERSES 1, 2. Hear this, all ye people: give ear, all ye inhabitants of the world: both low and high, rich and poor, together.

THE Hebrew people were for a long time the religious *ear* of the whole earth. What they heard, they heard not for themselves only, but for "all the inhabitants of the world. Both low and high, rich and poor together," were as deeply interested in what they heard at the mouth of their prophets, as they themselves were. "Hear this," is God's command to every descendant of Adam in regard to every doctrine, precept, and promise of his word. The truth he revealed to his prophets is catholic truth. He confined the revelation to his own people, only until He came, who is the centre, sun, and soul of the whole system, when he gave the command, "Go ye into all the world, and preach the gospel to every creature."

Mark xvi. 15. Thus that which was originally designed for all, found its way to all.

VERSES 3, 4. My mouth shall speak of wisdom; and the meditation of my heart shall be of understanding. I will incline mine ear to a parable: I will open my dark saying upon the harp.

The wisdom and understanding of which the writer here speaks, is the knowledge of divine things which is from above. The words indicate that what he is about to say is not a dictum of his own, but of the Divine Spirit. "I will incline mine ear to a parable"—a listener before he was a speaker. The parable of which he speaks, is this whole psalm, wherein the Divine Spirit compares the earthly condition of the righteous and the wicked, and shows the righteous that, however much the wicked may sometimes have the advantage over them in temporal, they shall in the end have dominion over the wicked in eternal blessings. This then is the "dark saying" which the divine singer proposes to open "upon the harp;" that is, the adversity of the righteous, and the prosperity of the wicked, considered in the prospect of eternity and human immortality. (See verses 14 and 15.) Whether or not he understood the import of his words as fully as we do, it is not for us to say. His subject may not have been a dark saying to his own mind, and he may have called it such only because he knew it would be dark to the minds of most hearers. Human immortality and future recompense is certainly not a dark saying to our minds, who see it in the light shed over it by the gospel.

VERSE 5. Wherefore should I fear in the days of evil, when the iniquity of my heels shall compass me about?

Critics propose, as required by the Hebrew, instead of "the iniquity of my heels," "the violence of my supplanters," treaders-down, tramplers, oppressors, of those dogging my every step to give me a trip and a fall. The old translation seems to give the true sense of the verse, which reads, "Wherefore should I fear in the days of evil, when iniquity shall compass me about, as at my heels?" The question implies a strong negative, that he should not fear, even when his enemies are doing their utmost to injure him. It should be all along borne in mind who the *I* of this verse is, that it is the person who says of the wicked in the 14th verse, "the upright shall have dominion over them in the morning:" and of himself in the 15th, "God will redeem my soul from the power of the grave: for he shall receive me." The speaker is a person who realizes that he has *one* interest, and that, his highest interest, which the wicked cannot reach nor affect, because *that* interest is in the safe-keeping of God himself.

VERSES 6–9. They that trust in their wealth, and boast themselves in the multitude of their riches; none of them can by any means redeem his brother, nor give to God a ranson for him; (for the redemption of their soul is precious, and it ceaseth for ever:) that he should still live for ever, and not see corruption.

Whatever else the rich man's wealth may purchase for him, it cannot purchase deliverance from the grave, either for himself or for one dear to him as a brother. It cannot redeem, nor ransom either, that he should still live for ever, and not see corruption. "The redemption of their soul is precious," and, so far forth as wealth can accomplish it, it ceases for ever—is a thing eternally beyond its reach.

This demonstrates the folly of making gold our hope, and fine gold our confidence. It cannot purchase us one moment's life. Men have bid high, bid millions for a few years, a few days, a few hours of life; but death was deaf to their offer. It is not with corruptible things, as silver and gold, that the soul is redeemed, but with the precious blood of Christ. 1 Pet. i. 18, 19. And yet the man of the world still trusts in his wealth to secure him immortality and bliss, though his own eyes should teach him the folly of it.

VERSE 10. For he seeth that wise men die, likewise the fool and the brutish person perish, and leave their wealth to others.

Why, then, should he not expect to depart, and leave his substance to others—to strangers? He cannot tell you why, and will still dream of an immortality on earth, if not in person, yet at least in name and estate, in family and wealth; for,

VERSE 11. Their inward thought is, that their houses shall continue for ever, and their dwelling-places to all generations: they call their lands after their own names.

This "inward thought" of men of the world that they will build up for themselves an earthly immortality through their families and estates, may not be avowed, still it is the secretly cherished thought of the heart, and the one thought to the realization of which all their undertakings are directed. It is for the realization of this that they think and act, join house to house, lay field to field, and "call their lands after their own names." This inward thought is seen in the efforts made by parents to give their children place and position in the world. If they can but secure for themselves and children wealth and worldly influence, riches and high social standing, they fancy their earthly bliss laid upon a foundation that cannot be shaken. Having the present well secured, and to their mind, they can think of the future only as the present repeated in always brightening colours.

VERSE 12. Nevertheless, man being in honour abideth not: he is like the beasts that perish.

"Being in honour"—in possession of everything the world lauds and admires, he "abideth not." Thoughtless as the beasts that perish, that have no future, death overtakes him as it overtakes them, wholly absorbed in the present. It was thus that death overtook the rich husbandman. "Being in honour," in the possession of everything that his heart coveted, he abode not therein. While the words, "Soul, thou hast much goods laid up for many years: take thine ease, eat, drink, and be merry," were yet in his mouth, God said to him, "Thou fool! this night thy soul shall be required of thee." Luke xii. 20. Hitherto this prosperous husbandman seems to have been wholly absorbed in hoarding, not stopping to enjoy his stores. At last, however, he determined to take his ease; and the very night in which he first thought of rest and enjoyment, his soul was required of him. So has it been with many thousand men of the world. Having at last acquired what they could regard an independency for children and old age, they retire to enjoy the fruit of their labours, but, before they have hardly tasted it, death dashes the cup from their lips. "Then whose shall those things be which they have provided?" Certainly not their own; they can carry nothing away with them. Probably not their children's; the hoardings of covetous selfishness seldom abide long in the same family. A secret curse rests upon such gains, and wastes them away, no one can tell how, or they pass at once into the hands of others. Neither they nor their children abide in the honours which they fancied they had secured beyond the reach of harm. So the rich husbandman died; and so the fool of our psalm died, with no more thought of a future beyond this life, than the unreasoning brute, that has no future. We may regard the parable of the prosperous husbandman as, in part, representing the character and destiny of the worldling of our psalm in picture, and designed by our Lord so to represent it; for so the majority of the world lives, and so the majority of it dies. Acting as if there were no future for man but that within the bounds of sense, they slave themselves as never bondman slaved, to hoard what they seldom enjoy; for while they are saying in their hearts, Many years! many years! God is answering them, This night!—thou fool! this night!

VERSE 13. This their way is their folly: yet their posterity approve their sayings. Selah.

"This their way" of devoting themselves soul and body to the acquisition of that which they may never enjoy, "is their folly"—yet their posterity approve their sayings, adopt their maxims of worldly policy, and live in the same way. It matters not how much like fools men may have lived, nor how much like brutes they may have died, they will not lack imitators. More servile followers of each other are nowhere to be found than among those we call "the world"—those "who have their portion in this life."

VERSE 14. Like sheep they are laid in the grave: death shall feed on them; and the upright shall have dominion over them in the morning; and their beauty shall consume in the grave from their dwelling.

"The grave from their dwelling." The margin renders these words, "The grave being an habitation to every one of them." However stately the dwelling each erects for himself as his earthly abode, he must leave it for his only permanent habitation, the grave. Hither they are driven and huddled together like sheep in a fold, or slaughter-house, and death feeds on them. They who fondly dreamed of an earthly immortality, become the food of death.

"And the upright shall have dominion over them in the morning." Here is a *morning* spoken of, as coming after the departure both of the wise man, and of the fool, to the grave. What morning must that be? Certainly no other than the morning of the resurrection. That is the morning when the upright shall have dominion over the wicked. The inequalities that existed in their lots on earth, will then be adjusted, and the upright have the better part. Theirs will be glory, and honour, and immortality; while shame and everlasting contempt will be the lot of those who chose not God as their portion.

VERSE 15. But God will redeem my soul from the power of the grave: for he shall receive me. *Selah.*

We cannot for a moment suppose that the speaker here expected to escape the decree, "Dust thou art, and unto dust shalt thou return." He knew he must suffer that—that, with those upon whom death would prey for ever, he must descend into "the house appointed for all living." Job xxx. 23. And yet he adds, "God will redeem my soul from the power of the grave." He speaks as one who was persuaded that God would raise him from the death of the grave to immortality. It has been contended, that a life beyond the grave was not revealed to the Old Testament saints. How any one could read this and the preceding verse, and deny the doctrine, we cannot see; for, as Calvin justly remarks, "He must be more than blind, that can get over this place, as if there were no mention made in it of the heavenly life." It was in no doubting terms that the ancient believer spoke of that life, saying, "Thou shalt guide me with thy counsel, and afterward receive me to glory." Ps. lxxiii. 24. It was in no doubting terms that Daniel spoke of the resurrection of the dead, and eternal judgment, saying, "Many of them that sleep in the dust of the earth shall awake, some to everlasting life, and some to shame and everlasting contempt." Dan. xii. 2. Our Lord's own words on the same subject are scarcely plainer, and more to the point, where he says, "The hour is coming, in the which all that are in their graves shall hear his voice, and shall come forth; they that have done good, unto the resurrection of life; and they that have done evil, unto the resurrection of damnation." John v. 28, 29. Our Lord's teaching here is but a re-affirming that of Daniel. St. Paul, too, declares that the Jews of his day held the doctrine of the resurrection, "both of the just and unjust," Acts xxiv. 15; and that their brethren, in times of persecution, had suffered martyrdom, in attestation of their conviction of its truth, Heb. xi. 35; and that Abraham "looked for a city which hath foundations, whose builder and maker is God." Heb. xi. 10. It is absurd to affirm, that the

Old Testament scriptures do not teach human immortality and future retribution.

VERSES 16, 17. Be not thou afraid when one is made rich, when the glory of his house is increased. For when he dieth, he shall carry nothing away: his glory shall not descend after him.

The man who has "an inheritance incorruptible, and undefiled, and that fadeth not away, reserved in heaven" for him, (1 Peter i. 4,) has small reason indeed to fear or envy the great and mighty of the earth. As compared with him, the richest of them are beggars: all that they have is in this world; and not one iota of it can they carry away with them. The moment they come to the grave, they enter on an inheritance of everlasting poverty. Not so the upright: the moment he comes to the grave, he enters into the possession of riches above what earth can grant, and lasting as the mind.

VERSES 18, 19. Though while he lived he blessed his soul: (and men will praise thee when thou doest well to thyself:) he shall go to the generation of his fathers; they shall never see light.

Here is the concluding touch in the description of the worldling's death—the evil that follows it. Hitherto he has been represented as one that abides not in his honours, and carries none of his earthly goods away with him. Up to this point, in the description of his death, it would seem to imply only a loss of earthly enjoyment. It is in this light that the parable of the prosperous husbandman represents his death. It goes not a step beyond, to tell us specifically of evils coming afterwards. Here, however, in speaking of the worldling's joining the assembly of his ancestors at his death, we have, in the words, "they shall never see light," an intimation of evils consequent upon death—of evils to which death leads, and of which it is the beginning. Never to see light, is never to know what happiness is. This then is to be added to the worldling's loss of all earthly good: he shall, in the world to which he goes, never see light; never know what happiness is. How sad must this change be to the man who, while he lived, could bless his soul; felicitate himself on wanting no earthly good that his heart coveted, and was praised by convivial companions for the princely manner in which he treated himself, and indulged every pleasure of sense. It is easy to perceive in this man—leaving every earthly good that his heart coveted, never to see light—the rich man of the parable of Dives and Lazarus. He evidently had every temporal blessing that his heart could wish: he was clothed in purple and fine linen, and fared sumptuously every day; but when he died, and was buried, he lifted up his eyes in hell, being in torments, pleading that Lazarus might be sent to him from heaven, with a drop of water to cool his burning tongue. Luke xvi. 19–25. What righteous man, what afflicted Lazarus, would envy such a man his lot in this world, to take therewith his lot in the world to come?

VERSE 20. Man that is in honour, and understandeth not, is like the beasts that perish.

Such is the conclusion at which inspired wisdom arrives, namely, that the man who makes not the securing of a blissful immortality the great aim of his earthly existence, makes no more account of himself than if he were verily a beast. He acts as if the divine endowment of reason were not his. All his acts convict him of being as unmindful of another life as the beasts for which there is no such life. Strange that such a noble creature as man is by native endowment, should thus degrade himself: a creature made in the moral and intellectual image of God, and capable, if he choose God as a portion of his soul, of advancing in the glory of that image till neither angel, nor archangel, shall stand higher than he. And yet, endowed with the honour of possessing a nature kindred to the Divine, and capable of sharing for ever in all its bliss and glories, it avails man nothing, if he "understandeth not," if he allow reason to slumber, and sense to control. Nor is the worst yet told. The man who lives not for immortality, dies not altogether as the brute dies—it would be well for him if he could so die—a death that ends at once all thought and all feeling—but he dies a *living* death, a death wherein thought and feeling are, without ceasing, intensely active, and work the soul at every moment a deeper wo. Read the dialogue between Abraham in heaven and the rich man in hell, and you will need no other proof that the death which the lost soul endures, robs thought of none of its power, and feeling of none of its intensity. Luke xvi. 19–31. May God, for the sake of his Son Jesus Christ, save us all from the fearful doom of having our immortal powers work us immortal wo.

LECTURE ON PSALM L.

VERSE 1. The mighty God, even the Lord, hath spoken, and called the earth from the rising of the sun even unto the going down thereof.

MANY commentators have interpreted this psalm as a description of the final judgment; others, as a description of what would take place at the Advent and during the personal ministry of the Messiah. Neither of these interpretations can be received as the right one. The right interpretation seems to be the following, viz. "The mighty God, even the Lord, who appeared in such power and majesty on Sinai, while *giving* the law to his people, has appeared in equal power and majesty on Mount Zion, to *explain* it to them, and teach them its spiritual import and uses." This seems to be the one great aim of the psalm; and to the explanation of the law and ritual about to be given, the whole "earth, from the rising of the sun even unto the going down of the same," is summoned to listen.

VERSE 2. Out of Zion, the perfection of beauty, God hath shined.

It is not in a physical and geographical, but in a *theological* sense, that Zion is here called "the perfection of beauty." It is so called because it was the mountain of God's *holiness:* because God shone there in a light more softened and effulgent than anywhere else on earth. He shone there in the law, in the ceremony, and in the sacrifice, and in each manifests himself as the One Being in whom all excellence dwells. It was there that he did continually what he promised Moses he would do, made all his goodness pass before his people, and proclaimed the name of the Lord, (Exod. xxxiii. 19,) a name in which, whether read in the revelation or the ritual, "truth, mercy, and justice, blend in infinite and indissoluble harmony." Exod. xxxiv. 5–7.

VERSES 3, 4. Our God shall come, and shall not keep silence; a fire shall devour before him, and it shall be very tempestuous round about him. He shall call to the heavens above, and to the earth, that he may judge his people.

"Our God," he who made a covenant with Abraham, and delivered the law from Sinai, shall come, "that he may judge his people;" subject their conduct to the tests of his law, in the presence of the whole universe beside, cited to attend, not as attesting, but as listening witnesses to the trial. And if needs be, in order to convince them that He who is now about to speak to them from Zion, is the same who spake to their fathers from Sinai, the same phenomena shall attend his appearance here as there. His voice shall be heard, "he shall not keep silence; a fire," too, "shall devour before him, and it shall be very tempestuous round about him." The mighty God, even the Lord, hath spoken. What hath he spoken? All that follows, beginning with the fifth verse and extending to the end of the psalm. His own first direct words are:

VERSE 5. Gather my saints together unto me; those that have made a covenant with me by sacrifice.

God calls his people *saints*—his holy ones—because he calls them to be such; their covenant obligations to him bind them to holiness and pureness of living. *Saints*, then, as the word is here used, indicates a covenant relation, rather than a moral quality. It is, then, those who knew and had assumed the vows of the law whom God here cites to trial for their manner of observing it in their worship of Him.

VERSE 6. And the heavens shall declare his righteousness: for God is Judge himself. *Selah.*

When God exercises the office of Judge in his own person, the heavens—celestial intelligences—can safely declare his righteousness; proclaim, even beforehand, the rectitude of his every judicial decision. The *Selah*, following the words "for God is Judge himself," is thought to indicate a solemn pause in the proceedings at this point, a brief, significant silence observed by the Judge, in order to give greater emphasis to his words that follow; which read,

VERSE 7. Hear, O my people, and I will speak; O Israel, and I will testify against thee: I am God, even thy God.

This verse may be regarded as the exordium of the trial. It gives us the names and relations of the parties. And although about to test them so severely by applying his law to their conduct in its broad spirituality, nevertheless God still calls Israel his people, and himself their God. This he no doubt does both by way of rebuke and of encouragement. It is always so; even in testifying against us, God still calls himself by some name that inspires hope. If in one breath he startles the soul with the words, "I will testify against thee," he soothes it in the next with the words, "I am God, even thy God." There is a blending of light in every aspect of his character.

The first class of delinquents in his Church to

whom God explains and applies his law in its spirituality, were those who, while offering every sacrifice required by the ritual of the tabernacle, were nevertheless formalists, wanting in piety to God. Vs. 8–15. The second class are those who, while quite as full and uniform in their sacrifices as the first, were nevertheless not only formal, but immoral; wanting not only in piety to God, but also in justice to man. Vers. 16–21. The first class seem to be arraigned for having violated the precepts of only the first table of the Decalogue; the second class for having violated the precepts of both. Addressing the whole first class as an individual, God says:

VERSES 8–12. I will not reprove thee for thy sacrifices or thy burnt-offerings, to have been continually before me. I will take no bullock out of thy house, nor he-goats out of thy folds: for every beast of the forest is mine, and the cattle upon a thousand hills. I know all the fowls of the mountains; and the wild beasts of the field are mine. If I were hungry, I would not tell thee: for the world is mine, and the fulness thereof.

It is not the offering of sacrifices continually that God reproves here; laws of his own enacting required it (Deut. xii. 5, 6;) and if it had been omitted, the omission would have received his severe condemnation. What he reproves here is something else—is the pagan, materialistic idea which seems to have crept into the Jewish mind, that God himself needed, and was in some way benefited by these continual sacrifices and offerings. To this gross misconception of the Divine nature, and the purpose of sacrifices, God indignantly replies, that if such things could in any wise promote his happiness, he needed not the help of the Jew to accomplish the desires of his heart, since everything that the Jew could bring to him as an offering or a sacrifice, was already his—"every beast of the forest, the cattle upon a thousand hills, the fowls of the mountains, and the wild beasts of the field, the world, and the fulness thereof." How absurd to suppose that such a God could need sacrifices for his own sake; or, if he did need them, that he would apply to any creature to make the offering. If he were in want, he need apply to none but himself to supply his wants; hence his words to man, "If I were hungry, I would not tell thee."

VERSE 13. Will I eat the flesh of bulls, or drink the blood of goats?

The questions of this verse demand for their answer an indignant and emphatic "No!" They are equivalent to God's saying, "I, the Lord, am a Spirit. Being such, material and bodily sacrifices cannot but be foreign to my very nature." This is conclusive that material offerings, as the flesh and blood of animals, could not be necessary to him, nor bring him refreshment, if he needed it. None but spiritual offerings could be agreeable to a purely spiritual Being. This brings us to the doctrine proclaimed by our Lord to the woman of Samaria, saying, "God is a Spirit; and they that worship him must worship him in spirit and in truth." John iv. 24. It is also the doctrine taught in the next verse of our psalm, which reads,

VERSES 14, 15. Offer unto God thanksgiving; and pay thy vows unto the Most High: and call upon me in the day of trouble; I will deliver thee, and thou shalt glorify me.

Paraphrase.—"Offer unto God"—not without it, but with the material and animal offering—"thanksgiving;" and so "pay thy vows unto the Most High."

Then "call upon me in the day of trouble: I will deliver thee, and thou shalt glorify me." Such is God's own interpretation of the import and uses of the various offerings and sacrifices of the tabernacle. They were pleasing to him, and useful to the worshipper, only as they were offered with *thanksgiving*, that is, with a grateful and believing heart. So offered, the sacrifice procured for the offerer the pardon of his sins; paid his "vows unto the Most High," fulfilled the requirements of the Divine law; and obtained for him God's sure promise of henceforth hearing and delivering him whenever he should call upon him in the day of trouble; and of so delivering him as to give him continual cause to glorify Him for his mercies. Thus early in the history of his Church did God proclaim the spirituality of its ritual, and protest against the *opus operatum* dogma in regard to its sacraments, that they convey the grace of life to the recipient, not only where faith is present and operative, but also where it is wholly wanting, if so be there be in the mind of the recipient no actual opposition, no positive disbelief. It is a dogma that ignores not only thanksgiving, but also repentance, faith, and obedience. "Offer unto God thanksgiving—and so pay thy vows unto the Most High." Implying, as it does here, repentance, faith, and obedience, this one word, *thanksgiving*, cannot but recall to every one familiar with it, a portion of the Communion Service of the Protestant Episcopal Church, where, in presenting Christ to the worshipper, as the vicarious sacrifice for his sins, we bid him, while receiving the sacred emblems in remembrance that Christ died for him, to feed on him in his heart by faith "with thanksgiving." We use words of the same import in presenting the cup, saying to the recipient, "Drink this in remembrance that Christ's blood was shed for thee, and be thankful." The teaching of our Communion Service is altogether in keeping with the teaching of the verse now before us. Who then can fail to see that any other, either offering, or receiving, as the great sacrifice for the sins of the world, must have been the emptiest formality, and utterly without value in the sight of God, who looketh only upon the heart.

VERSES 16—20. But unto the wicked God saith, What hast thou to do to declare my statutes, or that thou shouldest take my covenant in thy mouth? Seeing thou hatest instruction, and castest my words behind thee. When thou sawest a thief, then thou consentedst with him, and hast been partaker with adulterers. Thou givest thy mouth to evil, and thy tongue frameth deceit. Thou sittest and speakest against thy brother; thou slanderest thine own mother's son.

We come now to the second class of delinquents in his Church, to whom God explains and applies the ritual law in its broad spirituality. This second class are deficient, not only in piety to God, but also in justice to man; they are not formal, but immoral, men, who, as Calvin forcibly remarks, "under a cloak of ceremonies conceal an unclean heart and a wicked life." Hence God describes this as wicked, as hating instruction and casting it behind their backs; as holding fellowship with thieves and adulterers; as wholly given up to framing deceit; and as habitually slandering their nearest kin, even an own mother's son. Says God to this wicked professor of his religion,

VERSE 21. These things hast thou done, and I kept silence; thou thoughtest that I was altogether such an one as thyself: but I will reprove thee, and set them in order before thine eyes.

"Set them"—thy sins—"in order before thine

eyes." And that he has certainly done in the dark catalogue of sins just repeated. The godless professor must certainly feel himself reproved when he reads that catalogue of sins as his own. It certainly should convince him that God is not "altogether such an one" as himself in his estimate of sin; that Divine forbearance cannot be construed into approval, nor Divine silence into forgetfulness.

VERSE 22. Now consider this, ye that forget God, lest I tear you in pieces, and there be none to deliver.

This verse is addressed to both classes of delinquents described in this psalm, and is a call upon each to flee without delay from the wrath to come, lest, like Esau, when they would inherit the blessing, they should find no place for repentance, though they should seek it carefully with tears. Heb. xii. 17. The last verse of our psalm is little else than a repetition and re-statement of the terms of salvation already set forth. It reads,

VERSE 23. Whoso offereth praise [thanksgiving] glorifieth me: and to him that ordereth his conversation aright will I show the salvation of God.

What God hath joined, let not man put asunder. If he hath joined a life of prayer and praise to holy obedience, we separate them at our peril. "Hath the Lord as great delight in burnt-offerings and sacrifices as in obeying the voice of the Lord? Behold, to obey is better than sacrifice, and to hearken, than the fat of rams." 1 Sam. xv. 22.

THE END.

www.ingramcontent.com/pod-product-compliance
Lightning Source LLC
LaVergne TN
LVHW021225110826
845150LV00002B/249

* 9 7 8 1 4 2 5 5 6 3 8 3 7 *